George Percy Badger, Lodovico de Varthema, John Winter Jones

The Travels of Ludovico di Varthema in Egypt, Syria, Arabia Deserta and Arabia Felix, in Persia, India, and Ethiopia

George Percy Badger, Lodovico de Varthema, John Winter Jones

The Travels of Ludovico di Varthema in Egypt, Syria, Arabia Deserta and Arabia Felix, in Persia, India, and Ethiopia

ISBN/EAN: 9783744754330

Printed in Europe, USA, Canada, Australia, Japan

Cover: Foto ©Andreas Hilbeck / pixelio.de

More available books at **www.hansebooks.com**

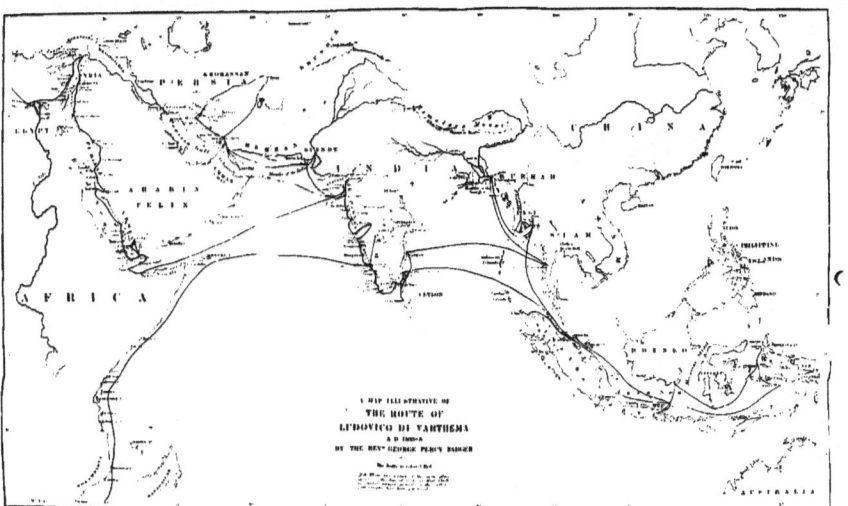

WORKS ISSUED BY

The Hakluyt Society.

THE TRAVELS OF
LUDOVICO DI VARTHEMA.

M.DCCCLXIII.

WORKS ISSUED BY

The Hakluyt Society.

THE TRAVELS OF
LUDOVICO DI VARTHEMA.

M.DCCCLXIII.

THE TRAVELS

OF

LUDOVICO DI VARTHEMA

IN

EGYPT, SYRIA, ARABIA DESERTA AND ARABIA FELIX,

IN PERSIA, INDIA, AND ETHIOPIA,

A.D. 1503 TO 1508.

Translated

FROM THE ORIGINAL ITALIAN EDITION OF 1510,

WITH A PREFACE,

BY

JOHN WINTER JONES, Esq., F.S.A.,

And Edited,

WITH NOTES AND AN INTRODUCTION,

BY

GEORGE PERCY BADGER,

LATE GOVERNMENT CHAPLAIN IN THE PRESIDENCY OF BOMBAY,
AUTHOR OF "THE NESTORIANS AND THEIR RITUALS,"
ETC., ETC., ETC.

WITH A MAP.

LONDON:
PRINTED FOR THE HAKLUYT SOCIETY.
M.DCCC.LXIII.

LONDON: T. RICHARDS, 37, GREAT QUEEN STREET.

TO THE

RIGHT HONOURABLE

SIR CHARLES WOOD, BART., G.C.B.,

HER MAJESTY'S SECRETARY OF STATE FOR INDIA,

THIS EDITION

OF THE EASTERN TRAVELS OF

LUDOVICO DI VARTHEMA,

AT THE BEGINNING OF THE SIXTEENTH CENTURY,

IS RESPECTFULLY DEDICATED

BY THE EDITOR.

COUNCIL

OF

THE HAKLUYT SOCIETY.

SIR RODERICK IMPEY MURCHISON, G.C.St.S., F.R.S., D.C.L., Corr. Mem. Inst. F., Hon. Mem. Imp. Acad. Sc. St. Petersburg, etc., etc., PRESIDENT.

REAR-ADMIRAL C. R. DRINKWATER BETHUNE, C.B.
THE RT. HON. SIR DAVID DUNDAS, M.P.
} VICE-PRESIDENTS.

J. BARROW, ESQ., F.R.S.
RT. HON. LORD BROUGHTON.
CAPTAIN CRACROFT, R.N.
SIR HENRY ELLIS, K.H., F.R.S.
JOHN FORSTER, ESQ.
R. W. GREY, ESQ., M.P.
T. HODGKIN, ESQ., M.D.
JOHN WINTER JONES, ESQ., F.S.A.
HIS EXCELLENCY THE COUNT DE LAVRADIO.
R. H. MAJOR, ESQ., F.S.A.
SIR CHARLES NICHOLSON, BART.
SIR ERSKINE PERRY.
MAJOR-GENERAL SIR HENRY C. RAWLINSON, K.C.B.
WILLIAM STIRLING, ESQ., M.P.

CLEMENTS R. MARKHAM, ESQ., HONORARY SECRETARY.

DIRECTIONS TO THE BINDER.

Map of Varthema's route . . . . . . to face title-page.
Section from Gastaldi's Map . . . . . „ page cxx.

TABLE OF CONTENTS.

PREFACE BY THE TRANSLATOR.

This translation made from the first Italian edition of 1510; truthfulness of Varthema's narrative, and simplicity of his style; later editions more or less faulty; the present version intended to be a faithful representative of the original text; Varthema's work immediately attracted attention, i-iii. Different editions and translations enumerated: Italian; Latin; German; Spanish; French; Dutch; English, iii-xvi.

INTRODUCTION BY THE EDITOR.

Deficiency of all the authorities as to Varthema's antecedents, xvii; not supplied by allusions in his dedication, xix; notice of the Lady Agnesina, Duchess of Albi and Tagliacozzo, to whom he dedicates, xix; Ramusio's preface has no information, and his edition a third-hand version, xxi; particulars derivable with more or less certainty from the narrative itself, xxii; his motives for travelling, xxiii; character of his narrative, xxiii; scanty recompense, xxiv.
Date of his leaving Europe, xxv; remarks on his notices of Cairo and Egypt under the Mamlúks, *ib.*; Syria and Damascus, xxvi; his enrolment as a Mamlúk, and reserve as to his profession of Islám, his Mussulman name (Yúnas or Jonah), and his knowledge of Muhammedanism, xxvi; remarks on such conformity to Islamism, xxvii; he joins the Hajj Caravan from Damascus, *ib.*; the only European who has reached Meccah by that route, xxvii; his sketches of the desert and Bedáwin, xxviii; his notice of a colony of Jews near El-Medinah, and the fact authenticated, *ib.*; his description of El-Medinah and correction of fables about Muhammed's coffin, xxix; his journey on to Meccah, xxx; his notice of the politics of the time confirmed by Arabic authorities, the *Kurrat El-Ayún* and *Ruah er-Ruah*, xxx-xxxv; his account of Meccah, its visitors, holy places, and ceremonies, xxxv; wonderful truth of his descriptions, as confirmed incidentally by Burckhardt and expressly by Burton, xxxvi.
Varthema escapes to Juddah from the Caravan, xxxvi-vii; his voyage down the Red Sea and arrival at Aden, xxxviii; suspected as a Christian spy and imprisoned, and sent to the Sultán of southern Yemen at Radáá, xxxix; corroboration of a part of Varthema's story here from the narratives of Portuguese acts of piracy at this time, xxxix—xli; outline of the contemporary politics of Yemen from Arabic authorities, xli—xliv, and incidental corroboration of Varthema's narrative, xliv; intervention of one of the Sultán's wives in Varthema's favour, and his pretended madness, xlv; morality of the harím, *ib.*; Varthema obtains leave to visit Aden, where he engages a passage to India, and spends the interval before its departure on an excursion through Yemen, xlvi; he is the first European traveller who has described that country, and scarcely any but

a

TABLE OF CONTENTS.

Niebuhr have followed, xlvi; abstract of his route, xlvii; returns to Aden, embarks, runs for Africa and visits Zaila and Berbera; truth of his descriptions, xlviii; circumstantial evidence of the season at which this voyage was made, xlix; Varthema crosses the Indian ocean to Diu in Guzerat; thence to Gogo; and thence westward to Julfar in the Persian Gulf, Máskat, and Hormuz, l; notices of Hormuz and its history, l, li.
Varthema's visit to Eri or Herat, lii; difficulty about his "large and fine river;" Shiráz, liii; his meeting with a Persian merchant "Cozazionor," who becomes his travelling companion; advantages of this to Varthema, liv; they start for Samarcand, but are turned back by the Sufi's persecution of the Shi'ás; confirmation of this from history, lv, lvi; Cozazioner proposes to give Varthema his niece in marriage, lvii; they reach Hormuz and embark for India, arriving at *Cheo* or Jooah on the Indus; they reach Cambay, lviii; truth of particulars regarding it.
Political state of Western India at this period, lviii; accession to the throne of Guzerat of Mahmúd Sháh, surnamed Bigarrah, who reigned during Varthema's visit, lix; Mussulman kingdom of the Deccan, its vicissitudes and subdivision; 'Adil Sháh of Bijapúr, Varthema's "King of Deccan," lx; the Brahminical kingdom of Bijayanagár; Ramráj of that state, Varthema's "King of Narsinga," lxi; Rajah of Cannanore; kingdom of the Zamuri Rajah or Zamorin, lxii; history of his preeminence as given by the Portuguese; Quilon, lxiii; Chayl; kingdom of Bengal under the Purbí sultáns.
Varthema's account of the Jains and the Joghis, lxiv; his description of Sultán Mahmúd's mustachioes confirmed by the Mussulman historians. Varthema's journey along the coast, inland to Bijapúr and back to the coast, and so to Cannanore, lxv; his abstinence from communication with the Portuguese already established there; visit to Bijayanagár, and remarks on his notices of the coinage; return to the coast and journey along it to Calicut, lxvi; fullness, truth, and originality of his descriptions of manners and peculiarities here, of the distinctions of castes and singular marriage customs, lxvii; remarks upon these.
Varthema and his companion quit Calicut by the Backwaters, for Kayan-Kulam and Colon or Quilon, lxix; thence to Chayl; position of the latter; city of Cioromandel, lxx, probably Negapatam; their visit to Ceylon; they proceed to Paleachet or Pulicat, lxxi; remarks suggested by the narrative as to the freedom of trade, and protection of foreign traders in India in those days, lxxi; many subordinate ports then frequented even by foreign vessels are now abandoned and have disappeared from the maps, lxxii; causes of the greater commercial centralization of the present day, and doubts whether the improvement of access to the old intermediate ports would not have been attended by better results; general prosperity which seems to have prevailed, and for which a much less equal distribution of property has now been substituted; impartial administration of justice in old India; the comparative costliness and tardiness of our system; humorous story in illustration related by an Arab merchant, lxxiv.
Sketch of the political geography of the Transgangetic Peninsula, lxxvi; Pegu, Siam, Ava, and Toungoo; the various kingdoms of Sumatra; "Moors" and "Pagans;" Java, lxxvii; sovereigns of the farther islands visited by Varthema.
The travellers sail from Pulicat to *Tarnassari* or Tenasserim, lxxviii; truthful features of the description; Varthema's notice of the Hornbill, lxxix; of extraordinary marriage usages; voyage to the "city of Banghella," lxxx; discussion as to the whereabouts of the city so indicated, with various quotations; wealth and abundance of products, lxxxii; meeting with Christians from the city of Sarnau, and probable identification of that place, from passage in Odorico; remarks on the interesting character of Fra Odorico's narrative, lxxxiii; these Christians advised

Vartheina's companion to visit Pegu with them, lxxxiv; description of
Pegu, lxxxv; Varthema's statement about the existence of Christians
there, lxxxv; interview with the King of Pegu, lxxxvi.
Departure for Malacca, lxxxvii; "Great River," viz. Straits of Malacca,
lxxxvii; character of the place and people, and corroboration of Varthema's narrative; Sumatra, lxxxviii; questions raised by the text
regarding coins and silk in that island; voyage to the Spice Islands
undertaken, xc; this part of the route never previously recorded by any
European, but it would be rash to say never travelled, xci; the Nutmeg
or Banda Islands; Monoch or the Moluccas; which of the latter did
Varthema visit? xcii; visit to Borneo, the part not determined, xciii;
curious particulars as to appliances for navigation, xciv; the Southern
Cross, xcv; and stories heard of apparently antarctic regions, xcv; curiosity
of the Sarnau Christians about Western Christendom; this may have
awakened Varthema's desires for home and the abandonment of his
false profession, xcvi; arrival at Java; a plea for the account of it
given by Varthema against Mr. Crawfurd's condemnation; mutilated
children, xcvii.
Return to Malacca and thence to Negapatam, and Calicut, xcviii; the
two Milanese gun-founders; Varthema's appearance as a physician, and
as Imám; his journey to Canuanore and escape into the Portuguese
garrison, xcix.
Varthema present at the sea fight off Cannanore, c; employed as factor
at Cochin; in the attack on Ponani; his knighthood; remarks on the
fanaticism and violence of the Portuguese.
Varthema finally quits India, ci; remarks on the rapid growth of the
Portuguese power in the East, and its rapid decay, cii; their religious
conquests have survived their temporal sovereignty, ciii; success of
Roman Catholic mission in India greater than that of the Reformed
churches, civ; remarks of Heber quoted.
Mozambique, cvi; summary of history of the Muhammedan settlements
on the coast of Eastern Africa from Krapf, cvii; the Portuguese rule
and its fall, cviii; inscription over the gateway of Mombása; rise of the
'Ammân Seyyeds of Máskat and Zanzibar, cx; Varthema's inland excursion at Mozambique, and the illustration it affords of the dealings of the
civilized with the uncivilized, cxi.
Varthema's arrival in Europe, and conclusion of his narrative, cxii.
The Editor's acknowledgments to various gentlemen, cxiii.
POSTSCRIPT. On the site of the ancient city of Bengala.
Further evidence as to the existence of Bengala as a city and port distinct
from Satgong and Chittagong, cxiv; some authors, however, mention the
two latter and not Bengala, cxvii; abstract of the data as to these three
cities afforded by the principal old maps in the British Museum, cxix;
Bengala appears for the last time in 1740; the site of Bengala, and its
probable destruction by the river as supposed by Rennell, cxx.
Advantages of Travel, from the Arabic.

TRAVELS OF LUDOVICO DI VARTHEMA.

(The headings in the larger type are those of the original text.)

Privilege of printing granted to Varthema by Raphael Bishop of Portueri
and Cardinal of St. George, the Pope's Chamberlain.

Dedication to Countess of Albi and Duchess of Tagliacozzo, 1-4.

First Chapter concerning Alexandria, 5.

TABLE OF CONTENTS.

Chapter concerning Cairo, 5, 6.
    Size of the city, 5; Sultan, Mamelukes, and Moors, 6.

Chapter concerning Baruti, Tripoli, and Aleppo, 6, 7.
    Sails to Baruti (Beyroot), 6; St. George and the Dragon, 7; goes to Tripoli, ib.; to Aleppo, ib.

Chapter concerning Aman and Menin, 8.

First Chapter concerning Damascus, 8-11.
    Beauty of Damascus, 8; Varthema learns Moorish (Arabic); Castle of Damascus; story of its builder, a Florentine, 9; government of Damascus under the Sultan of Cairo, and oppressive exactions, 10; watchmen, 11.

Second Chapter concerning said Damascus, 11, 12.
    Riches; fruits and flowers; water and fountains, 11; Mosque of St. Zachariah; legendary sites of St. Paul's history and others, 12.

Third Chapter concerning [the Mamelukes in] Damascus, 13-15.
    Mamelukes, their training, pay, and customs, 13; rudeness to ladies; dress of ladies; divorces; cheese, milk, and goats, 14; truffles; dress of Moors; Mameluke oppression; Christian merchants, 15.

BOOK CONCERNING ARABIA DESERTA.

Chapter showing the route from Damascus to Mecca, wherein some Arabs are concerned, 16-19.
    Varthema joins the caravan to Mecca in the character of a Mameluke; travels to Mezeribe, 16; Zambei a great Arab lord; his plundering excursions; Arabs described, 17; numbers in the caravan, and its marshalling; length of the journey to Mecca; food of camels; halts to water, 18; fights with the Arabs at watering places; excellence and skill of the Mamelukes as soldiers, archers, and horsemen, 19.

Chapter concerning the city of Sodom and Gomorrah, 19-21.
    Valley of Sodom; barren and blood-red soil, 19; deaths from thirst in the caravan; mountain with a well, and fight with 24,000 Arabs; camel intrenchment, 20; black-mail paid; fight renewed and many Arabs killed, 21.

Chapter concerning a mountain inhabited by Jews, 22-25.
    Mountain in which dwelt Jews, naked, short and black, 22, 23; tank of water, and turtle-doves, 24; arrives at Medinathalnabi (El-Medinah); barrenness round it; palm-garden; fables about Mahomet's tomb denied, 25.

Chapter concerning where Mahomet and his Companions were buried, 26-28.
    The mosque described; books of Mahomet and his Companions, 26; tombs of Mahomet, Haly, Babacher, Othman, Aumar, and Fatoma, 27; dissensions of Mahometan sectaries, 28.

Chapter concerning the Temple and Sepulchre of Mahomet and his Companions, 28-31.
    Superior of the Mosque tries to trick the caravan, 28; Varthema's Arabic, 29; pretended supernatural illumination of the sepulchre, 30; no truth about the loadstone, 31.

TABLE OF CONTENTS.

Chapter concerning the journey to go from Medina to Mecca, 31-35.
Pilots of the caravan, 31; well of St. Mark, 32; sea of sand (which should have been mentioned before the Jews' mountain) and its dangers, 33; remarkable mountain and grotto, 34; two fights with Arabs; arrival at Mecca; four brothers fighting for the lordship thereof, 35.

Chapter showing how Mecca is constructed, and why the Moors go to Mecca, 35-37.
Description of Mecca, 35; its governors; caravan enters the city, 36; barrenness round the city renders it dependent for food on foreign parts, 37.

Chapter concerning the merchandize in Mecca, 38.

Chapter concerning the pardoning in Mecca, 38-41.
The Great Temple or Mosque described, 38; the tower (El-Käaba), 39; the well, 40; ceremonies performed by the pilgrims, 41.

Chapter concerning the manner of the sacrifices in Mecca, 42-46.
Sacrifices of sheep at a mountain; poor pilgrims, 42; discourse of the Cadi; returns to Mecca; stone-throwing, and legend of its origin, 44; doves of Mecca, 45.

Chapter concerning the unicorns in the Temple of Mecca, not very common in other places, 46-49.

Chapter concerning some occurrences between Mecca and Zida, a port of Mecca, 49-52.
Varthema recognized as a European by a certain Moor, 49; but professes to be a Mahometan convert, 50; the Moor conceals him in his house, and the Damascus caravan departs, 51; whilst Varthema goes with another caravan to Zida (Juddah), 52.

Chapter concerning Zida, the port of Mecca, and of the Red Sea, 52-54.
Zida described; Varthema hides in a mosque, 52; agrees with a ship-master going to Persia, and sails, 54.

Chapter showing why the Red Sea is not navigable, 54.

THE SECOND BOOK.—OF ARABIA FELIX.

Chapter concerning the City of Gezan [Gàzàn], and of its fertility, 55, 56.

Chapter concerning some people called Baduin [Bedàwin], 56-57.

Chapter concerning the island of the Red Sea called Chamaram [Camràn], 57, 58.
The island and its productions, 57; the mouth of the Red Sea, and island of Belmendo (Bàb el-Mandeb); arrival at Aden, 58.

Chapter concerning the city of Aden, and of some customs respecting the merchants, 59, 65.
Aden described; intense heat; Castle (of Seerah), 59; mode of securing the Sultan's dues from ships; Varthema denounced as a Christian spy, and put in irons, 60; sent to the Sultan at a city called Rhada (Radàà), 61; dialogue with the Sultan; the author

professes to be a Mahomedan, but cannot utter the creed, and is cast into prison, 63; Sultan's guard of Abyssinians; their dress and arms, 64; camels and tents, 65.

Chapter concerning the partiality of the women of Arabia Felix for white men, 65-68.
The Queen's kindness to Varthema, 65; he feigns madness, 66, 67; he is removed to the palace, 68.

Chapter concerning the liberality of the Queen, 68-73.
The Queen makes much of him, but he evades her advances, 68-70; she procures his release from the Sultan, 71; he goes to Aden and engages a passage to India, 73.

Chapter concerning Lagi, a city of Arabia Felix, and concerning Aiaz, and the market in Aiaz, and the castle Dante, 73-75.
Whilst the ship delays he travels over Arabia Felix; to Lagi (Láhej), 73; Aiaz ('Az'az), 74; Mahomedan sects; strong city of Dante (Damt), 75.

Chapter concerning Almacarana, a city of Arabia Felix, and of its abundance, 75-77.
Goes to Almacrana (El-Makrânah), a city on a mountain, 75; great reservoir; and the Sultan's treasure kept there, 77.

Chapter concerning Reame, a city of Arabia Felix, and of its air, and of the customs of the inhabitants, 77, 78.
Goes to Reame (Yerim), 77; fat-tailed sheep; seedless grapes; longevity of people, 78; fashion of horns.

Chapter concerning Sana, a city of Arabia Felix, and of the strength and cruelty of the King's son, 78-80.
Goes to Sana (Sanäa), 78; the Sultan's endeavours to capture it, 79; the Sultan of Sana's mad son, who eats human flesh, 80.

Chapter concerning Taesa and Zibit and Damar, very large cities of Arabia Felix, 80-82.
Goes to Taesa (Ta'ez), 80; its antiquity and buildings, 81; goes to Zibit (Zebîd); goes to Damar (Dhamâr), 82.

Chapter concerning the Sultan of all the above-mentioned cities, and wherefore he is called by the name of Sechamir, 83, 84.
The name explained; the Sultan puts no one to death but in war; but had thousands in prison.

Chapter concerning apes, and some animals like lions very hostile to man, 84, 85.
Returns to Aden, 84; finds a mountain with numerous apes, and destructive animals like lions (supposed hyenas), 85; goes on board ship.

Discourse touching some places of Ethiopia, 85.
An accident sends them to the coast of Ethiopia, where they enter the port of Zeila (Zaila).

Chapter concerning Zeila, a city of Ethiopia, and of the abundance of it, and concerning some animals of the said city, such as sheep and cows, 86-88.

Traffic of Zeila, slave trade, &c., 88; products; oil of zerzalino; fat-tailed Berbera sheep, 87; twisted-tailed sheep; stag-horned cows; one-horned cows; the Sultan, his soldiers, &c., 88.

Chapter concerning Barbara, an island of Ethiopia, and of its people, 88-90.

Arrival at Barbara (Berbera), 88; sails for Persia, 90.

THE BOOK CONCERNING PERSIA.

Chapter concerning Diuobandierrumi, and Goa, and Giulfar, lands of Meschet, a port of Persia, 91-93.

After twelve days reaches Diuobandierrumi (Diu in Guzerat), 91; goes to Goa (Goghá), 92; to Giulfar (Julfár in the Persian Gulf), 93; and Meschet (Máskat).

Chapter concerning Ormus, a city and island of Persia, and how they get very large pearls at it by fishing, 94, 95.

Chapter concerning the Sultan of Ormus, and of the cruelty of the son against the Sultan his father, his mother, and his brothers, 96-99.

The Sultan's eleven sons, the eldest a devil, the youngest simple, 96; the former murders his father, mother, and brothers, except the youngest; he tries to get rid of two powerful favourites of his father, and is slain by one of them, 97, 98; who causes the younger brother to be proclaimed Sultan, 99; the many merchants of Ormus.

Chapter concerning Eri in Corozani, of Persia, and of its riches, and of the abundance of many things, and especially of rhubarb, 99-101.

Varthema passes to Persia, and travels to Eri (Herát) in Corazani (Khorassán), 99; abundance of silk and rhubarb; population, 101.

Chapter concerning the river Eufra, which I believe to be the Euphrates, 101-103.

Arrives at a large river called by the people Eufra (? Pulwán), 101; reaches the city Schirazo (Shiráz); turquoises and rubies from Balachsam (Badakhsán), 102; musk, and its power when pure; character of the Persians; liberality and kindness of Cozazionor (Khawája ——), a Persian merchant who proposes that Varthema should travel with him; they set out towards Sambragante (Samarcand), 103.

Chapter concerning Sambragante (as it is called), a very large city like Cairo, and of the persecution by the Soffi, 103, 104.

The greatness of Sambragante and its king, 103; but they are hindered from going thither by the Soffi's (Sháh Ismá'íl es-Súfí's) violence against believers in Bubachar, Othman, and Aumur (viz. Sunnis); Cozazionor proposes to give Varthema his beautiful niece Samis (Shams) to wife, 104; they return to Eri, and thence to Ormus, and take ship for India, where they arrive at the port of Cheo (Jooa in the Indus delta).

TABLE OF CONTENTS.

THE FIRST BOOK CONCERNING INDIA.

Chapter concerning Combeia, a city of India, abounding in all things, 105-107.
> The Indus, and city of Combeia (Cambay), 105; its spices (or drugs), 106; cotton; and precious stones, 107.

Chapter concerning the estate of the Sultan of the very noble city of Combeia, 107-110.
> Sultan Machamuth (Mahmûd Bigarrah), 107; the Guzeratis, their virtues and dress, 108; the Sultan's pomp and elephants, 109; his huge mustachioes; his daily eating of poison, and spurting it on those he desires to kill; his embraces fatal, 110; great trade and riches of Cambay, 111.

Chapter concerning the manner of living and customs of the King of the Joghe, 111 113.
> The Pagan king of the Joghe, his people, and their pilgrimages, 111; their dress, and various acts of devotion, and reputed sanctity, 112; their wars with Sultan Machamuth, 113.

Chapter concerning the city of Ceval [Chaul] and its customs, and the bravery of its people, 113, 114.

Chapter concerning Dabuli, a city of India, 114, 115.

Chapter concerning Goga, an island of India, and the King of the same, 115, 116.
> Varthema and his companion go to Goga (Goa), 115; *Pardai* a gold coin of the country (pagodas); Mameluke garrison and their wars with the King of Narsinga, 116; goes on to the city of Decan.

Chapter concerning Decan, a very beautiful city of India, and its many and various riches and jewels, 117, 118.
> The city of Decan (Bîjapûr) and its Mohamedan King, 117; beautiful palace and houses; splendour of the court, 118; mountain from which diamonds are dug; veiled ladies.

Chapter concerning the activity of the King in military affairs, 118.
> His wars with Narsinga; his navy hostile to Christians; Varthema goes to Bathacala, 118.

Chapter concerning Bathacala, a city of India, and of its fertility in many things, and especially in rice and sugar, 119, 120.
> Bathacala (Batheal, Beitkul, or Sedashevaghur), 119; its trade and fertility, 120; absence of horses, mules, and asses; Varthema goes to Anzediva island.

Chapter concerning Centacola, Onor, and Mangolor, excellent districts of India, 120-122.
> Arrives at Centacola (Uncola in North Canara), 120; at Onor (Honahwar), 121; its productions, fine air, and longevity of the people, 122; Mangolor.

TABLE OF CONTENTS.

Chapter concerning Canonor, a very great city in India, 123-125.

The King of Portugal's castle at Canonor, 123; importation of horses, 124; spices (properly so called) begin; the King's Naeri (Nairs) and their costume; the travellers take their way to the kingdom of Narsinga, and reach the city of Bisinegar, 125.

Chapter showing Bisinegar, a very fertile city of Narsinga in India, 125-128.

Great size and defences of Bisinegar (Bijayanagâr), 125; a paradise of a place, 126; the power of the Pagan King; his horsemen and elephants; equipment of the war elephant; his docility, 127; his dread of fireworks; how elephants were employed in Varthema's presence at Canonor to beach a ship; the absence of joints a fable; description of the animal, and power of his trunk, 128; height of the elephant; pace, and how they are mounted.

Chapter showing how elephants generate, 129-131.

They generate in secret marshes, 129; parts of an elephant eaten in some countries; various values of elephants; their great discretion; riches of the King of Narsinga; dress of the people and the king; his coinage, 130; lions; the Portuguese honoured in Narsinga, 131; return to Canonor, and go to Tormapatani.

Chapter concerning Tormapatani, a city of India; and concerning Pandarani, a place one day distant; and concerning Capogatto, a similar district, 131-134.

Tormapatani (Dormapatam), 131; misery of the people, 132; timber for ships; houses worth half a ducat; Pandarani; Capogatto, 133; go to Calicut; has reserved till now the description of the manners of the preceding places (because similar to those of Calicut), but he will now describe that kingdom, for the King of Calicut, called Samory, is the most important, 134.

THE SECOND BOOK CONCERNING INDIA.

Chapter concerning Calicut, a very large city of India, 135, 136.
Description of the city and poverty of the houses.

Chapter concerning the King of Calicut, and the religion of the people, 136-139.

The king worships the devil, 136; why, 137; description of the devil's chapel and images of Deumo and Sathanas; rites and ceremonies of the Brahmins in worshipping, 138.

Chapter concerning the manner of eating of the King of Calicut, 139-141.

The King's food first offered to Deumo, 139; and how the Brahmins wait on the King when eating, 140; and carry their relics away and give them to the black crows, 140.

Chapter concerning the Brahmins, that is the priests of Calicut, 141.
The Brahmins are the chief persons of the faith; royal marriage custom.

TABLE OF CONTENTS.

Chapter concerning the Pagans of Calicut and of what classes they are, 141, 142.
Classes of the Pagans, 141; Brahmins; Naeri (Nairs); Tiva, or artisans, 142; Mechua, or fishermen; Poliar, who collect pepper, wine, and nuts; Hirava, who plant rice; degradation of the two last before Brahmins and Naeri.

Chapter concerning the dress of the King and Queen, and others of Calicut, and of their food, 143.

Chapter concerning the ceremonies which they perform after the death of the King, 143, 144.
Succession goes to sister's son, 143; reasons for this, 144; customs on the King's death; betel eating.

Chapter showing how the Pagans sometimes exchange their wives, 145-147.
Varthema shows his Malayalim, 145; dialogue between two merchants exchanging wives; polyandria of the other classes of pagans, 146.

Chapter concerning the manner of living, and of the administration of justice among the Pagans, 147, 148.
How they eat, 147; punishments; impaling; fines; curious mode of enforcing payment of debts.

Chapter concerning the mode of worship of the Pagans, 149.
Their matutinal washing; prayers; and customs of cooking, &c.

Chapter concerning the fighting of these people of Calicut, 149-151.
Army of the King, 149; dress, 150; customs of battle; the Naeri (Nairs), 151; customs as to burning and burial; money of Calicut; great variety of nations found trading there; great numbers of Moors (Mohamedans).

Chapter concerning the manner of navigating in Calicut, 152-154.
Mode of ship-building, 152; timber, 153; sails; anchors of marble; seasons of navigation; names of the different classes of vessels, 154.

Chapter concerning the palace of the King of Calicut, 155, 156.
The palace and its small value, 155; why they cannot dig foundations, 156; the King's jewels, and his bad humour, with the reasons thereof; his treasures.

Chapter concerning the spices which grow in that country of Calicut, 157, 158.
Pepper described, 157; ginger, 158; myrobalans.

Chapter concerning some fruits of Calicut, 159-163.
Fruit called ciccara (jack), 159; amba (mango); corcopal (?), 161; fruit like a medlar; comolanga (?); malapolanda (plantain), 162.

Chapter concerning the most fruitful tree in the world, 163-166.
The tenga (cocoa-nut tree), 163; its many uses, 164; the nuts; sub-

TABLE OF CONTENTS.

stance like flax which is woven, 165; another made into cords; charcoal; excellent water contained in the nut; oil; sap drawn and used for wine; the cutting down of these trees not forgiven, 166; mode of cultivation; the oil of zerzalino (sesamum).

Chapter concerning the practice they follow in sowing rice, 166, 167.
Ploughing, sowing, and devil-dancing, 167.

Chapter concerning the physicians who visit the sick in Calicut, 167.
Devil-dancers employed to visit the sick, 167; potion of ginger.

Chapter concerning the bankers and money-changers, 168-170.
Their balances and touchstones, 168; the brokers, and their curious mode of bargaining with the fingers; weights used in trade, 170.

Chapter showing how the Poliari and Hirava feed their children, 171-173.
Singular treatment of the children, 171; their agility; the many animals and birds of Calicut, 172; parrots; starlings (or mainas); apes and their tricks.

Chapter concerning the serpents which are found in Calicut, 173.
Great marsh serpents (crocodiles), 173; venomous serpents; protection of them; protection of cows, 174; superstitions.

Chapter concerning the lights of the King of Calicut, 174, 175.
Vases used in the king's house for lamps described, 174; feasting customs on expiry of mourning, 175.

Chapter showing how a great number of people came to Calicut on the 25th of December to receive their pardon, 175-177.
Temple in a tank, 175; manner of the sacrifice; the great Sathanas; the vast number assembled, 177.

THE THIRD BOOK CONCERNING INDIA.

His companion cannot sell his goods, because of the war with the King of Portugal, 178; they go by a beautiful river (backwater) to Caicolon, 179; Christians of St. Thomas, 180; go to Colon (Quilon), 182; and thence to Chayl, 184; pearl-fishery.

Chapter concerning Cioromandel, a city of India, 186-188.
City of Cioromandel, 186; body of St. Thomas, 187; miracle at his tomb; war with the King of Tarnassari, 188; Varthema and his companion go to Zailon (Ceylon).

Chapter concerning Zailani, where jewels are produced, 188-190.
Four kings in the island, 188; their wars, 189; elephants; rubies, 190; mining customs; excellent fruits.

Chapter concerning the tree of the canella [cinnamon], 191-194.
Cinnamon-tree described, 191; Adam's Peak; no rice in Ceylon, 192; dress and character of the people, 193: no artillery; flowers; summoned to show their goods to the King, 194.

TABLE OF CONTENTS.

Chapter concerning Paleachet, a country of India, 194, 195.
    Paleachet (Pulicat), 194; its trade, 195; war with Tarnassari; they set out for that place.

Chapter concerning Tarnassari, a city of India, 196-199.
    Description of Tarnassari (Tenasserim), 196; the King's wars with Narsinga and Banghella (Bengal) 198; his army; products of the country.

Chapter concerning the domestic and wild animals of Tarnassari, 199-202.
    Animals detailed, 199; bird with great beak (hornbill), 200; great cocks and hens; cock-fighting; goats, remarkable sheep, &c.; buffaloes, 201; great bone of a fish; dress of the people.

Chapter showing how the King causes his wife to be deflowered, and so also the other pagans of the city, 202-204.
    White men employed, 202; dialogue between merchants and the author's companion recited.

Chapter showing how the dead bodies are preserved in this city, 204.
    Burning of the dead and preservation of the ashes, 204; odoriferous woods, &c., used in burning, 205.

Chapter showing how the wife is burnt alive after the death of her husband, 206-208.
    Description of the ceremonies of widow-burning, 206, 207; another custom of proving affection, 208.

Chapter concerning the administration of justice which is observed in Tarnassari, 209.
    Punishment of murder, 209; conveying, &c.; the King heir to foreign merchants; funeral customs of Moorish merchants.

Chapter concerning the ships which are used in Tarnassari, 210.

Chapter concerning the city of Banghella, and of its distance from Tarnassari, 210-212.
    They go to Banghella (some city of Bengal), 210; the Moorish Sultan and his great army, 211; great plenty in the country, 212; wealthy merchants; names of the stuffs exported.

Chapter concerning some Christian merchants in Banghella, 212-214.
    Christian merchants from a city called Sarnau, 212; their dress, 213; their belief, mode of writing, observances; they offer to take Varthema and his companion to a good market, 214; these go with the Christians to Pego (Pegu).

Chapter concerning Pego, a city of India, 215.
    The city of Pego, 215; Christians employed by the King, 217; animals, 218; parrots; timber (teak); great canes; rubies from Capellan; the King's wars with Ava; they go in search of the King, 219; but return to Pego, and are admitted to an interview when he comes back victorious.

TABLE OF CONTENTS.

Chapter concerning the dress of the King of Pego above-mentioned, 219-222.

The King described, and his jewels, 219; Varthema's companion shows his corals, 220; and presents them to the King, 221; the King gives rubies in return; his wealth and liberality, 222; products of his country; approach of the King of Ava; women burning themselves.

Chapter concerning the city Malacha and the river Gaza, otherwise Gange, as I think, and of the inhumanity of the men, 223-228.

Go to Melacha (Malacca), 223; great river more than twenty-five miles wide, called Gaza (the Straits of Malacca); Sumatra; Sultan of Melacha; tributary to the King of Cini (Siam), 224; great amount of shipping; trade and produces, 225; the people described, 226; their violence and insubordination, 227; the travellers go to Pider (Pedir) in Sumatra, 228.

Chapter concerning the island of Sumatra, and concerning Pider, a city of Sumatra, 228-232.

Circumference of Sumatra, 229; he identifies it with Taprobane; the inhabitants and their customs, 230; their money, 231; great elephants, 232.

Chapter concerning another sort of pepper, and concerning silk and benzoin, which are produced in the said city of Pider, 233, 234.

Pepper and long pepper, 233; silk, 234; benzoin.

Chapter concerning three sorts of aloes-wood, 234-237.

Three kinds of aloes-wood, viz., calampat, loban, and bochor, 235; the first and best chiefly purchased in Gran Cathai, in Cini, Macini, Sarnau, and Giava, 236.

Chapter concerning the experiment with the said aloes-wood and benzoin, 238.

The Christians show by experiment the excellence of kalampat and of benzoin; lacca-wood used for dying red.

Chapter concerning the variety of dealers in the said island of Sumatra, 238.

Beautiful work in gold, 238; numerous money-changers, 239; timber; great junks, with prows each way; swimmers, and fireworkers.

Chapter concerning the houses, and how they are covered in the said island of Sumatra, 240-243.

Houses covered with turtle shells, 240; great elephants' teeth, 241; very great serpents; they wish to see spices growing, but are informed that the nutmegs and cloves grow much further off; their Christian companions teach them what they must do to go there, 242; they buy two small vessels, and persuade the Christians to accompany them, 243.

Chapter concerning the island of Bandan, where nutmegs and mace grow, 243, 244.

Pass many islands, 243; arrive at Bandan, 244; description of the

TABLE OF CONTENTS.

people, and of the nutmeg-tree; stupidity of the people; determine to go to the clove island.

Chapter concerning the island of Monoch, where the cloves grow, 244-246.
Reach the island of Monoch (Moluccas), 245; the clove-tree described, 246.

Chapter concerning the island of Bornei, 246-248.
The Christians propose to show them the largest and richest island in the world (apparently Java), 247; but they must first go to another island called Bornei (Borneo); which they reach accordingly, 248; the Christians are charmed with Varthema's conversation about the saints, and wish him to go home with them; notices of Bornei; they charter a vessel for Giava.

Chapter showing how the mariners manage the navigation towards the island of Giava, 248-251.
The captain carries compass and chart with lines, 249; how he navigated thereby, but tells them how beyond Giava there are some races who sail by certain stars opposite to the north (antarctic); and that there the day is only four hours long, and 'tis colder than in any part of the world, 251.

Chapter concerning the island of Giava, of its faith, manner of living and customs, and of the things which grow in the said Island, 251-255.
Arrive at Giava, 251; religion of the island; its products, 252; character and features of the people, 253; birds; dress of the people; arms, 254; blowpipes; food.

Chapter showing how in this island the old people are sold by their children or their relations and afterwards are eaten, 255-257.
Fathers when aged sold in the market for food, 255; sick persons killed and sold, 256; Varthema's comrade takes alarm.

Chapter where, at midday, the sun casts a shadow in the island of Giava, 257, 258.
The sun casts a shadow to the south in June, 257; their fear of being eaten; purchase of emeralds and mutilated children, 258.

Chapter concerning our return, 258-263.
Charter a junk and return to Malacha, 258; part with the Christians of Sarnau, to the great grief of these, 259; sail to Cioromandel, and take another ship to Colon (Quilon); they proceed to Calicut, where Varthema finds two Milanese Christians who made ordnance for the king; Varthema plays the hypocrite, pretending to be a Mussulman saint, and is much venerated, 262.

Chapter showing how I made myself a physician in Calicut, 263-266.
Varthema called to visit a silk merchant, 263; his medical practice, 264; and its success; his fame as a saint spreads, but he keeps up secret communication with the Christians, 265.

TABLE OF CONTENTS.

Chapter concerning the news of the ships of the Portuguese which came into Calicut, 266.
> Two Persian merchants of Cannanore report the arrival of the Portuguese fleet there, and the commencement of a fort; Varthema pretends to denounce them, 266.

Chapter showing how the Moors summon to the church those who are of their sect and faith, 267, 268.
> Takes occasion to describe the call to prayer (*adhán*), 267; Varthema sets forth (as Imám) to lead the prayers of the congregation in the mosque; gives his version of the prayer (*Fátihah*); pretends illness, and his comrade proposes his going to Cannanore for change, 268.

Chapter concerning the flight from Calicut, 268-270.
> Varthema after doubts and fears sets out by sea with the two merchants of Cannanore, 268; they are stopped by the Nairs; they start by land till they find a boat which takes them to Cannanore, 270; where a friend of his (Mussulman) comrade receives him hospitably.

Chapter showing how I escaped from Cananor to the Portuguese, 270-274.
> He makes his way to the Portuguese factory, and takes refuge with Don Lorenzo de Almeyda, 271; to whom he relates all the preparations at Calicut; and is then sent to the Viceroy at Cochin, 272; the Viceroy receives him well and gives him a safe conduct for the two Milanese; he makes many attempts to induce them to escape alone with their jewels and money; but their avarice causes delays and they are betrayed, 273; the Moorish merchants combine to bribe the King of the Gioghi, who was then at Calicut, to have them murdered, 274; Varthema protects the son of one of them, who dies a year later.

Chapter concerning the fleet of Calicut, 274-280.
> Description of the great fleet which issued from the ports of Calicut, 274; the Viceroy's son having but eleven ships to meet them, 275; he exhorts his officers and men; the chaplain follows with a discourse and absolution; but the main fight takes place next day near Cannanore, 277; gallantry of Captain Joan Sarrano and of Captain Simon Martin, 278; rout and pursuit of the Calicut fleet, 279; great slaughter of the enemy; bravery of the Portuguese; and joy of the Viceroy, 280.

Chapter showing how I was sent back to Canonor by the Viceroy, 280-286.
> Varthema made factor by the Viceroy and sent to Cannanore, 280; King of Cannanore dying, the new king is hostile, 281; war breaks out and the fort is beleaguered from April to August, 282; when they are relieved by the fleet from Portugal; miraculous aid hinted at, 284; superstition of the Moors, 285; enchanters among them, 286.

Chapter concerning the assault of the Portuguese upon Pannani, 286-288.
> Varthema obtains leave to go to Europe, 286; but first takes part in the assault on Pannani, 287; desperate fighting; Varthema is knighted by the Viceroy, 288; return to Cannanore.

TABLE OF CONTENTS.

THE BOOK CONCERNING ETHIOPIA.

Chapter concerning the various islands in Ethiopia, 289, 290.

They sail from India, and arrive at Mozambich, 289; notices of Melindi, Mombaza, Chiloa (Kilwah or Quiloa), Zaphala (Sofála), Gogia (Angoxa), Pati (Paté), Brava, the islands of Socotra, of Cumero (Comoro), and Penda (Pemba), 290.

Chapter concerning the island of Mozambich and its inhabitants, 291-296.

Products of Mozambich are gold and oil, 291; natives, their low state, 292; wild elephants, 293; extraordinary speech of the negroes; barter with them, 294; proceed on their voyage, passing the island of San Lorenzo (Madagascar); the Portuguese conversions in India merit success for the king's arms.

Chapter concerning the Cape of Good Hope, 296-298.

Pass the Cape of Good Hope at a distance of 200 miles, 296; pass near St. Helena, where they see two great and extraordinary fishes, 291; find the island of Ascension, and certain stupid birds thereon; begin to see the north star; reach the islands of Astori (Azores); and Lisbon; Varthema has an interview with the King of Portugal, 298, who confirms his patent of knighthood; Varthema proceeds to Rome.

PREFACE,

BY THE TRANSLATOR.

THE following translation has been made from the first edition of Varthema's work printed at Rome in the year 1510, or, as stated in the colophon: "Nel Anno M.D.X. a di · vi de Decembrio." It is impossible to peruse Varthema's narrative and not feel a conviction that the writer is telling the truth, that he is recording events which actually took place, and describing men, countries and scenes which he had examined with his own eyes. There is a manifest absence of all attempt at composition. The tale is told with a charming simplicity and all the concise freshness of a note-book, and the author has evidently not stopt to consider whether the word he used was Bolognese, Venetian, or "Lingua Toscana." Neither has he felt any qualms of conscience as to his grammar. This latter circumstance has occasionally rendered the meaning of a passage somewhat doubtful. The printers also have added their mite to the obscurity by sometimes uniting two words or sentences together, or separating one word or sentence into two, or by leaving out a word altogether. This edition, however, is the only one which gives Varthema's text truly. Even the Latin translation by Archangelus Madrignanus (a monk of the abbey of Clairvaux), which was finished on the 25th day of May 1511, or within six months after the publication of the first Italian edition, is not always an exact exponent of Varthema's text. Later editions vary still more, and the English translation, which is given in Eden's Collection of Voyages and Travels, printed at London in 1577, is extremely imperfect: many passages are totally at variance with the original, and many others are omitted. It has, therefore, been thought advisable by the Council of the HAKLUYT SOCIETY that a new version should be executed, which should as far as possible be a faithful representative of the original work. With this object in view, the translator has endeavoured to preserve the quaint dry style of the author. This must be his excuse for retaining some expressions which are hardly suited to the refinement of the present day, and for not omitting some anecdotes which a writer in modern times would hardly venture to record. They, however, afford an additional voucher for the truth of the narrator: it is impossible to imagine them to be inventions, and they only make us feel the more assured that we are really travelling with Varthema, and sharing with him in all his adventures. His work at once attracted attention. It was, as stated above, immediately translated into Latin, shortly afterwards into German, then into Spanish and French, again into

German, then into Dutch and English, a third time into German, and again into Dutch in the middle of the 17th century.

All the early editions, as well of the original Italian as of the translations of this work, are extremely rare and costly. The consequence is, that there is, perhaps, no work which has been so frequently reproduced, of which the lists given by bibliographers are so inaccurate and imperfect. They have been obliged to copy one from another without the means of testing the accuracy of their statements. The translator has had the advantage of seeing most of the editions of which he gives the titles, and has described them somewhat fully for the benefit of those to whom the originals may not be conveniently accessible.

The following is a list of the most important editions of this work :—

Italian.

1. Itinerario de Ludouico de Varthema Bolognese nello Egypto, nella Surria, nella Arabia deserta & felice; nella Persia, nella India & nella Ethiopa. La fede, el uiuere, & costumi de tutte le prefate Prouincie con Gratia & Privilegio infra notato.

Colophon.—Stampato in Roma per maestro Stephano guillireti de Loreno & maestro Hercule de Nani Bolognese, ad instātia de maestro Lodouico de Henricis da Corneto Vicētino. Nel Anno M.D.X. a di · vi. de Decembrio. 4°.

This edition contains 102 leaves, besides the title, 100 of which are numbered, and the two leaves containing the last page of the privilege, and the first three pages of the table being unnumbered. This is the first Italian edition, and is of excessive rarity. Until recently, very few bibliographers were aware of its existence. A copy is in the Grenville Library in the British Museum.

2. Itinerario de Ludouico de Varthema Bolognese nello egypto nella Suria; nella Arabia deserta et felice nella Persia nella India et nella Ethiopia Le fede, el viuere et costumi de tutte le p̄fate prouincie. Cū Priuilegio.

Colophon.—Impresso in Rome per Mastro Stephano Guillireti De Lorēno Nel anno M.D.XVIJ adi . xvi de Junio Cum gratia et Priuilegio del S. Signore N. S. Leone. p̄. p̄. X. in suo anno quinto. 8°.

This edition contains title, seven leaves of preliminary matter (viz. the privilege and table of contents), and 123 leaves of text not numbered. Signatures A ij to Q vj.

The Privilege is dated 10th of June 1517. In this Privilege it is stated that licence is given to Stephanus Guillereti de Lothoringia to print the book, " Ludovico defuncto, neminem ex heredibus superesse qui ex nova impressione vel jactura vel injuria afficiatur." It is also stated that all the copies of the former impression were sold.

The only known copy of this edition is in the Grenville Library.

Mr. Grenville, in a note upon this copy, speaking of some of the editions of the book, says :—

" It was a third time printed in Italian, at Venice in 1518, and this third Italian edition is by Haym, and most of the books of bibliography, described as the first. In truth, the two first Italian editions of 1510 and 1517 are so rare, that I find no notice whatever of either of them, except in Croft's Catalogue, No. 8045—8046, and quoted by Brunet from Croft's. This copy [of the edition of 1517] comes from the Blandford sale; it had been bought at Croft's sale. I have seen no copy but this of this edition. It is unknown to Panzer, Maittaire, Haym, &c."

3. Itinerario De Ludouico De Varthema Bolognese ne lo Egypto, ne la Suria, ne la Arabia Deserta & Felice ne la Persia ne la India ne la Ethiopia. La fede el viuere & costumi de tutte le p̄fate p̄uīcie, Nouamēte imp̄sso.

Colophon.—Stampata in Venetia per Zorzi di Rusconi Milanese: Regnando linclito Principe Miser Leonardo Loredano: Nella incarnatiōe del nr̄o signore Jesu xp̄o M.D.XVII. adi vi del Mese de Marzo. 8°.

This edition is printed in double columns, and contains ninety-two unnumbered leaves. Signatures A ii to M. The table of contents occupies four pages, and commences on the verso of sig. M.

This edition was printed in 1518, new style, the year then commencing on the 25th of March. A copy is in the Banksian Library in the British Museum.

4. Itinerario De Ludouico De Verthema Bolognese ne lo Egypto ne la Suria ne la Arabia Deserta e Felice ne la Persia ne la India: e ne la Ethiopia. La fede el uiuere e costumi de tutte le p̄refate prouincie. Nouamente impresso.

Colophon.—Stampata in Milano per Ioanne Angelo Scinzenzeler Nel Anno del signor M.CCCCXIX. Adi vltimo de Mazo. 4°.

This copy contains fifty-eight unnumbered leaves. Signatures a ii. to g iii. The colophon is printed on a separate leaf, and is followed by two leaves of the table of contents.

A copy of this edition is in the Royal Library in the British Museum.

5. Itinerario De Ludouico De Verthema Bolognese ne lo Egypto ne la Suria ne la Arabia Deserta & Felice ne la Persia ne la India: & ne la Ethiopia La fede el uiuere & costumi de tutte le prefate prouincie. Nouamente impresso.

The type in the *colophon* has got shifted. It reads:—

 Sta
M.CCC mpata in Milano per Johanne Angelo
Scinzenzeler nel Anno del Signor
CCXXIII. adi. xxx. de Aprile. 4°.

This edition contains title, forty-one leaves numbered II to XLII, and two leaves of table of contents not numbered. Signatures A ii to F ii.

A copy of this edition of 1523 is in the Grenville Library.

6. Itinerario de Ludouico De Varthema Bolognese nello Egitto, nella Soria nella Arabia deserta, & felice, nella Persia, nella India, & nela Ethyopia. Le fede el viuere, & costumi delle prefate Prouincie. Et al p̄sente agiontoui alcune Isole nouamēte ritrouate.

Colophon.—Stampato in Vinegia per Francesco di Alessandro Bindone, & Mapheo Pasini compani, a santo Moyse al segno de Langelo Raphael, nel M.D.XXXV. del mese d'Aprile. 8°.

The Itinerary of Varthema terminates on the recto of page 89, with the following words:—

"Qui Finisse lo Itinerario de Ludovico de Varthema Bolognese, de li paesi et Isole la Fede el vivere et costumi loro. Nuovamente per lui visto in piu parte."

Followed by—

"Qui comencia lo Itinerario de Lisola de Iuchatan nouamente retrouata per il Signor Joan de Grisalue Capitan Generale de Larmata del Re de Spagna e p̄ il suo Capellano cōposta."

This edition consists of 103 leaves, of which 99 are numbered; the title-page, and table of contents, and device at the end, are not numbered. The colophon is printed at the end of the table; the device occupies a separate leaf, and represents the "Archangelus Raphael" leading with his right hand "Tobiodo," (who is represented as a little child with a large fish in his hand), and having on his left Tobit's dog.

The Itinerary of the Island of Yucatan is printed in this edition of Varthema for the first time.

A copy of this edition is in the Grenville Library.

7. Itinerario de Ludovico De Varthema Bolognese nello Egitto, nella Soria, nella Arabia deserta, & felice, & nella Persia, nella India, & nella Ethyopia. Le fede, el viuere, & costumi delle prefate Prouincie. Et al Presente Agiontovi alcune Isole nuouamente trouate.

Colophon.—In Venetia per Matthio Pagan, in Frezzaria, al segno della Fede. 8º.

The type in the colophon has got shifted. This edition reads page for page with that of 1535. One has evidently been closely reprinted from the other.

Mr. Grenville was of opinion that this edition was printed in 1518. This, however, must be a mistake, as Matthio Pagan or Pagano printed at Venice between the years 1554 and 1569 (see also " Saggio di Bibliografia Veneziana, composto da E. A. Cicogna." Venezia 1847), and his name is not found in any list of printers prior to that date. The circumstance which renders it important to fix the date of this edition is that of the " Itinerario de l'Isola de Juchatan," being printed for the first time with the work of Varthema. If Mr. Grenville be correct, then the Itinerary was printed in 1518 ; if not, it was not printed until 1535. It is not included in any edition bearing a date prior to that of 1535.

A copy is in the Grenville Library.

Varthema is also inserted by Ramusio in his " Primo volume delle navigationi et viaggi nel qual si contiene la descrizione dell' Africa, et del paese del prete Janni con varii viaggi dal Mar Rosso a Calicut et infin all' isole Molucche dove nascono de spetierie," &c. Venetia, 1550. Fol. Ramusio had evidently never seen the first or second editions, as he tells us that he had made use of the Spanish translation from the Latin, in order to correct the corrupted text then in use. It may naturally, therefore, be supposed that such a process cannot have restored the language of the original.

Boucher de la Richarderie (" Bibliothèque Universelle des Voyages ") mentions an edition in Italian printed by Rusconi at Venice in 1520, and another printed at the same place in 1589 ; and Ternaux Compans inserts in his " Bibliothèque Asiatique et Africaine " the title of an edition printed by Scinzenzeler at Milan in 1525 in 4°. Beckmann (*Vorrath*) mentions an edition printed at Venice in fol. in 1563.

Latin.

We have already said that the travels of Varthema were translated into Latin within a few months after the appearance of the Italian edition, the dedicatory epistle of the translator bearing the date " Mediolani octavo caleñ. Junias MDXI." [25 May, 1511.] Although there is no date to this edition, it was most probably printed in the year the dedication bears date, or very shortly afterwards. The title is as follows:—

Ludovici Patritii Romani novum Itinerarium Æthiopiæ: Ægypti: vtriosque Arabiæ: Persidis: Siriæ: ac Indiæ: intra et extra Gangem. 4°.

The dedicatory epistle bears the following inscription:—

Reverendissimo in Christo Patri Domino Domino Bernardino Carvaial episcopo Sabino: Sancte crucis in Hierusalem Cardinali amplissimo: Patriarchæ Hyerosolimeo: ac utriusque philosophiæ monarchæ eminentissimo, Archangelus Carævallensis.

In this epistle the translator gives a rapid geographical sketch of the various parts of the world, showing the interest and importance of Varthema's work, which, he says, " tuis auspiciis effectus est romanus et, quasi serpens, exuto senio elegantioreque sumpto amictu juvenescit."

Colophon.—" Operi suprema manus imposita est auspitiis cultissimi celebratissimiq: Bernardini Carauaial hispani. Epī sabineñ. S.R.E. Cardīalis cognomēto sancte crucis amplissimi. quo tpe quibus nunq̃ : antea bellis : Italia crudelē īmodū uexabat."

This edition consists of sixty-two numbered leaves, besides eight preliminary leaves. Sigs. AA. A. to I v.

Ternaux Compans (*Bibliothèque Asiatique et Africaine*) gives the title of an edition of Madrignanus's translation of 1508; but this is clearly a mistake, the Italian not having been printed until 1510, and the epistle to the Latin translation bearing date 1511.

A copy of the edition of 1511 is in the Grenville Library.

Another Latin edition was printed at Nuremburg in 1610, and again at Francfort in 1611. It was also inserted in the " Novus Orbis" of Grynœus.

German.

Four years after the Latin translation a German version was published with the following title :—

1. Die Ritterlich vn̄ lobwirdig rayss des gestrengen vn̄ über all ander weyt erfarnen ritters vnd Lantfarers herren Ludowico vartomans vō Bolonia Sagent vō den landen, Egypto, Syria, vō bayden Arabia, Persia, India, vn̄ Ethiopia vō den gestalte, sytē vn̄ dero menschen leben vnd gelauben. Auch von manigerlay thyeren vöglen vnd vil andern in den selben landen seltzamen wūderparlichen sachens. Das alles er selbs erfaren vn̄ in aygner person gesehen hat.

Colophon.—Auss welscher zungen in teytsch transferyert und seligklichen volend worden in der Kayserlichen stat Augspurg in Kostung und verlegung des Ersamen Hansen Millers der jar zal Christi 1515. An dem. sechzehen den Tag des Monatz Junij. 4°.

This edition consists of 76 leaves not numbered.

Signatures a ii to t. iii. The printer's device occupies the last leaf.

A copy is in the Grenville Library.

2. Die Ritterlich und lobwürdig reiss des gestrengen vn̄ über all ander weyt-ērfarnē Ritters vn̄ landtfarers herrē Ludowico Vartomans vō Bolonia Sagend von den landen, Egypten, Syria, von beiden Arabia, Persia, India, vnd Ethiopia, von den gestalten, sitten vnd dero menschen leben vnd glauben. Auch von manigerley thieren, vöglen vnd vil andern in den selben landen seltzamen wunderbarlichen sachen. Das alles er selbs erfaren vnd in eygner person gesehē hat.

Colophon.—Auss Welscher zungen in Teutsch transfferiert. Unnd selighlichen volendet unnd getruckt in des Keyserlichē Freystat Strassburg. Durch den Ersamē Johannem Knobloch, Als man zalt vō der geburt Christi unsers herrē mccccxvj. Jar. 4º.

This edition contains 113 unnumbered leaves. Signatures A ij to X. v.

A copy is in the British Museum.

Both these editions are copiously illustrated with engravings on wood.

Panzer (*Annalen der älteren Deutschen Literatur*, p. 421,) gives the following:—

"3. Die Rittertich vnd lobwirdig raiss des gestrēgen vnd über all ander weyt erfarnen ritters vn̄ landfarers, herren Ludowico Vartomans von Bolonia. Sagent vō den landen Egipto. Syria, vō bayden Arabia. Persia. India. vn̄ Ethiopia. Das alles er selbs erfaren vnd geschen hat." *Colophon.*— "Getruckt in der kaiserlichen stat Augspurg, in der jar zal Christi m.d.xviii." 4º.

Panzer is of opinion that this translation may have

been made by Michael Herr. It will be shown, however, hereafter, that this cannot have been the case. It was reprinted at Augsburg in 1530.

In 1532 Simon Grynæus published at Basle, in folio, a collection of voyages and travels, under the title, "Novus orbis regionum ac insularum veteribus incognitarum una cum tabula cosmographica et aliquot aliis consimilis argumenti libellis," in which he included the Latin translation of Varthema. This collection was translated into German by Michael Herr, under the title, "Die New Welt," and printed at Strasburg in 1534. In the introductory epistle to Regnart Count of Hanau, he says, that if he had met with the German translation of Varthema (whom he calls Varthoman) before he had made his own, he should have been glad to have been spared his trouble. It is clear, therefore, that Herr did not make the German translation published in 1515 and 1516. Herr's translation was executed from the Latin— that of 1515 from the Italian.

Another translation by Hieronymus Megiserus, historiographer of the Elector of Saxony, was printed at Leipzig in 1610, with the following title :—

"4. Hodeporicon Indiæ Orientalis; das ist, Warhafftige Beschreibung der anschlich Lobwürdigen Reyss, Welche der Edel gestreng und weiterfahrne Ritter, H. Ludwig di Barthema von Bononien aus Italia bürtig, Inn die Orientalische und Morgenländer, Syrien, beide Arabien, Persien, und Indien, auch in Egypten und Ethyopien, zu Land und Wasser persönlich verrichtet : Neben eigentlicher Vermeldung Vielerley Wenderbahren Sachen, so er darinnen gesehen und erfahren, Alss da seynd mañigfaltige sorten von Thieren und Gewächsen, Dessgleichen allerhand Volcker sitten, Leben, Polycey, Glauben, Ceremoinen und gebräuch, sampt anderer seltzamen denckwürdigen dingen, daselbst zu sehen: Und endlich, Was er für angst, noht und gefahr in der Heidenschafft vieler ort aussgestanden: Alles von jhme H. Barthema selber in Italianischer Sprach schrifftlich verfasst und nu aus dem Original mit sonderm fleiss verdeutscht: Mit Kupferstücken artlich geziert, und auffs new in Truck verfertiget: Durch Hieronymum Megiserum. Leipzig. 1610. 8 ."

This edition is copiously illustrated with maps and plans engraved on copper by H. Gross. A copy is in the British Museum.

Ternaux Compans has inserted in his *Bibliothèque* the title of an edition of Megeserus's translation, printed at Augsburg in 4° in 1608. This date may be correct, as the preface to the edition of 1610 is dated 1 October 1607. He also mentions an edition printed at Francfort by H. Gulferichen in 1548. An edition was also printed at Leipzig in 1615.

Spanish.

The first edition of the Spanish translation was printed in 1520, and the translator, Christoval de Arcos, informs us that he made it from the Latin version, because he could not procure the Italian. He recommends those who doubt the truth of Varthema's relation to go and see for themselves; and to those who may find fault with his translation, he excuses himself on account of the obscurity of the Latin from which it was made. The title is:—

Itinerario del venerable varon micer Luis patricio romano: en el qual cuēta mucha parte de la ethiopia Egipto: y entrābas Arabias: Siria y la India. Buelto de latin en romance por Christoual de arcos clerigo. Nuncia hasta aqui impresso en lengua castellana.

Colophon. Fue impressa la presente obra enla muy noble y leal cuidad Seuillapor Jacobo crōberger aleman. Enel año dela encarnaciom del señor de Mill y quincentos y veynte. Fol.

This edition consists of fifty-four numbered leaves (from II to LV), besides the title, and also the colophon, which is printed on a separate leaf. The book is printed in double columns. Signatures a iii to g v.

A copy of this edition is in the Grenville Library. Brunet states that this translation was reprinted at Seville in 1523 and 1576 in folio, and Ternaux Compans mentions an edition printed at Seville in 1570.

French.

No separate translation into French has been published of this work, but a French translation is printed in the "Description de l'Afrique, tierce partie du monde contenant ses royaumes, regions, viles, cités, chateaux et forteresses: iles, fluves, animaux tant aquatiques que terrestres, &c. Escrite de notre tems par Jean Leon, Africain." Tome second: "Contenant les Navigations des capitaines Portugalois et autres faites audit païs, jusques aux Indes, tant orientales que Occidentales, parties de Perse, Arabie Heureuse, pierreuse et deserte. . . . L'assiette desdits païs, iles, royaumes et empires: Les figures, habits, religion et façon de faire des habitans et autres singularités cy devant incogneues." Lyons, 1556. Fol.

Dutch.

The Novus Orbis of Grynæus was again translated, and this time into Dutch by Cornelis Ablijn, and printed at Antwerp in 1563 in folio. The translator addresses his work to William Prince of Orange, and, speaking of the original, announces his own labours in the following words :—

"Dwelck ich Cornelis Ablijn openbaer notarius residerende inder vermaerder coopstadt van Antwerpen, door bede van sommige vrienden wt der Hoochduytscher in deser Nederduytscher oft Brabantsche taelen getranslateert ende oveghesedt hebbe."

This translation, therefore, is further removed from the original than any of the others. The privilege is dated 1561.

De uytnemende en seer wonderlijcke zee-en-Landt-Reyse vande Heer Ludowyck di Barthema, van Bononien, Ridder, &c., gedaen Inde Morgenlanden, Syrien, Vrughtbaer en woest Arabien, Perssen, Indien, Egypten, Ethiopien, en andere. Uyt het Italiens in Hoogh-duyts vertaelt door Hieronymum Megiserium, Cheur-Saxsens History schrijver. En vyt den selven nu eerstmael in't nederdeuyts gebracht door. F. S. Tot Utrecht, 1654. 4º.

A copy of this edition is in the British Museum.

Meusel, " Bibliotheca Historica," vol. 2, pt. 1, p. 340, says that the German translation of Megiserus was translated into Dutch, and printed at Utrecht in 1615 in 4º; and Ternaux Compans inserts in the " Bibliothèque" the title of another edition printed at Utrecht in 4º by W. Snellaert in 1655.

English.

In 1577 Richard Eden published a collection of voyages and travels in 4°, which he entitled "The History of Travayle in the West and East Indies," &c., in which he included the Itinerary of Varthema with the following title:—

" The navigation and vyages of Lewes Vertomannus, Gentleman, of the citie of Rome, to the regions of Arabia, Egypte, Persia, Syria, Ethiopia, and East India, both within and without the ryver of Ganges, etc. In the yeere of our Lorde 1503: conteynyng many notable and straunge thinges, both hystoricall and naturall. Translated out of Latine into Englyshe by Richarde Eden. In the yeare of our Lord 1576."

A short extract, greatly abridged, from Varthema's work, is also inserted in " Purchas his Pilgrimage." London, 1625-6. Fol.

J. WINTER JONES.

Dec. 10, 1863.

INTRODUCTION,

BY THE EDITOR.

WHO WAS LUDOVICO DI VARTHEMA? Unfortunately, scarcely any record of him is forthcoming except what he tells us himself. I have searched every available repository of such information, to learn something of his antecedents, and have searched in vain. Zedler finds no place for him in his *Universal Lexicon*; our own Biographical Collections pass him over; and all that the French have to say is this:—
" *Vartomanus*, gentilhomme Bolonais, et patrice Romain, fut un voyageur célèbre dans le xvie siècle. Il est presque inconnu dans le nôtre, parce que l'abbé Prévost, et ceux qui ont écrit l'histoire des voyages, ont négligé de parler du sien, quoiqu'il soit un des plus importants pour l'histoire de la géographie, et pour l'histoire en général."[1] I had hoped to glean some stray notices of him in the writings of his own countrymen; but they are as barren of what we wish to know as the rest. Zurla[2] does not even mention him in his Dissertation on the most illustrious Italian

---

[1] *Biographie Universelle, Ancienne et Moderne*, Paris, 1827.
[2] *Di Marco Polo e degli altri Viaggiatori più illustri, Dissertazione da* P. AB. D. PLACIDO ZURLA, 2 vols. Venezia, 1818.

travellers; and Fantuzzi, the only Italian historian who devotes more than a few lines to him, begins his article on "*Lodovico Bartema*" with an admission which I have been obliged to imitate, and ends it by erroneously stating that our author's *Itinerary* was first published at Venice, and by hazarding a doubt respecting his return to Italy,—a fact which is plainly stated at the conclusion of his narrative. Fantuzzi's notice is as follows:—" Of this person, we know nothing beyond what the Co. Valerio Zani has written in the Preface to the *Genio Vagante*, tom. i. p. 32, viz., that Lodovico Bartema, a Bolognese by birth, flourished in the sixteenth century,—that he left Bologna for Venice, from whence he crossed over into Asia, and arrived first at Alexandria," *etc.* " This is all we learn from the Co. Valerio Zani in the abovenamed Preface, subsequent to which we possess no information about Lodovico Bartema; hence, we do not know whether he returned to Italy, or where he died, except that, inasmuch as his *Itinerary* was printed for the first time in Venice, we are led to believe that he did return thither; for it is not easy to suppose that he sent his manuscripts from Portugal to be printed in Italy, which they appear to have been during his lifetime."[1]

[1] The following is appended to the foregoing extract in a footnote:—" This writer's name is spelt in different ways. In his *Itinerary* comprised in the edition of Ramusio, by Ferdinando Leopoldo del Migliore in the *Firenze Illustrata*, p. 310, and in P. D. Abondio Collina's Dissertation *De acus nautica inventore*, contained in the *Commentarj dell' Accadem. dell' Instituto*, tom. ii.

This is very unsatisfactory, and the deficiency is not supplied by any incidental allusions in the author's dedicatory epistle. Agnesina, the illustrious lady to whom he dedicates his *Itinerary*, was the fourth daughter of Federico di Montefeltro, Count and second Duke of Urbino, by his second wife Battista Sforza, and was married in 1474 to Fabrizio Colonna, Lord of Marino, Duke of Albi and Tagliacozza. Of the lady Agnesina, Dennistoun says: " She inherited the talents and literary tastes which had descended to her mother, and transmitted them to a still more gifted daughter, the illustrious Vittoria Colonna, Marchioness of Pescara."[1] Her brother, whose

part iii. p. 382, he is called *Lodovico Bartema;* but in the title-page of the edition of the said *Itinerary*, from the edition of 1535, of Bumaldi, in the *Biblioth. Bonon.*, p. 158, of Orlandi's *Notizia degli Scritt. Bologn.*, he is styled *Lodovico Vartema.* This is noticed by the Co. Mazzuchelli; but it must be borne in mind, that the permutation of the letters *B* and *V*, in pronunciation, is very common with the Portuguese and Spaniards, as has been the case, moreover, among almost all nations in almost every age. So, likewise, the ancient Florentines used to say *Voce* and *Boce*, *Voto* and *Boto*, and so forth. By Konig, in the *Biblioth. Vetus et Nova*, p. 831, he is called *Lodovicus Vartomannus*, alias Varthema. Doni, in his *Libreria*, p. 33, styles him merely *Lodovico Bolognese;* and Simlero, in his *Epit. Biblioth. Gesneri*, p. 121, has *Lodovico da Bologna.* Besides Mazzuchelli, who speaks of him in his *Scrittori d'Italia*, he is also mentioned by Sig. Ab. Tiraboschi, in his *Storia della Letter. d'Italia*, tom. vii. part i. p. 211." FANTUZZI's *Notizie degli Scrittori Bolognesi*, Bologna, 1781.

[1] *Memoirs of the Dukes of Urbino*, vol i. p. 277. Writing of Battista, Agnesina's mother, the same author remarks:—" She was a remarkable instance of the transmission of talent by female descent. Her great grandmother, Battista di Montefeltro [daughter

genius and acquirements are justly eulogized by Varthema, was Guidobaldo, who succeeded to the dukedom on the death of his father in 1482, and died on the 11th of April 1508. As he appears to have been living at the time the Dedication was written, it must have been prepared immediately after the author's return to Italy.[1]

of Count Antonio di Montefeltro,] was conspicuous among the ladies of high birth, whose acquirements gave illustration to her age. By cotemporary authors, her talents and endowments are spoken of in most flattering terms, whilst her character is celebrated for piety and justice, benignity and tranquillity. Though married to a man of miserable character, she had a daughter, Elisabetta Malatesta, who inherited her misfortunes as well as her genius. Elisabetta's daughter was Costanza Varana, the associate of scholars and philosophers, whose gifts she is said to have rivalled, notwithstanding an early death that deprived her infant Battista of a mother's care." The latter, the mother of Agnesina, displayed remarkable talents while yet a child, and subsequently made rapid acquisition of solid knowledge. She was married to Count Federigo, Duke of Urbino, in 1459. (See *Id.*, pp. 206-7.) According to Litta, the lady Agnesina died in 1522, while returning from a visit to the Sanctuary at Loreto. Her brother Guildobaldo having been deprived of the dukedom by Leo X., her son Ascanio Colonna, Duke of Palliano, was subsequently invested with that dignity by Clement VII.; but the bull of the former pope not having been carried into effect, he never succeeded to Urbino. See LITTA, *Famiglie Celebri Italiani*, tom. ii. tavola vii.

[1] I am inclined to think, indeed, that the Dedication may have been intentionally antedated, otherwise Varthema must have had an extraordinary quick passage from India; for as he left Cannanore on the 6th December 1507, stayed fifteen days at Mozambique and two at the Azores, there only remain three months and eighteen days for the homeward voyage, and for the preliminaries connected with the preparation of his book, or at least of the

One would have thought that Ramusio might have picked up some information respecting the early life and subsequent career of our author; but his " Discorso Breve" to Varthema's book is briefer than many of the notices prefixed to other far less important Voyages and Travels contained in his valuable Collection. Moreover, it is clear that the first authorized edition of the *Itinerary*, printed at Rome in 1510, was either unknown to him or beyond his reach; since he tells us that his revised exemplar was prepared from a Spanish version made from the Latin translation,—a third hand process, which accounts for the many variations existing between his copy and the original Italian edition. The following is all that he says:—

"*This* Itinerary *of Lodovico Barthema, a Bolognese, wherein the things concerning India and the Spice Islands are so fully and so correctly narrated as to transcend all that has been written either by ancient or modern authors, has hitherto been read replete with errors and inaccuracies, and might have been so read in future, had not God caused to be put into our hands the book of Christoforo di Arco, a clerk of Seville, who, being in possession of the Latin exemplar of that Voyage, made from the original itself, and dedicated to the Most Reverend Monsignor Bernardino, Cardinal Carvaial of the Santa Croce, translated it with great care into the Spanish language, by the aid of which we have been enabled to correct in many places the present book, which was originally written by the author himself in our own vulgar tongue, and dedicated to the Most Illustrious Madonna*

---

dedicatory epistle, up to the death of Duke Guidobaldo, which, according to Dennistoun, occurred on the 11th of April 1508.

Agnesina, one of the preeminent and excellent women of Italy at that period. She was the daughter of the Most Illustrious Signor Federico, Duke of Urbino, and sister of the Most Excellent Guidobaldo, wife of the Most Illustrious Signor Fabricio Colonna, and mother of the Most Excellent Signor Ascanio Colonna and of the Lady Vittoria, Marchioness Dal Guasto, the ornament and light of the present age. And the aforesaid Lodovico divided this volume into seven Books, in the First of which he narrates his journey to Egypt, Syria, and Arabia Deserta. In the Second, he treats of Arabia Felix. In the Third, of Persia. In the Fourth, Fifth, and Sixth, he comprises all India and the Molucca Islands, where the spices grow. In the Seventh and last, he recounts his return to Portugal, passing along the coast of Ethiopia, the Cape of Good Hope, and several islands of the Western Ocean."

In this dearth of all external aids, we are obliged to have recourse to the narrative itself; but even there, the materials for constructing a biographical sketch of its author are scanty in the extreme. He tells us on one occasion (p. 263), that his father was a physician; but as he was acting a part when that statement was made, little reliance can be placed upon it. On another, he claimed a knowledge of casting artillery (p. 50); and although the circumstances under which the pretension was advanced are calculated to throw a doubt on its truth, it is not improbable that Varthema had been brought up to the profession of arms, or had at some antecedent period served as a soldier, since he incidentally remarks, in a subsequent chapter, (p. 280), that he had been present at several battles in his time. This conjecture is further supported by the particular attention which he pays to the military organization and peculiar weapons of the different people described in the course of his narrative. The only additional intimation which he lets drop of his private history gives us to understand that he was a married man, and was the father of several children (p. 259).

The motives which led him to undertake this journey are briefly set forth in the dedication of his *Itinerary*. He had an insatiable desire of becoming acquainted with foreign countries, not unmixed with ambition for the renown which had been awarded to preceding geographers and travellers; but being conscious, withal, of his inaptitude to attain that object by reading, " knowing himself to be of very slender understanding" and disinclined to study, he " determined, personally, and with his own eyes, to endeavour to ascertain the situations of places, the qualities of peoples, the diversities of animals, the varieties of the fruit-bearing and odoriferous trees of Egypt, Syria, Arabia Deserta and Felix, Persia, India, and Ethiopia, remembering well that the testimony of one eye-witness is worth more than ten thousand hearsays." His surprising travels in search of this knowledge are recorded in the accompanying narrative with an ingenuousness and honesty, and his personal adventures with a ready wit and humour, which do credit to his head and heart; the remarkable success of his book is attested by the successive editions which were called for in the course of a few years after its first publication, and its translation into several European languages; but what reward was reaped by the enterprising traveller himself, beyond the barren honour of knighthood conferred upon him by Don Francisco de Almeyda after the battle of Ponani, and subsequently confirmed by Don Emanuel of Portugal, we have no means of ascertaining. As far as we know, the copyright of his *Itinerary*, secured to himself and to his heirs for ten years, officially granted at the special mandate of Pope Julius II., by the Cardinal Chamberlain of the Court of Rome, as appears from the document attached to the first edition of 1510, was the only recompense bestowed upon him by his admiring but parsimonious countrymen.

Turning from the author to the author's book, I do not see how I can better introduce it than by rapidly leading the reader over the route pursued, halting here and there to illustrate the traveller's journeyings by brief sketches of the history of the countries visited, and the different people with whom he came in contact. The antecedent investigations of Dr. Vincent and Dr. Robertson, and the very recent researches of Mr. R. H. Major, who in his able Introduction to *India in the Fifteenth Century* has done much towards exhausting the subject of the ancient intercourse with India prior to the discovery of the route *viâ* the Cape of Good Hope, must be my excuse for not venturing to supplement their learned essays in that line,—a task, moreover, for which I am utterly unqualified. With this candid admission, I shall now pass on to the narrative under review.

Varthema appears to have left Europe towards the end of 1502, and reached Alexandria about the beginning of the following year, from whence he proceeded by the Nile to Cairo. In his brief remarks on that city, he corrects the exaggerated idea of its extent which seems to have prevailed in the West even after his time; for we find Giovan Leoni Africano enumerating it as "une delle maggiore e mirabili città che siano nel mondo."[1] His summary account of the people and government is surprisingly accurate:—"The inhabitants are Moors [Arabs] and Mamlûks. The lord over them is the Grand Sultan, who is served by the Mamlûks, and the Mamlûks are lords over the Moors." Egypt, at the time, was governed by the Borjëeh Mamlûk Sultân, El-Áshraf Kansooh el-Ghôrî, whose territories comprised Syria as far as the Taurus in Cilicia on the north, and the Euphrates on the east. Already, the Turks under Bayázîd II. had attempted to wrest Egypt from the hands of the Mamlûks; but their invasion in 1490 resulted in nothing beyond the annexation of Tarsús and Ádana. It remained for Bayazid's second son, Selîm I., surnamed El-Yáûz, about thirty years later, to put an end to a military dynasty which for upwards of two centuries and a half had usurped the authority of the 'Abbaside Khalifs, whose representative in the person of El-Mustánsik b'Illâh must have been residing in Egypt, in comparative obscurity, at the period of our author's visit.

From Egypt Varthema sailed to Syria, landed at

[1] Ramusio, vol. i. p. 83.

Beyroot, and travelled by Tripoli to Aleppo. He notices the concourse of Persians and other foreigners at the latter place, which, until the route *viâ* the Cape of Good Hope became the great highway to and from India, was one of the principal stations of the overland transit trade between the Mediterranean on the one side, and Persia and the Persian Gulf on the other. Passing through Hamâh, the Hamath of Scripture, and Menîn in the vicinity of Helbon, still famous for the quality of its grapes, he arrived at Damascus, where he appears to have sojourned several weeks, and to have made good use of his time in acquiring some knowledge of colloquial Arabic. Here, he became acquainted with the Mamlûks of the garrison, and by means of money, according to his own statement, induced a captain of that body, who was a renegade Christian, to attach him to a company under his command; but he cautiously reserves, what is highly probable, that a profession of Islamism was exacted as a necessary condition of his enrolment among the Mamlûks. Whether on assuming the new name of Yûnas, (Jonah,) he underwent any more special initiation than that of repeating the simple formula, "There is no god but the God, and Muhammed is His Apostle," does not transpire; but the sequel of his narrative proves, that he had been tolerably well instructed in the outward ceremonies of Islâm, and by practice, combined with an inquiring disposition, and a great facility in adapting himself to circumstances, eventually attained as correct an insight into the doctrines of the Korân as is possessed by the generality of Mussulmans.

This is not the place to discuss the morality of an act, involving the deliberate and voluntary denial of what a man holds to be the Truth in a matter so sacred as that of Religion. Such a violation of conscience is not justifiable by the end which the renegade may have in view, however abstractedly praiseworthy it may be; and even granting that his demerit should be gauged by the amount of knowledge which he possesses of what is true and what false, the conclusion is inevitable, that nothing short of utter ignorance of the precepts of his faith, or a conscientious disbelief in them, can fairly relieve the Christian, who conforms to Islamism without a corresponding persuasion of its verity, of the deserved odium which all honest men attach to apostasy and hypocrisy.

Forming one of the Mamlûk escort of the *Hajj* Caravan, Varthema set out from Damascus on the 8th of April 1503 on the march towards El-Medinah. Among the few Europeans who have recorded their visits to the Holy Places of the Mussulmans, he is still the only one who has succeeded in reaching them by that route. Joseph Pitts of Exeter in A.D. 1680, Ali Bey in 1807, Giovanni Finati in 1811, Burckhardt in 1814, and Burton in 1853, all penetrated into the Hijâz and returned therefrom by the Red Sea. In this respect, therefore, our author's narrative is unique; nevertheless, we have the means of testing its authenticity by the *Hajj* Itinerary from Damascus compiled with so much care by Burckhardt. This has been attempted in the annotations on the text of the present edition, and the result is alike confirmatory of Varthema's intelligence and accuracy. A journey of thirty days through a desert, which Sir John Maundeville and other travellers long after him would have filled with images of their own marvellous imaginations, is recounted in the sober colouring of a tourist of our own times, enlivened ever and anon with vivid sketches of the wild country and tribes through which the Caravan wended its solitary way. His description of the Bedawîn, of their marauding incursions and mode of warfare, is minutely correct, and the picture which he portrays of an Arab encampment is as true to life now as it was three centuries and a half ago.

Among the most interesting incidents contained in this portion of Varthema's peregrinations is the Caravan halt near " a mountain inhabited by Jews," within three days' march of El-Medînah. The stature of these people, which he limits to two feet in height, was either taken on trust from his Muhammedan companions, or estimated irrespective of the distance at which he saw them; but tinged with borrowed fable as this part of his narrative undoubtedly is, the existence of a Jewish colony in that locality for ages anterior to his time is a well authenticated fact, though every trace of them, beyond an unfounded rumour that their descendants still existed there, performing in secret all the ceremonies of their religion, had disappeared when Burckhardt visited the Hijâz. Arabian authors refer the foundation of the settlement to different periods extending as far back as the days of Moses; but the most probable account is that their first immigration occurred after the devastation of Judea by the armies of Nebuchadnezzar, and that the colony was enlarged by successive bands of refugees in after times down to the destruction of Jerusalem by Titus, and the persecutions to which they were subjected under the Emperor Adrian.

On entering El-Medînah, " wishing to see every thing," our traveller's party engaged the services of a *Muzawwir*, or guide, whose duty it doubtless was then, as it is still, to instruct the pilgrims in the appointed ceremonies of the *Hajj*, as well as to accompany them in the character of ordinary *ciceroni*. The principal object of interest here was the tomb of Muhammed, and with one or two minor exceptions, attributable probably to his imperfect knowledge of Arabic, our author's detailed description of the interior and exterior of the Mosque is strikingly verified by the later accounts of it as given by Burckhardt and Burton. He takes occasion, moreover, in the course of his observations, to correct the absurd notion, which prevailed extensively in those days, that the Prophet's coffin was made of metal, and hung in mid air by the attraction of a powerful magnet.

Another superstition which the party ventured to question on the spot, was the supernatural light which the more credulous Moslems believe to issue from the sepulchre of their Prophet, as firmly as pious Christians of the Greek rite believe in the fable of the Holy Fire as it is manufactured at Jerusalem.

The discussion which took place on this subject between the Captain of the Mamlûks and certain Sherîfs of the Mosque reveals the renegade's general disbelief in Muhammedanism; though it may well be doubted whether such an unreserved manifestation of it could have been attempted with impunity except by a person in his position.

The character of the townspeople, which is proverbially bad, elicits from Varthema the epithet of " canaglia," and expressing equal disgust at " the vanities of Muhammed," which form the staple attractions to the pilgrim visitors at El-Medînah, or The City, *par excellence*, he resumes his onward journey towards Meccah, which was accomplished in ten days. The intervening country appears to have been in a very unsettled state, for he records two skirmishes with large bands of Arabs, and ascribes the cause to the prevalence of a great war between four brothers who were fighting for the lordship of Meccah. In a subsequent chapter, whilst describing Juddah, he mentions incidentally that the government of that town was administered by one of the brothers of " Barachet," who was then the ruling " Sultan of Meccah."

By the latter designation, we are undoubtedly to understand the " Sherîf," which title, as applied to the Arab ruler of Meccah, has entirely superseded the more ancient one of " Amir." The particular family from which candidates for that dignity were elected claim, in common with several others which assume the same honourable distinction, to be the descendants of Hasan, the eldest son of 'Ali, through his two sons Zaid and Hasan el-Musanna; but the first historical notice which we possess of their territorial jurisdiction in the Hijâz, is given by Ibn Shubnah, during the reign of the Ayyubite princes in Yemen, who records that in his time El-Medînah and Meccah were severally governed by two members of that family, each bearing the title of "Amîr."[1] Although exercising almost sovereign power within the limits assigned to them, the Sherîfs were avowedly subordinate to the successive Khalîfs of the Omeyya and 'Abbaside dynasties, and subsequently to the Mamlûk Sultâns of Egypt, whose prerogative it was to recognize their authority by investing them annually with a robe of honour. This suzerainty, in his time, is casually adverted to by Varthema, who speaks of the lord of Juddah and the Sultan of Meccah as being "subject to the Grand Sultan of Cairo."

But a supremacy which, in effect, was barely nominal, seldom availed to maintain public order in the Hijâz, more especially whenever rival factions among the Sherîfs contended for the chief magistracy of Meccah. Such family feuds were of constant occurrence, and one was actually in progress at the time of our traveller's visit, and his incidental remarks on the subject are so strikingly corroborated by native historical records, as to merit special illustration. The following passages, translated from the *Kurrat el-Ayûn*, an Arabic manuscript Chronicle of

---

[1] See D'HERBELOT, sub voce *Meccah*.

Yemen, besides substantiating the statements of Varthema, afford a general view of the political condition of the Hijâz at the period referred to:—

"A.H. 906. In the month of Zul' Käadah of this year, [corresponding with parts of May and June, A.D. 1500,] a battle took place between the Sherîf Hazä'a bin Muhammed bin Barakât and his brother Barakât ibn Muhammed, the lord of the Hijâz, wherein the latter was overcome and put to flight, the Egyptian escort seizing all his property, and depriving him of everything. The cause was as follows:— When El-'Adil Tûmân Bey, lord of Egypt, succeeded El-Ashraf Janblât, he expelled an amîr of the latter named Kansooh el-Mâhmady, known as El-Burj, who proceeded to Meccah; but neither the Sherîf nor the Kâdhi, nor any of the nobles, took any notice of him, fearing the displeasure of Tûmân Bey. On the death of Tûmân Bey, he was succeeded by El-Ashraf Kansooh el-Ghôrî, who forthwith sent a letter to El-Burj, appointing him Nâib of Damascus. Thereupon the Sherîf went to pay his respects to him; but he refused to receive him on account of his former conduct. Hazä'a being then at Meccah, Kansooh el-Burj instigated him to assume the government of Meccah, and to place his brother Barakât over it [as his subordinate.] To this end he directed him to go to Yembo, and sent word to the Amîr of the Egyptian *Hajj* to meet him there, to make over to him the imperial firmâns, and to invest him with the imperial robe. This was accordingly done; and Hazä'a put on the robe which had been brought for his brother Barakât, and dressed his brother El-Jâzâni in the clothes which he himself wore when he presided with his brother Barakât. He then proceeded with the Egyptian caravan towards Meccah, accompanied by about one hundred of the Sherifs of the Benu-Ibrahîm. On hearing this, Barakât went out as far as the Wâdi Markâ to meet them, when a battle ensued wherein

Hazä'a was routed several times, about thirty of his followers were killed, and some parts of the caravan plundered. The Egyptian escort then charged with Hazä'a, whereupon Barakât fled, leaving his son Abu'l-Kasam and several of his soldiers dead on the field. After this, the Egyptians entered the house of Barakât, seized all he had, his women included, whom they also plundered. Barakât took refuge in Juddah, and Hazä'a entered Meccah with the Egyptian escort; but the city became much disturbed, outrages and fear increased on the roads, and the pilgrims who had come by sea returned home; consequently the *Hajj* was very small, and the Sherîf Barakât did not perform it. When the *Hajj* was over, Hazä'a reflected that the cause of all this mischief was owing to his contention with his brother Barakât; and fearing lest he might be attacked by him in Meccah, he accompanied the Damascus caravan to Yembo, whither Barakât pursued him; but the escort protected Hazä'a against him. So Barakât returned to Meccah, and peace and security were reëstablished among the people and on the roads.

"But the year following [A.D. 1501] Hazä'a and Barakât again encountered each other in a place called Táraf el-Burkà, when the latter was overcome, and his brother Abu-Dä'anaj, with seven of the Sherîfs of the Benu-Nima, together with fourteen of the Turks on his side, were killed. On this occasion Hazä'a had with him three thousand two hundred horsemen, and Barakât only five hundred. The latter fled till he reached Salkhat el-Ghoráb, and Hazä'a went to Juddah, where he proclaimed an amnesty to the inhabitants, and appointed Muhammed ibn Râjah ibn Sámbalah his deputy, and one of his slaves governor in Juddah, and sent his brother, El-Jâzâni, to Meccah, to settle matters in that quarter, whither he subsequently followed him with a military force. Some time after, a robe of investiture and a firmân were sent to him from Egypt, and he took up his residence in Meccah.

"On the fifteenth of the month of Rajab, [25th December 1501,] Hazä'a ibn Muhammed ibn Barakât was removed to the mercy of God, and his brother El-Jâzâni succeeded him, through the influence of the Kâdhi Abu es-Sa'ûd ibn Ibrahîm ibn Dhuheirah.

"A.H. 908. In the month of Shä'abân of this year [corresponding with January A.D. 1502] there was a fierce battle between the Sherîf el-Jâzâni and his brother Barakât at Munhenna, to the eastward of Meccah, in which the Sherîf Barakât was thoroughly routed, and all the principal men of his armies killed, he himself escaping with only a few adherents.

"In the month of Rajab of the same year [December A.D. 1502] the Sherîf El-Jâzâni ibn Muhammed ibn Barakât was killed near the gate of the Käabah by a band of Turks, on account of some outrages which he had committed, and they set up in his place his brother Humeidhah. Towards the end of that same year [between March and May 1503] the Sherîf Barakât fled from Egypt [by which it would appear that he had been taken there as a prisoner] with the connivance of the Amîr ed-Duweidâr,[1] and brought with him a large army, which he collected from among the Beni Lâm, the Ahl esh-Shark, and the Findiyîn, and he prevented the people from performing the *Wakûf*,[2] until the Amîr of the *Hajj* gave him four thousand *ashrafi* to clear the road between them and the [place of the] *Wakûf*; whereupon he was able to accompany the people to Arafât and Muzdelifah and Mina;[3] but in the meantime the followers

---

[1] This was the first dignitary of the state, after the sovereign, during the regency of the Mamlûks. The office corresponded with that of the Grand Wazír among the Turks, and the court of the Amîr ed-Duweidâr was almost equal to that of the Sultàn.

[2] One of the ceremonies connected with the Pilgrimage, which is performed at Arafât. See p. 43.

[3] See note 1 on p. 45.

of Barakât plundered a caravan from Juddah, near the gates of Meccah."

The facts thus recorded are corroborated by the author of the *Ruăh er-Ruăh*, another Arabic chronicle of a later date; but these extracts amply suffice to attest the truth of Varthema's incidental remarks respecting the feud which existed between the rival brothers Barakât, and the general insecurity of the country resulting therefrom. Moreover, a careful comparison of dates, as they may be gathered from our traveller's journal, with those given in the above quotations, renders it highly probable that the Arabs whom the caravan encountered between El-Medînah and Meccah, (see p. 35,) and those also who caused the precipitate rush from Arafât, (see p. 44,) consisted of adherents of one or other of the contending factions.

To return to our review of the narrative. Entering Meccah with the *Hajj*, Varthema proceeds to give an account of the city and its inhabitants, noticing particularly the great number of foreigners who had arrived there from the east and west, "some for purposes of trade, and some on pilgrimage for the pardon of their sins"; and the various commodities which were imported by them from Africa, the western coast of India, and the Bay of Bengal. Next, he takes us into the Great Mosque, describing the Kä'abah and the well Zemzem, with the various ceremonies performed there; and thence he accompanies the pilgrims to Arafât, and returns with them in haste through the Valley of Mina, where he witnessed the customary lapidation of the "Great Devil."

d 2

Considering that our author is the first European traveller on record who visited the holy places of the Muhammedans, and taking into account how scanty must have been his previous knowledge of the history and distinctive doctrines of Islâm, his description of Meccah and of the *Hajj* may fairly claim to be regarded as a literary wonder. With but few exceptions, his minutest details are confirmed by later and far more learned writers, whose investigations on the whole have added comparatively little to the knowledge which we possess of the Mussulman pilgrimage through the pages of Varthema; and the occasional correspondence between some of his statements and those of Burckhardt is so striking, as to give rise to the conjecture that that enterprising traveller had perused his book either before or after his own journey into the Hijâz. Burton, whose eastern learning and personal experience of the *Hajj* constitute him a most competent judge, bestows this well merited encomium on our author's narrative:—"But all things considered, Ludovico Barthema, for correctness of observation and readiness of wit, stands in the foremost rank of the old oriental travellers."[1]

The *Hajj* over, Varthema being anxious to visit other countries, or disinclined to return by the same route he had come, meditated escape from his companions. Fortune favoured the design by throwing in his way a Mussulman trader who had been to Europe, and who agreed to aid him in the attempt,

[1] *Personal Narrative of a Pilgrimage to El-Medinah and Meccah*, vol. ii. p. 352.

on learning that he intended to manufacture "large mortars," to be used by the Moslems against the infidel Portuguese, and in consideration of having his goods passed free of duty out of Meccah, through our author's influence with the commander of the Mamlûks. He also furnished him with directions how to reach the court of the King of the Deccan, from which latter circumstance it is clear that Varthema had already contemplated a journey to India. Departing himself with the caravan, the Mussulman confided his charge to the care of his wife, with instructions to despatch him, on the following Friday, by the Indian *káfila* proceeding to Juddah. According to his own statement, Varthema succeeded in gaining the affections of his kind hostess and her young niece, both of whom held out strong inducements for him to remain; but he prudently "declined all their offers, on account of the present danger," and started towards the coast with the caravan, " to the no small regret of the said ladies, who made great lamentations."

At Juddah, our traveller took refuge in a mosque, which was crowded with indigent pilgrims, and, fearing detection, pretended sickness, and even abstained from going abroad except by night in search of food. Nevertheless, his brief account of the place is quite correct, and judging from the number of vessels then in the harbour, which he estimates at one hundred, " great and small," the commerce of the port must have been much larger at that time than it is now,—a result mainly attributable to the

Cape route having subsequently diverted much of the trade between India and Europe from its older channel *viâ* Egypt.

In his description of the voyage down the Red Sea, (which he naïvely remarks is not red,) during which the vessel only sailed by day owing to the numerous coral-reefs and shoals which lie off the coast, Varthema mentions their landing at Jâzân, now an unfrequented place, but at that time one of the principal ports of southern Arabia; then their skirmish with some wild Bedawîn, who are as wild still; next, their touching at the island of Camrân, which he tells us was subject to the " Sultan of the Amanni," meaning the Imâm of Sanäa, but whose territories were invaded a few years later by a combined Egyptian and Turkish army whose fleet anchored in that very place; and finally the passage through the Straits of Bâb el-Mandeb, and their safe arrival at Aden. Here, the day following, being suspected as a Christian spy in disguise, he was forthwith laden with irons, and placed in confinement together with another individual, apparently a fellow-passenger, whose name and country, however, do not transpire. Three days after, some refugees from a ship, which had been captured by the Portuguese, arriving at Aden, the suspicions of the inhabitants were confirmed, and it was only through the personal intervention of the deputy governor, who decided that the case should be referred to the Sultân, that they were saved from the vengeance of the infuriated inhabitants. Accordingly, after a delay of sixty-five days, the two captives were mounted on one camel, still in chains, and sent under an escort to Radâä, eight days' journey from Aden, where they underwent a preliminary examination before the Sultân; but Varthema failing to pronounce the Muhammedan formula of faith, either through fear, or, as he says, "through the will of God," he and his companion were again cast into prison.

Leaving them there to chew the bitter cud of repentance, it will not be out of place to notice the coincidence connected with the proceedings of the Portuguese in the Indian seas at this period, and the misfortunes which they entailed on our enterprising traveller.

In a note on the text of this part of the narrative, I have adduced a passage from an Arabian historian, to the effect that in the year A.D. 1502, seven native vessels had been seized by the Franks between India and the island of Hormuz, and most of the crews murdered. I am inclined to believe, however, that the case in which the refugees were concerned may be gathered more definitely, partly from Greene's *Collection*, and partly from the journal of Thome Lopez. The former has the following :—

"Stephen de Gama being arrived on the coast of India, near Mount Deli, to the north of Kananor, he met a ship of great bulk, called the *Meri* [probably *Miri, i.e.* state property,] belonging to the Sultân of Egypt, which was very richly laden, and full of Moors of quality, who were going to Mekka. The ship being taken after a vigorous resistance, the General went on board, and sending for the principal

Moors ordered them to produce such merchandizes as they had, threatening them, otherwise, to have them thrown into the sea. They pretended all their effects were at Kalekût; but one of them having been flung overboard, bound hand and foot, the rest, through fear, delivered their goods. All the children were carried into the General's ship, and the remainder of the plunder given to the sailors. After which, Stephen de Gama, by Don Vasco's order, set fire to the vessel; but the Moors, having broken up the hatches under which they were confined, and quenched the flames with the water that was in the ship, Stephen was commanded to lay them aboard. The Moors, having been made desperate with the apprehension of their danger, received him with great resolution, and even attempted to burn the other ships.

"Night coming on, he was obliged to desist without doing his work; but the General gave orders, that the vessel should be watched, that the passengers might not, by favour of the darkness, escape to land, which was near. All night long the poor unhappy Moors called on Muhammed to help them, but the dead can neither hear nor succour their votaries. In the morning, Stephen de Gama was sent to execute his former orders. He boarded the ship, and, setting fire to it, drove the Moors into the poop, who still defended themselves; for some of the sailors would not leave the vessel till it was half burnt. Many of the Moors, when they saw the flames approach them, leaped into the sea with hatchets in their hands, and, swimming, fought with their pursuers. Some even made up to, and attacked, the boats, doing much hurt; however, most of them were at length slain, and all those drowned who remained in the ship, which soon after sunk. So that of three hundred persons, (among whom were thirty women,) not one escaped the fire, sword, or water."[1]

[1] GREENE's *Collection of Voyages and Travels*, vol. i. pp. 51-2.

If this is the same act of piracy recorded by Thome Lopez, which appears tolerably certain, it occurred on the 29th of September 1502. The main incidents are identical, and he dilates with admiration on the gallant defence made by the Arabs, and stigmatizes the conduct of the Portuguese admiral as cruel and barbarous. But as all the unfortunate Arabs perished on that occasion, the case alluded to in Varthema's narrative, wherein several ships are said to have been captured and some of the crews to have escaped, must be a different one, though perhaps both were connected. The desideratum is supplied by Thome Lopez, who, in continuation of his account of the previous engagement, describes the chase of four Moorish ships immediately after, of which three escaped, and one was stranded, and the capture of two others on the 22nd and 26th of October following.[1] The six or seven months which elapsed between these outrages and Varthema's arrival at Aden, would allow time for any of the surviving crews to reach that place, and the coincidence thus established is another striking example of the accuracy of our author's statements.

In order to illustrate this still further, it will not be irrelevant to the subject to give a general outline of the political condition of Yemen at that period, referring the reader to the annotations on the text for the corroboration of particular facts mentioned in the course of the original narrative.

During the reign of the more warlike Khalifs, the

[1] See Ramusio, vol. i. pp. 136-38.

turbulent tribes of Yemen appear to have been kept in tolerable subjection; but towards the end of the tenth century the authority of the 'Abbasides became virtually extinct, and the country was divided into a number of petty sovereignties, each assuming different titles, and exercising various degrees of territorial jurisdiction. This state of things continued till the accession of Salâh ed-Dîn, the first of the Ayyubite Sultâns, whose brother Toorân Shâh captured Sanäa, the capital of the province, about A.D. 1173, and reduced many of the independent chiefs both in the interior and on the coast to submission. Successive princes of that family continued to exercise a limited supremacy over Yemen long after the dynasty had been superseded by the Bâharite Mamlûks of Egypt; but the country gradually relapsed into complete anarchy until about A.D. 1429, when the government was seized by two brothers of the Beni Tâhir, named severally Shams ed-Dîn 'Ali and Salâh ed-Dîn 'Amir surnamed El-Melek edh-Dhâfir, claiming descent from the Koreish tribe, who eventually succeeded in taking possession of Sânäa, and in establishing their joint sway over the southern provinces of Yemen. The capital, however, was soon after retaken by its former governor Muhammed ibn Nâsir, and in a fruitless attempt to recover it Salâh ed Dîn 'Amir lost his life.

The surviving brother was succeeded in 1454 by Mansûr Tâj ed-Dîn 'Abd el-Wahhâb, on whose death in 1488 the government fell into the hands of his nephew 'Amir ibn 'Abd el-Wahhâb, who was the ruling sovereign of southern Yemen during the time of Varthema's visit.[1] On the accession of 'Amir ibn 'Abd el-Wahhâb the government of the peninsula, according to the author of the *Ruăh er-Ruăh*, was divided as follows:—" The Tehâma, and Zebîd, and Aden, and Láhej, and Ábyan, as far as Radáä, were under 'Amir. Sanäa and its districts were subject to Muhammed ibn el-Imâm[2] en-Nâsir. Kaukabân and its districts under El-Mutahhir ibn Muhammed ibn Suleimân. Esh-Shark, and Edh-Dhawâhir, and Sá'adah, with their dependencies, were divided between El-Muwéyyed, the Sherîfs of the Al el-Mansûr, and the Imâm el-Mansûr, Muhammed ibn 'Ali es-Serâji el-Wáshli."

[1] He mentions him by name as "Sechamir" or Sheikh 'Amir. See p. 83.

[2] In a religious sense, this title ordinarily designates the leader of the services in the Mosque, and as the Khalifs were recognized as spiritual as well as temporal presidents, they early adopted it. When the authority of the 'Abbasides declined in Yemen, it was assumed by the regents at Sanäa, who moreover usurped that of *Amir el-Mu'amanin*, or Lord of the Faithful. In course of time, however, other rulers of Yemen seem to have called themselves "Imâm;" so that eventually it came to signify nothing more than a presiding prince, or one having authority over subordinate chiefs. At the present day, it would be difficult to trace the right of bearing the distinction to lineal descent; in fact, those who now use it in Yemen cannot lay claim to it on that score. On the other hand, in 'Ammân it appears to have been conferred, by the general consent of the people, for some real or fancied excellence in the person of the sovereign; and it is remarkable that whereas all the predecessors in the dynasty of the late Seyyed Sa'îd bore the appellation, he himself was never so styled except by Europeans, and his successor at Máskat is known only by the title of "Seyyed." I may also add that the title of "Imâm" has frequently been given to renowned authors, either because they have at some period taken the lead in the religious services of the Mosque, or on account of their acknowledged learning and piety.

It is easy to imagine, from the bare enumeration of these petty chiefdoms, that the country at this period was in a most distracted state; but the genius and military prowess of 'Amir soon effected a great change. One after another, most of the inland chiefs submitted to his sway, and in A.D. 1501 he made an attempt to capture Sanäa, but was ignominiously repulsed. Determined, however, not to abandon the project which he had conceived of removing the only impediment to his complete ascendancy over Yemen, he two years after collected a vast army, which according to the *Ruăh er-Ruăh* consisted of 180,000 men, including 3,000 cavalry, and after a severe conflict entered the capital in triumph.

Comparing the dates given by the Arabian historian with the probable time of Varthema's arrival at Radää, there can be no doubt that the 80,000 troops which he saw reviewed there, and which he tells us marched two days after towards Sanäa, headed by the Sultân, was a portion of the army which shortly after, as has just been stated, succeeded in capturing that city. The coincidence is as perfect as it was undesigned, and the inference substantiates with the highest proof the authenticity of our author's narrative.

After a similar digression, wherein he describes in detail the arms and military equipment of the Sultan's army, Varthema invites us to return to his prison.[1] There he would probably have languished for an in-

[1] Prisons in many parts of the East are attached to the palace or residence of the governor.

definite period but for the intervention of one of the Sultân's wives, whom he honours with the title of "queen," who, impelled by various motives, interested herself in his behalf, and employed her maidens to minister to his necessities. But Varthema, intent on effecting his escape, and reasonably doubtful whether the queen's liberality alone was likely to promote that object, drew lots with his companion which of the two should feign madness,[1]—a stratagem of ancient date, if not of authority, (see 1 Sam. xxi. 13—15.) The lot fell on our traveller, and if in the course of his simulation he sometimes transgressed the bonds of decency, the freaks were not inconsistent with his assumed character; and his examination by two hermits, or sheikhs, who were sent for to decide on the case, would probably have resulted in a confirmation of his sanctity, but for the practical joke which he imprudently played on the persons of the venerable examiners, which sent them scampering from the prison, exclaiming: "He is mad! He is mad! He is not holy!"

The amusement which these eccentricities afforded the Sultâna and her attendants is so inconsistent with our notions of female modesty as to be almost incredible; nevertheless, if the inner life of many native *harîms* were similarly exposed to view, it would exhibit ladies of rank revelling in scenes far more revolting than those described in the "Chapter concerning the

[1] It is a popular superstition throughout the East to attribute madness to the influence of a separate spirit acting upon the maniac.

Partiality of the Women of Arabia for White Men." What else, indeed, could reasonably be expected? Brought up without education, confined to the seclusion of the women's apartments, and debarred from sharing in public amusements, it is not surprising that the uncultivated mind of eastern females should follow its natural bent, and seek to satisfy the longing for enjoyment, inherent in us all, by kindred gratifications.

The queen was evidently convinced from the outset that our hero's madness was merely a feint; but he very discreetly resisted all her consequent blandishments, only availing himself of them as might best conduce to his own ends. Simulating sickness, he obtained her consent to visit a holy man at Aden renowned for miraculous cures, and was furnished, moreover, by her liberality with a camel and the very opportune gift of twenty-five *ashrafi*[1] for the journey. On reaching Aden, he forthwith engaged a passage on board a native ship which was to sail for India, *viâ* the Persian Gulf, in the course of a month, and, taking advantage of that interval to escape from the notice of the Adenites, he set out on an excursion into the interior.

In the subsequent pages, I have annotated so fully on the text of this part of our author's wanderings, that it would be superfluous to notice any details here. The Arabic MS. Chronicles already mentioned and Niebuhr's voyages, conjoined with personal experience derived from natives of the country, have been my principal guides in illustrating his trip

---

[1] The *ashrafi* appears to have been equivalent to a ducat, or about 4s. 6d. of our money.

into Yemen; in fact, I am not aware that any others, in the shape of general travels, exist, unless it be the very meagre account given by Ibn Batûta in the fourteenth century. Varthema is undoubtedly the first European who has left us a description of this portion of Arabia, and between his time and the present, Niebuhr as far back as 1761, (with the exception of several brief personal narratives of the route between Mokha and Sanäa, and a trip from thence to Mâreb by Mons. Arnaud in 1843,) is the only European traveller who has penetrated into the country more than a few miles from the sea-coast. Even Niebuhr's journey, performed in comparative security and luxury, does not embrace so large an extent of Yemen as that of our author; but wherever his testimony or that of others was available, it substantiates in a remarkable manner the accuracy of Varthema's observations. The annexed abstract of his route conveys, in a tabular form, the different towns visited, with their approximate distances:—

	General Direction.	Miles.
Aden to Damt,[1] *viâ* Lâhej and 'Az'az	N.W.	120
Damt to Yerim, *viâ* El-Makrânah	E.	40
Yerim to Sanäa	N.	70
Sanäa to Ta'ez	S.	110
Ta'ez to Zebid	N.E.	70
Zebid to Dhamâr	E.N.E.	65
Dhamâr to Aden	S.	120
	Total	595

[1] In a note on the text (p. 75) I have identified this place, which Varthema calls " Dante," with Niebuhr's *Dimne;* but on second thoughts I think it more likely that it represents his *Denn*, which he describes as " une petite ville, avec une bonne citadelle, et une place de foire." *Voy. en Arabie*, vol. iii. p. 214.

On his return to Aden, of which place he gives a very accurate description, Varthema again sought refuge in a mosque under pretence of sickness; but when the time for departure arrived, he was smuggled on board by the conniving Arab skipper, who doubtless received some of the queen's *ashrafi* which Her Majesty had given for a different purpose. Sailing towards the Persian Gulf, the vessel probably encountered one of those north-westerly gales which, at the season of the year when I have calculated the voyage to have been made, blow for several days together along the north-east coast of Arabia. Being obliged to veer, they ran with a fair wind for the north-east coast of Africa, anchoring first at Zaila, from whence they subsequently proceeded to the contiguous snug port of Berbera.

Varthema's account of Zaila comprises all that there is to be said of the place. He notices the large number of Abyssinian slaves which were exported from thence to different parts,—a traffic which has only been arrested within the last few years; the various produce which found its way there from the interior; some of the animals peculiar to the country; and his description of the Sômâli inhabitants is true to life still. Except that he erroneously calls Berbera an island, (wherein he possibly translated from the Arabic *jezîrah*, a term which the natives also apply to a peninsula, and sometimes conventionally to havens on the mainland,) his brief account of that locality also, and of the pastoral habits of the people, is equally truthful.

Though originally bound for the Persian Gulf, the Arab skipper most probably picked up some additional freight at the above-mentioned places for India, between which and the north-east coast of Africa a considerable trade is still carried on, chiefly by Borah merchants of Guzerat and Cutch. This commerce, which in more ancient times appears to have been conducted through the intermediate ports of Hadhramaut on the north-east coast of Arabia, eventually took the more direct route across the Indian ocean, and was in full play when the Portuguese first found their way to the Red Sea. The fact of the skipper having made for Zaila proves that the voyage occurred during the north-east monsoon, which is the only season for foreign trade there, the coast being generally dangerous throughout the opposite or south-westerly monsoon.

In twelve days, the vessel reached the small island of Diu in Guzerat, which Varthema calls " Diu bander-er-rumi," *i.e.*, Diu the Port of the *Rúm*, and describes with his usual accuracy. The suffix, which I have not met with elsewhere, was probably a conventional designation among the Arabs owing to so many "Turkish merchants," (more correctly, Circassians, Affghâns, and Persians,) being resident there. The familiar intercourse which existed between that part of Western India and the opposite coast of Arabia is attested by incidental notices occurring in Arabian chronicles of the time.

From Diu, the ship proceeded up the Gulf of Cambay to Gogo, and from thence steered across the Indian Ocean, doubling Mussendom, to Julfâr, an Arab town on the western side of that promontory, which was subsequently occupied by the Portuguese as a station for the pearl-fishery. Here, a retrograde movement was made by redoubling Mussendom in order to reach Máskat, of which place our author barely gives the name, and the next port gained was Hormuz, where he appears to have sojourned for several days.

The eligibility of that island, situated directly in the line of the Indian trade, *viâ* the Persian Gulf, appears to have given it considerable importance as a commercial emporium at a very early period. If it was the Nekrokis of Benjamin of Tudela, which is highly probable though his description of that place is most perplexing, it was largely frequented by traders to and from India in the middle of the twelfth century. A century later, Marco Polo makes it the resort of many merchants who brought thither spices, pearls, precious stones, elephants' teeth, " and all other precious things from India;" and 'Abd er-Razzák, sixty years prior to our traveller, says that " the merchants of the seven climates all make their way to this port." Varthema's account of the island, —its situation near the mainland, its utter barrenness and yet withal its prosperity as " a chief maritime port, where sometimes as many as three hundred vessels are assembled,"—is in perfect accordance with these preceding travellers, and he describes the mode of fishing for pearls just as it exists at the present day.

INTRODUCTION.   li

All this is now changed, and Hormuz, like the Tyre of Scripture, is little better than a rock for fishermen to spread their nets on. It was captured by the Portuguese under Albuquerque in 1508, who were in turn expelled in 1662 by the Persians, aided by a British fleet, during the reign of Shâh Abbâs, who caused the colony to be removed to Gombrûn on the opposite mainland, and dignified it with the name of Bander Abbâs. The intervention of Great Britain in this affair is thus judiciously commented on by Sir John Malcolm :—

"If the English ever indulged a hope of deriving permanent benefit from the share they took in this transaction, they were completely disappointed. They had, it is true, revenged themselves upon an enemy they hated, destroyed a flourishing settlement, and brought ruin and misery upon thousands, to gratify the avarice and ambition of a despot, who promised to enrich them by a favour, which they should have known was not likely to protect them, even during his life, from the violence and injustice of his own officers, much less during that of his successors. The history of the English factory at Gombroon, from this date till it was abandoned, is one series of disgrace, of losses, and of dangers, as that of every such establishment in a country like Persia must be. Had that nation either taken Ormuz for itself, or made a settlement on a more eligible island in the gulf, it would have carried on its commerce with that quarter to much greater advantage ; and its political influence, both in Persia and Arabia, would have remained unrivalled."[1]

We are now to accompany our traveller through a part of the journey where the landmarks of his route

[1] *History of Persia*, vol. i. p. 547.

are less distinctly traceable. We must, of course, suppose him to have crossed over to the mainland; but how far he had penetrated into the interior when he writes : " Departing thence, I passed into Persia, and travelling for twelve days I found a city called Eri," is not specified. Nevertheless, as I see no cause to question his visit to Eri, the ancient name of Herât, and as it is tolerably certain that he could not have reached that place in the time given, we may reasonably infer either that an error has in this instance crept into the original narrative, or that Varthema dates his departure from a point which he has omitted to record. As far as his rather summary account of Herât goes,—of the city, its productions, its manufactures, and its population,—his information is perfectly correct; and that fact, taken in conjunction with a subsequent avowal that he described Samarcand by report only, may be fairly regarded as a proof of his veracity; for if he was disposed to misrepresent in the one case, there is no reason why he should not have done so in the other.

Twenty days' march from Herât brought our traveller to " a large and fine river, called Eufra," which " on account of its great size" he supposes to be the Euphrates. As he was then three days distant from Shirâz, to which city the onward road lay " to the left hand" of his Eufra, I have supposed him to have struck on the Pulwân at or near Merghâb, a little to the southward of which town there appears to be a highway, leading by Istakâr, to a point below the junction of the Pulwân with the Bendemir, from whence it is continued to Shiráz. Should this identification be correct, (and I can suggest no other, unless he pursued a route by Neyríz and Bakhtegân, mistaking the neighbouring lake which goes by those names for a river,) Varthema must unquestionably be charged with exaggeration, as neither the Pulwân nor the Bendemir is entitled to the epithet of " a large and fine river."

Arrived at Shiráz, which our author describes as a great mart for turquoises and Balass rubies, remarking, however, that those stones were not produced there, but came, as was reported, from a city called " Balachsam" (Badakshân,) accident threw him in the way of a Persian merchant called "Cazazionor," by whom he was recognized as a fellow-pilgrim at Meccah, and whose friendly overtures on the occasion were destined to exert a powerful influence in shaping his subsequent course.

We, who carry with us on our travels circular notes or letters of credit negotiable in any part of the globe, can form a very inadequate conception of the difficulties which an adventurer under Varthema's circumstances must have encountered in making his way from one place to another. He never alludes directly to the subject, but his management may be gleaned from incidental passages occurring in his narrative. At the outset, he appears to have had a supply of money, for he bribed the Captain of the Mamlûks to admit him into that corps. While with them, he probably received pay and shared in their exactions, which, with any remains of his original funds, sufficed to take him to Aden. From thence, he was sent into the interior, as the saying is, at Government expense, and the liberality of the Arabian sultâna furnished his viaticum as far as Shiraz; for, it may be remarked, that there is not the slightest evidence to prove his having engaged in any commercial transactions up to that period, and, if he did so subsequently, it was merely as sleeping partner to his Persian benefactor. Be that as it may, his encounter with the latter was a piece of good fortune, without which it may fairly be questioned whether he would have been able to extend his travels as far as he did. On the other hand, the Persian merchant, who appears to have been a wealthy trader in jewels, was evidently glad to secure an intelligent companion in the projected journey, and his oriental hospitality looked for no other recompense. Instances of such generosity are not as uncommon in the East as in the West, and the experience of Varthema in this respect forms a striking contrast to that of Don Alonzo Enriquez de Guzman in the course of his European travels during the same century.[1]

The first place for which our travellers started in company was Samarcand, whether with the intention of limiting the trip to that city, or of making their way from thence to India, does not appear. However, they had not proceeded far when they were obliged to return, because "the Soffi was going through this country putting every thing to fire and

[1] HAKLUYT SOCIETY'S PUBLICATIONS, *The Life and Acts of Don Alonzo de Guzman*, translated and edited by C. R. Markham.

flame; and especially he put to the sword all those who believed in Bubachar and Othman and Aumar, who are all companions of Mahomet; but he leaves unmolested those who believe in Mahomet and Ali." Here, we have another undesigned coincidence with contemporary Persian history which deserves special notice. Isma'il es-Sûfî, the first of the Sufawîan dynasty, was the son of the famous Sheikh Haidar, the son of Juneid the great grandson of Seif ed-Dîn, who claimed descent from 'Ali by Hussein his second son, whose branch, according to the Persians, is that of the Imâms. Haidar's mother was the daughter of Hasan Beg, the first of the Turkmân dynasty called Bayandûrî, who furnished his son-in-law with an army to avenge the death of his father Juneid, who had been killed in battle with Ferukhzâd king of Shirwân; but Haidar lost his life in the attempt, his two sons Isma'îl and 'Ali Mîrza were made prisoners, and most of his adherents destroyed. Haidar's two sons were afterwards set at liberty by Rustam Beg, the grandson of Hasan Beg, who succeeded his uncle Yä'acûb. The subsequent portion of 'Ismai'îl's career illustrative of our narrative, I translate from D'Herbelot :—

"At this period there were among the Mussulmans scattered throughout Asia an infinite number of people who professed publicly the sect of 'Ali, and especially the distinctive form of it ascribed to Haider, which Sheik Sûfî one of his illustrious ancestors had raised into high repute. Isma'îl Sûfî, hearing that there were a great many of these in Caramania, which is the ancient Cilicia, repaired thither, and raised a levy of seven thousand men attached to the sect, and more particularly devoted to his family, because either they or their fathers had been delivered out of the hands of Tamerlane through the intercession of Sheik Sûfî.

"Young Isma'il, who was then only fourteen years old, undertook with this handful of men to wage war with Ferukhzâd, king of Shirwân, a province of Media, whom he regarded as the murderer of his father. This enterprise was so successful, that he challenged and slew his enemy, seized his kingdom, and thereby gained a position which opened Asia to his ambition.

"This first essay in arms took place A.H. 906, corresponding exactly with A.D. 1500, and the following year Isma'il attacked and took the city of Tabrîz, obliging Alvend, the grandson of Usuncassan [Hasan Beg] who reigned there, to flee and shut himself up in Baghdad; but that sultân was forced to leave that city also and take refuge in Diarbekir, where he died, A.H. 910, and Baghdad fell into the hands of Isma'il.

"In A.H. 908, [A.D. 1052,] Isma'il Shâh, after making himself master of Tabrîz, Media, and Chaldea, turned his arms against Persia, where another grandson of Usuncassan reigned, named Murâd Beg, or 'Amrâth son of Yü'acûb Beg. This prince, finding himself vigorously attacked by his adversary, wished to decide the contest by a general engagement. Leaving Shirâz with that object, he marched towards Hamadân, where the battle took place, wherein he was overcome and obliged to flee to Baghdad, as his cousin Alvend had done before him.

"In A.H. 909, [A.D. 1503,] Isma'il having besieged Murâd in Baghdad, the latter took to flight, and running from one province to another was ultimately slain by the soldiers of Isma'il."[1]

---

[1] *Bibliothèque Orientale*, sub voce ISMAEL.

INTRODUCTION.   lvii

The disturbed state of the country consequent on these intestine politico-religious contests may reasonably be inferred, and as they were at their height during Varthema's sojourn in Persia, his incidental notice of them, as interrupting his journey to Samarcand, is entitled to be regarded as a strong internal proof of the truthfulness of his narrative.

The Persian merchant became so much attached to our traveller during the abortive attempt to reach Samarcand, that on their return to Shiráz he intimated to the latter his intention of giving him the hand of his niece, who was called " Samis, that is, the Sun," and so far transgressed Mussulman etiquette in his favour as to present him personally to the damsel, with whom Varthema "pretended to be much pleased, although his mind was intent on other things." He tells us, however, that his destined bride was " extremely beautiful, and had a name which suited her ;" and lest the designation should be considered a misnomer, it must be remembered that the Sun takes the feminine gender in most of the oriental languages.

Starting afresh from Shiráz, the two travellers reached Hormuz, where they embarked for India, and in due course anchored " at a port which is called Cheo, near to a very large river called the Indus, which Indus is near a city called Combeia." Faulty as Varthema's geography is of that part of the coast, there is no difficulty in identifying his " Cheo" with Joah, or Kow, a village on one of the estuaries of the Indus about four miles from the sea, which is still frequented by native boats trading with

Scind. His account of Cambay, however, which is the next port gained,—of the city; its situation near another river (the Myhee;) the produce of the district, comprising abundance of grain, "an immense quantity of cotton" and manufactured silk stuffs, with which between forty and fifty vessels were laden every year; and the cornelians and chalcedonies for which Cambay is still famous;—in all these particulars his description is as applicable now as it was then. Moreover, the extraordinary tides called the *Bore*, which prevail in the Gulf of Cambay, are recognizable in his remarks on that subject, although he erroneously makes the waters "rise in the reverse of ours," that is, "when the moon is on the wane."

Before accompanying our author any farther, it may serve to illustrate his subsequent progress, and obviate needless repetition, if we take a general view of the political state of Western India at this period.

Till the end of the fourteenth century, Guzerat was a dependency of the Affghân or Ghôrî empire of Hindustân, and in A.D. 1391 Nâsir-ed-Dîn Muhammed Shâh bin Firûz Shâh, the ruling emperor, appointed Dhâfir Khân viceroy over that province; but the disorders which subsequently ensued among the successors of Fîrûz Shâh induced Dhâfir Khân to throw off his allegiance to the court of Delhi, and in 1408 he declared himself independent under the title of Muzáffir Shâh. Three years later, he was poisoned by his grandson Ahmed Shâh, who succeeded him on the throne of Guzerat, and the sovereignty continued in the same family till the accession of Mahmûd Shâh, surnamed Bigarrah, who was the reigning sultân when Varthema reached Cambay.

The next native state with which our narrative brings us in contact is the Mussulman kingdom of the Deccan, comprising several dependencies in the Concan, of which the principal appear to have been Dabul and Goa, ruled by tributary governors, and extending as far south on the coast as the vicinity of Varthema's " Bathacala." Towards the end of the fifteenth century, the different principalities forming this kingdom were still subject to the Bahmâni sultâns of Kalberga, or Ahsunabâd, a dynasty founded by 'Alâ-ed-Dîn Bahmâni, a servant at the court of Muhammed Shâh Toghlâk, the Ghôrî Emperor of Hindustân, who about A.D. 1347 conquered all the Deccan and established his capital at Kalberga. But during the reign of Mahmûd Shâh II., (A.D. 1482—1518,) the fourteenth of the Bahmâni dynasty, the territories of this state were divided by the revolt of several of its subordinate governors: Fath'-Allah 'Imâd Khân, of Berar, appropriated that province; Ahmed Nizâm Shâh, of Ahmednagar, followed his example; Kâsim Berîd, the Shah's minister, made himself master of Bidar, or Ahmedabâd; and Yûsuf 'Adil Khân seized upon Bîjapûr. The latter personage was the reputed son of Murâd II. of Anatolia, who on the accession of his elder brother Muhammed, and while yet a child, was sent secretly into Persia by his mother to escape the law which ordained that only one son of the reigning family should be suffered to live. Brought up until sixteen years old among the disciples of the famous Sheikh Sûfî, he subsequently determined to try his fortune in Hindustân, became one of the body-guard in the royal household at Kalberga, and eventually governor of Bijapûr. Taking advantage of the dissensions which arose at that period in the Bahmani empire, and supported by a strong party in the state, he assumed independence with the title of 'Adil Shâh. This event occurred in A.D. 1501, and as his reign lasted for ten years, he is undoubtedly the "King of the Deccan" referred to by Varthema in his description of Bijapûr.

After passing the maritime provinces of Bijapûr, our narrative brings us into the territories of Bijayanagâr, which at the period under review comprised several tributary dependencies on the Western coast extending from Bathacala, or Batheal, near or identical with the more modern town of Sedashevaghur, on the north, and Mangalore on the south. This Brahminical kingdom of the Carnatic, having its capital at Bijayanagâr on the Toongabudra, and which in more ancient times included the greater part of the peninsula, had been deprived of several of its provinces by the encroachments of the Mussulman sovereigns of the Deccan; nevertheless, at the beginning of the sixteenth century it was still a powerful state, and exercised jurisdiction over a number of tributary râjahs on the Coromandel coast as far north as the Kistnah. At that time, the affairs of the kingdom were administered by Ramrâj, whose accession to the regency is thus narrated by Ferishta:—

"The government of Beejanuggur had remained in one family, in uninterrupted succession, for seven hundred years; when Seeroy dying was succeeded by his son, a minor, who did not live long after him, and left the throne to a younger brother. He also had not long gathered the flowers of enjoyment from the garden of royalty, before the cruel skies, proving their inconstancy, burned up the earth of his existence with the blasting winds of annihilation. Being succeeded by an infant, only three months old, Heemraaje, one of the principal ministers of the family, celebrated for great wisdom and experience, became sole regent, and was cheerfully obeyed by all the vassals of the kingdom for forty years; though, on the arrival of the young king at the age of manhood, he had poisoned him, and put an infant of his family on the throne, in order to have a pretence for keeping the regency in his hands. Heemraaje at his death was succeeded in office by his son Ramraaje, who having married a daughter of Seeroy, by that alliance greatly added to his influence and power. By degrees, raising his own family to the highest ranks, and destroying the ancient nobility by various intrigues, he at length aspired to reign in his own name, and totally to extirpate the family of Seeroy."[1] This Ramraaje, or Ramrâj, was the person whom Varthema designates as "the king of Narsinga" in the account of his visit to Bijayanagâr.

Adjoining the littoral provinces of the latter, on the south, was the small independent rajahship of

[1] Scott's *Ferishta*, vol. i. p. 262.

Cannanore, beyond which began the kingdom of the Tamuri Râjah, commonly called the Zamorin, whose territories extended as far south as Ponani, and who appears to have exercised certain rights of suzerainty over the contiguous state of Cochin. The origin of the preëminence of the Zamorin, as collected from the early Portuguese historians, is as follows:—
"About 600 years ago, Malabar was all united under one prince, whose name was Sarana Perimal. In his time, the Moors (Arabs) of Mekka discovered the Indies; and coming to Koulan, [Quilon,] which was then the royal seat, the king was so taken with their religion, that not content with turning Mohammedan, he determined to go on a pilgrimage to Mekka, and there spend the remainder of his life. Before his departure, he divided his dominions among his kindred, reserving only twelve leagues of land lying near the sea. This, just before he embarked, he gave to his page, who was a relation, ordering it to be inhabited, in remembrance of his embarking there. He also gave him a sword and his cap as ensigns of state, and commanded all the other princes, among whom he had divided his territories, to acknowledge him as their Samorîn or Emperor, except the kings of Koulan and Kananor; but forbid all to coin money but this Emperor. After this, he embarked where Kalekut now stands: on which account the Moors took so great an affection to the place, that thenceforward they deserted the port of Koulan, and would never since lade goods at any but that of Kalekut, which by this means became the greatest

mart in all India for all sorts of spices, drugs, precious stones, silks, calicoes, silver, gold, and other commodities."[1] Varthema's account of the predominant authority exercised by the Zamorin on the Malabar coast, coincides generally with the foregoing, and with all other writers on the subject.

Passing down the coast, our narrative brings us to Quilon, which it describes as the capital of an independent Hindu rajahship, comprising the maritime districts as far as Cape Comorin on the south, and extending beyond that cape to "Chayl" towards the north-east.

Intermitting any further notice of the prevailing government on the Coromandel coast, which, as has already been stated, was ruled generally by deputies subject to the Râjah of Bijayanagâr, the only Indian kingdom remaining to be noticed is that of Bengal. Incorporated towards the end of the twelfth century with the Ghôrî or Patan empire of Hindustân, Bengal was formed into a separate province under Kutb ed-Dîn, the second Emperor, and placed under the administration of Muhammed Bakhtiâr Khiljî, governor of Berar, who is considered as the first Sultán of the Purbî dynasty. According to some authors, Bengal threw off its allegiance to the Empire under Nâsir ed-Dîn Baghra about the end of the fourteenth century; whilst others postpone its sovereignty to the reign of Fakhr ed-Dîn Iskandar, who is said to have assumed independence A.D. 1340.

The succession continued in the same family till

[1] Greene's *Collection of Voyages and Travels*, vol. i. p. 29.

the province was subjugated by Akbar in 1573, and at the period of Varthema's visit the reigning Sultân was 'Alâ ed-Dîn Husein Shâh bin Seyyed Ashraf, who held his court at Lucknouti or Gour, situated on the left bank of the Ganges, about twenty-five miles below Rajemal.

We must now return to our traveller whom we left at Cambay. His account of the Jains of Guzerat, and of the habits and customs of the Joghi ascetics, is as interesting as it is accurate, while his description of the person of the reigning sovereign supplies another remarkable instance of his great observation and veracity:—"The said Sultan has mustachios under his nose so long that he ties them over his head as a woman would tie her tresses." According to 'Ali Muhammed Khân, the historian of Guzerât, Sultân Mahmûd received his surname of "Bigarrah," the name applied to a cow with twisted horns, because his mustachios were long and curled in a similar way.

From Cambay the travellers sailed along the coast to Chaul in the Northern Concan, and then to Goa, from whence they started to Bîjapûr, which Varthema styles, after the province, the "city of Decan," where they arrived in seven days. His description of this capital,—of its inhabitants, the splendour of the the Sultân's court, the magnificence of his palace, his military prowess, and the number of foreign mercenaries enrolled in his army, as also his wars with the neighbouring Râjah of Bijayanagâr,—is fully corroborated by the history of the times as recorded by

Ferishta, as well as by the monuments of its former extent and grandeur which still mark the site of the once famous city of Bîjapûr.

Returning to the coast, our travellers touched at Bathcal, Uncola, and Honahwar, in North Canara,—places of greater trade then than they are now,—from whence they proceeded to Cannanore, where Varthema mentions the presence of the Portuguese, who had arrived three years prior to his visit: the first occasion being that of Cabral in 1501, and the next of any importance that of Vasco de Gama in 1503, when he obtained permission to establish a factory in the harbour. It is noticeable that our author appears to have eschewed all intercourse with the resident Europeans at this time, though Cannanore was eventually the place where he sought their protection. He was evidently not yet tired of his adventurous mode of life, and his assumed profession of Islâm might have been suspected by his companion, and his future aim thereby thwarted, had he established amicable relations with the Portuguese.

Fifteen days' journey inland from Cannanore brought the travellers to Bijayanagâr, where they remained some time. After describing the city, its noble site, and the hunting grounds in the neighbourhood, our author's narrative is taken up with a full account of the elephants maintained by the Râjah, detailing the various uses to which they were applied, their armour when employed in war, their surprising intelligence, and the manner of their propagation. He also gives the names of the different coins cur-

f

rent in the country, with their relative value, on comparing which with a similar list supplied by the Arabian traveller 'Abd er-Razzák sixty years before, some changes appear to have been made in the interval in the silver and copper money; but the gold coinage had undergone no alteration, unless it was the withdrawal of the *Varáha*, or Double Pagoda, from circulation.

Returning to Cannanore, the party proceeded along the coast to Tormapatani, Pandarani, and Capogatto. The first of these places is undoubtedly the "Dormapatam" of Hamilton, situated near the Tellicherry river. The two last I have been unable to identify satisfactorily with the names of any existing towns; but they are distinctly mentioned by Baldæus as occurring between Cannanore and Calicut, and appear to have occupied the sites of Hamilton's "Burgara" and "Cottica," answering to the "Bergara" and "Cotta" of D'Anville, and the "Vadacurry" and "Kotacull" of Buchanan and Arrowsmith. Vasco de Gama landed at this Pandarani, (which must not be confounded with a place which then bore a similar name, to the south of Calicut, but now called Ponani,) when he paid his first visit to the Zamorin.

Our adventurers made a long stay at Calicut, and an entire book of Varthema's narrative is taken up with reminiscences of the memorable things observed there. Its topography, trade, agriculture, animal and vegetable productions, the court and state of the Zamorin, the administration of justice, the Brahmins, the religion of its inhabitants, their every-day worship

and funeral services, their division into castes, the
influence acquired there by the foreign and native
Muhammedans, their mode of navigation and warfare,—all these subjects are treated of in detail,
and with more than ordinary care, forming together
a most complete domestic history of what he calls
" the place of the greatest dignity in India." Bearing
in mind that all this matter is original, and that
many of the particulars noted were communicated to
Europe for the first time through our author's
writings, one cannot but express surprise at the extent
of his observation and the depth of his researches.
What strikes us most is the generally clear insight
which he obtained into some of the abstruse doctrines
of Hinduism, and the correct account which he gives of
the mode of succession to the sovereignty, the oligarchy
of the *Nairs*, and the distinctions between the subordinate castes down to the half savage *Poulias* or
Poulichees. Not less remarkable is his description of
the extraordinary relations, sanctioned by usage if
not by law, existing between the *Nambouris*, or
highest caste, and the wife or wives of the Zamorin,
which, coupled with the picture which he draws of
the polyandry prevailing among the *Nairs*, reveals a
state of social depravity as revolting as it is lament-
ably true.

Through what medium did Varthema acquire all
this information, so diffuse in detail and yet so
authentic? He had no books of reference, and his
prejudiced Mussulman companions alone would undoubtedly have led him into frequent misrepresenta-

tions regarding the *Káfirs*. The only inference we can draw is, that he did not confine his inquiries to them, but associated familiarly with the Hindús also, and, being endowed with uncommon perspicacity, was enabled to separate the true from the false, and to present us with a narrative almost unrivalled for originality of investigation and accuracy of statement among the published travels of his age. Moreover, how did he compile his book? Did he keep a journal, noting down day by day his acquired experience, or did he trust to recollection alone? If the latter, the retentiveness of his memory would not be the least qualification for the task which he accomplished with such surprising exactness.

The suspension of trade at Calicut, owing to the hostile proceedings of the Portuguese on the coast, was a serious drawback to Cogiazenor's mercantile speculations, apparently causing him and Varthema to leave the place sooner than they had otherwise intended. In describing their onward progress, the latter says: "We departed and took our road by a river, which is the most beautiful I ever saw, and arrived at a city called Cacolon, distant from Calicut fifty leagues." This river was unquestionably what is known to sailors as the "Backwater of Cochin," formed by the inland confluence of different streams with the numerous estuaries along the coast, by which, especially during the rainy monsoon, navigation is practicable in a line parallel with the shore. It seems very likely that the journey was continued by the same mode of conveyance as far as Quilon, for Varthema tells us, in a subsequent part of his narrative, that they went from that place to Calicut by this same " river" on their return from the Indian Archipelago. "Cacolon," the modern Kayan Kulam, and the *Coilcoiloan* of Hamilton, is described by the latter, in his time (1688—1723) as "a little principality contiguous to Porkah," which our author calls "the island of Porcai," probably from its being almost insulated by the " Backwater of Cochin." At Kayan Kulam he fell in with the " Christians of St. Thomas," or Nestorians, the ancestors of the native Christian community still existing in Malabar, and notices briefly some of their ritual differences from the Church of Rome. Quilon, the town next gained, and which Varthema calls "Colon," he describes as fertile in fruits but not in grain, and speaks of the king as being very powerful, and a great friend of the Portuguese, which is true, for they had obtained permission to settle a factory there two years prior to his visit.

Leaving Quilon, our travellers rounded Cape Comorin, and proceeded in a north-easterly direction to " Chayl," noticing by the way the pearl-fishery near Tuticorin. Chayl, I take to represent the " Calligicum" of Pliny, and the " Kolkhi" of the author of the *Periplus*, and appears to have been situated near the promontory forming one side of the Pamban Passage.[1] Their next voyage was to the city of

[1] I have identified it with Barbosa's "Cael," which he locates on the mainland " after passing the province of Quilicare [Killikarai] towards the north-east," and also with Hamilton's " Coil," (see note I, on p. 184); but I do not find the name in that neigh-

"Cioromandel," "distant from Colon seven days' journey by sea, more or less, according to the wind," and subject to the Rájah of Bijayanagâr. From the indications given, I presume this to be Negapatam, though, if right in the conjecture, it was a place of greater commercial importance then than it is now. Departing thence, and passing a gulf where there were many rocks and shoals, (the Palk Strait,) they reached Ceylon, and from Varthema's description of the locality as being situated near a large river, surrounded by cinnamon-plantations, and in the neighbourhood of high mountains, I infer that they landed at Colombo. Though their stay here was short, owing to some jealousy of Cogiazenor on the part of a resident Arab merchant, our author managed to collect a considerable amount of general information respecting the island. He mentions the intestine wars which prevailed between four rival kings,—a fact corroborated by Sir J. E. Tennent and other historians; the various gems found there; the cultivation of cinnamon; Adam's Peak, and the tradition associated with it among Mussulmans; the dress of the people, their ignorance of fire-arms, and the weapons in use among them, with which, however, "they did not kill each other overmuch, because they are cowardly fellows."

Three days' sail from Ceylon brought our party

bourhood in any of the modern maps. Colonel Yule identifies Barbosa's Cael with a Coilpatam near the Tinnevelly river; but I think that position is too far south to correspond with Varthema's "Chayl." See *Friar Jordanus*, p. 40.

to "Paleachet," the modern Pulicat, about twenty-two miles north of Madras, then subject to the Narsinga, or Rajah of Bijayanagâr. The neighbouring district is represented as abounding in grain, and the port as largely frequented by "Moorish" merchants. Varthema also mentions that "the country was at fierce war with the king of Tarnasseri,"—a statement which I have been utterly unable either to question or to confirm for want of any historical records, known to me, of any such international hostile relations between the rulers on the Coromandel coast and those of the Burmese peninsula.

Before accompanying our travellers from the shores of Hindustan, I venture to submit a few brief observations on the narrative under review, as far as it treats of that continent.

Notwithstanding the civil wars which prevailed at the time, the external commerce of the country, except in the single instance attributed to the proceedings of the Portuguese fleet off Calicut, appears to have been carried on without interruption, and to have been subject to no restrictions beyond the levy of a fixed customs duty at the place of entry or embarkation. Moreover, foreign merchants residing at the seaports, or periodically visiting them, seem to have enjoyed perfect immunity in person and property, to have been under the special protection of the local authorities, and were withal wholly free in the exercise of their religion. The principal seaports on the western side were Cambay and Calicut; on the Coromandel coast, Negapatam, Pulicat, and Masulipatam;

and, farther east, *Banghella* near the eastern mouth of the Ganges, and Satgong on the Hooghly; but between these were numerous subordinate depôts, occupied originally on account of their harbours, and as affording more direct communication with different points in the interior, which were much frequented not only by coasting craft, but by vessels engaged in the foreign trade. Many of these ports, some of which were selected for factories by the early European traders to India, have been abandoned, and even the names of a few of those mentioned by Varthema have disappeared from the modern maps. One cause of this is doubtless assignable to a considerable share of the external commerce, in which a great many native boats were engaged, having been diverted from the Red Sea and Persian Gulf to the route *viâ* the Cape of Good Hope. The larger vessels employed in that transport required deeper anchorage, and sought the most eligible harbours, whither the trade followed them; whilst the gradual absorption of the native states by the British Government tended still further to promote commercial centralization. That the trade of the country has progressively increased is certain; nevertheless, it may fairly be questioned whether it would not have increased in a higher ratio had good roads been more generally substituted for those numerous outlets on the coast which, by the combined operation of the causes aforesaid, were eventually disused and forsaken. This conjectural inference is confirmed by the fact, that notwithstanding the efforts which have been made of late years to facilitate inland intercommunication, the desirableness of adding to the existing harbours has originated several schemes for improving several of the old ports and for creating new ones.

Another inference deducible from our narrative is the uniform prosperity which prevailed among the inhabitants. Excepting the case of the outcast *Poulias* of Malabar, the different classes of the population appear to have been in a thriving condition, and we read of no systematic oppression on the part of their rulers. These, and the higher ranks of the community, are represented as being very opulent; but their riches served to support large establishments of retainers, and being wholly expended in the country contributed to promote the general well-being of the people. It may fairly be doubted, indeed, whether in this respect the natives of India, on the whole, have benefited by their subjection to British rule. Larger fortunes are perhaps amassed by private individuals, but the domestic changes which a different system of government has introduced have closed many of the outlets through which the wealth of the few found its way among the many; besides which, no insignificant portion of the incomes realized in the country is now taken out of it and disposed of elsewhere. In consequence of this altered state of things, property is becoming more unequally distributed, and the native population is gradually assimilating itself to the European model. It remains for the future to decide whether the results in the East will correspond with the workings of the social organism of the West.

Varthema's reiterated encomium on the impartial administration of justice, wherein he corroborates the testimony of ancient Greek and Roman authors, reveals another striking feature in the Indian polity at this period. That no declension, in that respect, has resulted from the supersession of the old native tribunals by British legislation cannot be doubted; nevertheless, the two systems are frequently contrasted by the people to the decided disparagement of the latter. The chief defect complained of, however, is the comparative tardiness of our law; for under the oriental mode of procedure, punishment follows hard on the offence, and cases are disposed of without the intervention of those intricate forms and delays, and without the heavy fees, which seem inseparable from a British law court. There are, unquestionably, many among the better informed natives who appreciate the even and solid justice ultimately aimed at and dispensed; but the masses revert with regret to the good old days when awards were attainable in much less time, and at far less cost, than at present. This subject reminds me of a wealthy Arab pearl merchant from the Persian Gulf, whom I met at Máskat upwards of two years ago, and who occasionally formed one of a party of evening visitors whose opinions I frequently endeavoured to elicit on points connected with British policy in the East. The theme under discussion was the administration of justice in India, in the course of which the Arab merchant, who was well acquainted with Bombay, spoke as follows, as nearly as I can remember his words:—"There can be no doubt that the government of the English is the best in the world, and no Eastern government can be compared to it. Their law too is excellent, and their judges and magistrates incorruptible; still, there are serious drawbacks in the way of obtaining justice. Knowing this by experience, I long forbore pressing a case against a man who was indebted to me to a large amount; but a Parsee acquaintance eventually persuaded me to put myself into the hands of an English lawyer who, he was sure, would get my claim settled promptly and economically, and moreover gave me a note of introduction to his legal adviser. Thanking him for his courtesy, but still wary of the machinery of the law, I took the note to a Banyan and begged him to read it for me. It contained this sentence:—'My dear ———, I send you a good fat cow; milk him well.' I need not tell you that my suspicions were confirmed, and that I preferred a voluntary compromise with my debtor, to an involuntary milking at the hands of the English advocate." The anecdote, whether true or fabricated, is illustrative of a very common notion among the natives respecting the obstacles in the way of securing prompt justice from a British court of law in India.

It is high time to revert to our travellers, but we must leave them a little longer in the house of the "Moorish" merchant at Pulicat, (who was delighted with the corals and saffron, figured-velvet and knives, which they had brought for sale,) while we take a cursory glance at the political condition of the countries whither they subsequently proceeded.

The principal monarchies in the great Burmese peninsula at this period were those of Pegu and Siam. The capital of the former was the city of the same name, and of the latter, Yûthya, or Odia, situated on the river Menam above the modern capital of Bangkok. The kingdom of Pegu appears to have comprised the sea-coast as far as the fifteenth degree of south latitude, and that of Siam the whole of the Malayan peninsula, the maritime districts of which were divided into three provinces, *viz.*, Tenasserim, Ligor, and Queda, ruled by semi-independent viceroys, of whom the chief was the viceroy of Tenasserim. It would seem, however, that Malacca, though subject to Siam, formed a separate jurisdiction under a Muhammedan deputy, whereas the governors of all the other provinces, like the mass of the people, were Buddhists. There were frequent wars at this time between Pegu and Siam, and between Pegu and the inland states of Ava and Toungoo, which before the end of the sixteenth century considerably modified the territories of the rival sovereigns.

The island of Sumatra was divided into several kingdoms, of which the principal were those of Achin and Pedir, though it is not improbable that the latter was tributary to the former. Most of the inland sovereigns professed Hinduism, and in Varthema's time the king of Pedir was a "Pagan;" but there were many "Moors" resident on the eastern coast, and Achin had embraced Islamism as early, at least, as the fourteenth century.

Java, also, was ruled by a number of petty Hindú kings, who were for the most part subject to a paramount sovereign, called "Pala-Udora" by Barbosa, who resided in the interior. According to the same authority, this personage was a "Pagan;" but Crawfurd assigns A.D. 1478 as the date when the principal Hindú state was overthrown by the Muhammedans. There were many "Moors" settled at the different seaports, and about this period Islamism appears to have been making rapid progress among the inhabitants of the maritime provinces.

Of the places visited by our travellers to the eastward of Java, there is but little to be remarked under this head. According to Varthema, the inhabitants of the Banda or Nutmeg Islands were "Pagans, who had no king, nor even a governor;" Barbosa makes them Moors and Pagans, and Pigafetta, Moors only; to which De Barros adds, that "they had neither king nor lord, and all their government depended on the advice of their elders." The people of the Moluccas were Pagans and Muhammedans, but most of the "kings" were of the latter denomination. Barbosa describes one of these sovereigns, however, as being "nearly a Pagan;" from which we may infer that the population generally, as regards religion, were in a state of transition between heathenism and Islâm. Of the prevailing government in Borneo, we know scarcely anything, beyond the fact that it comprised a number of petty independent states, which were chiefly subject to heathen rulers. The inhabitants of the place where Varthema landed were Pagans, as were those of the island generally; but Crawfurd adduces evidence to prove that many of the Malay and Javanese settlers had embraced Islamism long prior to this period.

Rejoining our travellers, we shall now proceed to accompany them in their subsequent wanderings. From Pulicat, they sailed to "Tarnassari," which I have found no difficulty in identifying with Tenasserim, although Dr. Vincent was disposed to locate it either at Masulipatam, or between that place and the Ganges. Varthema's description of this city,— its situation on the southern bank of a large river, forming a good port; the military power of the king, who maintained a standing army of 100,000 men, whose weapons were bows and lances, swords and shields, some of the latter made of tortoise-shell; the animal and vegetable productions of the country; the domestic habits of the people generally;[1] the

[1] Varthema describes the cocks and hens at Tenasserim (p. 200) as the largest he ever saw; and among the domestic usages of the people, he speaks of their eating out of "some very beautiful vessels of wood." (p. 201.) Colonel Yule informs me that the big cocks and hens, and very handsome vessels of lackered wood, are notable features in Burmah at the present day. He also suggests whether the word "Mirzel," which he has found applied to an Indian dye in a work written by a Dutch author twelve hundred years ago, and which seems to indicate the brazil-wood, one of the products of Tenasserim, may not have originated the Italian "verzino," which Varthema uses to describe the dye, but the etymology of which I have failed to discover. (See note on p. 205.) The quotation with which he has kindly supplied me is as follows:—"Tinctura quædam, *Mirzel* illis dicta, qua panni elegantissimo colore jecorario sive castaneo inficiuntur." Whereon he remarks: "Now, has the *illis dicta* any foundation? It might

peculiar dress of the Brahmins, or, more correctly, Buddhist priests; the amusement of cock-fighting; the concremation of the dead bodies of the kings and principal Buddhists, and the prevailing practice of *Sati*, or widow-burning, with their attendant rites;— all these subjects are treated of in detail, and with an accuracy which is amply confirmed by the testimony of subsequent writers. Among the birds enumerated by our author, there is one "much larger than an eagle," with a yellow and red beak, "a thing very beautiful to behold," the upper mandible of which was made into sword-hilts. Professor Owen considers that this parti-coloured bill applies to the *Buceros galeatus*, of which a jewelled bowl, belonging to the crown jewels of the Ottoman Sultan, is formed; but which tradition had believed to have been made from the beak of the fabulous Phœnix.

Varthema devotes a whole chapter to the description of an extraordinary usage among the people of Tenasserim, connected with their marriages, in which the concurrence of foreigners was importunately solicited, and illustrates it by the personal experience of his party. Extravagant and obscene as the custom is, its prevalence in the Burmese provinces is confirmed by writers of a later date, and evidence is not wanting of its existence up to a very recent period.

help us to the origin of the words *brazil* and *verzino*. Drury or Ainslie would give the synonymes." I have searched through both writers in vain for an Indian name anything approaching that of *Mirzel* either in form or sound, and am therefore inclined to think that it is nothing more than a native corruption of *Verzino*.

A voyage of eleven days from Tenasserim brought our travellers to the "city of Banghella." In my annotations on the text (p. 210,) I have inferred that this place was the ancient *Gour* on the Ganges; but the following judicious remarks, which Colonel Yule has been good enough to transmit to me, lead me to doubt the accuracy of that identification. He observes:—"I think it is to be deduced from what Varthema says, that the 'city of Banghella' was a seaport, and therefore could not be Gour. In an old Dutch Latin geography book, which I have chanced on in the *salle* of this hotel, (Hotel Royal, Genoa,) with wonderfully good maps, by J. and C. Blaen, (no title; date about 1640, as Charles I. is spoken of as reigning,) I find *Bengala* put down as a town close and opposite to *Chatigam* (Chittagong.) I don't lay much stress on this; but I suspect it was either Chittagong, or Satgong on the Hoogly, which was the great port one hundred years later, and also in Ibn Batûta's time." By *Satgong* I presume the Colonel indicates Ibn Batûta's *Sâdkâwân*, which the latter describes as "the first town he entered," [in Bengal,] and as being "large and situated on the sea-shore."[1] But the following quotation from Patavino, whose work was published in 1597, seems to upset my friend's deduction as well as my own; for it also describes *Bengala* as a town distinct from either Gour, or Chittagong, or Satgong. He writes:—
"GOVRO vrbs Regia habitatio fuit, et BENGALA urbs quæ regioni nomen dat, inter vniversæ Indiæ

[1] LEE's *Translation*, p. 194.

præclarissimas connumeratur. Præter has iuxta maris ripam ad ostia Chaberis insignia emporia *Catigan* et *Satigan* iacent, quæ centum propemodum leucis ab invicem distant."¹ I find, moreover, on further investigation, that Rennell likewise recognizes *Satgong* and *Banghella* as distinct towns, and gives some clue towards determining the position of the latter. The former he describes as follows:—" Satgong or Satagong, now an inconsiderable village on a small creek of the Hoogly river, about four miles to the northwest of Hoogly, was, in 1566, and probably later, a large commercial city, in which the European traders had their factories in Bengal. At that time, Satgong river was capable of bearing small vessels; and I suspect, that its then course, after passing Satgong, was by way of Adaumpour, Omptah, and Tamlook; and that the river called the Old Ganges was a part of its course, and received that name while the circumstance of the change was fresh in the memory of the people. The appearance of the country between Satgong and Tamlook countenances such an opinion." Of the other place, which seems to be Varthema's *Banghella*, he says: " In some ancient maps, and books of travel, we meet with a city named *Bangella*; but no traces of such a place now exist. It is described as being near the eastern mouth of the Ganges,² and I conceive that the site of it has been

---

¹ *Geog. Univ. tum Vet. tum Novæ absolutissimum opus*, p. 258.
² It is so placed in several of the old maps belonging to the British Museum. For some further notes on this subject, the reader is referred to the *Postscript* at the end of this *Introduction*.

carried away by the river, as in my remembrance a vast tract of land has disappeared thereabouts. Bengalla appears to have been in existence during the early part of the last century."[1]

To return from this digression: Varthema represents *Banghella* as one of the finest cities he had hitherto seen. The Sultán was a Muhammedan, and had a standing army of 20,000 men. Here they found the richest merchants they had ever met; the principal exports were cotton and silk stuffs, which were woven by men and not by women; the country abounded in grain of every kind, sugar, ginger, and cotton, and was, withal, the best place in the world to live in. In this latter particular, our author's statement is corroborated by the experience of Ibn Batûta nearly two centuries before, who says: "I never saw a country in which provisions were so cheap. I there saw one of the religious of the West, who told me that he had bought provisions for himself and family for a whole year with eight dirhems,"[2] or about twenty-four shillings of our money!

At *Banghella* our adventurers met two Christians from the city of *Sarnau* in Cathay, a place which I was unable to identify when writing the notes, but for which I have since discovered, what appears to me, a very probable representative in one of the letters of Fra Odorico (A.D. 1318), who, in his account of "Catay," speaks of Christians inhabiting that

[1] *Memoir of a Map of Hindoostan*, p. 57.
[2] Lee's *Translation*, p. 194.

province in considerable numbers, and mentions that of the 4,009 doctors who attended on the "Gran Cane," eight were Christians. He then adds:— "During the winter, this lord resides at Cabalec, [Kanbalù=Pekin,] but at the beginning of summer he leaves it to take up his abode in a city called *Sanay*, situated towards the north, a very cold locality and habitation, and in removing from the one place to the other, he goes in wonderful state."[1] This quotation is from the narrative which Fra Guglielmo di Solona professes to have taken down from Fra Odorico's own lips, at Padua, in the year 1330. In the other account, which is also preserved by Ramusio, and which appears to have been written by the missionary Friar himself, this summer-palace of the Great Khân is called *Sandoy*; but the names of the same places are so differently spelt in the two exemplars as frequently to defy identification without the aid of the accompanying narrative. In this instance, there can be no doubt that *Sanay* and *Sandoy* represent one and the same locality; and although it is beyond me to decide which is the more correct orthography, I deem it tolerably certain that the place so called was identical with Varthema's "city of Sarnau."

There is so much interesting matter in these early travels of Fra Odorico, that it is to be hoped some competent hand will prepare an annotated translation of them for the HAKLUYT SOCIETY. A striking feature in the two narratives, which evidently de-

[1] RAMUSIO, vol. ii. p. 251.

scribe the same journey, is that one of them, *viz.*, that written by Fra Guglielmo, contains an account of several places on the western coast of India between *Thana* (Tanna) and Cape Comorin, including *Alandrina* (Fandaraina=Pandarani?) and *Mebor* (Malabar,) and also of *Sumoltra* (Sumatra?) and *Iana* (probably for *Iaua*=Java?) as far as *Hicunera*, a large island in the ocean towards the south about 2,000 miles in circuit, from whence the traveller proceeds to *Silam*, (Ceylon,) then to *Dadin*, an island one day distant, and next, after a navigation of many days, to *Manzi* on the frontiers of China; whereas, in the other exemplar, most of these intermediate places are omitted, and the writer goes direct from *Tana* (Tanna) to *Nicoverra*, and then to *Mangi* by *Diddi*. Whence this discrepancy? Was the additional matter an interpolation of a later date? The subject deserves a thorough investigation.

The two Sarnau Christians whom our travellers encountered at *Banghella* had evidently come to that part of India for trading purposes, and as Varthema describes them as writing from right to left, they were probably Nestorians. On seeing the branches of coral which Cogiazenor had for sale, they advised him to accompany them to Pegu, as being the most eligible market for such articles; and the party accordingly set off together on a voyage of "about one thousand miles,"[1] during which they "passed a gulf

[1] It is somewhat strange that Varthema should make the distance between his *Banghella* and Pegu three hundred miles more than he interposes between Tenasserim and *Banghella*. See pp. 213, 214.

towards the south," (Martaban,) and in due time reached their destination.

Varthema correctly describes the Pegu of his day as a great city, situated to the west of a beautiful river, containing " good houses and palaces built of stone, with lime," and as being enclosed within a wall. The old town has long since disappeared, but Symes tells us that its extent may still be traced by the remains of the ditch which surrounded it, and that the bricks from its ruins now pave the streets of the new town. Among the vegetable productions of the kingdom, its splendid timber-trees and enormous bamboos, and, among the animals, the abundance of civet-cats, are particularly noticed. The chief merchandize of the place was in jewels, and the mines of Capellan, which Tavernier a century and a half later locates in a mountain twelve days' journey from Sirian, are mentioned as the great source of rubies.

In his account of the Peguese army, our author makes the singular statement that it contained one thousand Christians like those found in Sarnau, meaning thereby Nestorians. As there is not the slightest evidence to prove that so large a number of native Christians ever existed in Pegu, I have been led to suppose that Varthema had heard that many of the soldiers, like the Buddhists in general, believed in a trinity, or, as Yule explains it in commenting on a similar remark made by Nicolò de' Conti, " the Triad of *Buddha, Dharma,* and *Sanga,*" and incontinently christianized them. The same writer, in another place, quotes the old Geographer in Ramusio as identifying the Hindû Triad with the Christian doctrine in personal detail:—" All the country of Malabar believes in the Trinity, Father, Son, and Holy Spirit, and this, beginning at Cambay, and ending at Bengal."[1]

Finding that the King was absent on an expedition against the King of Ava, our party hired "a ship, made all of one piece," and set forth in search of him, their course being, as may be presumed, down the river of Pegu and then up the Irawaddy. Not being able to reach Ava on account of the war, they retraced their steps, and on the return of the King five days after were admitted to an audience of His Majesty, who was so bedizened with jewels that, if seen by night, " he appears to be a sun." The Christians, who acted as interpreters on the occasion, apprised him of the merchandize which Cogiazenor had brought for sale; but that business was deferred to the day after the next, " because the next day the King had to sacrifice to the devil for the victory which he had gained" over his Avan enemies. The account which Varthema gives of the subsequent interview reveals the craft of the Persian in placing his corals at the King's disposal for the mere honour of having them accepted by royalty. The artifice was eminently successful; for although the King was unable to pay in ready cash, owing to the heavy expenditure occasioned by two years' war, he gave the wily merchant a handful of rubies for his corals, and presented the Christians with two rubies each.

[1] *Friar Jordanus*, p. 24, *note*.

"Wherefore," remarks our author, "he may be considered the most liberal King in the world;" adding for our information that his principal revenue was derived from the lac and sandal-wood, brazil-wood and cotton, which the country produced in great abundance. Five days after, news arrived that the King of Ava was marching to attack the King of Pegu, and as the latter left the city with a large army to encounter him, our party embarked on board a ship and in eight days reached Malacca.

Near this place was a river twenty-five miles wide, called "Gaza." This was undoubtedly the Straits of Malacca, which are about that width between the mainland and the opposite island of Rupat, and the name is most probably a contraction of *Boghâz*, the common Arabic designation of a strait. As Varthema describes their course from Pegu as being "towards the west," he had evidently a very incorrect idea of the geography of the peninsula. The country about Malacca was not very fertile, but it abounded in fruits and different kinds of birds and animals, and the commerce carried on at the port was very extensive, for "more ships arrived there than at any other place in the world." The natives generally were a bad race, and foreign merchants slept on board their ships to avoid assassination. Distinct from the more civilized community of the place, who dressed after the manner of Cairo, there was another class who set the local authorities at defiance, and who did not care to reside on land because they were "men of the sea." I have pointed out in my annotations on the text how strikingly this part of Varthema's narrative is corroborated by the learned researches of Mr. Crawfurd. "Men of the Sea" is the literal translation of the Malay *Orang-laut*, or sea-gipsies, who are to be found sojourning from Sumatra to the Moluccas. The only habitations of this people are their boats, and they live exclusively by the produce of the sea, or by the robberies which they commit on it.

The next place to which our party proceeded was Pider in the island of Sumatra, which Varthema locates about eighty leagues from the mainland,—a correct estimate if measured from the coast directly opposite, but nearly twice that distance from Malacca. After portraying the physical features of the people, and remarking that their religion and customs, that of *Sati* included, were like those of Tenasserim, Varthema describes the currency as consisting of gold, silver, and tin coins, "all stamped, having a devil [idol] on one side, and something resembling a chariot drawn by elephants on the other." This statement is somewhat in opposition to Mr. Crawfurd, who says that the natives of the Archipelago generally had no coined money prior to the arrival of the Europeans; but this conclusion is modified by the exception of Java, and more especially of Achin, where he states that a gold coin existed inscribed with Arabic characters, bearing the names of the sovereigns under whom it was struck, from which it may be inferred that the date of coinage was subsequent to the establishment of Islamism in that province.

Still, as Ibn Batûta found a Muhammedan sovereign reigning at Sumatra in the fourteenth century, and as Achin was most likely the place which he touched at in that island, there is nothing incredible in Varthema's account of the different coins current at Pedir in his time; for Pedir is the next adjoining province to Achin, and was probably at some period tributary to that state. It is possible, however, that some of these coins were imported in the course of trade with the continent of India, for Varthema describes one street of Pedir as occupied by five hundred money-changers, and associates the remark with the great number of foreign merchants who carried on an extensive traffic at the place. As a colony of Hindûs still exists at Malacca, whose profession it is to try gold by the touch and to refine it, it is not unlikely that the money-changers at Pedir were also natives of India; and, if so, the importation of Indian money is readily accounted for. Perhaps some one learned in oriental *numismata* may succeed, where I have failed, in identifying the devices on Varthema's stamped money of Pedir with some of the old Hindû coins.

In his enumeration of the natural productions of Sumatra, our author includes most of those peculiar to the island, such as pepper, specifying the long pepper, of which he gives a detailed description; benzoin; different qualities of sandal-wood, the eagle-wood of commerce; and silk, both domestic and wild. With regard to the latter article, Crawfurd says, in commenting on a similar statement made by De Barros, that it is probably an error, as he is not aware of any kind of silk being produced in the islands of the Archipelago; and as I can suggest nothing to modify this wide discrepancy, I must just leave it as it is, and rejoin our travellers in their onward journey.[1]

A desire on the part of Cogiazenor to see the place where the nutmegs and cloves were produced, induced him and Varthema to put themselves under the guidance of their two Christian companions, who were now anxious to return to their own country, but who eventually consented to accompany them, on hearing that Varthema had been a Christian, and had seen Jerusalem, where he had been purchased as a slave, and brought up as a Mussulman. This fabricated story so delighted the simple Sarnau couple, that they endeavoured to persuade Varthema to go with them to China, promising that he should be made very rich there, and be allowed the free exercise of his adopted faith. Cogiazenor objected to the latter arrangement, informing them that his companion was the destined husband of his bright-eyed niece "Samis," which finally settled the matter. Smaller boats being required for the projected trip,

---

[1] Varthema also mentions that many of the houses in Sumatra were covered with shells of sea turtles,—a remark which I have been able to illustrate by the researches of Mr. R. H. Major (see *note* 1, on p. 240). But the colossal tortoise of Diodorus Siculus, and even the *Colossochelys Atlas* of the British Museum, is outdone by one described by Fra Odorico in a country which he calls "Zapa," somewhere in the Indian Archipelago. He says: "And in this place I also saw a turtle of wonderful size like the *cuba* or *trullo* [the square tower] of [the church of] Saint Anthony at Padua"! RAMUSIO, vol. ii. p. 248.

wherein there were no dangers to be apprehended from pirates, though the Christians could not promise them immunity from the chances of the sea, two *sampans*, ready manned, were bought by the Persian for 400 *pardai*, (about £280,) and after taking on board a stock of provisions, including the best fruits which Varthema had ever tasted, the party sailed from the island of Sumatra.

We are now to follow our adventurers on a route never before traversed by Europeans, or, more safely, of which no European before him has left any record.[1] "About twenty islands" were passed during the voyage, leading us to infer that they steered along the coast of Java, and in fifteen days they arrived at "Bandan," one of the Banda or Nutmeg group. The inhabitants are represented as being "like beasts:" they had no ruler, neither was any law necessary, "because the people were so stupid, that if they wished to do evil they would not know how to accomplish it." Nevertheless, they must have been within the area of the trade at that period, and in frequent contact with a superior civilization,

---

[1] As far as I can recollect, Marco Polo and Fra Odorico are the only Europeans, prior to our author, who have given us a personal account of any of the countries to the east of the Malayan peninsula, yet neither of them travelled to the eastward of Borneo. Nevertheless, it is by no means improbable that stray foreigners from the West may have been there long before Varthema. Until very lately, I believed with the rest of the world that Burton was the first European who visited Hurrur; but Padre Sapeto affirms that he himself was there some years before Burton, and that several other Europeans had resided at the place half a century antecedent to his time.

for "money circulated there as at Calicut." The only production of the island was the nutmeg, which grew spontaneously, and was common property, each person gathering as much as he chose. The tree, nut, and mace, are described with Varthema's usual accuracy, and he states that the market price of twenty-six pounds of nutmegs was half a *carlino*, or about three pence of our currency.

Leaving Bandan, the next place gained was "Monoch,"[1] a distorted form of *Maluka*, the proper collective name of the Moluccas, which they reached in twelve days. Mr. Crawfurd remarks that Varthema "seems to consider the Moluccas as one island, including probably under this name the great island of Gilolo."[2] This is hardly so; for our author mentions expressly "other neighbouring islands where cloves grow," but says "they are small and uninhabited." It is impossible to decide with certainty which of the islands the party landed at, but as it is described as being "much smaller than Bandan," I have conjectured that it was either Ternaté or Tidor. The inhabitants are represented as being worse than those of Bandan, but lived much in the same style. The only object of interest here was the cloves,—an object which, as Mr. Crawfurd correctly says, "mainly prompted the European nations of the fifteenth century to the discovery of the New World." Varthema gives a very fair account of the clove tree, the soil in

---

[1] I perceive that, by an oversight, I have written "*Maluch*" for *Monoch* in the 23rd line of the note on p. 247.
[2] *Descriptive Dictionary of the Indian Islands*, etc., p. 64.

which it flourished, and the simple manner of gathering the spice. The price of the cloves was double that of the nutmeg, but they were sold by measure "as the people did not understand weights." He says the country was very low, which is only true of the latitude of the Moluccas; and that was evidently our author's meaning, for he immediately subjoins: "and the north star is not seen from it."

After a short stay at "Monoch," the Christians proposed to conduct our travellers to "the largest island in the world;" for so they designated Java, proving how ignorant they were of its relative size. But they must first go to "Bornei," or Borneo, and procure a large ship there, "because the sea is more rough." As this precaution would have been uncalled for had the party taken the same route as that by which they had come, I was at first inclined to suppose that they might have sailed through the Macassar Strait; but that would not agree with the course pursued, which Varthema says was "constantly to the southward." Hence, I have been led to infer that the Java Sea was the rougher passage indicated; though one fails to see the necessity for their having taken the route by Borneo, when they might have reached Java without touching there at all, unless, indeed, the Christians had some particular object in visiting that island. Unluckily, the space of two hundred miles, which Varthema interposes between the Moluccas and Borneo, affords no clue to determine the route, as the nearest extremities of those two places are more than twice that distance apart, which leads to the conjecture that by some mischance the word *miles* has been substituted for *leagues*. However this may be, the place where they disembarked was certainly in the highway of trade, for " a very great quantity of camphor" was shipped from it every year. Varthema heard that this substance was the gum of a tree, but not having seen the tree himself, he abstains from asserting the truth of the report.

Chartering a vessel at " Bornei," the party pursued their course towards the south. The captain,—who was probably a Malay, for Varthema and the Persian communicated with him through the Christians, whereas, had he been an Arab, they would not have required an interpreter,—" carried the compass and magnet after our manner, and had a chart which was all marked with lines perpendicular and across." Mr. Markham assumes that the compass was of European manufacture, its index pointing to the north, and not like that of the Chinese pointing to the south. It may be so; nevertheless, I have not yet met with any conclusive proof that the Easterns borrowed the use of the compass, as they now have it, from the West. However, as the polar star was invisible, Cogiazenor inquired of the master how he navigated. To which he replied, that he steered by his compass, which was adjusted to the north; but, pointing out " four or five stars, among which he said there was one which was *opposite* to our north star," he stated that on the other side of the said island, towards the south, [Java?] there were " some other races who navigate by the said four or five stars opposite to ours." There can be no doubt that the constellation of the Southern Cross is here indicated; but the additional information respecting other races to the south, " where the day lasted only four hours," which would be about 15° to the southward of Van Diemen's Land, is most interesting. It is highly improbable that the Malay could have guessed at phenomena so true, and yet so different to anything which he himself had experienced; still, from whence did he derive his knowledge, superficial as it was? In a note which Mr. R. H. Major kindly drew up for me on this chapter, he remarks:—"This reference to Australia is the more remarkable, as it precedes, in time, those early indications of the discovery of that country which I have shown to exist in manuscript maps of the first half of the sixteenth century, although the discoverers' names, most probably Portugese, and the date of the discovery, as yet remain a mystery." The mystery of the old Malay's knowledge will never be revealed: Varthema might have aided us in the matter by pursuing his inquiries, but he winds up his record of the skipper's communications with the exquisite peroration: " On hearing this, we were much pleased and satisfied"!

The tedium of the voyage between Borneo and Java was relieved by the anxious inquiries of the Christians respecting their brethren in the far West. On this subject Varthema had much to communicate which would be deeply interesting to them; and when he told them " of the Volto Santo at St. Peter's, and of the heads of St. Peter and St. Paul, and of many other saints," his ingenuous listeners would fain have taken him back with them to their country. It is by no means improbable, that this friendly converse had some influence in determining our traveller to bring his wanderings to a close at the first favourable opportunity. He had slaked his thirst for adventure by seeing parts of the globe which no other European of his day had yet visited, and the associations of kindred and home, and of the things which he once regarded as sacred, revived as they were by these discussions, made him long to throw off the trammels of a profession which was now becoming a burden to him.

Five days' sail from Borneo brought the vessel to Java, but at what place on the island the party landed is uncertain; doubtless, it was somewhere on the northern coast. The king and all the people were "Pagans," and although one class of the community consisted of "the most trustworthy men in the world," there was another class still so barbarous as to be addicted to the practice of eating human flesh. Mr. Crawfurd ridicules the latter idea, which would perhaps have been preposterous had our travellers touched at one of the more civilized maritime towns; but that, as it appears to me, was not the case: first, from this recorded statement respecting the subsistence of cannibalism, which, as I have shown in my notes, prevailed in other parts of the Archipelago at this period. Secondly, because the inhabitants were all Pagans, whereas most of the frequented ports contained many Muhammedans who had introduced a superior civilization together with their religion. Thirdly, because in such localities fire-arms were well known, while the natives where our party disembarked were quite ignorant of artillery, their only weapons being bows and darts of cane, and the peculiar *Sumpitan,* or blow-pipe. And, lastly, these separate considerations receive general confirmation from the absence of all mention in Varthema's narrative that the place which they visited was one of trade,—a circumstance which he never omits to record whenever such was the case.

Before quitting Java, Cazazionor purchased a couple of young children who had undergone the cruel operation regarded as desirable for fitting them to become attendants on a Mussulman *harim.* The barbarous practice, which also prevailed in different parts of India at this period, was most probably introduced into these countries with Islâm, and many "Moorish merchants" are said to have made a trade of buying and preparing these wretched victims for exportation to foreign markets.

Crossing over to Malacca, steering at first to the eastward to avoid the surrounding islands, our travellers there took leave of the Sarnau Christians, with sincere regret on both sides, and from thence proceeded to "Cioromandel" (Negapatam), where they engaged a *sampan* to take them to Quilon. At that place Varthema found twenty Portuguese, and would gladly have made his escape to them, "but they were very few," and the eyes of some Mussulmans who knew

h

him to be *Hajji* were upon him. At Quilon they embarked on the "river" (see p. lxviii. *ante,*) and in ten days reached Calicut.

At Calicut, our author met two Milanese, who had deserted from the Portuguese at Cochin, and were there employed in casting artillery for the Zamorin. Varthema concerted with these renegades how to effect their escape, but the attempt was surrounded with difficulties on all sides, and he was obliged to trust to his own resources. Long practice had made him fertile in expedients, and an adept at dissimulation, and on this occasion he set himself up as a Muhammedan santon, affecting abstinence from animal food, (though he clandestinely helped the Milanese to consume two brace of fowls every day,) and a severity of demeanour consistent with his assumed character. As such, he was consulted in the case of a sick friend of Cazazionor, and requested to prescribe for him. The narrative of his mode of treating the patient, as recorded in the chapter entitled "How I made myself a physician in the town of Calicut," is as extravagant as it is ludicrous. Fortunately, the sick man survived the severe treatment to which he was subjected, and the success of his amateur medical practice greatly enhanced our author's repute, insomuch that he was solicited to act the part of *Imám,* and lead the prayers of the congregation in the mosque. Conceiving that his saintliness was now generally established, he next simulated sickness, and suggested that a change of air might be beneficial. Cazazionor, who appears to have been wholly blinded by his companion's deceit, readily gave his consent, and furnished him with letters of recommendation to a friend at Cannanore. Varthema narrowly escaped detention by the Zamorin's Nairs at the place of embarkation, but his good star was in the ascendant, and after travelling some distance along the coast, he eventually picked up a boat which carried him to his destination. Under the hospitable roof of Cazazionor's acquaintance, he breathed more freely, and after reconnoitering the spot where the Portuguese fort was in course of erection, he availed himself of the next favourable opportunity to place himself under the protection of the garrison. Lorenzo de Almeyda, the Viceroy's son, who was there at the time, gave a hearty welcome to one who was so well able to describe the warlike preparations which were being made at Calicut to oppose the Portuguese, and after discussing such matters with him for several days, sent him on board a galley to his father at Cochin, who also gave him an honourable reception, and remanded him to Cannanore to use his best endeavours in behalf of the two Milanese at Calicut. His efforts, however, to effect their liberation were unsuccessful. The unfortunate men were betrayed by the spy he employed to communicate with them, and were barbarously murdered by a crowd of infuriated Joghis in their own house at Calicut.

The sequel of our author's Indian career may be told in a few words. He appears to have been present at a great naval engagement between the Portuguese and the Zamorin's fleet off Cannanore, and was subsequently employed for a year and a half as factor at Cochin. He also describes the siege of the Portuguese fort at Cannanore by the justly-incensed population, which occurred during his tenure of office, and the opportune relief of the beleaguered garrison by the fleet under Tristan de Cunha. He also took part in the attack on Ponani, and in the destruction of the Zamorin's ships which were anchored there, and after the battle was, with several others, dubbed a knight by the Viceroy Don Francisco de Almeyda, the gallant Captain Tristan de Cunha acting as his sponsor on the occasion. His account of these different operations is replete with interesting details, and its general authenticity is fully corroborated by numerous undesigned coincidences between his narrative and the records of later Portuguese historians. Unfortunately, one is unable to deduce any reflection, from Varthema's independent testimony, palliative of the unwarrantable proceedings of the Portuguese towards the native states on the western coast of India at this period. Those proceedings, the offspring of national ambition and selfishness, were carried out in a spirit of barbarity mingled with fanaticism which outraged the first principles of justice, and disgraced the religion which it was one design of such conduct to promote. Would that the history of our own first transactions in India were unstained by any such blemishes! Let us hope that some, at least, of those early faults have been atoned for, and that the remainder will be forgotten in the future prosperity of an empire which has been justly called the brightest jewel in the diadem of Britain's glorious Queen.

On the 6th of December 1507, our traveller finally left Cannanore with the homeward-bound ships, on board the *San Vicenzo*, a vessel belonging to one Bartolomeo Marchioni, a Florentine resident at Lisbon. While on the voyage, he takes a brief retrospect of the recent conquests of the Portuguese in the East, and predicts a glorious future for that monarchy owing to the simultaneous efforts which were made, under its immediate auspices, to promote Christianity among the natives of India. "Ten, and even twelve, Pagans and Moors were baptized every fête day" at Cochin alone, and the work of conversion, which was being zealously prosecuted, was everywhere crowned with signal success. The prognostication, as regards territorial aggrandizement, was speedily realized; for, fifteen years later, the Portuguese had made themselves masters of the principal ports on the Malabar and Coromandel coasts, of parts of Ceylon and the Malayan peninsula, and also of the Moluccas. Their possession of Malacca in the east, and their settlements at Diu and Goa on the west, enabled them to engross the entire trade, including that of the Persian Gulf on the one side, where they held the important island of Hormuz, and that of China, Japan, and the Indian Archipelago on the other. Their ships frequented every port, and their merchandize was to be found from the Cape of Good Hope to the river of Canton; while along this immense line of coast they had established a chain of forts and factories, where their traffic was carried on and protected, unrivalled and uncontrolled. The commercial empire of the Portuguese in the East, whether considered in the dimensions which it attained, the brief space in which it was consolidated, its opulence, the splendour with which its government was conducted, or the very slender powers with which it was formed, is unique in the history of nations.

But the dominion thus acquired was as short-lived as the sincere piety, the generous courage, and the indefatigable energy which had created it. No longer animated by the spirit of the original conquerors, their successors, heedless of the common cause, became indolent, debauched, and effeminate, and strove solely for their own individual profit. Officers and soldiers were without subordination, discipline, or patriotism, and the governors, corrupt themselves, found it their interest to foment divisions among their countrymen. These intestine cabals alone, combined with the oppression which was exercised towards the natives, would have sufficed in time to disintegrate the newly-formed empire; but its downfall was precipitated by the appearance of a formidable enemy from without. The revolted Dutch, interdicted by a decree of Philip II., of Spain and Portugal, from all commercial relations with those kingdoms, seized every opportunity of harassing and humiliating their former masters, and, taking advantage of the anarchy which pervaded the Portuguese colonies in the East, boldly prosecuted their trade in that quarter, and determined at length to expel their rivals. In the course of a few years they deprived them of the Moluccas, the Spice Islands, Amboyna, Tidor, Ceylon, and Malacca. The English, also, who had now begun to claim a share of the spoils, wrested from them Surat and other parts of Guzerat, and in conjunction with the Shâh of Persia drove them from the island of Hormuz, while the Imâm of Máskat expelled them from 'Ammân, and from many of their settlements in East Africa. And now, Macao in China, with Diu, Goa, and Damân on the Guzerat and Canarese coasts, are the only fragments which remain to them of an empire which Alexander coveted but could not win.

The religious conquests of the Portuguese, however, have survived their temporal sovereignty, and the descendants of the first converts, with large additions won over to the Church of Rome by the zeal of subsequent missionaries, are still to be found scattered over the continent of India, and more especially in the Madras Presidency, the scene of their earliest efforts at evangelization, where their numbers are very considerable. Political influence, emanating from every department of the Government, was undoubtedly used at the outset to promote Christianity among the natives; for that, indeed, was one of the avowed objects of the invaders, who professed to be as anxious to destroy the strongholds of heathendom, as to secure territorial dominion. But the withdrawal of State coöperation, consequent on the extinction of Portuguese supremacy, was not followed, as might have been expected, by any general apostacy of the proselytes; on the contrary, though arrested for a time, the work of conversion progressed, and fresh native churches were formed, whose members at the present day far outnumber the converts to Protestantism made by the combined efforts of Dutch, American, and English missionaries, of all denominations.

How are we to account for this remarkable phenomenon in the history of Christianity in India? Whence comes it that Roman Catholic missions there have ever been more successful than missions from the Reformed Churches? Whence, that their converts, a feeble folk though they be, have persistently clung to their adopted faith amidst all the political changes which have surrounded them, the social influences which both directly and indirectly have been levelled against them, and the strenuous exertions which have been put forth to win them over to a purer creed? And, supposing the case, that British domination in India were to terminate as suddenly as did that of the Portuguese, is it probable that two centuries later there would be found amidst its ruins native communities professing the Reformed religion as we now find congregations of native Christians firmly attached to the Church of Rome? One of our own Bishops in India, after describing some of the old Portuguese churches in the neighbourhood of Bombay makes the following remarks:—" They are melancholy objects to look at, but they are monuments, nevertheless, of departed greatness, of a love of splendour far superior to the anxiety for amassing money, by which other nations have been chiefly actuated, and of a zeal for God which, if not according to knowledge, was a zeal still, and a sincere one. It was painful to me, at the time, to think, how few relics, if the English were now expelled from India, would be left behind of their religion, their power, or their civil and military magnificence."[1] During the forty years which have elapsed since the late lamented Heber penned these lines, a great advance has been made in our own civil and political *status* in India, and much has undoubtedly been done to improve the secular and intellectual condition of the people generally; but as regards the diffusion of our religion among the natives, how insignificantly little has been effected, especially when compared with the profuse and expensive machinery which for the last century has been set in motion to that end!

I would be understood as alluding to this subject in its purely human point of view, and wholly apart from all supernatural or Divine affinities; but even under that aspect, the reflections which it is calculated to evoke deserve the serious consideration of such as believe that Christianity alone can regenerate India, and particularly of those who, whether in this country or on the spot, are engaged in promoting its extension among our fellow-subjects in that vast continent.

To discuss this interesting topic more fully would be foreign to a work like the present, and perhaps an apology is due for the foregoing intrusion of it. Readily granting the same, I return again to the narrative of our Europe-bound traveller.

[1] Bishop Heber's *Journal*, vol. iii. p. 91.

After a course of "about three thousand miles" from Cannanore, the *San Vincenzo* reached Mozambique on the east coast of Africa, or, as the country was then called, "Ethiopia." They saw "many lands" on the way, where the King of Portugal held strong fortresses, but whether they landed at those places or not is uncertain. Varthema enumerates Malindi, Mombâsa, Kilwah, Sofâla, Paté, and Brâva, but omits all mention of Mukdishu and Lâmu on the continent, and the adjacent islands of Zanzibar and Pemba, which latter is called by the Arabs Jezîrat el-Khadhrâ, or the Green Island. Most of these localities had been captured by the Portuguese before our author's arrival, and several of them were well garrisoned. The conciliatory policy adopted by Vasco de Gama when he first visited this coast in 1498 had been reversed by his successors, whose arrogant pretensions, inspired by a thirst after gold and conquest, soon brought them into collision with the inhabitants, who were eventually obliged to succumb to the superior arms of the invaders. Almost all the places above-mentioned were at this period in the hands of the Arabs, whose original settlements on the coast must have taken place at a very early period. Eschewing the knotty question of the locality of the Scriptural " Ophir," which some have attempted to identify with Sofâla, and whether Solomon was supplied with " ivory, apes, and peacocks," by Arab traders between Eziongeber and the east coast of Africa, the reader will find in the following quotation from the researches of Dr. Krapf a valuable summary of the more authentic history of these foreign colonists.—

" It is well known that the Muhammedan Arabs, during the first period of their history, for 150 years, overran a large section of Asia, Africa, and Europe, and that soon after the death of their prophet Muhammed they fell a prey to political and religious dissensions, and the defeated party resolved to abandon the land of their birth. Where was a better home to be found than the fruitful strand of Eastern Africa? There they were already known, and would be safe from the pursuit of their fanatical conquerors. It seems that the first settlements of the kind were made in various points of the East-African coast in the year 740 by the Emosaids, or adherents of Said, a great grandson of Ali, the prophet's cousin and son-in-law. Said, proclaimed Caliph by the rebels, was defeated and slain, on which his adherents were obliged to seek safety in flight, and it was in East Africa that they found refuge. In the works of various Arabian historians and geographers, for several centuries afterwards, we find interesting notices of these Arab settlements. From all these notices it is to be gathered, that the Muhammedan Arabs founded political and religious states or towns in Eastern Africa, and that their migration to that country was sometimes voluntary, sometimes forced upon them. Among these Arabian states or towns the most prominent are: Mukdîshu, Kilwah, Brâva, Malindi, and Mombâsa. Mukdîshu was supreme in the north, while Kilwah was queen of the south, from Zanzibar to Sofâla. With the declining power of these two states and towns, Malindi and Mombâsa, situated midway between them, appear to have increased in influence and importance. Mukdîshu seems to have been founded between A.D. 909-951 ; and Kilwah between A.D. 960-1000. It is likely from the narrative of the famous Ibn Batûta,[1]

---

[1] [See LEE's *Translation*, pp. 55-57.]

who visited Mombâsa about A.D. 1330, that the Wanîka [a native tribe] had not then settled in the vicinity of the coast. . . .

"These Arabian cities and communities were prosperous, and in some degree civilized; but they were deficient in military organization. They had not been founded by conquerors, but by traders, emigrants, and exiles, who behaved peaceably to the natives, and so developed and established their influence slowly, but at the same time more surely. They were pacific colonists, and by the trade and commerce which they originated, the natives of the interior could not but recognize the advantage of peaceful intercourse with the strangers, and be glad of their presence. . . . But the Arabs were not to remain for ever in exclusive possession of the knowledge, the commerce, and the power of Eastern Africa, —a possession which would have led them to rule and to convert the whole of Southern Africa. Providence interposed, and at the right time led into those waters and to that coast a Christian power, to check the progress and weaken the influence of Muhammedanism."

The subsequent domination of this " Christian " power, and its baneful results, are thus described:—

"In East Africa, Portugal enriched herself by levying tribute and taxes, in addition to her enormous gains from the gold-mines of Sofâla; but East Africa received nothing in return. She ruled the East-Africans with a rod of iron, and their pride and cruelty had their reward in the bitter hatred of the natives. In Eastern Africa, the Portuguese have left nothing behind them but ruined fortresses, palaces, and ecclesiastical buildings. Nowhere is there to be seen a single trace of any improvement effected by them. No wonder that the Portuguese rule was of short duration, and that it fell as quickly as it had risen. John IV. had, indeed, restored independence to Portugal in 1640; but he could no longer save his colonies. In 1620, Portugal had already lost the island of Hormuz, and its loss was the more felt, because it gave the Arabs of Omân courage and leisure to extend and to strengthen their influence in the Persian Gulf and in Eastern Africa. Portugal had no longer men like Albuquerque, capable of restoring the fallen influence of their country in those seas. All were now alike corrupt and incapable. In India and its waters, England and Holland had appeared, and with their appearance the star of Portugal had to sink to the horizon."

Some idea of the hostile relations which existed between the Portuguese and the natives towards the middle of the seventeenth century, may be gathered from an inscription over the gateway leading into the fortress of Mombâsa. I had not time to transcribe it during my short stay at that island in December 1860, but relied on a copy in my possession, which I believe was taken by Dr. Krapf. The following is a translation of the original Portuguese:—

"*In* 1635, *Chief Captain Francisco de Xeiras de Cabreira, aged* 27 *years, after having commanded this fortress for four years, rebuilt it, and raised this corps-de-garde. And he reduced into submission to His Majesty the coast of Malindi, where a tyrant king had sprung up, and made the kings of Tondo, Mandra, Lazieva, and Jaca, tributaries. He also visited Paté and Sio with a punishment never before witnessed in India, levelling the walls thereof to the ground. He imposed a fine on the Muzungulos, and punished Pemba and its rebel people, killing the petty king, who had been set up by them and by others of note, obliging the* Pariahs *to pay to His Majesty the tribute which they had evaded for years. For these services, he was raised to the dignity of Fidalgo of His Majesty's Household, having previously received, for other similar services, the decoration of the Knight of the Order of Christ, an annuity of a thousand* Reis, *and six years' tenure of the Governorship of Jafampatas and four of that of Beligas, with the faculty of making all [appointments] therein during his lifetime.* [*This inscription was raised*] A.D. 1639, *when Pedro de Silvoa was Viceroy.*"

" We have still to show how the authority of the Arabian princes of Omân first rose, and gradually replaced that of the Portuguese along the East-African coast. Omân comprises the north and south-eastern portions of Arabia, which lie on the Gulf of Persia and the Indian Ocean. In the year 1624, after great disorders and dissensions, Omân and its inhabitants became subject to the rule of a sagacious and energetic Imâm, Nàsir bin Murshid, the Yä'arabite. After establishing his sovereignty in Omân, he planned the complete expulsion of the Portuguese from their Arabian and African possessions. . . . His victories over the Portuguese were continued by his cousin and successor, Sultân bin Seif bin Mâlik, who took Máskat in 1658, leaving the Portuguese then no seaport of any consequence on the coast of Arabia. His second son, Sultân Seif, who defeated his brother Bel'arab and usurped the throne, at the request of the people of Mombâsa, sent a fleet to Eastern Africa, captured Mombâsa, Zanzibar, and Kîlwah, and laid siege to Mozambique in 1698. He placed a governor in Mombâsa who was nominally subject to Omân. After the fall of Mombâsa, the Portuguese on the East-African coast were everywhere massacred or expelled; and there was an end of their sovereignty from Cape Delgado to Cape Gardafui. Even the town of Mukdîshu, which had retained its independence during the period of the Portuguese rule, placed itself under the protection of the princes of Omân."[1]

The different towns and forts on the coasts, together with the adjacent islands, from Cape Delgado

[1] KRAPF'S *Travels and Missionary Labours in Eastern Africa*, pp. 521-29.

to Mukdishu, still remain in the hands of the 'Ammân Seyyeds or Sultans; but by a recent arrangement the African territories have been detached from the parent state, and placed under the sovereignty of Seyyed Mâjid, a younger son of the late Seyyed Sä'îd, known to Europeans as the Imâm of Máskat, his eldest brother Seyyed Thoweynee retaining possession of 'Ammân.

But it is high time to rejoin our party whom we left at Mozambique. During their fifteen days' residence at that island, they made several trips on the mainland, and Varthema gives a graphic description of the physiognomy of the aboriginal *Makuas*, their strange jargon, and peculiar and scanty costume. The excursionists carried torches to frighten the elephants which abounded in the neighbourhood, but, notwithstanding this precaution, they were chased by three dams followed by their young, and only escaped by running up a mountain. On this occasion also, they met some natives who dwelt in caves, and our author's account of their bartering with them reveals the cupidity of the foreigners and the simplicity of the barbarians. The former had the dishonesty to demand thirty bullocks for a bombardier's rasor and a little bell, with the addition of a shirt which Varthema incontinently divested himself of for the sake of obtaining a meal of fresh meat. They were eventually content with fifteen head of cattle, on the understanding, however, that the owners should conduct the animals to the top of the mountain. On the way, and while these Christians were exulting over their extortionate bargain, a great noise was heard which was supposed to arise from a warm discussion among the natives, as to which of their number should become the happy possessor of the little bell. What a picture of civilized and uncivilized humanity! Europe and Africa!

Madagascar, or the Island of San Lorenzo, as it was then called, was sighted on the voyage to the Cape, beyond which the vessels composing the fleet were scattered by a furious storm, and did not meet again till they reached Portugal. That in which our author sailed passed under St. Helena and Ascension, at which latter place he notices the swarms of boobies which alighted on the deck, and were easily taken with the hand. Next, they reached the Azores, remaining for two days at the island of Terceira, and finally arrived at Lisbon,—in Varthema's case, after an absence from Europe of about five years. He leaves to the conception of his readers the delight which he experienced at being once more within easy reach of home, while he himself sets off on a visit to Don Emanuel of Portugal. That deservedly " Fortunate" monarch welcomed the enterprising traveller to his court, where he detained him several days listening with pleasure to the interesting tale of his discoveries and adventures, and was graciously pleased to confirm the honour of knighthood which had been conferred upon him by the Viceroy of India after the battle of Ponani. Receiving his Majesty's permission to depart, Varthema hurried away to the land of his birth, and takes leave of us from the city of Rome as abruptly as I bring my following him to a close.

In the annotations on the text, I have specified my obligations to Professor Owen, to J. J. Bennett, Esq., and to R. H. Major, Esq., of the British Museum, and also to C. R. Markham, Esq., for their prompt aid where my own knowledge was at fault. A similar recognition is due to J. Winter Jones, Esq., my colleague in the preparation of this work, for his uniform kindness in aiding me in my part of the task. To J. Crawfurd, Esq., whose learned researches into the history of that region were my principal guide in tracing our author's route through the Indian Archipelago, I owe my best thanks. And last, though not least, I feel deeply indebted to my friend Colonel H. Yule, C.B. for many useful suggestions, and, moreover, for having volunteered to compile the Table of Contents, and also the valuable Index at the end of this volume, which may justly elicit the encomium, *finis coronat opus*.

I had designed to write an Introduction, but have, I fear, written a book. The mistake will be unaccompanied with regret, if the attempt be found useful to the Members of the HAKLUYT SOCIETY in illustrating the early and wonderful travels of old LUDOVICO DI VARTHEMA.

GEORGE PERCY BADGER.

London,
7, Dawson Place, Bayswater,
    November 1863.

POSTSCRIPT.

ON THE SITE OF THE ANCIENT CITY OF *BENGALA*.

I am surprised to find that in transcribing a quotation from Barbosa respecting the City of *Bengala*, (note 3 on p. 210,) I omitted a part of his account which, had the passage been more carefully studied, might have prevented my erroneous identification of Varthema's *Banghella* with the capital of *Gour*, and afforded me at the same time a clue to the position of the former town. Premising that Barbosa was travelling from west to east, and had just before described the kingdom of Orixa, (Orissa,) and the *Guengua*, or Ganges, whereby the Hoogly branch is clearly indicated, he proceeds to say:—

"Beyond the Ganges, onward towards the East, is the kingdom of *Bengala*, wherein there are many places and cities, as well inland as on the sea-coast. Those in the interior are inhabited by Gentiles, who are subject to the king of *Bengala*, who is a Moor; and the stations on the coast are full of Moors and Gentiles, among whom are many merchants and traders to all parts. For this sea forms a gulf which bends towards the north, at the head of which is situated a great city inhabited by Moors, which is called *Bengala*, with a good port. The inhabitants thereof are white men, who are well-disposed. In the same city there are many foreigners from all parts, including Arabia, Persia, and Abyssinia. The country being very extensive, and the

climate temperate, many persons frequent it, and all are
great merchants, who possess large ships made like those of
Mecca, and some like those of China, called *Giunchi*, which
are very large, and carry large cargoes, and with these they
navigate towards Coromandel, Malabar, Cambaia, Tarnasseri,
Sumatra, Zeilam, and Malaca, and they trade with all kinds
of merchandize from one place to the other." RAMUSIO,
vol. i. p. 315.

The foregoing extract, taken in conjunction with
Varthema's narrative, is satisfactory evidence that a
city called *Banghella* or *Bengala* existed at this period,
that it was a seaport of considerable trade, and was
situated beyond the Hooghly, at the head of the gulf
known in those days as the Gulf of Bengal. It is
remarkable that Barbosa makes no allusion whatever
either to *Satigam* or *Chatigam*, (Satgong and Chittagong;) but in the *Sommario de' Regni*, etc., as given
by Ramusio, the former place is mentioned under the
name of *Asedegam*, and some further particulars are
supplied respecting the city of *Bengala*. After describing the kingdom of *Bengala*, the author subjoins:—

"Of the seaports of the kingdom, the principal is in the
city of *Bengala*, from which the kingdom takes its name.
One goes in two days from the mouth of the Ganges to the
city, which [Mouth of the Ganges] now goes by the name of
Sino Gangetico or *Gulf of Bengal*, and in the best roadsteads
the water is three *braccia* deep. The city contains about
40,000 hearths, and the king has a residence there at all
times, which is the only one covered with tiles, and is built
with well-made bricks.

"There is also another port, called *Asedegam*, towards the
kingdom of *Orixa*, which is a good port, with a wide en-

trance, where there is a good and wealthy city, containing many merchants, and about 10,000 hearths. These are the principal mercantile cities of *Bengala*." RAMUSIO, vol. i. p. 333.

As far as my researches go, these are the only circumstantial accounts which we possess of the ancient *Bengala*, subsequent to which I find it mentioned by Purchas and Mandelslo, but by no other writers. Mandelslo does not appear to have visited it personally, and merely enumerates it among the principal cities of the then kingdom of Bengal. (See a quotation from his *Voyages* in the note on p. 211.) Purchas has the following :—

"The kingdome of Bengala is very large, and hath of coast one hundred and twentie leagues, and as much within land. *Francis Fernandes* measureth it from the confines of the kingdome of Ramu or Porto Grande [Chittagong] to Palmerine, ninety miles beyond Porto Pequene, in all six hundred miles long. The river Chaberis, (which some call Guenga, and think it to be the ancient Ganges,) watereth it: it is plentiful in rice, wheat, sugar, ginger, long-pepper, cotton and silke, and enjoyeth a very wholesome ayre. The inhabitants neere the shoare are, (for the most part,) Mahumetans, and so also was the king, before the Great *Mogore*, (one likewise of his owne sect,) conquered him. Gouro, the seat royall, and *Bengala*, are faire cities. Of this, the Gulfe, sometimes called *Gangeticus*, now beareth name *Golfo di Bengala*. Chatigan is also reckoned amongst these cities." *Voyages*, vol. v. p. 508.

Of the travellers subsequent to Barbosa, Cæsar Fredericke (A.D. 1563) represents *Satigan* as a flourishing commercial port, and locates it 120 miles from the mouth of the Ganges (Hooghly,) but he does not allude either to *Bengala* or *Chatigam*. (Ramusio, vol. i. p. 392.) Ralph Fitch, twenty years later, describes both *Satagan* and *Chatigan*, and tells us that *Chatigan* was called "Porto Grande" by the Portuguese; but he says nothing about *Bengala*. In Hamilton's time, A.D. 1688—1723, the town of Hooghly appears to have succeeded *Satigan* as the chief seaport on the western branch of the Ganges, for he represents the former as "driving a great trade, because all foreign goods are brought thither for import, and all goods of the product of Bengal are brought hither for exportation," which circumstance sufficiently accounts for his not naming *Satigan*. "Chittagoung, or, as the Portuguese call it, Xatigam," he describes at some length, but he never mentions the city of *Bengala*, which the earlier writers located at no great distance from that town. (See Pinkerton, vol. ix. p. 414-16. Vol. viii. p. 415.)

Turning from the travellers to the historians of the period under review, one is surprised to find the same omission. De Barros, as quoted by Ramusio, in describing the Ganges, says:—

"Its first mouth, which is on the West, is called *Satigan*, from a city of that name situated in its streams, where our people carry on their mercantile transactions. The other, which is on the East, comes out very near another and more famous port called *Chatigam*, which is frequented by most of the merchants who arrive at and depart from this kingdom." Ramusio, vol. i. p. 390.

De Faria y Souza is equally explicit with regard to *Satigan* and *Chatigan*, but never alludes to *Ben*-

gala. After indicating the line of coast between the Hooghly and the eastern branch of the Ganges, he writes :—

"Within this interval is contained the Bay of *Bengala*, called by some *Sinus Gangeticus*, because the river Ganges, after watering the country of *Bengala*, falls into this bay about the latitude of 23 degrees. . . . Though the river Ganges has many mouths, the two most remarkable are called *Satigan* to the west, and *Chatigan* on the east, near one hundred leagues distant from each other."

And, again :—

"This river [Ganges] has its springs in the mountains of Great Tartary, from whence it runs to the southward near 600 leagues, and divides India into two parts, *Intra* and *Extra* Gangem. In the mouth that falls into the sea to the eastward is the city *Chatigam*, on that to the westward *Satigam*. The principal city is *Gouro*, seated on the banks of Ganges, three leagues in length, containing one million two hundred thousand families, and well fortified." *Portuguese Asia*, translated by STEVENS, vol. i. pp. 96-97, 416-17.

The absence of all allusion to *Bengala* by travellers and historians generally subsequent to Varthema and Barbosa, with the exception of Mandelslo and Purchas, is the more remarkable from the fact of its appearance, together with *Chatigam*, in most of the early maps of Asia and of India, and its reproduction by succeeding cartographers for nearly two centuries later. The following is a list of the principal maps belonging to the British Museum, arranged in chronological order, wherein both cities are noted :—

Map.	Author.	Date.	Orthography.
Asia	Gastaldi	Venetia, A.D. 1561	Bengala and Catigan.
India	Kœrius	Amst., 1620	Bengala, Chatigam.
Asia	Speed	London, 1626	Bengala, Chatiga.
Asia	Bleauw[1]	Amst., 1640	Bengala, Chatagam.
India	Mariette	Paris, 1650	Bengala, Chatigam.
India	Bleauw	Amst., 1660	id.
Asia	Visscher	Amst., 1657	id.
Asia	Berey	Paris, 1671	Bengala, Chatiga.
Asia	De Witt	Amst., 1680	Bengala, Chatigam.
Asia	Dankerts	Amst., 1690	id.
Asia	Sanson	Paris, 1696	id.
India	Visscher	Amst., 1710	id.
Asia	Mathys	Amst., 1715	id.
India	Seutter	Augs., 1730	id.
Hindoostan	id.	id., 1730	id.
Asia	Ottens	Amst., 1740	id.

To the above I may add that in the map of *India Orientalis* attached to Patavino's *Geography*, (date, A.D. 1597,) *Bengala* is marked as a town situated at the head of the gulf, on the right bank of the eastern mouth of the Ganges. It also occupies the same position in *Hondius his Map of the East Indies*, as given in Vol. i. of Purchas.

The following cartographers, immediately succeeding Ottens, omit the city of *Bengala*, and the name does not reappear in any map of a subsequent date:—

Asia	Hasius	Nurnberg, 1744	Satigan [for Chatigam].
India	Mayer	id., 1748	Chatigan.
Hindoostan	Blair	London, 1773	Chittagong or Shatigan.

The time when *Bengala* thus ceases to be repre-

---

[1] This is most probably the map referred to by Colonel Yule, (see p. lxxx. *ante*.) He writes the author's name *Bleau*, misprinted *Blean*; but in the copy of the map in the British Museum it is spelt as above.

sented in the maps corresponds with Rennell's statement, that the city " appears to have been in existence during the early part of the last century." (See p. lxxxi. *ante*.)

The next subject which calls for inquiry is the site of this ancient *Bengala*. All the maps enumerated in the first of the foregoing lists, with the exception of the oldest one by Gastaldi, locate *Bengala* either on the north-east, due east, or south-east of *Chatigam*. Now, if the relative situation of the two cities corresponded with one or other of these descriptions, it is difficult to conceive how the site of *Bengala* could have been carried away by the river, as Rennell supposes, and that of *Chatigam*, or Chittagong, left intact. Reverse the position of the two places, and such a result would not only be probable, but would moreover serve to account for the present greater depth of the Gulf of Bengal in that direction as compared with the delineations of it given in the old maps, and also for the increased distance which now appears to exist between Chittagong and the eastern mouth of the Ganges. Singularly enough, Gastaldi does so transpose the sites of the two cities, placing *Catigan* on the south-east of *Bengala*, as will be seen from the accompanying section copied from his map.

This alone is but slender ground whereon to form an hypothesis; nevertheless, the inference which I am disposed to draw therefrom receives support from the manner in which De Barros and De Faria y Souza describe the Ganges in the extracts already quoted from their writings. Both profess to indicate its two

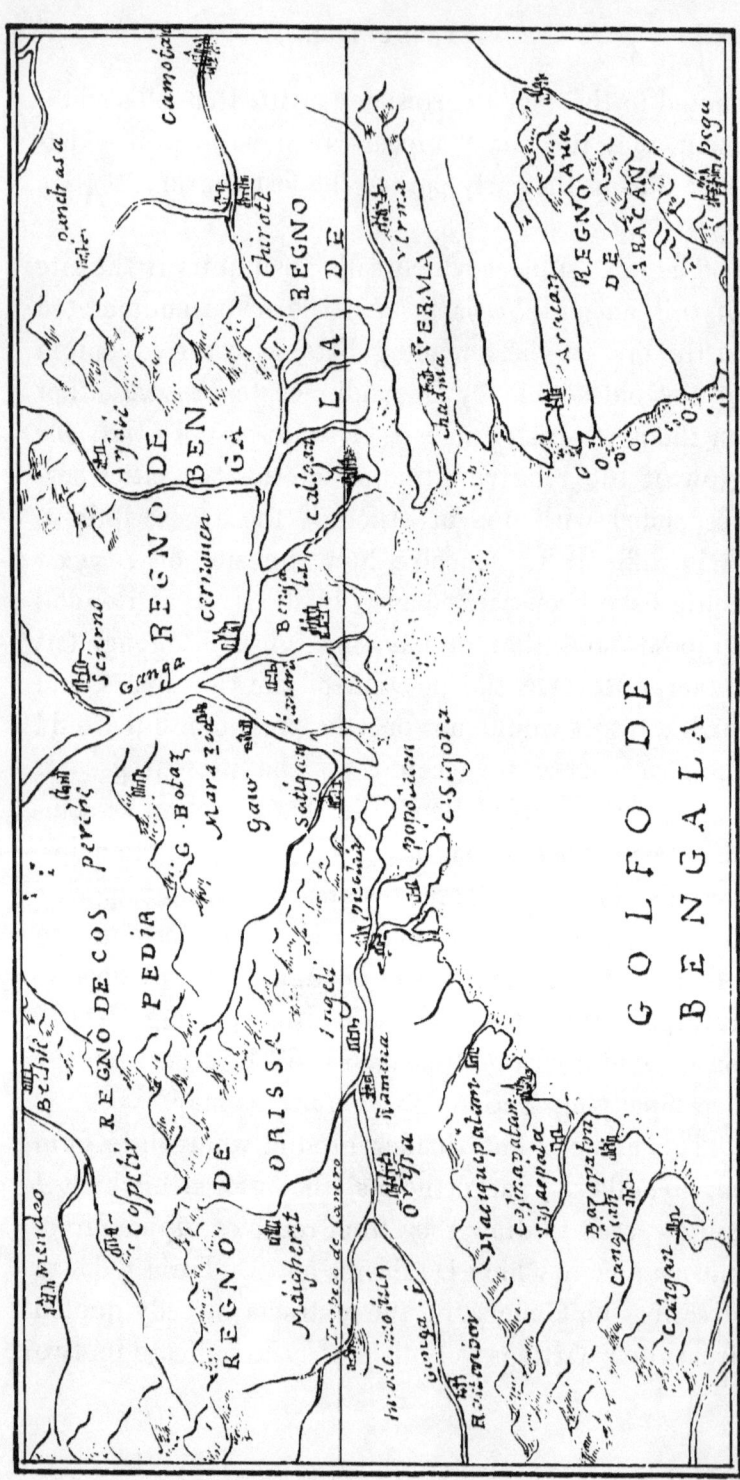

SECTION FROM GASTALDI'S MAP OF ASIA, A.D. 1561.

extremities where it debouches into the sea, and in doing so both select *Satigan* as its western and *Chatigam* as its eastern boundary; whereas, had *Bengala* been to the south-eastward or southward of *Chatigam*, it is presumable that, standing as Barbosa tells us it did on the mouth of the nether Ganges, they would have chosen it, rather than *Chatigam*, to mark the eastern termination of that river.

In the absence, therefore, of any direct proof to the contrary, beyond the not very reliable information contained in the old atlases, I am inclined to infer that *Bengala* occupied a position between the Hattia and Sundeep islands, situated at the present mouth of the Brahmaputra, which I conceive to be the eastern branch of the Ganges of the earlier geographers, and have so placed it, marked with a star, in the map attached to this volume. That I may be mistaken is more than possible; but it is worth while hazarding an erroneous opinion on a subject of this nature, if it were only for the sake of eliciting ulterior research and discussion, which may result in defining the correct site of the ancient city of *Bengala*.

G. P. B.

ADVANTAGES OF TRAVEL.[1]

Go, traverse distant lands, in each you'll find
Some in the place of those you leave behind :
Some, it may chance, of more congenial hearts,—
    Sympathy is life's charm,—its bane *ennui*,—
    No honour lies in inactivity,—
Then quit your home, go, range in foreign parts.
The stagnant puddle foul and fetid grows,
Healthful and clear the running fountain flows :
Unless the changes of the moon on high
Revealed the future to the sage's eye,
He would not watch her aspect in the sky :
Unless he left his den, the forest-king
    Would win no trophies of the sylvan war :
Unless the arrow parted from the string,
    It could not hit the destined mark afar :
The *Tibr*,[2] when from its native mine cast forth,
Appears as vile unprofitable earth ;
    The aloës-wood enjoys but slight esteem
In its own land,—mere fuel for the hearth ;
Let either quit the country of its birth,
    The one, an ore all-coveted we deem,
The other, a perfume of priceless worth.

---

[1] Translated from the Arabic. For the English versification, the Editor is indebted to the Rev. P. G. Hill.

[2] *Tibr* means unwrought gold, either in the form of dust or nuggets. The word is also applied to designate native ores generally.

THE ITINERARY

of Ludovico di Varthema, of Bologna,
in Egypt, in Syria, in Arabia Deferta and
Felix, in Perfia, in India, and in
Ethiopia. The religion, mode of life,
and cuftoms, of all the aforefaid
Provinces, with the Grace
and Privilege hereinafter
mentioned.

[For the Publishers' names and date of publication, see the end of the volume on p. 298.]

[PRIVILEGE.]

[*Translated from the original Latin by the Editor.*]

RAPHAEL, by Divine grace, Bishop of Portueri, Cardinal of Saint George, Chamberlain of our Most Holy Lord the Pope, and of the Holy Roman Church, to all and singular, by whatsoever name called, and with whatsoever dignity or office invested, and to all others whom it does or may concern, to whom these our letters may come,—Peace in the Lord for ever.

Whereas among other subjects and sciences which, as well by the inspiration of genius as by art and experience, promote the benefit, usefulness, and enjoyment of mankind, and by transmission from hand to hand are enlarged and illustrated, the description and measurement of the world and of parts of the earth, which the Greeks call Cosmography, Geography, Topography, Geometry, and other like names, do not hold the last place, and yield no less pleasure than profit; on which account those who have devoted themselves to such studies have always been held in the highest honour, and have been abundantly rewarded.—Therefore, whereas our well-beloved friend Ludovico Vartomanus of Bologna, who (as we are assured) has for the space of seven years travelled over the most remote and hardly-known regions of Asia and Africa, and has largely written in the vernacular tongue of their sites, seas, rivers, pools, lakes, forests, mountains, cities, lands, people, and their established manners, rites, laws, and other memorable things, and has corrected many places, (as one may well do who sees all with his own eyes, and has not merely heard thereof or received it from others,) in Ptolemy, Strabo, Pliny, and other most famous writers, and has also added much to what others have written thereon up to this time.—It is our pleasure, being moreover advised thereto by many other Most Reverend Cardinals of the Apostolic See, that what he has committed to writing and collected into a volume, should be printed for the public use and study of the things therein contained, and that it should be held worthy, not only of praise and commendation, but of ample reward. We, being desirous (as is meet) to assist him as far as we are able, and to recompense his industry with all due favours, do, by these presents, proclaim, decree, and inhibit, in virtue of a mandate from our Most Holy Lord the Pope in person, communicated to us by word of mouth to that effect, and by the authority of our Chamberlain's office, that all Printers who shall be applied to by the said Ludovico, that they print his writings on his own request or that of any of his heirs; and that all other Printers abstain from printing them, and that no Printers or persons of any other condition whatsoever, either of themselves, or through any other or others, shall dare or presume to sell the printed books or volumes of the said Ludovico, without the consent of the said Ludovico or of his acknowledged heirs, for the space of ten years to come, to be reckoned from the date of their first impression; and, further, that they lend no aid, counsel or countenance, to either Printers or Venders of the same, against the wishes of the said Ludovico and his heirs, under the penalty of one hundred ducats of gold to be exacted for every counterfeit and from every one so counterfeiting, without any other declaration of the fact, through the medium of the Apostolic Chamber, to be applied to the use of the said Ludovico or his heirs. We further command and inhibit, under the same penalty, all those whom it may concern, that this our edict, decree, and will, be executed in like manner at the instance of the said Ludovico, or of his successors and heirs, for the space of the aforesaid ten years, against all and every one who, in any manner, or under any pretext, shall be guilty of counterfeit,—the Apostolical constitutions, ordinances, statutes, and customs, even when confirmed by oath, also the privileges and licenses granted to any persons whatsoever, under any words or form of words, notwithstanding.

Given at Rome, at our Palace of Saint Laurence in Damaso, the xviith day of November M.D.X., with the usual seal of our Chamberlain's office appended.

MATTHEUS BONFINIS, *Secretarius*.

THE TRAVELS OF
LUDOVICO DI VARTHEMA.

TO THE MOST ILLUSTRIOUS AND MOST EXCELLENT LADY THE COUNTESS OF ALBI AND DUCHESS OF TAGLIACOZZO, MADAME AGNESINA FELTRIA COLONNA, LUDOVICO DI VARTHEMA OF BOLOGNA WISHES HEALTH.

THERE have been many men who have devoted themselves to the investigation of the things of this world, and by the aid of divers studies, journeys, and very exact relations, have endeavoured to accomplish their desire. Others, again, of more perspicacious understandings, to whom the earth has not sufficed, such as the Chaldeans and Phœnicians, have begun to traverse the highest regions of Heaven with careful observations and watchings; from all which I know that each has gained most deserved and high praise from others and abundant satisfaction to themselves. Wherefore I, feeling a very great desire for similar results, and leaving alone the Heavens as a burthen more suitable for the shoulders of Atlas and of Hercules, determined to investigate some small portion of this our terrestrial globe; and not having any inclination (knowing myself to be of very slender understanding) to arrive at my desire by study or conjectures, I determined, personally, and with my own eyes, to endeavour to ascertain the situations of places, the qualities of peoples, the diversities of animals, the varieties of the fruit-bearing and odoriferous trees of Egypt, Syria, Arabia Deserta and Felix, Persia, India and Ethiopia, remembering well that the testimony of one eye-witness is worth more than ten heard-says. Having then, by Divine assistance, in part accomplished my object and examined various provinces and foreign nations, it appeared to me that I had done nothing if I kept hidden within myself the things I had witnessed and experienced, instead of communicating them to other studious men. Wherefore I bethought myself to give a very faithful description of this my voyage, according to my humble abilities, thinking thereby to do an action which would be agreeable to my readers; for that, whereas I procured the pleasure of seeing new manners and customs by very great dangers and insupportable fatigue, they will enjoy the same advantage and pleasure, without discomfort or danger, by merely reading. Reflecting, then, to whom I might best address this my laborious little work, you, Most Illustrious and Most Excellent Lady, occurred to me as being a special observer of noteworthy things, and a lover of every virtue. Nor did my judgment appear to me vain, considering the infused learning transferred by the radiant light of that Most Illustrious and Excellent Lord the Duke of Urbino your Father, being as it were to us a sun of arms and of science.

I do not speak of the very Excellent Lord your Brother, who (although still a young man) has so distinguished himself in his Latin and Greek studies as to be spoken of as almost a Demosthenes and a Cicero. Wherefore, having derived every virtue from such broad and clear streams, you cannot do other than take pleasure in honourable works and entertain a great desire for them. He who can justly appreciate them, would willingly go with his corporeal feet where he flies with the wings of his mind, remembering that one of the praises awarded to the most wise and eloquent Ulysses was, that he had seen many customs of men and many countries. But as your Ladyship is occupied with the affairs of your Most Illustrious Lord and Consort (whom, like another Artemisia, you love and respect), and about the distinguished family which, with admirable rule, you adorn by your graces, I say it will suffice if amongst your other good works you will feed your mind with this fruitful, although, perhaps, unpolished reading, not acting like many other ladies who lend their ears to light songs and vain words, taking no account of time, unlike the angelic mind of your Ladyship, which allows no moment to pass without some good fruit. Your kindness will easily supply all want of skill in the connection of the narrative, grasping only the truth of the facts. And if these, my labours, should prove agreeable to you and meet with your approbation, I shall consider that I have received sufficient praise and satisfaction for my long wanderings, my rather fearful exile, during which I have endured, innumerable times, hunger and thirst, cold and heat, war, imprisonment, and an infinite number of other dangerous inconveniences, and shall gain fresh courage for that other journey which I hope to undertake in a short time; for having examined some parts of the countries and islands of the east, south, and west, I am resolved, if it please God, to investigate those of the north. And thus, as I do not see that I am fit for any other pursuit, to spend in this praiseworthy exercise the remainder of my fleeting days.

THE TRAVELS,

ETC.

THE FIRST CHAPTER, CONCERNING ALEXANDRIA.

The same desire to behold the various kingdoms of the world which has urged on others, excited me also to a similar enterprise; and inasmuch as all countries have been very much laid open by our people, I deliberated in my own mind that I would see those which had been the least frequented by the Venetians. Wherefore spreading our sails to a favourable wind, and having implored the Divine aid, we committed ourselves to the sea. When we came to Alexandria, a city of Egypt, I, longing for novelty (as a thirsty man longs for fresh water) departed from these places as being well known to all, and, entering the Nile, arrived at Cairo.

THE CHAPTER CONCERNING CAIRO.

On my arrival in Cairo I, who had been previously much astonished at the account of its size, came to the conclusion that it was not so large as it had been reported to be. But its size in circumference is about equal to that of Rome. It is true, however, that it contains very many more habitations than there are in Rome, and that the population is larger. The mistake which many have made is this, that there are several hamlets outside the walls of Cairo which some believed to be within the circuit of Cairo itself; this, however, cannot be the case, for they are distant some two or three miles, and are distinct villages.[1] I shall not enter into any long account of their faith and manners, because everyone knows that they are inhabited by Moors[2] and Mamelukes. The lord over them is the Grand Sultan,[3] who is served by the Mamelukes, and the Mamelukes are lords over the Moors.

THE CHAPTER CONCERNING BARUTI,[4] TRIPOLI, AND ALEPPO.

I say nothing about the riches and beauty of the aforesaid Cairo and of the pride of the Mamelukes, because they are well known to all our countrymen. I sailed thence into Syria; and first to Baruti, the distance from the one place to the other by sea is 500 miles. In that Baruti I remained several days. It is a country thickly inhabited by the Moors, and is well supplied with everything. The sea breaks against the walls, and you must know that the district is not entirely surrounded by walls, but only in some parts, that is to say, towards the west and towards the sea.[5]

[1] *Misr el-'Ateekah* or Old Misr, corrupted by Europeans into "Old Cairo," and the large suburb of Boolák, are probably the "distinct villages" indicated.

[2] The author frequently uses this term as laxly as we do that of "Arabs," and sometimes as synonymous with "Mussulmans."

[3] As Varthema commenced his travels A.D. 1503, Egypt was still under the rule of the Borjeëh or Circassian Mamlûks, and the "Grand Sultan" of the text must have been Sultân el-Ghôree of that dynasty. Contemporaneous with him in Egypt was the Khalîfa el-Mustansik b'Illâh of the 'Abbasîeh or Abbaside Caliphs, who, however, had long ceased to exercise more than a nominal sovereignty over the country.

[4] Beyroot is still written and pronounced as above by the Levantines and Italian residents in Syria.

[5] Until very recently Beyroot was completely enclosed on the land side by a wall, whereas there is only a small extent of wall "towards the sea." Possibly, at the period of our author's visit, some parts of the

I did not see anything there worthy to be recorded, excepting an ancient building, which, they say, was inhabited by the daughter of the king when the dragon wanted to devour her, and where St. George killed the said dragon.[1] This ancient building is all in ruins; and I departed thence, and proceeded in the direction of Tripoli in Syria, which is two days' journey towards the east. This Tripoli is subject to the Grand Sultan,[2] and all are Muhammedans, and the said city abounds in everything. And I departed thence and went to Aleppo, which is eight days' journey inland, which said Aleppo is a very beautiful city, and is under the Grand Sultan of Cairo, and is the mart [scala] of Turkey and Syria, and they are all Muhammedans. It is a country of very great traffic in merchandize, and particularly with the Persians and Azamini,[3] who come as far as there. This

former had been levelled, and were subsequently restored by the Ameer Fakhr ed-Din, who repaired and strengthened the fortifications in the beginning of the seventeenth century; and he may have mistaken for a wall the numerous ancient columns which form the foundation of the quay, and against which the sea frequently beats with great violence.

[1] The legend of St. George and the Dragon has been attached to this locality since the Crusades, and the remains of an old brick building, situated about two miles from Beyroot, on the road to Jebail, are still pointed out as occupying the exact site of the renowned encounter. Varthema describes it as it is now, "an ancient building in ruins," though d'Arvieux, in 1660, speaks of a chapel of St. George in this neighbourhood which had been converted into a mosque, and Pococke repeats the same in 1738. If a Christian chapel ever existed here, the Muhammedans, in converting it into a mosque, would not scruple to retain the original dedication, as the *Nabi Jerjees* (the Seer George) is regarded as an orthodox saint by all Mussulmans.

[2] Of Cairo, of course, as the whole of Syria at the time was subject to the Mamlûk sovereign of Egypt.

[3] This is, doubtless, a distorted plural form of '*Ajami*, a Persian, the Italian initial *z* being used to express the *j* sound of the Arabic, just as in the sequel we find "Zida, cioè porto della Meccha," where Juddah (Jiddah) is obviously indicated. Also "xii *zornate*," for xii giornate. The phrase "Persians and Azamini," moreover, is not altogether a pleonasm; since the latter term, in the original, has a wide signification, and denotes the natives generally of all the countries comprehended

is the route which is taken to go into Turkey and Syria by those who come from Azemia.

THE CHAPTER CONCERNING AMAN[1] AND MENIN.[2]

And I departed thence and went towards Damascus, which is distant ten short days' journey. Midway there is a city which is called Aman, in which there grows a vast quantity of cotton, and very good fruit. And near to Damascus, sixteen miles distant from it, I found another district called Menin, which is situated on the summit of a mountain, and is inhabited by Christians of the Greek Church, who are subjects of the lord of Damascus. In this place there are two very beautiful churches, which are said to have been erected by Helena, the mother of Constantine. Very excellent fruits grow there, and most especially good grapes; and here also there are very beautiful gardens and fountains. I departed thence, and went to the most noble city of Damascus.

THE FIRST CHAPTER CONCERNING DAMASCUS.

Truly it would not be possible to describe the beauty and the excellence of this Damascus, in which I resided some

under the Persian empire. Besides which, the word "'Ajami" conveys the same idea among the people of the East as "Barbarian" did with the ancient Greeks, and "Gentile" among the Jews.

[1] The modern town of Hamah, the Hamath of Scripture, the Epiphania of the Greeks and Romans, and the birthplace of Abu'l-Feda, the eminent Arabian geographer and historian, which lies midway on the caravan route between Aleppo and Damascus, is obviously indicated. It is somewhat surprising that Varthema does not mention the river Orontes, which bisects the town.

[2] Menin is situated ten miles from Helbon, still famous, as of old, for the quality of its grapes. (See Ezek. xviii. 28.) The vine is the chief

months in order to learn the Moorish language, because this city is entirely inhabited by Moors and Mamelukes and many Greek Christians. Here I must give an account of the government of the lord of the said city, which lord is subject to the Great Sultan of Cairo. You must know that in the said city of Damascus there is a very beautiful and strong castle, which is said to have been built by a Florentine Mameluke at his own expense, he being lord of the said city. And, moreover, in each angle of the said castle, the arms of Florence are sculptured in marble. It is surrounded by very wide fosses, and has four extremely strong towers and drawbridges, and powerful and excellent artillery are constantly mounted there.[1] Fifty Mamelukes, in the service of the Grand Sultan, are constantly quartered with the governor of the castle. This Florentine was a Mameluke of the Grand Sultan; and it is reported that in his time the Sultan was poisoned, and could find no one who could relieve him of the said poison, when it pleased God that this Florentine should cure him. For this service he gave him the said city of Damascus, and thus he came to build the castle. Afterwards he died in Damascus; and the people held him in great veneration as a holy man, possessing great knowledge, and from that time forward the

product of the district, which abounds also in fountain-streams tributary to the Barada. One of these streams takes its rise at Menîn. Christians of the orthodox Greek rite are more numerous in this neighbourhood than in any other part of Syria.

[1] The citadel of Damascus is an extensive quadrangular fortress, with towers, surrounded by a deep fosse. I remember noticing several sculptured escutcheons built into the exterior wall of the city during my visit in 1835, when a portion of the same was being demolished by Ibrahim Pasha to furnish materials for a military hospital; but the tradition of the Florentine is quite new to me, neither do I find it alluded to by any of the older or more recent travellers in Syria. In its present form the castle is evidently of Saracenic origin, though its foundations probably date from a very early age. There is nothing improbable, however, in the story of a renegade Christian having rebuilt or restored it.

castle has always been in the possession of the Sultan. When a new Sultan succeeds to the throne, one of his lords, who are called *Amirra*,[1] says to him: "Lord, I have been for so long a time your slave, give me Damascus, and I will give you one hundred thousand, or two hundred thousand, teraphim[2] of gold." Then the lord grants him this favour. But you must know, that if in the course of two years the said lord does not send him 25,000 teraphim, he seeks to kill him by force of arms, or in some other manner; but if he makes him the said present, he remains in the government. The said lord has always ten or twelve lords and barons of the said city with him, and when the Sultan wants two or three hundred thousand teraphim from the lords or merchants of the said city, who are not treated with justice, but whom they vie with each other in oppressing by robbery and assassination (for the Moors live under the Mamelukes like the lamb under the wolf), the said Sultan sends two letters to the governor of the said castle, one of which simply enjoins him to bring together in the castle such lords or merchants as he may think proper. And when they are assembled, the second letter is read, the object of which is immediately carried out, whether for good or for evil. And in this manner the said lord seeks to obtain money. Sometimes the said lord becomes so powerful that he will not go into the castle; whereat many barons and merchants, feeling themselves in danger, mount their horses and retire towards Turkey.[3] We will say no more upon this subject, excepting that the men of the guard of the said castle, in each of the four great towers, are always on the watch. They make

[1] Ameer.

[2] In the Third Chapter concerning Damascus, and in some editions, this word is spelt "Saraphi" and also "Sarahpi." I take it to be the *Sherif* or *Ashrafi*, an old Arabian ducat.

[3] In some editions it is the Lords and Merchants who are said to refuse to go into the castle when they have become powerful, and this appears to be the more correct reading.

no cry during the night, but each has a drum, made in the shape of a half-box,[1] upon which they beat vigorously with a stick, and each answers the other with these said drums. He who delays answering for the space of a *pater noster*, is imprisoned for a year.

THE SECOND CHAPTER CONCERNING THE SAID DAMASCUS.

Now that we have seen the customs of the Lord of Damascus, it is necessary that I should make mention of some circumstances relating to the city, which is extremely populous and very rich. It is impossible to imagine the richness and elegance of the workmanship there. Here you have a great abundance of grain and of meat, and the most prolific country for fruits that was ever seen, and especially for fresh grapes, during all seasons. I will mention the good and the bad fruits which grow there. Pomegranates and and quinces, good: almonds and large olives, extremely good. The most beautiful white and red roses that were ever seen. There are also good apples and pears and peaches, but with a very bad taste, the reason of which is that Damascus abounds much in water.[2] A stream runs through the city, and the greater number of the houses have very beautiful fountains of mosaic work. The houses are

---

[1] The *báz* or small *tabl*, still generally used by the *Musahhirs*, who traverse the streets during the Ramadhán, to announce the hour of the *Sahoor*, or last meal of the early dawn.

[2] It is rather surprising that no mention is made of oranges and apricots, the former being very plentiful, and the latter by far the most abundant produce of the orchards round Damascus, and one of its chief articles of export; but as Varthema left the city early in April, that fruit was not in season.

Roses, from which the rich perfume of the *'atar* is extracted, are extensively cultivated in a part of the great plain about three miles from the city.

dirty externally, but within they are very beautiful, adorned with many works of marble and porphyry.

In this city there are many mosques. One, which is the principal, is as large as St. Peter's at Rome. It has no roof in the centre, but the surrounding parts are covered in. It is reported that they keep there the body of St. Zachariah the prophet, and they pay him very great honour. In the said mosque there are four principal doors of metal, and within there are many fountains. Again, we see where the canonica stood, which belonged formerly to the Christians, in which canonica there are many ancient works in mosaic.[1] Again, I saw the place where they report that Christ said to St. Paul, "Saule, Saule, cur me persequeris?" which is without the city, about a mile from one of the gates thereof. They bury there all the Christians who die in the said city. Again, there is that tower in the wall of the district where (as they say) St. Paul was imprisoned. The Moors have many times rebuilt it, but in the morning it is found broken and thrown down, as the angel broke it when he drew St. Paul out of the said tower. I also saw the house where (as they say) Cain slew Abel his brother, which is a mile without the city in the opposite direction, on the side of a hill in a large deep valley.[2] We will now turn to the liberty which the said Mamelukes enjoy in the said city of Damascus.

[1] The "Masjid Yahya" or "Jamiia Beni Umeyya" (the Temple of John or the Mosque of the Ommiades), a part of which is generally supposed to have formed a Christian church dedicated to St. John the Baptist, the son of Zechariah. This is still regarded as the adytum or most sacred portion of the building, and is believed by Muhammedans to contain the head of the aforesaid Apostle. A peristyle, supported on splendid Corinthian pillars, surrounds the quadrangular court, in which there are several marble fountains for religious ablution. Buckingham, like Varthema, speaks of the mosque as having been a church dedicated to St. Zechariah.

[2] These and several other absurd local traditions, such as the house of Ananias, the grave of the martyr George who assisted St. Paul to escape through a window in the wall, and a cleft in the rock, about a

CHAPTER THE THIRD, CONCERNING THE MAMELUKES IN DAMASCUS.

The Mamelukes are renegade Christians, who have been purchased by the said lord. Certain it is that the said Mamelukes never lose any time, but are constantly exercising themselves either in arms or in letters, in order that they may acquire excellence. And you must know that every Mameluke, great or little, has for his pay six saraphi per month, and his expenses for himself, his horse, and a family; and they have as much more when they are engaged on any warlike expedition.[1] The said Mamelukes, when they go about the city, are always in companies of two or three, as it would be a great disgrace if they went alone. If they accidentally meet two or three ladies, they possess this privilege, or if they do not possess it they take it: they go to lay in wait for these ladies in certain places like great inns, which are called Chano,[2] and as the said ladies pass before the

---

mile from the city, through which the Apostle evaded his pursuers, are still current among the monks and Christians at Damascus.

[1] Browne's account of the Mamlûks in Egypt in 1722, coincides in the main with the foregoing description. "These military slaves are imported from Georgia, Circassia, and Mingrelia. A few have been prisoners, taken from the Austrians and Russians, who have exchanged their religion for an establishment...Particular attention is paid to the education of these slaves. They are instructed in every exercise of agility or strength, and are in general distinguished by the grace and beauty of their persons...They have no pay, as they eat at the table in the house of their master...Any military officer may purchase a slave, who becomes *ipso facto* a Mamlûk. After a proper education, the candidate thus constituted a Mamlûk, receives a present of a horse and arms from his master, together with a suit of clothes, which is renewed every year in the month of Ramadhân." Browne was assured that during the eleven years preceding his visit, sixteen thousand white slaves, of both sexes, were imported into Egypt. *Travels in Africa, Egypt, Syria,* etc., pp. 53-56, 76.

[2] *Khâns*, buildings generally designed for the accommodation of merchants and their goods. In some instances the principal bazaars are held in the khâns.

door each Mameluke takes his lady by the hand, draws her in, and does what he will with her. But the lady resists being known, because they all wear the face covered, so that they know us, but we do not know them. The Mameluke says to her, that he wishes to know who she is, and she replies: "Brother, is it not enough that you do with me what you will, without desiring to know who I am?" and she entreats him so much that he lets her go. And sometimes they think that they take the daughter of the lord, when in fact they take their own wives; and this has happened while I was there. These ladies go very well clad in silk, and over it they wear certain white garments of wool, thin and bright like silk, and they all wear white buskins and red or purple shoes, and many jewels around their heads, and in their ears, and on their hands. These ladies when they are married, at their own will and pleasure, that is, when they do not wish to remain with their husbands any longer, go to the cadi of their faith and cause themselves to be talacare,[1] that is, to be separated from their husband; and then they take another, and he takes another wife. Although they say that the Moors have five or six wives, I for my part have never seen any who had more than two or three at the most. These Moors for the greater part eat in the streets, that is, where the clothes are sold; they have their food cooked and eat it there, and there are very many horses, camels, and buffalos, and sheep and goats. There is here an abundance of good fresh cheese; and if you wish to purchase milk, there are forty or fifty goats, which go every day through the district, and which have ears more than a span in length. The master of these goats takes them up into your chamber, even if your house have three stories, and

---

[1] An Italianized infinitive of the Arabic *talak*, to divorce. According to Muhammedan civil law a woman cannot repudiate her husband against his will, unless it be for some grievous fault or cruelty on his part, and even in that case a formal decision of the Kádhi is necessary to dissolve the union.

there in your presence he milks as much as you please into
a handsome tin vessel.¹ And there are many milch goats.
Here, again, is sold a great quantity of truffles: sometimes
twenty-five or thirty camels arrive laden with them, and in
three or four days they are sold. They come from the
mountains of Armenia and Turkey.² The said Moors go
clothed in certain long and wide garments, without girdles,
made of silk or cloth, and the greater number wear breeches
of wool and white shoes. When a Moor meets a Mameluke,
although he may be the principal merchant of the place, he
is obliged to do honour and give place to the Mameluke,
and if he do not so he is bastinadoed. The Christians have
there many warehouses, which contain cloths, and silk and
satin, velvets, and brass, and all merchandize that is required; but they are ill treated.³

¹ The long-eared goats of Damascus are correctly described, and the custom of hawking them about the streets still prevails.
² Truffles (Arab. *Kama*) are found in large quantities, at certain seasons of the year, along the banks of the Euphrates and Tigris, and are transported by the Bedawîn long distances. The price at Mosul and Baghdad varies from one to six shillings the '*okkah* of four pounds.
³ Until within the last few years Varthema's Moors or Mussulmans at Damascus were quite as overbearing in their conduct towards the Christians as the Mamlûks were in his time. As late as 1835 a haughty Seyyed insisted on my descending from the pavement into the street while he passed, and he literally foamed at the mouth with rage because I declined obeying him.

THE BOOK CONCERNING ARABIA DESERTA.

THE CHAPTER SHOWING THE ROUTE FROM DAMASCUS TO MECCA, WHEREIN SOME ARABS ARE CONCERNED.

The matters relating to Damascus having been here described perhaps more diffusely than was necessary, opportunity invites me to resume my journey. In 1503, on the 8th day of April, the caravan being set in order to go to Mecca, and I being desirous of beholding various scenes and not knowing how to set about it, formed a great friendship with the captain of the said Mamelukes of the caravan, who was a Christian renegade, so that he clothed me like a Mameluke and gave me a good horse, and placed me in company with the other Mamelukes, and this was accomplished by means of the money and other things which I gave him; and in this manner we set ourselves on the way, and travelled three days to a place which is called Mezeribe,[1] and there we remained three days, in order that the merchants might provide themselves, by purchase, with as many horses as they required. In this Mezeribe there is a lord who is named

---

[1] El-Mezarib, where, according to Burckhardt, the pilgrim caravan to Meccah generally remains encamped for ten days to collect stragglers, obtain supplies, and pay the accustomed tribute to the different Arab tribes for the passage of the caravan through the desert. *Travels in Syria*, pp. 240-242.

Zambei,[1] and he is lord of the country, that is to say, of the Arabians; which Zambei has three brothers and four male children, and he has 40,000 horses, and for his court he has 10,000 mares. And he has here 300,000 camels, for his pasture-ground extends two days' journey. And this lord Zambei, when he thinks proper, wages war with the Sultan of Cairo, and the Lord of Damascus and of Jerusalem, and sometimes, in harvest time, when they think that he is a hundred miles distant, he plans some morning a great incursion to the granaries of the said city, and finds the grain and the barley nicely packed up in sacks, and carries it off. Sometimes he runs a whole day and night with his said mares without stopping, and when they have arrived at the end of their journey they give them camels' milk to drink, because it is very refreshing. Truly it appears to me that they do not run but that they fly like falcons; for I have been with them, and you must know that they ride, for the most part, without saddles, and in their shirts, excepting some of their principal men. Their arms consist of a lance of Indian cane ten or twelve cubits in length with a piece of iron at the end, and when they go on any expedition they keep as close together as starlings. The said Arabians are very small men, and are of a dark tawny colour, and they have a feminine voice, and long, stiff, and black hair. And truly these Arabs are in such vast numbers that they cannot be counted, and they are constantly fighting amongst themselves. They inhabit the mountain and come down at the time when the caravan passes through to go to Mecca, in order to lie in wait at the passes for the purpose of robbing the said caravan. They carry their wives, children, and all

[1] Burckhardt enables me to identify this with Zäabi or Ez-Zäabi, the patronymic of the principal Arab family in this district. He says: "At three hours from Mezarîb is the village of Ramtha,...the sheikh of which is generally a santon, that dignity being in the family of Ez-Zäabi, who possess there a mosque of the same name."—*Ibid.* Appendix iii.

their furniture, and also their houses, upon camels, which houses are like the tents of soldiers, and are of black wool and of a sad appearance.[1]

On the 11th of April,[2] the said caravan departed from Mezeribe; there were 35,000 camels, about 40,000 persons, and we were sixty Mamelukes in guard of the said caravan. One third of the Mamelukes went in advance of the caravan with the standard, another third in the centre, and the other third marched in the rear. You must understand that we performed our journey in this wise. From Damascus to Mecca is a journey of forty days and forty nights: thus, we set out from Mezeribe in the morning and travelled for twenty hours. At that point certain signals made by the captain were passed from band to band that the whole company should stop where they then found themselves, and they pass twenty-four hours in unloading, and feeding themselves and their camels. And then they make signals, and the camels are immediately laden again. And you must know that they give the said camels for food only five loaves of barley-meal, uncooked, and each of about the size of a pomegranate,[3] and then they mount their horses and journey all night and all the following day for the said twenty-two hours, and then for twenty-four hours do as before. And every eight days they find water, that is, by digging in the earth or sand; also, certain wells and cisterns are found, and at the end of the eight days they stop for one or two days, because the said camels carry as great a burthen as two

---

[1] A most graphic and correct description of the predatory and warlike customs of the desert Arabs, and of their physical and social peculiarities. The picture is throughout true to the life at the present day.

[2] This is either an error, or Varthema meant thereby to reckon his travelling days only; otherwise, as he left Damascus on the 8th of the month, was three days in reaching Mezarib, and remained there another three days, the date should be April 14th.

[3] The meal or flour is made into a paste and then formed into a ball. Cameleers throughout the East, especially on long journeys, adopt the same mode of baiting their animals.

mules, and they only give the poor animals drink once in every three days. When we halted at the said waters we always had to fight with a vast number of Arabs, but they never killed more than one man and one lady, for such is the baseness of their minds, that we sixty Mamelukes were sufficient defence against forty or fifty thousand Arabs; for pagans, there are no better people with arms in their hands than are the Mamelukes. You must know that I had excellent experiences of these Mamelukes during the journey. Amongst others, I saw a Mameluke take one of his slaves and place a pomegranate on his head, and make him stand twelve or fifteen paces distant from him, and at the second trial strike off the pomegranate by a shot from a bow. Again, I saw another Mameluke, running at full gallop, take off his saddle and place it upon his head, and afterwards return it to its original place without falling, and always at full gallop. Their saddles are made according to our usage.

THE CHAPTER CONCERNING THE CITY OF SODOM AND GOMORRAH.

And when we had travelled twelve days we found the valley of Sodom and Gomorrah. Verily the Scriptures do not lie, for one sees how they were destroyed by a miracle of God; and I say that there are three cities which were on the top of three mountains, and around them to the height of three or four cubits is still seen what appears to be blood, like red wax mixed with earth. Of a truth, I believe, upon what I have seen, that they were a wicked people, for all around the entire country is desert and barren. The earth produces no one thing, nor water; and they lived upon manna and were punished, for not acknowledging the benefits they received; and by a miracle everything is still seen in ruin. Then we passed that valley, which was at least twenty miles, and there died there from thirst thirty-three persons, and many were buried in the sand who were not quite dead, and they left only their faces uncovered.[1] Afterwards we found a little mountain, near which was a well, whereat we were well pleased. We halted upon the said mountain. The next day, early in the morning, there came 24,000 Arabs, who said that we must pay for their water.[2] We answered that we could not pay, for the water was given by God. They began to fight with us, saying that we had taken their water. We fortified ourselves, and made a wall of our camels,[3] and the merchants stood within the

[1] After twelve days' journeying our traveller must have passed the valley of the Dead Sea proper, but being in the neighbourhood it was natural that he should refer to the Scriptural narrative of the destruction of Sodom and the other cities of the Plain. Besides which, it is now ascertained that the depression about the Dead Sea is but a section of a continuous valley, extending between Bâniâs, at the foot of Jebel esh-Sheikh, and the head of the Gulf of 'Akabah. True, Varthema's route, if he followed that of the Hajj at the present day, was about twenty miles to the eastward of the Wâdi 'Araba (the name which the valley takes to the south of Petra); but it is not surprising that he should have confounded therewith a dreary and difficult pass which branches off from the central chain of mountains, and which is known as the 'Akabet esh-Shâmi, for with that I am disposed to identify his "Valley of Sodom and Gomorrah." Burckhardt gives this as the twelfth day's journey of the pilgrims from Damascus, and describes it as follows: "The Hadj route, as far as Akabet Esh-Shami, is a complete desert on both sides. The mountain chain continues about ten hours to the west of the Hadj route... Here the Hadj descends a deep chasm, and it takes half an hour to reach below... The mountain consists of a red grey sandstone, which is used at Damascus for whetstones." [Was it this colour of the geological formation which Varthema's vivid or pious imagination converted into "what appeared to be blood, like red wax mixed with earth"?]—*Travels in Syria*, Appendix iii.

[2] The caravan was now in Edom, traversing a section of the route taken by the Israelites when they turned "northward" to "pass through the coast of the children of Esau," with whom they were commanded "not to meddle," but peaceably "to pass through the coast," and to "buy meat and water of them for money." (See Deut. ii. 3-6.) Payment for water is still exacted by the descendants of Esau in the same locality at the present day.

[3] A prevailing custom among the Bedawin when defending themselves

said camels, and we were constantly skirmishing, so that they kept us besieged two days and two nights, and things came at last to that state, that neither we nor they had any more water to drink. They had completely surrounded the mountain with people, saying that they would break through the caravan. Not being able to continue the fighting, our captain consulted with the Moorish merchants and we gave them (the Arabs) 1200 ducats of gold. They took the money, and then said that 10,000 ducats of gold would not pay for their water, and we knew that they wanted something else besides money. So our prudent captain arranged with the caravan, that all those men who were capable of bearing arms should not ride on the camels, and that each should prepare his arms. The morning having come, we put forward all the caravan, and we Mamelukes remained behind. We were in all three hundred persons, and we soon began to fight. One man and one lady were killed by bows on our side, and they did us no further harm. We killed of them 1600 persons.[1] Nor is it to be wondered at that we killed so many of them : the cause was, that they were all naked and on horseback, without saddles, so that they had a difficulty in turning on their way.

against an attack. The right fore-leg is first bent at the knee, and firmly secured with the leading halter so as effectually to prevent the camel rising. The animals are then made to lie down in close contact, their mass serving as a rampart, the space between the shoulders as embrasures, and their bodies as rests for the matchlocks of the defenders.

[1] Probably an exaggeration, though Strabo records a battle between the Roman army under Ælius Gallus and the Arabians of the southern part of the Hijâz, with a loss of two only of the former and ten thousand of the latter. Lib. xvi.

THE CHAPTER CONCERNING A MOUNTAIN INHABITED BY JEWS.[1]

At the end of eight days we found a mountain which appeared to be ten or twelve miles in circumference, in which

[1] This is a most interesting subject, and deserves more than a cursory notice. Our traveller describes the locality as being three days' journey from El-Medînah, which brings it to about "Hedye," given in Burckhardt's Itinerary as the twenty-fourth halt of the modern Hajj from Damascus, and four hours distant from Khaibar, "whither the people of the caravan often go to buy provisions." *Travels in Syria*, Appendix iii.

Mons. Caussin de Perceval has collected together the various notices found in the principal Arabian historians respecting the first Jewish colony in the Hijâz, from which it will be seen that Khaibar was one of their most important settlements. According to Ibn Khaldoon, the original immigrants formed part of an army sent by Joshua against the Amâlica (Amalekites), which, after destroying that people, took possession of their country, and occupied Yathrib (El-Medînah), Khaibar, and the surrounding places.

Others, and among them the author of the *Aghâni*, make the original colonists to have consisted of a large body of troops which Moses, on reaching Syria, had despatched against the Amâlica, with order to exterminate them utterly; but that having spared the young son of the Amalekite king, Arcam, the Israelites refused to receive them on their return from the expedition. Whereupon they retraced their way back to the Hijâz, and finally settled at Yathrib, Khaibar, and the adjoining districts.

Caussin de Perceval, in noticing the striking resemblance which this narrative bears to the Scriptural account of the Amalekite king Agag, whose life was spared by the soldiers of Saul against the positive command of the prophet Samuel, remarks that if the Arab tradition is founded on any historical truth connecting the fact of the disobedience of the Israelitish troops with the establishment of a Jewish colony in the Hijâz, it would serve to fix the date of that emigration to the time of Saul, or four centuries after Moses.

Other Arabian historians assert that the emigration did not take place till after the fall of Zedekiah, the last king of Judah, and the devastation of Judea by the armies of Nebuchadnezzar, when many Jewish families sought refuge in the Hijâz. Personal experience enables me to add that such also is the prevailing tradition among the Jews of Yemen of their original settlement in that country.

From these various accounts it is natural to infer that the Jewish

mountain there dwell four or five thousand Jews, who go naked, and are in height five or six spans, and have a fe-

colony in the Hijâz was formed by several successive immigrations in very remote times, and that it received new accessions by similar immigrations of a more recent date, one of which, specially noticed by the author of the *Aghâni*, may be referred either to the period of the reduction of Judea into a Roman province by Pompey, B.C. 64, to the destruction of Jerusalem by Titus, A.D. 70, or to the cruel persecution of the Jews under Adrian, A.D. 136. It is, indeed, highly probable that on each of those occasions many fugitive Jews from Judea sought an asylum with their co-religionists in the Hijâz.

The existence of a considerable Jewish population in the district indicated by Varthema at the period of Muhammed is a well-authenticated historical fact. His cursory description of the particular locality is equally correct; and the enmity of the resident Jews towards the Muhammedans appears to have been inherited by them through many generations. Referring to that period, Caussin de Perceval says: "The Jewish race was still powerful. They possessed, between three or four days' journey from Medînah, a fertile territory, abounding in grain and date-trees, and protected by several forts, the principal of which, called El-Cammoos, was situated on a mountain difficult of access. The district occupied by these strongholds was denominated KHAIBAR, a word which Arabian authors take to signify a castle. [More probably a confederation or colony, from the Hebrew חבר (khabar) *to be confederated*]. Its population was composed of different families, which had been established in the country from time immemorial. The Jews of Khaibar had manifested an active and implacable hatred towards the Prophet and his followers. United by an old alliance with their neighbours the Bedawîn descendants of Ghatafân, they laboured incessantly to stir up the hostility of that and other adjacent tribes against Muhammed."

In the month of Muharram of the seventh year of the Hijrah (12th April—12th May, A.D. 628) Muhammed led an army in person against Khaibar, and after a severe conflict, which lasted for several days, succeeded in capturing all the forts in that and the surrounding districts, and in reducing the Jews to abject submission. At first, they merely begged that their lives might be spared, promising to quit the country forthwith; but they were subsequently permitted to remain as simple farmers of the soil, binding themselves to give half of the produce to its new Mussulman proprietors. It was expressly stipulated, however, that their future expulsion should depend on the will of the Prophet.

Though it is generally believed that 'Omar, on his succession to the Khalifate A.D. 634, availed himself of this proviso to banish the Jews from the country, in order to execute an injunction said to have been

minine voice, and are more black than any other colour.
They live entirely upon the flesh of sheep, and eat nothing
else. They are circumcised, and confess that they are Jews;
and if they can get a Moor into their hands, they skin him
alive. At the foot of the said mountain we found a tank of
water, which is water that falls in the rainy season. We
loaded with the said water 16,000 camels, whereat the Jews
were ill-pleased; and they went about that mountain like
wild goats, and on no account would they descend into the
plain, because they are mortal enemies of the Moors. At
the foot of the mountain, by the said water, there were six
or eight feet of beautiful thornbushes, in which we found
two turtledoves, which circumstance appeared to us like a
miracle, inasmuch as we had travelled fifteen days and

given by Muhammed when dying, that two religions were not to be
tolerated in Arabia; nevertheless, it is tolerably certain that they continued to occupy the neighbourhood of Khaibar in considerable numbers
up to a very recent period. As late as 1762, Niebuhr was informed that
that district was still inhabited by several independent Jewish tribes, who
had sheikhs of their own like other Arabs. Burckhardt mentions the
old colony of the Jews at Khaibar, but says that it had disappeared,
though there still existed an unfounded belief at Meccah and Juddah
that their descendants still existed there, strictly performing the duties
of their religion. They seem, indeed, to have become extinct as a separate
race, for Burton was assured that there is not a single Jewish family now in
Khaibar, adding: "it is, indeed, the popular boast in El-Hejaz that, with
the exception of Jeddah (and perhaps Yembo), where the Prophet never
set his foot, there is not a town in the country harbouring an infidel. This
has now become a point of fanatic honour; but if history may be trusted,
it has become so only lately." *Pilgrimage to Meccah and El-Medinah*,
vol. ii. p. 118, *note*. See also CAUSSIN DE PERCEVAL, *Histoire des Arabes
avant l'Islamisme, etc.*, vols. ii. 641-644; iii. 193-201, 444. NIEBUHR,
Description de l'Arabie, pp. 326, 327.

Varthema evidently miscalculated the effects of distance in diminishing objects; hence, I presume, his fabulous measurement of the Jews at
five or six spans in height, and his failing to see the scanty cloth round
their loins, which still constitutes the only garment of the common
Bedawin of the Hijâz. As to complexion, if those seen by our traveller
were like the generality of the Jews in Yemen, he aptly describes it as
"more black than any other colour." In that respect they are not to be
distinguished from the Arab Bedawîn.

nights and had not met with a single animal or bird. The next day we resumed our journey, and in two days time arrived at a city which is called Medinathalnabi.[1] Near that city, at a distance of four miles, we found a well, by which the caravan halted for a day, and at this well each person washed himself, and put on clean linen to go into the said city, which contains about three hundred hearths, and is surrounded by walls made of earth.[2] The houses within are constructed with stone walls. The country around the said city lies under the curse of God, for the land is barren, with the exception that about two stones' cast, outside the city, there are about fifty or sixty feet of palmtrees in a garden,[3] at the end of which there is a certain conduit of water, which descends at least twenty-four steps, of which water the caravan takes possession when it arrives there.[4] Now, some who say that the body of Mahomet is suspended in the air at Mecca must be reproved; I say that it is not true. I have seen his sepulchre in this city, Medinathalnabi, in which we remained three days, and wished to see everything.[5] The first day we went into the city, at the entrance by the door of their mosque, and each of us, small or great, was obliged to be accompanied by some per-

[1] Medinat en-Nabi, the City of the Prophet.
[2] These earthen fortifications, according to Burton, were built by order of Kasim el Daulat el Ghori. The wall is now of stone, "well-built of granite and lava blocks, in regular layers, cemented with lime."
[3] "This alludes to the gardens of Kuba. The number of date-trees is now greatly increased." BURTON, *ut supra*.
[4] Burckhardt, in his plan of El-Mediuah, marks these "steps leading down to the canal in different parts of the town." Burton supposes the water to come from a spring in the date-groves of Kuba. "It flows down a subterranean canal, about thirty feet below the surface. In some places the water is exposed to the air, and steps lead to it for the convenience of the inhabitants."
[5] This absurd story, so long current in Christendom, but utterly unknown to Mussulmans, is supposed by Niebuhr to have originated from the position, one above the other, which the three enshrined tombs are represented as occupying in the rude drawings of the mosque made by native artists.

son,[1] who took us by the hand, and led us where Mahomet was buried.

THE CHAPTER CONCERNING WHERE MAHOMET AND HIS COMPANIONS WERE BURIED.

The mosque is made square in this manner: being about one hundred paces long, and eighty wide, and it has around it two doors on three sides, and the roof made arched, and there are more than 400 columns made of burnt stone, all whitened, and there are about 3,000 lighted lamps burning on one side of the arches.[2] On the right hand, at the head of the mosque, there is a square tower, about five paces on every side, which tower has a cloth of silk around it. At the distance of two paces from the said tower there is a very beautiful grating of metal, where persons stand to see the said tower; and at one side, on the left, there is a little door which leads you to the said tower, and in the said tower there is another little door, and by one of the doors there are about twenty books, and on the other side there are twenty-five books, which are those of Mahomet and of his Companions, which books declare his life and the commandments of his sect.[3] Within the said door

[1] A guide, called *Dalîl* or *Muzawwir*.

[2] Burckhardt makes the dimensions 165 paces in length by 130 in breadth. Burton calls it "a parallelogram about 420 feet in length by 340 broad." The former says: "It forms an open square, surrounded on all sides by covered colonnades, with a small building in the centre of the square......The columns are of stone; but being plastered white it is difficult to decide what species......The roof of the colonnade consists of a number of small domes." The latter styles it "a hypæthral building with a spacious central area, called El Sahn, El Hosh, El Haswah, or El Ramlah, surrounded by a peristyle with numerous rows of pillars, like the colonnades of an Italian monastery. Their arcades, or porticoes, are flat-ceilinged, domed above with the small 'Media Naranja,' or half-orange cupola of Spain."

[3] "Near the south-east corner stands the famous tomb, so detached

there is a sepulchre, that is, a pit under ground, wherein
was placed Mahomet, also Haly, and Babacher, and Othman, and Aumar, and Fatoma. Mahomet was captain, and
he was an Arab. Haly was son-in-law of Mahomet, that is,
he was the husband of Fatoma, who was the daughter of
Mahomet.[1] Babacher was he of whom we should say that

from the walls of the mosque as to leave between it and the south wall
a space of about twenty-five feet, and fifteen feet between it and the
east wall. The enclosure [Varthema's 'tower'] forms an irregular
square of about twenty paces, in the midst of the colonnade, several of
its pillars being included within it. It is an iron railing painted green
...the railing is of good workmanship, in imitation of filagree, and is
interwoven with open-work inscriptions of yellow bronze...What appears
of the interior is merely a curtain carried round on all sides, resembling
a bed, which is of the same height as the railing, and fills nearly the
whole space...This veil is a rich silk brocade of various colours, interwoven with silver flowers and arabesques. A band of inscriptions in
gold characters runs across the middle."—BURCKHARDT.

" The *Hujrah*, or Chamber, as it is called, from the circumstance of its
having been Ayisha's room, is an irregular square of from fifty to fifty-five feet in the south-east corner of the building, and separated on all
sides from the walls of the mosque by a passage about twenty-six feet
broad on the south side, and twenty on the eastern...Inside there are,
or are supposed to be, three tombs facing the south, surrounded by stone
walls, or, as others say, by strong planking. Whatever this material may
be, it is hung outside with a curtain, somewhat like a large four-post bed.
The outer railing is separated by a dark narrow passage from the inner
one, which it surrounds, and is of iron filagree, painted of a vivid grass
green, whilst carefully inserted in the verdure, and doubly bright by
contrast, is the gilt or burnished brass work forming the long and graceful letters of the Suls character, and disposed into the Moslem creed,
the profession of unity, and similar religious sentences. This fence has
four gates...they are constantly kept closed, except the fourth."—
BURTON.

The foregoing extracts prove the remarkable correctness of Varthema's
brief description of this mosque. Neither of the two enterprising travellers, however, throws any light on the books mentioned by him as existing in the vicinity of the Hujrah. The mosque library, according
to Burton, is now kept in large chests near the Bab el Salam.

[1] Muhammed, 'Ali, Abubekr, 'Othmân, 'Omar, and Fàtimah. Here
Varthema is in error, for it has never been believed by Mussulmans
that either 'Ali or 'Othmân was buried in the Prophet's mosque.
Burton says : " The sepulchre or cenotaph of Fàtimah is outside the

he was cardinal, and wanted to be pope.[1] Othman was one of his captains. Aumar was another of his captains. And these said books treat about each of his people, that is, of the said captains; and on this account it is that this *canaille* cut each other to pieces, for some wish to act according to the commandments of one, and some of another, and thus they do not know how to make up their minds; and they kill each other like beasts about these heresies, for they are all false.

THE CHAPTER CONCERNING THE TEMPLE AND SEPULCHRE OF MAHOMET AND HIS COMPANIONS.

In order to explain the sect of Mahomet, you must know that over the said tower there is a cupola, in which you can walk round the top, that is, outside.[2] You must understand

enceinte and the curtain which surrounds her father's remains." Burckhardt describes it thus: "Near the curtain of the Hejrah [Hujrah], but separated from it, though within the precincts of the railing, which here, to admit it, deviates a little from its square shape, is the tomb of Sitna Fatima, the daughter of Mohammed and wife of Ali. But some difference of opinion exists whether her remains actually rest here, or in the burial-ground called Bakya, beyond the town."

[1] I know of no passage in Abubekr's life which merits this remark. He was throughout the firm ally of Muhammed, and on the death of the latter proposed two candidates, 'Omar and Abu-'Obeidah, as most worthy to succeed him. It was mainly through the intervention of 'Omar, who recognized his superior claims as the special favourite of the Prophet, as his sole companion in the cave at Thor, and as having been designated by Muhammed to preside at the public prayers when he saw his end approaching, that the dignity of being his first successor was accorded to the aged Abubekr.

[2] The dome over the *Hujrah*, or Chamber, containing Muhammed's tomb. "Above the hujrah is the green dome, surmounted outside by a large gilt crescent springing from a series of globes. The glowing imaginations of the Moslems crown this gem of the building with a pillar of heavenly light, which directs from three days' distance the pilgrims' steps towards El-Medinah."—BURTON, *Pilgrimage to El-Medinah and Meccah*, vol. ii. pp. 73, 74.

the trick they played off upon the whole caravan the first evening we arrived at the tomb of Mahomet. Our captain sent for the superior of the said mosque, to whom he said: that he should show him the body of Nabi—this Nabi means the Prophet Mahomet—that he would give him three thousand seraphim of gold; and that he had neither father nor mother, nor brothers nor sisters, nor wife nor children, neither had he come to purchase spices or jewels, but that he had come to save his soul, and to see the body of the Prophet. Then the superior answered him with great violence, and rage, and pride, saying: " How do those eyes of yours, which have done so much evil in the world, desire to see him for whom God has created the heavens and the earth!" Then answered our captain: "Sidi intecate el melic;" that is to say, Sir, you say true;[1] but do me a favour, let me see the body of the Prophet, and immediately that I have seen it, I will pull out my eyes for the love of him. And Sidi[2] answered: "O Sir, I will tell you the truth. It is true that our Prophet wished to die here, in order to set us a good example; for he could well have died at Mecca had he so willed, but he desired to exercise poverty for our instruction; and as soon as he was dead, he was carried at once into heaven by the angels, and he says that he is equal with God." Our captain said to him: " Eise Hebene Marian phion?" that is, Jesus Christ the son of Mary, where is he? The Sidi answered: " Azafel al Nabi," that is, at the feet of Mahomet.[3] Our captain answered:

[1] *Sidi, anta tahki el-melieh.* Sir, you say well. I shall correct the orthography and mistranslations of Varthema's romanized Arabic, preserving the barbarisms of the original. The orthography varies in different editions, but in all it is execrably bad.

[2] Meaning the *Sherîf* belonging to the mosque.

[3] *Isa ibn Mariam fain hu?* Jesus, the Son of Mary, where is He? *Asfel en-Nabi.* Below (or under) the Prophet. Burton, having before him only the translation of these words, as he found it, unaccompanied by the Arabic, in Eden's *History of Travels*, supposes the reply

"Besbes, hiosi,"[1] that is, enough, enough! I will not know more. Then the captain came out and said to us: "See where I wanted to throw away three thousand seraphim!" In the night time, at three o'clock, there came into the camp about ten or twelve of those old men of that sect, for the caravan was encamped near the gate, two stones' cast off, and these old men began to cry out, some in one part and some in another: "Lei la illala, Mahometh resullala; lam Nabi, hia la, hia resullala, stasforla!" that is, God pardon me. "Leilla illala," means, God was, God will be; and "Mahometh resullala" is, Mahomet, the messenger of God, will rise again; "lam Nabi" signifies, O Prophet! O God! "hia resullala" means, Mahomet will rise again; "stasforla" signifies, God pardon me.[2] Our captain and we, hearing this noise, immediately ran with our arms in our hands, thinking they were Arabs who wanted to rob the caravan, saying to them: "What is this you are crying out?" for they made just such a noise as is heard amongst us Christians when a saint performs a miracle. These old men answered: "Inte mar abser miri igimen elbeit el Naby uramen il sama?" that is, Do you not see the brilliant light which comes out of the sepulchre of the Prophet?[3] Our captain said: "I do

to refer to the burial-place of Christ, and justly remarks that in that sense it is incorrect, since no Moslem ever believed that Christ left his body in this world. My own impression is, that it merely conveys the speaker's belief of Christ's inferiority to Muhammed, either locally or in rank, when the question was propounded.

[1] *Bass, bass.* Enough, enough; but I cannot decipher the "hiosi," unless it is a corruption of the vulgar *mush 'awaz,* I don't want [any more].

[2] *La ilah illa Alláh ; Muhammed Rasûl Alláh. Ya Nabi ! Hayya Alláh ! Hayya Rasûl Alláh ! Istaghfir lana !* There is no god but God. Muhammed is the Prophet of God. O Prophet! Salute God! Salute the Prophet! We invoke forgiveness!

[3] *Anta ma tabsur en-nûr* [alladhi] *yaji min beit en-Nabi wara min essama ?* Do you not see the splendour proceeding from the house of the Prophet beyond the heavens? The superstition that a supernatural light issues from Muhammed's tomb is still popular among pious Moslems.

not see anything;" and he asked all of us if we had seen anything, and we answered: " No." One of the old men replied: " Are you slaves?" that is, Mamelukes. The captain said: " Yes, they were slaves." The old man answered: " Oh, sirs! you cannot see these celestial things because you are not well confirmed in our faith." Our captain replied: " Lami ianon ancati telethe elphi seraphi: vualla anemaiati chelp menelchelp," which means, " Oh, fools, I was willing to give you three thousand ducats, by God, but I won't give you them now, you dogs, sons of dogs."[1] You must know that these lights were certain artificial fires which they had cunningly lighted on the top of the said tower to make us believe that they were lights which issued from the sepulchre of Mahomet; wherefore our captain ordered that none of us should on any account enter the said mosque. And you must know (I tell it you for a truth) there is no coffin of iron or steel, nor loadstone, nor any mountain within four miles. We remained there three days in order to give rest to the camels. The people of the said city supply themselves with the provisions which come from Arabia Felix, and from Cairo, and from Ethiopia by sea, for from thence to the sea is four days' journey.

THE CHAPTER CONCERNING THE JOURNEY TO GO FROM MEDINA TO MECCA.

Now we being tired of these things and vanities of Mahomet, prepared ourselves to pass onwards, and with our pilots, great observers of their compasses and charts,[2] neces-

[1] *Ya majnún! ana 'aiiti thaláth elf ashrafi! W' Alláh, ana ma 'aiiti. Kelb bin el-kelb.* You fool! I give three thousand ducats! By God, I will not give. You dog, son of a dog.

[2] *E con nostri Piloti delle sue bussole e carte al corso del mare necessarie grandi obseruatori cominciamo a caminare per mezo giorno."* The passage is obscure. If it means, as I conclude it does from a similar statement a few lines farther on, that the guides in the Hijáz used such

sary when traversing the sea, began the journey southwards, and we found a very fine well in which there was a great quantity of water, which well, the Moors say, was made by St. Mark the Evangelist, by a miracle of God, on account of the want of water which prevails in that country. This well was dry at our departure.[1] [I must not forget to mention our

instruments in order to direct their course between El-Medinah and Meccah, it is unquestionably absurd. Our traveller may have been led into the erroneous inference by seeing the leaders of the caravan consulting small portable compasses, called *Kiblah-námeh*, to ascertain the true *Kiblah*, or prescribed point to which they should turn during prayer. Nevertheless, the comparison which he here institutes leads to the conjecture that the Arabs who navigated the Red Sea at this period, one year at least before the appearance of the Portuguese in that quarter, were in possession of the mariner's chart and compass, which he expressly tells us in a later chapter were used on board the vessels in which he sailed from Borneo to Java. It is to be regretted that Varthema did not record the name by which the native pilots designated the compass. That of *Bushla* or *Busla*, from the Italian *Bussola*, though common among Arab sailors in the Mediterranean, is very seldom used in the eastern seas. *Daïrah* and *Beit el-Ibrah* (the Circle, or House of the Needle), are the ordinary appellatives in the Red Sea. In the Persian Gulf, *Kiblah-námeh* is in more general use.

[1] There are four roads leading from El-Medinah to Meccah; but it is impossible, from Varthema's brief description, to decide with certainty which was taken by his caravan. "St. Mark's well" affords no clue, as the name of that Apostle is utterly unknown to the Mussulmans of the Hijáz at the present day; nevertheless, its occurrence in connexion with this locality is somewhat remarkable. Has the tradition a much earlier origin? Eusebius makes St. Mark the first Bishop of Alexandria, and the patriarchal see of Egypt has borne that title ever since. Ecclesiastical historians further assert that one Pantænus, a teacher of divinity, was sent by Julianus, bishop of Alexandria, to preach the Gospel in Arabia towards the end of the second century. Ibn Khaldûn and the author of the *Aghâni* state that several of the Arab tribes between Egypt and Palestine professed Christianity at the time of Muhammed; and the destruction of an Abyssinian army before Meccah, A.D. 570, is a well authenticated historical fact. Now, as the first introduction of Christianity into Arabia is referrible to the zeal of the patriarchal see of St. Mark in Egypt, to which the Abyssinian church has always been ecclesiastically subject, it is just possible that the occurrence of the Apostle's name, as mentioned by Varthema, may be a traditional relic handed down from the earliest Christians in the Hijâz.

meeting with the sea of sand, which we left before we found the mountain of the Jews, and through which we travelled five days and five nights.[1] Now you must understand all about this. This is a very large level plain, which is full of white sand as fine as meal, where, if unfortunately the wind should blow from the south as you come from the north, all would be dead men, and although we had the wind with us we could not see each other at a distance of ten paces. The men ride on camels in certain wooden boxes,[2] in which they sleep and eat, and the pilots go in advance with their compasses as they do at sea. And here many died from thirst, and a great many died because when they dug and found water they drank so much that they burst; and here mummies are made.[3] When the wind blows from the north this sand collects against a very large mountain, which is a spur

---

[1] Burton remarks on this chapter generally, that "It is impossible to distinguish from this description the route taken by the Damascus caravan in 1503. Of one thing only we may be certain, namely, that between El-Medinah and Meccah there are no 'seas of sand.'" *Ibid.* p. 358. I am of opinion that the passage which I have placed between brackets is retrospective, and refers to a part of the journey between Damascus and El-Medinah, for Varthema describes his having left the sea of sand *before* he came to the Mountain of the Jews. Burckhardt's brief description of the stages on the present Hajj route does not enable me to identify the precise locality; but I think it should be looked for between El-Akhdar, the sixteenth stage from Damascus, and Hedye or Khaibar (the Mountain of the Jews), three days from El-Medinah; for in a note attached to El-Akhdar, in his enumeration of the caravan halts, Burckhardt says: "Two or three hundred years ago the Hadj route went to the east of the present route, and it is even now called *Darb esh-Sharki*, the Eastern Road."

[2] The *Shugduf*, the *Taktrawán*, the *Shibriyah*, and the *Mahaffah*, vehicles of different construction, borne by camels, and used by the more wealthy pilgrims in making the Hajj.

[3] "Wonderful tales are still told about these same mummies. I was assured by an Arabian physician, that he had broken a fowl's leg, and bound it tightly with a cloth containing man's dried flesh, which caused the bird to walk about, with a sound shank, on the second day."— BURTON, *ibid.* p. 361. *n.*

of Mount Sinai.[1] When we were at the top of the said mountain we found a door [or doorway] of the said mountain made by the hand of man. On the left side upon the top of the said mountain there is a grotto to which there is a door of iron. Some say that Mahomet stopped there to pray. At this door

[1] Burton, having inferred that Varthema was describing a part of the route between El-Medinah and Meccah, supposes this to be Jebel Warkan, on the sea-route to the latter place. For the reason already given, I prefer identifying it with the mountains in the vicinity of Hedjer (more correctly, El-Hijr), which, though with great latitude, may be styled an offshoot of Sinai. I am confirmed in this opinion by our author's somewhat romantic account of the ancient remains existing there, and the traditions with which they are associated. Burckhardt's description of them is as follows : " The most interesting spot on the caravan route between Damascus and Medinah, within the limits of Arabia, appears to be Hedjer, or, as it is sometimes called, Medayen Saleh, seven days north of Medinah. This place, according to many passages of the Koran (which has a chapter entitled Hedjer), was inhabited by a gigantic race of men, called Beni Thamoud, whose dwellings were destroyed because they refused to obey the admonitious of the prophet Saleh. In circumference, Hedjer extends several miles ; the soil is fertile, watered by many wells, or running streams. ...An inconsiderable mountain bounds this fertile plain on the west, at about four miles' distance from the ground where the pilgrims' caravan usually encamps. In that mountain are large caves cut out of the rock, with sculptured figures of men and various animals, small pillars on both sides of the entrances, and, if I may believe the Bedouins, numerous sculptures over the doors."—*Travels in Syria*, Appendix vii. According to the Korân, (chap. vii.), the destruction of the Thamudites was accompanied by "a terrible noise from heaven," and Muhammed's own conduct, on the occasion of his expedition against El-Hijr, shortly after his destruction of the Jews at Khaibar, served to perpetuate among his followers a dread of that signal example of the Divine vengeance, for he refused to let them drink at one of the wells in the valley, bidding them flee the accursed spot. The vivid imagination of pious Moslems still attributes supernatural noises, "like violent and repeated claps of thunder," to the desolate abode of those ancient Troglodytes, and it may fairly be presumed that these and similar traditions, and the fact of a chapter of the Korân being entitled " El-Hijr," —subjects which his Muhammedan companions would freely discuss while in that vicinity,—gave rise to the fable with which this part of Varthema's narrative is disfigured.

a very great noise is heard. We passed this said mountain with great danger, so much so that we thought we should never arrive at this place.] Then we departed from the said well and travelled for ten days, and twice we fought with 50,000 Arabs, till at length we arrived at Mecca, and there was a very great war, one brother with another, for there are four brothers, and they fought to be Lords of Mecca.[1]

THE CHAPTER SHOWING HOW MECCA IS CONSTRUCTED, AND WHY THE MOORS GO TO MECCA.

We will now speak of the very noble city of Mecca, what it is, its state, and who governs it. The city is most beautiful, and is very well inhabited, and contains about 6,000 families. The houses are extremely good, like our own, and there are houses worth three or four thousand ducats each. This city is not surrounded by walls.[2] A quarter of a mile distant from the city we found a mountain where there was a road cut by human labour.[3] And then we descended into

---

[1] The remarkable coincidence of this casual remark with the historical record of the period has been fully noticed in the Introduction.

[2] "The city is open on every side; but the neighbouring mountains, if properly defended, would form a barrier of considerable strength.... The mode of building is the same as that adopted at Djidda, with the addition of windows looking towards the street: of these many project from the wall, and have their framework elaborately carved or gaudily painted. Before them hang blinds made of slight reeds...Every house has its terrace."—BURCKHARDT'S *Travels in Arabia*, vol. i. pp. 189, 190.

[3] Burton identifies this with the Saniyah Kuda, a pass opening upon the Meccah plain. It is, doubtless, the same as that described by Burckhardt in the following extract: "Opposite to this building [a house belonging to the Sherif Ghâleb], a paved causeway leads towards the western hills, through which is an opening that seems artificial. El-Azraki applies the name of Jebel el-Hazna to this part of the mountain, and says that the road was cut through the rock by Yahia ibn Khold ibn Barmak. On the other side of the opening, the road descends into the plain of Sheikh Mahmoud, so named from the tomb of a saint, round which the Syrian pilgrims generally encamp."—*Ibid.* p. 234.

the plain. The walls of the said city are the mountains, and it has four entrances. The governor of this city is a Sultan, that is, one of the four brothers, and is of the race of Mahomet,[1] and is subject to the Grand Sultán of Cairo. His three brothers are always at war with him. On the 18th of May we entered into the said city of Mecca; we entered from the north, and afterwards we descended into the plain. On the side towards the south there are two mountains which almost touch each other, where is the pass to go to the gate of Mecca. On the other side, where the sun rises, there is another mountain pass, like a valley,[2] through which is the road to the mountain where they celebrate the sacrifice of Abraham and Isaac, which mountain is distant from the said city about eight or ten miles.[3] The height of this mountain is two or three casts of a stone by hand, and it is of some kind of stone, not marble, but of another colour. On the top of this said mountain there is a mosque according to their custom, which has three doors. At the foot of the said mountain there are two very beautiful reservoirs of water. One is for the caravan from Cairo, and the other for the caravan from Damascus; which water is collected there from the rain and comes from a great distance.[4] Now,

[1] A Sherif. "In Arabia the Sherif is the descendant of Hasan through his two sons, Zaid and Hasan el-Musanna."—Burton's *Pilgrimage to el-Medinah*, etc. Vol. ii. p. 257, *n*.

[2] "This is the open ground leading to the Muna Pass."—*Ibid.* p. 362, *n*.

[3] "An error. The sacrifice is performed at Muna, not at Arafat, the mountain here alluded to."—*Ibid.* p. 362, *n*.

[4] Burckhardt's account of Arafát reads like an amplification of Varthema's briefer description. "This granite hill, which is called Jebel er-Rahme, rises on the north-east side of the plain, close to the mountains which encompass it, but separated from them by a rocky valley. It is about a mile or a mile and a half in circuit: its sides are sloping, and its summit is nearly two hundred feet above the level of the plain... On the summit is shown the place where Mohammed used to take his station during the hadj; a small chapel [Varthema's 'mosque'?] formerly stood over it, but it was destroyed by the Wahabys...Several large

let us return to the city. At the proper time we will speak of the sacrifice which they make at the foot of the said mountain. When we entered into the said city we found the caravan from Cairo, which had arrived eight days before us, because they had not travelled by the same route as ourselves. In the said caravan there were sixty-four thousand camels and one hundred Mamelukes. You must know that, in my opinion, the curse of God has been laid upon the said city, for the country produces neither grass nor trees, nor any one thing.[1] And they suffer from so great a dearth of water, that if every one were to drink as much as he might wish, four *quattrini* worth of water daily would not suffice them.[2] I will tell you in what manner they live. A great part of their provisions comes from Cairo, that is, from the Red Sea. There is a port called Zida [Juddah], which is distant from the said city forty miles. A great quantity of food also comes there from Arabia Felix, and also a great part comes from Ethiopia. We found a great number of pilgrims, of whom

reservoirs lined with stone are dispersed over the plain : two or three are close to the foot of Arafāt...They are filled from the same fine acqueduct which supplies Mecca, and the head of which is about one hour and a half distant in the eastern mountains."—*Travels in Arabia*, vol. i. pp. 40-42. Burton says the Meccans have a tradition that the water comes from Baghdad.

[1] " Moslems who are disposed to be facetious on serious subjects often remark, that it is a mystery why Allah should have built his house in a spot so barren and desolate."—BURTON, *Ibid.* Vol. ii. p. 363, *n*.

[2] " With respect to water, Mecca is not much better provided than Djiddah. There are but few cisterns for collecting rain, and the well water is so brackish, that it is used only for culinary purposes...The famous well of Zemzem, in the Great Mosque, is indeed sufficiently copious to supply the whole town ; but, however holy, its water is heavy to the taste, and impedes digestion...The best water in Mecca is brought from the vicinity of Arafat, six or seven hours distant. The supply which it affords in ordinary times is barely sufficient for the use of the inhabitants, and during the pilgrimage sweet water becomes an absolute scarcity. A small skin of water, two of which skins a person may carry, being then often sold for one shilling, a very high price among Arabs." —BURCKHARDT'S, *Travels in Syria*, vol. i. pp. 193-195.

some came from Ethiopia, some from India Major, some from India Minor, some from Persia, and some from Syria. Truly I never saw so many people collected in one spot as during the twenty days I remained there. Of these people some had come for the purposes of trade, and some on pilgrimage for their pardon, in which pardon you shall understand what they do.

THE CHAPTER CONCERNING THE MERCHANDIZE IN MECCA.

First we will speak of the merchandize, which comes from many parts. From India Major there come a great many jewels and all sorts of spices, and part comes from Ethiopia; and there also comes from India Major, from a city called Bangchella,[1] a very large quantity of stuffs of cotton and of silk, so that in this city there is carried on a very extensive traffic of merchandize, that is, of jewels, spices of every kind in abundance, cotton in large quantites, wax and odoriferous substances in the greatest abundance.

THE CHAPTER CONCERNING THE PARDONING IN MECCA.

Now let us turn to the pardoning of the said pilgrims. In the midst of the said city there is a very beautiful temple, similar to the Colosseum of Rome, but not made of such large stones, but of burnt bricks, and it is round in the same manner; it has ninety or one hundred doors around it, and is arched, and has many of these doors.[2] On entering the said

[1] Bengal, pronounced Bangala by the Arabs(!).
[2] Joseph Pitts, who visited Meccah in 1608, describes the Great Mosque as having "about forty-two doors to enter into it,—not so much, I think, for necessity, as figure; for in some places they are close by one another." Ali Bey says: "The temple has nineteen gates with

temple you descend ten or twelve steps of marble, and here
and there about the said entrance there stand men who sell
jewels, and nothing else. And when you have descended
the said steps you find the said temple all around, and everything, that is, the walls, covered with gold.[1] And under the
said arches there stand about 4,000 or 5,000 persons, men
and women, which persons sell all kinds of odoriferous
things; the greater part are powders for preserving human
bodies,[2] because pagans come there from all parts of the
world. Truly, it would not be possible to describe the
sweetness and the odours which are smelt within this temple.
It appears like a spicery full of musk, and of other most
delicious odours. On the 23rd of May the said pardon
commences in the above-mentioned temple. The pardon is
this: Within the said temple, and uncovered, and in the
centre, there is a tower, the size of which is about five
or six paces on every side,[3] around which tower there is

thirty-eight arches." Burckhardt, in 1814: "The gates of the mosque
are nineteen in number, and are distributed about without any order of
symmetry. As each gate consists of two or three arches or divisions,
separated by narrow walls, those divisions are counted in the enumeration of the gates leading into the Kaabah, and thus make up the number
thirty-nine." Burton says: "The principal gates are seventeen in number. In the old building they were more numerous." The latter fact,
coupled with Burckhardt's description of the double and triple division
in each gate, may account for Varthema's approximate estimate, and
might have spared him Burton's remark thereon, who calls it "a prodigious exaggeration."

[1] "Seven [or, according to Burton, eight] paved causeways lead from
the colonnades towards the Kaabah or Holy House in the centre...The
whole area of the mosque is on a lower level than any of the streets surrounding it. There is a descent of eight or ten steps from the gate on
the north side into the platform of the colonnade, and of three or four
steps from the gate on the south side."—BURCKHARDT'S *Travels in
Arabia*, vol. i. p. 247.

[2] "I saw nothing of the kind, though constantly in the Haram at
Meccah."—BURTON.

[3] The *Kāabah* is here described. Burckhardt calls it "an oblong
massive structure 18 paces in length, 14 in breadth, and from 35 to 40

a cloth of black silk.¹ And there is a door all of silver, of the height of a man, by which you enter into the said tower. On each side of the door there is a jar, which they say is full of balsam, and which is shown on the day of Pentecost.² And they say that that balsam is part of the treasures of the Sultan. On each side of the said tower there is a large ring at the corner.³ On the 24th of May all the people begin, before day, to go seven times around the said tower, always touching and kissing each corner.⁴ And at about ten or twelve paces distant from the said tower there is another tower, like one of your chapels, with three or four doors. In the centre of the said tower there is a very beautiful well, which is seventy fathoms deep, and the water is brackish.⁵ At this well there stand six or eight

---

feet in height." Burton says it is 18 paces in breadth, and 22 in length; but as the Käabah was entirely rebuilt as it now stands in 1627, these measurements afford no test of the accuracy of Varthema's statement.

¹ The *Kiswah*, or curtain covering the Käabah. Burton says that the material now is a mixture of silk and cotton. It is renewed annually at the time of the Hajj.

² The door of the present Käabah, according to Burckhardt, is "wholly coated with silver, and has several gilt ornaments; upon its threshold are placed every night various small lighted wax candles, and perfuming pans filled with musk, aloe-wood, etc."

Giovanni Finati (1814) restricts the opening of the Käabah to once a year. Burckhardt says it is opened two or three times a year. Burton, that " the house may now be entered ten or twelve times a year gratis; and by pilgrims, as often as they can collect, amongst parties, a sum sufficient to tempt the guardians' cupidity."

Varthema was probably thinking of Good Friday and the Easter which follows, and connecting in his mind the Muhammedan sacrifices at Arafât with the solemnities of those Christian seasons, when he spoke of " the day of Pentecost."

³ " These are the brazen rings which serve to fasten the lower edge of the *Kiswah*, or covering."—BURTON.

⁴ " Then commenced the ceremony of *Tawâf*, or circumambulation.... I repeated, after my Mutawwif, or cicerone : ' In the name of Allah, and Allah is omnipotent ! I purpose to circuit seven circuits unto Almighty Allah glorified and exalted.'"—BURTON.

⁵ " A true description of the water of the well Zemzem." BURTON. The

men appointed to draw water for the people. And when the said people have gone seven times around the first tower, they go to this well, and place themselves with their backs towards the brink of the well, saying: "Bizmilei crachman crachin stoforla aladin," which means, In the name of God, God pardon me my sins.¹ And those who draw the water throw three bucketsful over each person, from the crown of their heads to their feet, and all bathe, even though their dress be made of silk. And they say in this wise, that all their sins remain there after this washing.² And they say that the first tower which they walked round was the first house that Abraham built.³ And all having thus bathed, they go by way of the valley to the said mountain of which we have before spoken, and remain there two days and one night. And when they are all at the foot of the said mountain, they make the sacrifice there.⁴

building which encloses the well (Varthema's "tower") was erected, according to Burckhardt, A.D. 1072. Burton estimates the distance between the well and the Käabah at forty cubits.

¹ *B'ism-Illáh er-rahmán er-rahim. Istaghfir lana.* In the name of God, the Pitiful, the Compassionate. Pardon us.

² "Many hadjis, not content with drinking it, strip themselves in the room, and have buckets of it thrown over them, by which they believe that the heart is purified as well as the body."—BURCKHARDT, *Idem.* vol. ii. p. 264.

³ "Mohammedan mythology affirms that the Käabah was constructed in heaven two thousand years before the creation of this world, and that it was then adored by the angels, whom the Almighty ordered to perform the *Tawaf*, or walk round it. Adam, who was the first true believer, erected the Käabah on earth on its present site, which is directly below the spot it occupied in heaven... The sons of Adam repaired the Käabah, and after the deluge Ibrahim [Abraham], when he abandoned the idolatry of his forefathers, was ordered by the Almighty to reconstruct it. His son Ismayl [Ishmael], who from his infancy resided with his mother Hadjer (Hagar) near the site of Meccah, assisted his father, who had come from Syria to obey the commands of Allah."—BURCKHARDT, *Idem.* p. 297.

⁴ Burton justly observes that there is great confusion in this part of Varthema's narrative, and gives the following as the consecutive order of the ceremonies: "On the 9th of Zu'l Hijjah, the pilgrims leave Mount Arafat. On the 12th, many hasten into Meccah, and enter the Käabah.

THE CHAPTER CONCERNING THE MANNER OF THE SACRIFICES IN MECCA.

Every generous mind is the most readily delighted and incited to great deeds by novel events. Wherefore, in order to satisfy many of this disposition, I will add concisely the custom which is observed in their sacrifices. Every man and woman kills at least two or three, and some four and some six sheep; so that I really believe that on the first day more than 30,000 sheep are killed by cutting their throats, facing the east. Each person gives them to the poor for the love of God,[1] for there were about 30,000 poor people there, who made a very large hole in the earth, and then put in it camels' dung, and thus they made a little fire, and warmed the flesh a little, and then ate it.[2] And truly, it is my opinion, that these poor men came more on account of their hunger than for the sake of the pardon; and as a proof that it was so, we had a great number of cucumbers, which came from Arabia Felix, and we ate them all but the rind, which we afterwards threw away outside our tent. And about forty or fifty of the said poor people stood before our tent, and made a great scrambling among themselves, in order to pick up the said rinds, which were full of sand. By this it appeared to us

---

They then return to the valley of Muna, where their tents are pitched, and sacrifice the victims. On the 10th, the tents are struck, and the pilgrims re-enter Meccah."

[1] "Others stood before their tents, and, directing the victim's face towards the Käabah, cut its throat, ejaculating: 'Bismillah! Allahu Akbar!'"

"It is considered a meritorious act to give away the victim without eating any portion of its flesh."—BURTON.

[2] This extempore style of cooking is common among the Bedawîn. Niebuhr describes it with his usual accuracy: "Quelquefois ils [les Arabes du désert] mettent une boule de pâte sur des charbons de bois allumés, ou sur du fumier de chameau séché; ils la couvrent soigneusement de ce feu, afin qu'elle en soit pénétrée; ensuite ils en ôtent les cendres, et la mangent toute chaude."—*Voyage en Arabie*, vol. iii. p. 46.

that they came rather to satisfy their hunger than to wash away their sins.[1] On the second day a cadi of their faith, like one of our preachers, ascended to the top of the said mountain and made a discourse to all the people, which discourse lasted for about an hour;[2] and he made in their language a sort of lamentation, and besought the people that they should weep for their sins. And he said to them in a loud voice: "Oh, Abraham, well-wished for and well-loved of God!" And then he said: "Oh, Isaac, chosen of God, friend of God, beseech God for the people of Naby!" and then were heard very great lamentations.[3] And when he had finished his sermon, the whole caravan rushed back into Mecca with the greatest haste, for at the distance of six miles there were more than 20,000 Arabs, who wanted to rob the caravan, and we arrived for the defence of

[1] Burton remarks that " this well describes the wretched state of the poor *Takruri* and other Africans, but it attributes to them an unworthy motive." He gives a still more revolting instance of their abject poverty, which occurred on the road between El-Medinah and Meccah: " After the long and sultry afternoon, beasts of burden began to sink in considerable numbers. The fresh carcases of asses, ponies, and camels, dotted the wayside: those that had been allowed to die were abandoned to the foul carrion-birds, the Rakham (vulture), and the yellow Ukab; and those whose throat had been properly cut, were surrounded by troops of Takruri pilgrims. These half-starved wretches cut steaks from the choice portions, and slung them over their shoulders till an opportunity of cooking might arrive. I never saw men more destitute."—*Ibid.* vol. iii. pp. 7, 8.

[2] The *Khutbat el-Wakfah*, or Sermon of the Standing, usually preached by the Kádhi of Meccah from Arafát, the orator taking his stand on the stone platform near the top. In Burckhardt and Burton's time the sermon lasted nearly three hours, *i.e.* from three p.m. till towards sunset.

[3] Joseph Pitts, the first Englishman who visited Meccah, describes a similar scene during the Hajj of 1680:—" It was a sight, indeed, able to pierce one's heart, to behold so many thousands in their garments of humility and mortification [clad in the white *ihrám*], with their naked heads, and cheeks watered with tears; and to hear their grievous sighs and sobs, begging earnestly for the forgiveness of their sins."—*A Faithful Account of the Religion and Manners of the Mahometans*, etc.

Mecca.[1] But when we had gone half way, that is, between Mecca and the mountain where the sacrifice is made, we found a certain little wall four fathoms high, and at the foot of the said wall a very great quantity of small stones, which stones are thrown there by all the people when they pass that way, for the objects which you shall hear. They say that when God commanded Abraham that he should go and sacrifice his son, he went before him, and he said to his son that he must follow after him, because it was necessary to fulfil the commandments of God. The son answered him: "I am well pleased to fulfil the commandment of God." And when Isaac[2] arrived at the above-mentioned little wall, they say that the devil appeared to him in the form of one of his friends and said to him: "My friend Isaac, where art thou going?" He answered him: "I am going to my father, who is waiting for me in such a place." The devil answered him: "Do not go, my son, for thy father will sacrifice thee to God and will put thee to death." And Isaac replied: "Let it be so; if such be the will of God, so let it be." The devil then disappeared, and a little farther on he appeared in the form of another dear friend of Isaac, and said to him the above-mentioned words. They relate that Isaac answered with anger: "Let it be so;" and

---

[1] On this particular occasion the return of the pilgrims may have been hastened by fear of an apprehended attack from the Bedawin; but the same rush, often attended with fatal results, occurs at every Hajj, and has given to that part of the ceremonies the name of *Ed-Defiia min Arafát*, the Hurry from Arafat. "Every man," says Burton, "urged his beast with might and main: it was sunset; the plain bristled with tent-pegs, litters were crushed, pedestrians trampled, and camels overthrown; single combats with sticks and other weapons took place;—here a woman, there a child, and there a camel were lost; briefly, it was a state of chaotic confusion." The cause of this precipitation is that, in accordance with the example of Muhammed, the *Salát el-'Esha*, or Prayer shortly after Sunset, should be said at the mosque of Muzdalifah about three hours distant.

[2] Here Varthema is in error. According to Muhammedan theology it was Ishmael and not Isaac who was ordered to be sacrificed.

took a stone and threw it in the devil's face: and for this reason, when the people arrive at the said place, each one throws a stone at the said wall, and then they go to the city.[1] We found in the street of the said city 15,000 or 20,000 doves, which they say are of the stock of that dove which spoke to Mahomet in the form of the Holy Spirit,[2] which doves fly about the whole district at their pleasure, that is, in the shops where they sell grain, millet, rice, and other vegetable productions. And the owners of the said articles

[1] "Bartema alludes to the 'Shaytan el Kabir,' the "Great Devil,' as the buttress at El Munah is called. His account of Satan's appearance is not strictly correct. Most Moslems believe that Abraham threw the stone at the 'Rajim,'—the lapidated one; but there are various traditions on the subject."—BURTON.

This custom of maledictory lapidation prevails elsewhere in the East. In 1835, while travelling from Sidon to Tyre, not far from the former place, my muleteer and another Mussulman who accompanied us each took up several small stones, at the same time giving me a handful, and requesting me to follow their example. Shortly after, we came in sight of a conical heap of loose pebbles and stones which stood in the road, on approaching which my companions hurled their stones at it with great vehemence, uttering simultaneously a long string of curses on the memory of a famous robber and murderer, who, as I afterwards learned, had been killed and buried there half a century before. It has often occurred to me since, that the ancient practice, recorded in the Old Testament, of raising a heap of stones, or cairns, over notorious criminals, may have been analogous to that which I have just mentioned, and was, perhaps, the origin of the rite instituted by Muhammed of casting stones at the places where Satan is said to have appeared to Abraham in the Valley of Muna (more properly, Mina). The language in which Scripture describes the execution of Achan is remarkable:—
" And *all Israel stoned him with stones*, and burned him with fire after they had stoned him with stones. *And they raised over him a great heap of stones* UNTO THIS DAY." Joshua vii. 25, 26. I think it may fairly be inferred from this account that the stoning on the occasion was not only general on the part of the Israelites, but that the action or ceremony was, or was intended to be, perpetuated. See also Joshua viii. 29; 2 Sam. xviii. 17.

[2] "A Christian version of an obscure Moslem legend about a white dove alighting on the Prophet's shoulder, and appearing to whisper in his ear whilst he was addressing a congregation."—BURTON.

are not at liberty to kill them or catch them. And if anyone were to strike any of those doves, they would fear that the country would be ruined.[1] And you must know that they cause very great expense within the temple.

THE CHAPTER CONCERNING THE UNICORNS[2] IN THE TEMPLE OF MECCA, NOT VERY COMMON IN OTHER PLACES.

In another part of the said temple is an enclosed place in which there are two live unicorns, and these are shown as

[1] "Meccah generally, but the mosque in particular, abounds with flocks of pigeons, which are considered the inviolable property of the temple, and are called the Pigeons of the Beit-Allah. Nobody dares to kill any of them when they enter private houses. In the square of the mosque several small stone basins are regularly filled with water for their use."—BURCKHARDT, *Travels in Arabia*, vol. i. p. 227.

When Muhammed, accompanied by Abubekr, fled from Meccah, he took refuge in a cave of Mount Thor, situated about three miles to the south of that city, to which spot he was traced by the emissaries of the hostile chiefs of the Koraish; but on noticing that a dove or pigeon had laid its eggs in the narrow passage, and that a spider had spun its web across it, they discontinued the search, remarking that if the refugees had entered there, the eggs would have been broken, and the web destroyed. The reverence for the pigeon which prevails among the Moslems of the Hijáz is supposed to originate in this tradition; nevertheless, Burton states that at El-Medinah it is sometimes used as an article of food. The same is true of many other parts of the East, but, as a general rule, Moslems everywhere have a superstitious notion that ill-luck is associated with the killing of pigeons.

[2] Burton remarks that these animals "might possibly have been African antelopes, which a *lusus naturæ* had deprived of their second horn," adding, "but the suspicion of fable remains." I was inclined, at first sight, to coincide in this opinion, and to conclude that Varthema saw merely two anomalous specimens of the Oryx, by no means an uncommon quadruped on the north-east coast of Africa, judging from the quantity of its horns brought to Aden by the Somalis. On further reflection, however, I am induced to believe that the "unicorns" which our traveller describes with so much exactness, and which were "shown

very remarkable objects, which they certainly are. I will tell you how they are made. The elder is formed like a

as very remarkable objects," were living representatives of a species of the antelope family, the existence of which is very generally doubted.

The following extracts on this interesting subject are from the notes of Dr. Edward Robinson, the learned American editor of Calmet's *Dictionary of the Holy Bible*, under the head of " Unicorn," who, among other authorities, quotes the above testimony of Varthema.

The figure of the unicorn is depicted, according to Niebuhr, on almost all the staircases found among the ruins of Persepolis. *Voyage en Arabie*, vol. ii. p. 109.

Pliny (*Hist. Nat.* viii. 21) in speaking of the wild beasts of India says: "The unicorn (*fera monoceros*) is an exceedingly fierce animal, resembling a horse as to the rest of its body, but having the head like a stag, the feet like an elephant, and the tail like a wild boar; its roaring is loud; and it has a black horn of about two cubits projecting from the middle of its forehead." With the exception of the Sacred Scriptures, these seem to be the chief ancient notices of the existence of the animal in question.

Don Juan Gabriel, a Portuguese colonel who lived several years in Abyssinia, assures us, that in the region of Agamos in the Abyssinian province of Damota, he had seen an animal of the form and size of a middle-sized horse, of a dark chesnut-brown colour, and with a whitish horn about five spans long upon the forehead; the mane and tail were black, and the legs short and slender. (LUDOLPH, *Hist. Æthiop.* lib. i. c. 10.) This account is confirmed by father Lobo, who lived for a long time as a missionary in Abyssinia. He adds, that the unicorn is extremely shy, and escapes from closer observation by a speedy flight into the forests. (*Voyage Hist. d'Abyssinie*, Amst. 1728, vol. i. p. 83, 291.)

Dr. Sparrman, the Swedish naturalist, who visited the Cape of Good Hope in 1772-6, gives an account of one Jacob Kock, who had travelled over the greater part of South Africa, and who had found on the face of a rock a drawing representing a quadruped with one horn. The Hottentots told him, that the animal there depicted was very like a horse, but had a straight horn on the forehead. They added that these animals were rare, that they ran with great rapidity, and were very fierce.

A more definite account of a similar animal is contained in the *Transactions* of the Zealand Academy of Science at Flushing. (Pt. xv. Middelb. 1792. Præf. p. lvi.) The account was transmitted from the Cape of Good Hope by Mr. Henry Cloete. It states that a bastard Hottentot, named Gerritt Slinger, related that while engaged with a party in pursuit of the savage Bushmen, they got sight of nine strange animals, and shot one of them. It resembled a horse, and was of a light-gray

colt of thirty months old, and he has a horn in the forehead, which horn is about three *braccia* in length. The other unicorn is like a colt of one year old, and he has a horn of about four *palmi* long.[1] The colour of the said animal resembles that of a dark bay horse, and his head resembles that of a stag; his neck is not very long, and he has some

colour, with white stripes under the lower jaw. It had a single horn, directly in front, as long as one's arm, and at the base about as thick. The hoofs were round like those of a horse, but divided below like those of oxen. Mr. Cloete mentions that several different natives and Hottentots testify to the existence of a similar animal with one horn.

The *Quarterly Review* for October 1820 (vol. xxiv. p. 120) contains a letter from Major Latter, commanding in the Rajah of Sikkim's territories, addressed to the Adjutant-General Nicol, wherein he explicitly states that the unicorn, so long considered a fabulous animal, actually exists at this moment in the interior of Thibet, where it is well known to the inhabitants, and is called by them the one-horned *tso'po*. They describe it as being as large as a middling-sized horse; fierce and extremely wild; seldom, if ever, caught alive, but frequently shot.

A paragraph in the *Calcutta Government Gazette*, August 1821, gives the following sequel to the foregoing: " Major Latter has obtained the horn of a young unicorn from the Sachia Lama, which is now before us. He expects shortly to obtain the head of the animal, with the hoofs and skin, which will afford positive proof of the form and character of the *tso'po*, or Thibet unicorn."

Whether Major Latter's expectation was ever realized, I am unable to say; but Professor Owen, whom I had the pleasure of consulting on the subject, regards the existence of the unicorn as mythical, to be classed with the mermaid and sea serpent, and he consequently infers that Varthema, however trustworthy on other matters of fact, was led astray in this instance, either through zoological ignorance, preconceived notions, or defective examination, or, perhaps, by a combination of these drawbacks. Not presuming, for a moment, to contest the learned professor's opinion, which is unquestionably founded on pre-eminent knowledge of this branch of science, I am still disposed, nevertheless, to rely on the credibility of Varthema, and to believe that he saw at Meccah two ordinary specimens of the famous unicorn, an animal which further research in the unexplored parts of Central Africa, or among the mountains of Thibet, may yet bring to light.

[1] Varthema's scale of measurements was probably Venetian. What it was in his time I have not ascertained. The modern *braccia* at Venice varies from 25.08 to 26.87 inches. The *palmo* is 3.937 inches.

thin and short hair which hangs on one side; his legs are slender and lean like those of a goat; the foot is a little cloven in the fore part, and long and goat-like, and there are some hairs on the hind part of the said legs. Truly this monster must be a very fierce and solitary animal. These two animals were presented to the Sultan of Mecca as the finest things that could be found in the world at the present day, and as the richest treasure ever sent by a king of Ethiopia, that is, by a Moorish king. He made this present in order to secure an alliance with the said Sultan of Mecca.

THE CHAPTER CONCERNING SOME OCCURRENCES BETWEEN MECCA AND ZIDA A PORT OF MECCA.

I must here show how the human intellect manifests itself under certain circumstances, in so far as it became necessary for me to exercise it in order to escape from the caravan of Mecca. Having gone to make some purchases for my captain, I was recognized by a Moor who looked me in the face and said to me: " In te menaine?" that is, " Where are you from?" I answered: " I am a Moor." He replied: " In te chedcab," that is, " You are not telling the truth." I said to him: "Orazalnabi Ancymuz lemma," that is, " By the head of Mahomet, I am a Moor." He answered: "Thale beithane," that is, " Come to my house;" and I went with him.[1] When I had arrived at his house, he spoke to me in Italian, and told me where I had come from, and that he knew that I was not a Moor, and he told me that he had

---

[1] *Anta min ain?* Where are you from?
Anta kadh-dhâb. You are a liar.
Wa-rás en-Nabi ana Muslim. By the head of the Prophet, I am a Moslem.
Taál ila beitana. Come to our house.

been in Genoa and in Venice, and gave me proofs of it. When I heard this, I told him that I was a Roman, and that I had become a Mameluke at Cairo. When he heard this he was much pleased, and treated me with very great honour, and as it was my intention to proceed further, I began to say to him, if this was the city of Mecca which was so renowned through all the world, where were the jewels and spices, and where were all the various kinds of merchandize which it was reported were brought there. I asked him this only that he might tell me why they had not arrived as usual, and in order not to ask him if the king of Portugal was the cause, he being Lord of the Mare Oceano [the Atlantic] and of the Persian and Arabian Gulfs. Then he began to tell me by degrees why the said articles had not come as they were accustomed to do. And when he told me that the king of Portugal was the cause, I pretended to be much grieved, and spoke great ill of the said king, merely that he might not think that I was pleased that the Christians should make such a journey.[1] When he saw that I displayed hostility to the Christians, he showed me yet greater honour, and told me everything point by point. And when I was well informed, I said to him: "O, my friend, I beg you, Menahamena lhabi,[2] to tell me some mode or way by which I may escape from the caravan, because my intention is to go to find those beings who are hostile to the Christians; for I assure you that, if they knew what I am capable of, they would send to find me even to Mecca." He answered me: "By the faith of our prophet what can you do?" I answered him that I was the most skilful maker of large mortars in the world. Hearing this he said: "Mahomet be ever

[1] According to the *Kurrat el-Ayún*, a manuscript History of Yemen in my possession, the Portuguese had seized seven native ships between India and the Persian Gulf, and massacred their crews, prior to Varthema's visit to Meccah. See note on p. 61.

[2] Probably *atmiiannak min en-Nabi*, I beseech you from (or, for the sake of,) the Prophet.

praised, who has sent us such a man to serve the Moors and God." So he concealed me in his house with his wife. And he begged me that I would induce our captain to drive out from Mecca fifteen camels laden with spices, and this he did in order not to pay thirty seraphim to the Sultan for the toll. I replied that if he would save me in this house, I would enable him to carry off a hundred camels if he had so many, for the Mamelukes have this privilege. And when he heard this he was much pleased. Afterwards, he instructed me in the manner in which I should conduct myself, and directed me to a king who is in the parts of India Major, and who is called the king of Deccan. When the time comes we will speak of that king. The day before the caravan set out he concealed me in his house in a secret place. In the morning, two hours before day, there went through the city a great quantity of instruments and trumpets, sounding according to their custom, and making proclamation that all the Mamelukes, under pain of death, should mount their horses and commence their journey towards Syria. Whereupon, my heart was seized with a great perturbation when I heard this proclamation, and I earnestly recommended myself with tears to the wife of the said merchant, and besought God that he would save me from such violence. On Tuesday morning the said caravan departed, and the merchant left me in his house with his wife; and he went with the caravan, and told his wife, that on the following Friday, she must send me away in company with the caravan of India which was going to Zida, which is a port of Mecca, forty miles distant. I cannot express the kindness I received from this lady, and especially from her niece of fifteen years old, they promising me that, if I would remain there, they would make me rich. But I declined all their offers on account of the present danger. When Friday came, I set out with the caravan at noon, to the no small regret of the said ladies, who made great lamentations, and at midnight we arrived at a certain city of Arabia, and remained there all night and until noon of the following day. On Saturday we departed and travelled until midnight, when we entered into the said port of the city of Zida.

THE CHAPTER CONCERNING ZIDA,[1] THE PORT OF MECCA, AND OF THE RED SEA.

This city is not surrounded by walls, but by very beautiful houses, as is the custom in Italy; we will, therefore, not dwell long on a description of it.[2] It is a city of very extensive traffic, because a great number of the pagan people come here; the reason being that neither Christians nor Jews are admitted.[3] When I had arrived at the said city I immediately entered into a mosque, that is, a temple, where there were at least 25,000 poor people, and I hid myself in a corner of the said temple, and remained there for fourteen days. All day long I remained stretched upon the ground covered up with my garments, and keeping up a constant groaning

[1] Jiddah, or, more correctly, Juddah.

[2] The present wall which surrounds Juddah on the land side was built by El-Ashraf Kansooh El-Ghôree, the Mameluke Sultan of Egypt, A.H. 917, or thirteen years after the date of Varthema's visit. The town is superior to any in the Hijâz: the houses are well built of stone and madrepore, and consist generally of two stories.

[3] The rule which excluded all but Muhammedans from Juddah has been practically rescinded within the last half century, and there are now several Christian merchants, chiefly Greeks, resident in the town. Niebuhr experienced greater civility there than in Egypt, but he was warned against approaching the gate leading to Meccah. At the period of Burckhardt's visit there were no Christians settled in Juddah, but a few Greeks from the islands of the Archipelago brought merchandize to the market from Egypt. He says: "In the time of the Sherifs they were much restricted, compelled to wear a particular dress, and prohibited from approaching the Meccah gate; but the Turks, having become masters of the Hijâz, abolished these restrictions, and a Christian now enjoys complete liberty there."

as though I were suffering intense pain in my stomach and body. The merchants said: "Who is that who is lamenting so?" The poor people who were near me said: "It is a poor Moor, who is dying." Every evening when night came I quitted the mosque and went to buy food. I leave you to judge whether or no I had an appetite, eating only once a day, and that very badly. This city is governed by the lord of Cairo. The lord of it is one who is a brother of Barachet, that is, of the Sultan of Mecca.[1] They are subject to the Grand Sultan of Cairo. There does not occur to me much to say here, for they are Moors. The land does not produce one single thing, and there is a great scarcity of water, that is to say, of fresh water.[2] The sea beats against the walls of the houses.[3] All sorts of necessaries are found here, but they come from Cairo, from Arabia Felix, and from other places. In this city there are always a great number of sick people, and they say that this is in consequence of the bad air of the place. It contains about five hundred families.[4] At the end of fourteen days I made an agreement

[1] This is another striking proof of Varthema's general correctness. The patronymic of the ruling Sherif of Meccah at the time was Barakát, of which family several notices, collected from Arabian historians, have already been given in the Introduction.

[2] With the exception of a few palm-trees near one of the mosques there is no vegetation of any kind in Juddah, and the country beyond is a barren desert. Rain water is carefully preserved in cisterns, with which many of the houses are provided; but most of that used for drinking is drawn from wells about one mile and a half distant on the southern side. Water, indeed, may be found everywhere in the vicinity at a depth of a few feet from the surface, but it is so brackish as scarcely to be drinkable.

[3] Only to a very small extent now, and that at high water, or, more correctly, according to the winds, by which the tides in the harbour are greatly influenced. This circumstance seems to corroborate Niebuhr's opinion that the sea had gradually receded from the town: the combined result, perhaps, of growing coral-reefs and silt. *Voyage en Arabie*, vol. i. p. 222.

[4] The population is much larger now. Ali Bey estimated it at 5,000, which was probably an exaggeration. Burton, on the authority of Mr. Cole, H.M. late vice-consul at Jiddah, states it to be 2,500, but thinks that figure too low.

with the master of a vessel which was going towards Persia, for in the said port there were about one hundred ships great and small. Three days afterwards we set sail, and began to navigate the Red Sea.

THE CHAPTER SHOWING WHY THE RED SEA IS NOT NAVIGABLE.

It will be understood that this sea is not red, but that the water is like that of any other sea. In this sea we sailed one day until the setting of the sun, because it is not possible to navigate it during the night time. And every day they proceeded in this manner until they arrived at an island called Chameram.[1] After this island you can proceed in safety. The reason why it is not possible to sail during night is, that there are many islands and many rocks, and it is necessary that a man should always be stationed on the top of the mast of the ship in order to see the route, which cannot be done during the night-time, and therefore they can only navigate during the day.[2]

[1] Camrân, generally written Camaran.

[2] The same precautions are still taken to avoid the numerous coral-reefs, sunken rocks, and dangerous patches, which exist between Leet, about ninety miles to the south of Juddah, and the island of Camrân. The navigation below the latter place is much more easy.

THE SECOND BOOK.
OF ARABIA FELIX.

THE CHAPTER CONCERNING THE CITY OF GEZAN,[1] AND OF ITS FERTILITY.

HAVING discoursed of the places, cities, and customs of the people of Arabia Deserta, as far as it was permitted me to see them, it appears to me that it will be proper, with brevity and more happily, to enter upon Arabia Felix. At the end of six days we arrived at a city which is called Gezan, which city has a very fine port; and we found there forty-five vessels belonging to different countries. This city is situated on the sea shore, and is subject to a Moorish lord, and is a district very fruitful and good, like Christian countries. Here there are very good grapes and peaches,

[1] Jeezân, or Gheezân, is situated in a fertile district, but the town has fallen into decay. It has a few stone buildings, but the principal part consists of grass huts, with pyramidal tops. It possesses a large fort, in a ruinous condition, and the small bazaar is now scantily supplied with such provisions as the natives use, the principal of which is the *dhurah* (Varthema's "dora"), a species of millet, extensively cultivated throughout Yemen, where it is called *tââm*. There is a good inner anchorage for small boats off the town. The dress of the male portion of the population, like that of the common Arabs of the country generally, consists of a cotton cloth, called a *footah*, worn round the loins. El-Edrisi states that the district of Jeezân was occupied by a family of the famous tribe of Ghassân (the Ghassanides,) which probably became extinct, or was made subject by the Imâms of Yemen, during the thirteenth century of our era. NIEBUHR, *Voyage en Arabie*, vol. iii. p. 232. See also MORESBY'S *Sailing Directions for the Red Sea*, pp. 27, 28.

quinces, pomegranates, very strong garlic, tolerable onions, excellent nuts, melons, roses, flowers, nectarines, figs, gourds, citrons, lemons, and sour oranges, so that it is a paradise. The inhabitants of this city go almost naked, and live after the manner of the Moors. There is here abundance of flesh, grain, barley, and white millet, which they call *dora*, and which makes good bread. We remained here three days in order to lay in provisions.

THE CHAPTER CONCERNING SOME PEOPLE CALLED BADUIN.[1]

Departing from the said city Gezan, we went for five days always in sight of land, that is to say, the land was on our left hand; and seeing some habitations on the sea shore, we disembarked fourteen of our people to ask for some provisions in exchange for our money. They answered our request by beginning to throw stones at us with slings, and these were certain people who are called Baduin: they were in number more than one hundred, and we were only fourteen. We fought with them for about an hour, so that twenty-four of them remained dead on the field, and all the others took to flight; for they were naked, and had no other arms than these slings. We took all that we could, namely, fowls, calves, oxen, and other things fit to eat. In the course of two or three hours the disturbance began to increase, as did also the inha-

[1] Bedouin, or more correctly Bedawín, sing. Bedawy. From the collective Bedu, properly 'a desert.' Hence the literal rendering is 'desert-men;' but the designation is frequently applied to Arabs who inhabit the open country in contradistinction to those who dwell in towns. In this instance, however, Varthema may have taken the term from the village El-Bedawi, there being one of that name midway between Jeezân and Camrán. Another locality in the neighbourhood, called Khabt el-Bakkâr, Niebuhr describes as being inhabited by some wandering families who were accused of plundering all travellers who came in their way. *Voyage en Arabie*, vol. iii. p. 233.

bitants of the said land, so that they were more than six
hundred, and we were obliged to withdraw to our ship.

THE CHAPTER CONCERNING THE ISLAND OF THE RED
SEA CALLED CHAMARAM.[1]

On that same day we took our course towards an island
called Chamaram, which island appears to be ten or twelve
miles in circumference, where there is a place containing
about two hundred families, which is inhabited by Moors.
In this said island there is sweet fresh water and flesh, and the
best salt I ever saw is made there. It has a port towards
the mainland, from which it is distant about eight miles.
This island is subject to the Sultan of the Amanni,[2] that is,
the Sultan of Arabia Felix, and we remained there two
days. We then steered towards the mouth of the Red Sea,
and for two days you can navigate in safety night and day,
but from the island to Zida you cannot navigate by night.
And when we had arrived at the said mouth, it really ap-

[1] Camrân is eleven miles long and from two to four broad. There are
seven villages on the island, consisting mostly of huts belonging to the
fishermen employed on the neighbouring pearl banks and turtle islands.
Several spots are under cultivation, good water is plentiful, and other
supplies, such as oxen and sheep, are tolerably abundant; for which
reasons, as well as on account of its secure harbour, the island is much
frequented by native vessels trading between the coasts of India and
Persia and the Red Sea.

[2] " Soldano delli Amanni." This was either the reigning Imâm of
Sanäa, or Sultân 'Amir ibn Abd el-Wahhâb. The latter, about this
period, was contesting the sovereignty of Yemen with the former, and
had already succeeded in wresting from him a large portion of the
southern districts, including the sea-board. As Varthema does not mention the term "Imâm," the ordinary designation of the rulers at Sanäa,
and which he must frequently have heard used, I apprehend that he
misconstrued the title into the name of a country or people, and then
Italianized it, distorting "Imâm" into "Amanni." Or, it may be a
contraction and corruption of [*Amír el-Mu*]*amanín*, (Lord of the Faithful,) another title common to all the Imâms of Sanäa.

peared as though we were within a hemmed-in house; for that embouchure is about two or three miles wide, and on the right hand thereof there is land about ten paces high and uninhabited, so far as we could perceive from a distance. On the left hand of the said embouchure there is a very high mountain, and it is of stone; and in the middle of the said embouchure there is a certain little uninhabited island which is called Bebmendo.[1] Those who wish to go to Zeilla take the route on the right hand, and those who want to go to Aden take that on the left hand; and this we did in order to go to Aden, and we always sailed in sight of land. From the said Bebmendo we arrived at the city of Aden in a little less than two days and a half.

[1] The narrowest part of the "Little Strait" is one and a half mile wide. Varthema's description of the low land on the African side, and the "very high mountain" on the Arabian side, (Bâb el-Mandeb Cape,) is remarkably correct. Native craft going from the Red Sea to Zeila, or any other ports on the former coast, still take the right or wider channel; those bound for Aden the left. By a pardonable misconception, however, he gives the name of the two Straits, "Babmendo," (Bâb el-Mendeb) to the small island which forms them, and which will be recognized at once as Perim, called by the natives, Mayûn.

The Arabs have a tradition respecting the formation of the Straits of Bâb el-Mandeb which, for its absurdity, surpasses very many of their extravagant legends. I quote the following from a manuscript in my possession, entitled *Târîkh Thaghr 'Aden* (a History of the Valley of Aden), written by the learned and devout Kâdhi, Aboo-Abdallah bin Ahmed Muhrim. He says: "Formerly from Kalzam [the Gulf of Suez?] to Aden, and beyond the mountains of Socotra, all was dry land: there was no sea, and no outlet; but when Alexander the Great, in his voyage round the world, came here, he opened a gulf wherein the sea flowed until it was arrested near the mountains of Bâb el-Mandeb, whereby Aden was surrounded by water, and nothing was visible there but the tops of the mountains jutting up into peaks......Then Alexander, (but others say, some other person,) cut a passage through Bâb el-Mandeb, whereby the water rushed in and filled the whole of El-Kalzam. When the rush was over, Aden rose up, and the waters about it were drained in the direction of Esh-Sham."

THE CHAPTER CONCERNING THE CITY OF ADEN, AND OF SOME CUSTOMS RESPECTING THE MERCHANTS.

Aden is the strongest city that was ever seen on level ground. It has walls on two sides, and on the other sides there are very large mountains. On these mountains there are five castles, and the land is level, and contains about five thousand or six thousand families.[1] The market is held at two o'clock in the night, on account of the intense heat in the city during the day.[2] At a stone's cast from this city there is a mountain, upon which stands a castle, and at the foot of this mountain the ships cast anchor.[3] This city

---

[1] The ruins of these towers still exist, also of the two walls, one of which extended along the shore of "Front Bay" (which appears to have been the principal harbour at that period), and the other over the heights commanding Bandar Hokkât, now called Holket Bay. These walls, connecting as they did the Mansûri heights on the north-east with the offshoots of the lofty Shamsân range on the south-west, completely enclosed the area where the town of Aden is situated, and which seems at one time to have been the crater of a volcano, forming a tolerably perfect circle from one to one mile and a half in diameter. According to the Arabian author last quoted, most of these fortifications were built by 'Othmân ez-Zenjíly, who was appointed governor of that district by Toorân Shah bin Ayyûb, brother of the famous Salâh ed-Dîn (Saladin), Sultan of Egypt, on his departure from Yemen in the year of the Hijrah 571, A.D. 1175. Ez-Zenjíly erected many other public buildings at Aden, some of which were standing when the British captured the place in 1839; but his rapacity rendered him odious to the inhabitants, and on hearing of the approach of Taghtakîn, another brother of Salâh ed-Dîn, who was sent with an army against Yemen, A. H. 579, he fled from Aden, and died at Damascus four years after.

[2] An incidental proof that Varthema was at Aden during the hot season, which lasts from May to October. By "two o'clock in the night," I understand two hours after sunset.

[3] The mountain here mentioned is the small island of Seerah, which has lately been joined to Aden by a causeway. The following absurd tradition respecting this spot is recorded by the author above quoted: " Cain, having killed his brother Abel, and being afraid of his father Adam, fled from India to Aden, and took up his abode on Seerah. Becoming sad at the separation from his home and relatives, Satan appeared

is extremely beautiful, and the capital of Arabia Felix. It is the rendezvous for all the ships which come from India Major and Minor, from Ethiopia and from Persia. All the ships which are bound for Mecca put in here. As soon as a ship comes into port, the officers of the Sultan of the said city board it, and desire to know whence it comes, the nature of its cargo, and when it left its own country, and how many persons there are on board. And when they have obtained all this information, they remove from the said ship the masts, sails, rudder, and anchors, and carry them all into the said city; and this they do in order that the said persons may not depart without paying the dues to the Sultan.[1] The second day after my arrival in the said city I was taken and put in irons, and this occurred through one of my companions, who said to me: "Christian dog, son of a dog." Some Moors heard this speech, and through this I was taken with great violence to the palace of the Vice-Sultan, and they immediately consulted whether they should at once put me to death, because the Sultan was not in the city. They said that I was a spy of the Christians. But as the Sultan of this country never puts any one to

to him, and presented him with sundry musical instruments, such as the lute, with which he managed to amuse himself." According to another tradition, the fire of the day of judgment is to spring from this rock; and the same author states that a well existed there up to a comparatively recent period, from the bottom of which flames used to issue, and that the end of a rope, let down by way of experiment in the presence of many witnesses, was found to be burnt on being drawn up. There is nothing improbable in this story, for the peninsula of Aden is undoubtedly of volcanic origin, and the same igneous agency still occasionally manifests itself among the Zebair islands in the Red Sea, and on the opposite coast of Africa.

The Portuguese, under Lopez Soarez de Albergaria, occupied the island of Seerah in 1516, and during their short stay repaired the old fort which stood on its summit, and further strengthened the position by enclosing it with a strong wall, the remains of which are still extant.

[1] This is a common custom with the native chiefs on the Arabian shores when they wish to detain a vessel.

death, these people respected my life, and kept me sixty-five days with eighteen pounds' weight of iron on my feet. On the third day after we had been taken, there ran to the palace forty or sixty Moors, belonging to two or three ships which had been captured by the Portuguese,[1] and who had escaped by swimming, and they said that we belonged to these Portuguese ships, and that we had come there as spies. For this fancy of theirs they ran to the palace in the greatest fury, with arms in their hands to slay us; but through the merciful intervention of God, those who guarded us fastened the door on the inner side. At this report the district rose in arms, and some desired that we should die and some not. At last the Vice-Sultan obtained that we should be spared. At the end of sixty-five days the Sultan sent for us, and we were both taken on a camel, still, however, with the said irons on our feet. We were eight days on the road, and were then presented to the Sultan at a city called Rhada. At the time when we arrived at the city the Sultan was reviewing eighty thousand men, because he was about to go to war with another Sultan of a city called Sana, which is distant from Rhada three days' journey.[2] This city lies

---

[1] The following passage, which I translate from the *Kurrat el-Ayûn*, confirms this statement: "In this year [A.H. 908=A.D. 1502, about one year before Varthema's arrival at Aden], the ships of the Sultan of the Franks made their appearance in the sea between India and the island of Hormuz. They seized seven vessels and murdered most of the crews."

[2] Radâä is situated about one hundred and sixty miles north of Aden, and sixty to the south of Sanäa. The town possesses a strong citadel and several detached forts, now in a very ruinous condition. The name in full is Radâä el-'Arsh.

The preparations for an expedition against Sanäa, incidentally mentioned by Varthema, are strikingly corroborated by the following extract from the *Kurrat el-Ayûn*: "In the month of *Safar* of this year [A.H. 910 = A.D. 1503-4] *El-Melek* Edh-Dhâfir, [*The Victorious King*, the surname given to 'Amir ibn Abd el-Wahhâb, the then reigning Sultan of Aden and southern Yemen], projected an attack on Sanäa, and made preparations accordingly. To that end he despatched several of his

partly on an acclivity and partly on the plain,[1] and it is very beautiful and ancient, populous and rich. When we were presented before the Sultan he asked me whence I came. I answered: "Anabletrom iasidi anaigi assalem menel Cayro anegi Medinathalnaby & Mecca & badanigi bledech cul ragel calem inte sidi scich hiasidi ane abdech Inte maarf sidi ane musolimim." That is, the Sultan said: 'Whence are you and what do you purpose doing?" I answered: "that I was a Roman, that I had become a Mameluke at Cairo, that I had been to Medina, to Naby, where Mahomet is buried, and to Mecca, and that then I had come to see his Highness; because through all Syria, and at Mecca, and at Medina, it was said that he was a saint, and if he was a saint, (as I believed), he must know that I was not a spy of the Christians, and that I was a good Moor and his slave."[2]

officers to the Tihâma to levy a force from among the Arabs, and in the month of *Rabiä el-Akhir*, a body of Arab horsemen, consisting of the Zäaliyyín, the Samiyyín, the Kahra, the Munâsika, the Wamâh, the Lamiyyín, the Küabiyyín, the Müazibah, and the 'Arshiyyín, proceeded to the seat of government. And in the same month our lord [the Sultan] marched towards Sanäa, stopping for some days at Radää el-'Arsh, from whence he went to Dhamâr, and on the twenty-second of the same month to Sanäa, before which city he halted with a very large army and many terrible engines of war, and he pressed the siege until the date hereinafter mentioned." It seems highly probably that Varthema's interview with the Sultan at Radää occurred during the short stay made by the latter at that place while on his march towards Sanäa.

[1] The passage in the original is: "Et e questa Citta parte in costa, parte in piano." As the town of Radää is nearly two hundred miles from the sea, Varthema undoubtedly uses the word "costa" in the sense given above, which is, moreover, locally correct. Dante affixes the same signification to it :—

"Lo sommo er' alto, che vincea la vista,
  E la costa superba più assai
  Che da mezzo quadrante al centro lista."

DEL PURGATORIO, *Canto* iv.

which Boccacio paraphrases thus: "L' acclività di essa costa rispetto al piano orizontale era assai maggiore di 45 gradi."

[2] *Ana* [*min*] *balád er-Rám, ya sídi. Anaáji asallim min el-Káhirah.*

Then said the Sultan: "Say, Leila ilala Mahometh resullala."[1] But I could not pronounce the words at all, whether such were the will of God, or through the fear which had seized me. The Sultan, seeing that I could not pronounce these words, commanded that I should be thrown into prison and kept with the greatest strictness by the men of eighteen castles, that is, four for each castle. They remained four days, and then were changed for four others from four other castles. And in this order they guarded me for three months, with a loaf of millet in the morning and one in the evening, although six of these loaves would not have sufficed me for one day, and sometimes I should have been well pleased if I could have had enough water.

Two days afterwards, the Sultan took the field, and marched to the said city Sana with his army, in which there were three thousand horsemen, sons of Christians, as black as Moors. They were of those of Prester John,[2] whom they

Ana aji Medinát-en-Nabi, wa-Meccah, wa-biïad ana aji baládak. Kul rajul kallam; Anta, sidi, sheikh. Ya sidi, ana abdak. Anta ma tüaraf, sidi, ana Muslim? "I am of the country of Rûm, my lord. I became a Muhammedan at Cairo. I came to El-Medinah of the Prophet, to Meccah, and then I came to your country. Every one says, sir, you are a sheikh. Sir, I am your slave. Do you not know, sir, that I am a Mussulman?"

[1] *La iláh illa Alláh; Muhammed Rasûl Alláh.* "There is no god but the God; Muhammed is the Prophet of God."

[2] That is, Abyssinians, "Prester John" being the fanciful name which the Portuguese had given to the Emperor of that people during the preceding century. The late Professor Lee, in a note on the title of "Rasûl" (*sent* or *commissioned*), which Ibn Batûta, in his *Travels*, says had been maintained by some of the Sultâns of Yemen up to his time because their grandfather was so called when *commissioned* as the Emir of Yemen by one of the Khalifs of the house of 'Abbâs, remarks as follows:—"A title of this sort seems to have originated the *Prester John* of Abyssinia, of which the missionary accounts said so much. A Tartar king seems also to have assumed this title, which in Persian was translated *Ferishta Ján*, John the Angel, probably because he had received Christianity. Hence the European 'Prester John;' but how this became ascribed to the King of Abyssinia, it is not easy to say, unless he had

purchased at the age of eight or nine years, and had them trained to arms. These constituted his own guard, because they were worth more than all the rest of the eighty thousand. The others were all naked, with the exception of a piece of linen worn like a mantle. When they enter into battle they use a kind of round shield, made of two pieces of cow hide or ox hide fastened together. In the centre of the said round shields there are four rods, which keep them straight. These shields are painted, so that they appear to those who see them to be the handsomest and best that could be made. They are about as large as the bottom of a tub, and the handle consists of a piece of wood of a size that can be grasped by the hand, fastened by two nails. They also carry in their hand a dart and a short and broad sword, and wear a cloth vest of red or some other colour stuffed with cotton, which protects them from the cold and also from their enemies. They make use of this when they go out to fight. They all also generally carry a sling for the purpose of throwing stones wound round their heads, and under this sling they carry a piece of wood, a span in length, which is called *mesuech*, with which they clean their teeth,[1] and generally from forty or fifty years downwards they wear two horns made of their own hair, so that they look like young kids.[2] The said Sultan also takes with his army five thou-

assumed the title mentioned here by our traveller which belonged to the King of Yemen." *Travels of Ibn Batúta*, p. 54, n.

[1] This custom still prevails throughout Yemen. The *Miswák*, which is generally carried about the head-dress, is made from the branch of an indigenous shrub, the wood of which is very fibrous, and is covered with a tough spongy bark, about an inch of which is cut off in order to allow the enclosed fibres to expand, thereby forming the tooth-brush. The *Indigofera pauciflora* is applied to a similar purpose in Scinde and by the Hindus of India.

[2] This style of wearing the hair is peculiar, I believe, to some of the tribes of central Yemen; but I have seen a similar *coiffure* among the African female slaves at Zanzibar. The Arabs nearer the coast, generally bind their long shaggy hair lightly on the top of the head, leaving the ends to form a large waving tuft.

sand camels laden with tents, all of cotton, and also ropes of cotton.[1]

CHAPTER CONCERNING THE PARTIALITY OF THE WOMEN OF ARABIA FELIX FOR WHITE MEN.

Having seen this army depart, let us return to my prison. In the said palace of the city there was one of the three wives of the Sultan, who remained there with twelve or thirteen very beautiful damsels, whose colour was more near to black than otherwise. This queen was very kind to me. I and my companion and a Moor, being all three in prison here, we arranged that one of us should pretend to be mad, in order the better to assist one another. Finally, the lot fell

---

[1] It is remarkable that in the foregoing account of the weapons borne by the Arabs no mention is made of fire-arms, and I find from the Chronicles of the *Kurrat el-Ayân*, and likewise from the *Ruâh er-Ruâh*, another MS. in my possession, that they were not generally known in Yemen before A.H. 921 = A.D. 1515, when they were introduced by the Egyptian expedition, and used with murderous effect on the inhabitants of the coast opposite Camrân, which island they had previously seized and fortified. A year later, the Egyptian forces were joined by a Turkish fleet and army under Suleiman Pasha, who had been sent by Sultân Selim to coöperate with them against the Portuguese; for the attack made on Yemen by the former does not appear to have been authorized by Kansooh el-Ghôree, the then reigning sovereign of Egypt. The following is a description given by the author of the *Kurrat el-Ayân* of the Turkish matchlock:—" The soldiers of the Lord of the *Room* were armed with musket-bows with which they took aim. It is a most wonderful weapon, and whoever confronts it must be overcome. It is something like a gun, only it is longer and thinner. It is hollow, and in this hollow is inserted a piece of lead as large as a lote berry, and it is filled with powder, and then discharged by means of a match at the bottom of the musket, and if it strikes any one he must perish, for it goes in at one side of him and comes out at the other."

Slings as well as bows and arrows had ceased to be used by the Arabs of Yemen as far back as Niebuhr's time. (*Voyage en Arabie*, vol. iii. p. 187, *n.*) They are now generally armed with matchlocks; those who do not possess that weapon carry a sword or spear; but all are provided with the *janbeah*, or curved dirk, worn in a girdle round the waist.

upon me to be mad. Having then taken this enterprise upon myself, it behoved me to do such things as were natural to madmen. Truly, I never found myself so wearied or so exhausted as during the first three days that I feigned madness. The reason was that I had constantly behind me fifty or sixty little children, who threw stones at me, and I threw stones at them. They cried out: "Iami iasion Iami ianun ;" that is to say: "Madman."[1] And I had my shirt constantly full of stones, and acted like a madman. The queen was always at her window with her damsels, and remained there from morning till evening to see me and talk with me; and I, being mocked by many men and merchants, taking off my shirt, went, quite naked as I was, before the queen, who took the greatest delight in seeing me, and would not let me leave her, and gave me good and sound food to eat, so that I gained my point. She also said to me: "Give it to those beasts, for if you kill them it will be their own fault." A sheep was passing through the king's court, the tail of which weighed forty pounds. I seized it and demanded of it if it was a Moor, or a Christian, or, in truth, a Jew; and repeating these words to it and many others I said: "Prove yourself a Moor and say: Leila illala Mahometh resullala;" and he, standing like a patient animal which could not speak, I took a stick and broke all its four legs. The queen stood there laughing, and afterwards fed me for three days on the flesh of it, than which I do not know that I ever ate better. Three days afterwards I killed, in the same manner as I had killed the sheep, an ass which was carrying water to the palace, because he would not become a Moor. Acting in the same manner by a Jew, I cudgelled him to such an extent that I left him for dead. But one day, being about to act in my usual manner, I came across one of those who had me in custody, and who was more mad than I was, who said to me: "Christian dog, son

[1] *Ya majnûn! Ya majnûn!* Madman! Madman!

of a dog." I threw a good many stones at him, and he began to turn towards me with all the children, and struck me with a stone in the breast which did me an ill service. I, not being able to follow him on account of the irons on my feet, took the way to my prison; but before I reached it he struck me with another stone in the side, which gave me much more pain than the first. I could easily have avoided both if I had chosen to do so, but I chose to receive them to give colour to my madness. And therefore I immediately entered my prison and blocked myself in with very large stones, and remained there two days and two nights without eating or drinking. The queen and the others feared that I might be dead, and caused the door to be broken open, and these dogs brought me some pieces of marble, saying: "Eat, this is sugar;" and some others gave me grapes[1] filled with earth, and said that it was salt, and I eat the marble and the grapes and everything, all together. On that same day, some merchants belonging to the city brought two men who were esteemed amongst them as two hermits would be amongst us, and who dwelt in certain mountains. I was shown to them, and the merchants asked these men: "Whether did it appear to them that I was holy or mad?" One of them said: "It appears to me that he is holy;" the other said it appeared to him that I was mad. In this way they kept disputing for more than an hour, and I, in order to get rid of them, raised my shirt and p—d over them both; whereupon they began to run away crying out: "Migenon migenon suffi maffis," that is, "He is mad, he is mad, he is not holy." The queen was at her window with her maidens, and seeing this they all began to laugh, saying: "O achala o raza al Naby ade ragel maphe donia methalon;" that is, "By the good God, by the head of Mahomet,

---

[1] Radàà is famous for its grapes. Most of those which are sent to the Aden market come from that district.

this is the most capital fellow in the world."[1] The next morning I found asleep him who had given me the two blows with the stones. I seized him by the horns,[2] and putting my knees upon the pit of his stomach, gave him so many blows upon the face that he was covered with blood, and I left him for dead. The queen remained standing at her window, exclaiming : " Kill those beasts." The governor of that city, discovering through many circumstances that my companions treacherously wished to escape, and had made a hole in their prison and removed their irons, and that I had not done so, and as he knew that the queen took great pleasure in me, he would not do me any injury until he had spoken with her; who, when she had heard everything, considered me in her own mind to be rational, and sent for me, and had me placed in a lower chamber in the palace without any door, but still with the irons on my feet.

CHAPTER CONCERNING THE LIBERALITY OF THE QUEEN.

The first night ensuing, the queen came to visit me with five or six of her damsels, and began to examine me, and I began to give her to understand by degrees that I was not mad. She, being a clever woman, saw that I was not at all mad, and began to make much of me; ordered a good bed after their fashion to be given me, and sent me plenty of good food. The following day she had prepared for me a bath according to their custom, with many perfumes, and continued these caresses for twelve days. Afterwards, she began to come down to visit me every night at three or four o'clock, and always brought me good things to eat. Enter-

[1] *Majnûn, majnûn; sûfi ma fîsh.* He is a madman ; he is not intelgent (or pious).
W'Allah, wa-râs en-Nabi, hâdha er-rajul ma fid-dûnya mithlu. By God, by the head of the Prophet, there is not one in the world like this man.
[2] That is, by the tufts of his hair.

ing where I was, she called me "Iunus tale inte iohan,"
that is, "Lodovico, come here, are you hungry?"¹ And I
replied: "E vualla," that is, "Yes,"² for the hunger which
was to come; and I rose on my feet and went to her in my
shirt. And she said: "Leis leis camis foch," that is, "Not
in that manner, take off your shirt."³ I replied: "Iaseti
ane maomigenon de lain," which is, "O, madam, I am not
mad now."⁴ She answered me: "Vualla ane arf in te habe-
denin te migenon inte mafdunia metalon," that is, "By God,
I know well that thou never wast mad, on the contrary, that
thou art the best witted man that ever was seen."⁵ In order
to please her I took off my shirt, and held it before me for
modesty's sake, and thus she kept me before her for two
hours, contemplating me as though I had been a nymph,
and uttering a lamentation to God in this manner: "Ialla
in te sta cal ade abiat me telsamps Inte stacal ane auset;
Ialla Ianaby iosane assiet: Villet ane asnet ade ragel abiath
Insalla ade ragel Iosane Insalla oel binth mit lade," that is,
"O God, thou hast created this man white like the sun,
thou hast created my husband black, my son also is black,
and I am black. Would to God that this man were my
husband. Would to God that I might have a son like this
man."⁶ And saying these words she wept continually and

¹ *Yûnas, tiâl; anta ju'ân?* Jonah, come; are you hungry?
² *Ay w'Allah,* a common expletive affirmation.
³ *Leis leis kamîs fôk.* No, no, not with your shirt on.
⁴ *Ya sitti, ana ma majnûn ilán.* Madam, I am not mad now.
⁵ *W'Allah, ana 'aüraf anta abadan anta majnûn. Anta ma fid-
dunya mithlak.* By God, I know that you were never mad. There is
not another in the world like you.
⁶ *Ya Allah! Anta khalakt hâdha abyad mithl esh-shams. Anta
khalaktani ana aswad. Ya Allah! Ya Nabi! zanji aswad: waladi
ana aswad: hâdha er-rajul abyad. In-shâa-Allah hâdha er-rajul zanji!
In shâa-Allah awallad ibn mithl hâdha.* O God! Thou hast created
this [man] white like the sun. Thou hast created me black. O God!
O Prophet! my husband is black; my son is black; this man is white.
Would that this man may become my husband! Would that I may
bear a son like this [man]!

sighed, passing her hands over me all the while, and promising me that, as soon as the Sultan returned, she would make him take off my irons. On the next night the queen came to me with two of her damsels and brought me some good food to eat, and said to me: "Tale Iunus," that is, "Come here, Lodovico;" "Ane igi andech," I replied. "Leis setti ane mochaet ich fio," that is, said the queen, "Lodovico, would you like that I should come and stay a little while with you." I answered: "No; that it was quite enough that I was in chains, without her causing me to have my head cut off." Then said she: "Let caffane darchi alarazane," that is, "Do not be afraid, for I will stake my own head for your safety." "In cane in te mayrith ane Gazella in sich: olla Tegia in sich olle Galzerana insich," that is, "If you do not wish me to come, shall Gazella, or Tegia, or Galzerana come?"[1] She only said this because she wished to come herself and remain with me in the place of one of these three. But I never would consent, because I thought of this from the time when she began to show me so many kindnesses. Considering also, that as soon as she had had her wish she would have given me gold and silver, horses and slaves, and whatever I had desired. And then she would have given me ten black slaves, who would have been a guard upon me, so that I should never have been able to escape from the country, for all Arabia Felix was informed of me, that is to say, at the passes. And if I had once ran away, I could not have escaped death, or

---

[1] *Taâl Yûnas.* Come hither, Jonah. *Ana aji andak.* I will come to you.
Leis [ya] sitti; ana mukayyad, jakfi. No, madam, I am in chains, and that is enough.
La takhâf, ana tarahi 'ala râsana. Do not be afraid; I take all the responsibility on my head.
In-kân an'a ma tarîd ana, Gazelle ansich; wa-illa Tâjiah ansich; wa-illa Gulzerâna ansieh. If you do not want me, I will call Gazelle; or I will call Tâjiah; or I will call Gulzerâna [for you].

chains for life. For this reason, therefore, I never would yield to her, and also because I did not wish to lose both my soul and body. I wept all night, recommending myself to God. Three days from that time the Sultan returned, and the queen immediately sent to inform me that if I would remain with her she would make me rich. I replied: "That if she would cause my chains to be taken off, and perform the promise she made to God and Mahomet I would then do whatever her highness wished. She immediately had me taken before the Sultan, who asked me where I wished to go when he had taken off my chains. I answered him: "Iasidi habu mafis una mafis, meret mafis uuellet mafis, ochu mafis octa mafis alla al naby Intebes sidi in te iati iaculane abdech," that is, "O lord, I have no father, no mother, no wife. I have no children, I have neither brothers nor sisters, I have only God, and the Prophet, and you, O lord : will it please you to give me food, for I wish to be your slave all my life?"¹ And I wept constantly. The queen was present all the time, and said to the Sultan : "Thou wilt have to render an account to God of this poor man, whom without any cause thou hast kept so long in chains. Beware of the anger of God." Said the Sultan : "Well, go where thou wilt, I give thee thy liberty." And immediately he had my chains taken off, and I knelt before him and kissed his feet, and then I kissed the queen's hand, who took me also by the hand saying : "Come with me, poor fellow, for I know that thou art dying of hunger." When I was in her chamber she kissed me more than a hundred times, and then she gave me many good things to eat. But I did not feel any inclination to eat, for I had seen the queen speak privately to the Sultan, and I thought that she

---

¹ *Ya sidi, abb ma fish; umm ma fish; marat ma fish; walud ma fish; akh ma fish; okht ma fish. Allah, en-Nabi, anta, bas, sidi. Anta titatini akul, ana abduk.* O lord, I have no father, no mother, no wife, no child, no brother, no sister. God, the Prophet, [and] you only. You give me food to eat, and I am your slave.

had asked me of the Sultan for a slave. Wherefore I said to
the queen: "I will not eat unless you promise to give me my
liberty." She replied: "Seut mi Ianu inte maarfesiati alla,"
that is, "Hold thy peace, madman, thou dost not know what
God has ordained for thee." "Incane inte milic inte amirra,"
that is, "If thou wilt be good thou shalt be a lord."[1] Now,
I knew the kind of lordship she wished to confer upon me;
but I answered her that she should let me get a little fatter,
and get back my blood, for the great fear I was in filled my
breast with other thoughts than those of love. She answered:
"Vuulla inte calem milic ane iaticullion beit e digege e amam
e filfil e cherfa e gronfili e iosindi," that is, "By God, thou
art right, but I will give thee every day eggs, hens, pigeons,
pepper, cinnamon, cloves, and nutmegs."[2] Then I recovered
my spirits somewhat at the good words and promises she
gave me. In order the better to restore me, I remained
fifteen or twenty days in her palace. One day she sent for
me and asked me if I would go hunting with her. I replied
in the affirmative and went with her. On our return I pretended to fall sick from weakness, and remained in this
feigned state eight days, while she continually sent persons

---

[1] *Askut, majnûn; anta ma tiiaraf aish jáati Allah.* Silence, madman;
you do not know what God will give.
In-kân anta malieh, anta amîr. If you are good, you [shall be] an
ameer.

[2] *W'Allah, anta titkállum malich: ana 'aütîk kul jôm baidh, wa-dujâj,
wa-hamâm, wa-filfil, wa-kirfah, wa-karanful, wa-jôz-Hindi.* By God,
you say well: I will give you every day eggs, fowls, pigeons, pepper,
cinnamon, cloves, and cocoa-nuts. The spices named are in common use
among the Arabs. It is not surprising that Varthema should have mistaken *Jôz-Hindi* for *nutmeg;* the word is so misapplied still by the
common Maltese and other Franks in Syria and Egypt. Ibn Batûta's
description of the cocoa-nut is quaint. He says: "It is like a man's
head; for it has something like two eyes and a mouth, and when green
is like brains, and its properties are, to nourish and quickly to fatten the
body, to make the face red, and greatly to stimulate to venery." And
in a subsequent chapter he more broadly than modestly describes the
effect of the incentive on himself. LEE's *Translation*, pp. 60,.176.

to visit me. One day I sent to inform her that I had made a promise to God and to Mahomet that I would visit a holy man who was in Aden, and who, they said, performed miracles; and I maintained that it was true in order to accomplish my object. She sent to tell me that she was well pleased, and ordered a camel and twenty-five seraphim of gold to be given to me, whereat I was much rejoiced. The following day I mounted and went to Aden in eight days, and immediately visited the holy man, who was worshiped because he always lived in poverty and chastity, and spent his life like a hermit. And, truly, there are many in that country who pass this kind of life, but they are deceived from not having been baptised.[1] When I had performed my devotions on the second day, I pretended to be cured by virtue of that holy man. Afterwards I wrote to the queen, that by the virtue of God and of that holy man I was cured, and since God had been so merciful to me I wished to go and see the whole of her kingdom. This I did because the fleet was in that place, and could not depart for a month. I spoke secretly with the captain of a ship, and told him that I wished to go to India, and if he would take me I would give him a handsome present. He replied: "That before he went to India he wished to touch at Persia." With that I was satisfied, and so we agreed.

THE CHAPTER CONCERNING LAGI, A CITY OF ARABIA FELIX, AND CONCERNING AIAZ, AND THE MARKET IN AIAZ, AND THE CASTLE DANTE.

The following day I rode for fifteen miles, and found a city which is called Lagi;[2] the place is level and very popu-

---

[1] According to contemporaneous Arabian historians, Yemen teemed with such devotees at the period referred to. The fashion, or piety, has considerably decreased within the last two centuries.

[2] Lahej, the place indicated, is about thirty miles to the north-west

lous. A vast number of date-trees grow here, there is also plenty of animal food and grain as with us. But there are no grapes here, and a great scarcity of firewood. This city is uncivilized, and the inhabitants are Arabs, who are not very rich. I departed thence and went to another city, which is one day's journey from the first mentioned, and is called Aiaz.[1] It stands upon two mountains, between which there is a very beautiful valley and a beautiful fountain, in which valley the market is held to which the men come from both the mountains. And very few of those markets are held without quarrels taking place. The reason is this: those who inhabit the mountain towards the north wish that those who inhabit the mountain towards the south should believe with them in Mahomet with all his companions; while these will only believe in Mahomet and Ali, and say that the other captains are false. For this reason they kill

---

of Aden. The name, though frequently applied to the town, designates more correctly the surrounding district, the former being generally called *El-Hawtah* by the Arabs, signifying a level spot. It is situated in a fertile plain, and is watered by the torrents which periodically descend from the mountains in its rear. The country is well cultivated and produces abundance of *dhurah*, sesamum, several kinds of pulse, and a small quantity of cotton, besides various culinary vegetables. It also affords good pasturage, and supplies the Aden market with excellent cows, sheep, and goats. It raises very little fruit, and, as Varthema remarks, no grapes grow there. At the period of his visit, Lahej was under the government of Sultàn 'Âmir ibn Abd el-Wahhàb, who ruled over the greater part of southern Yemen. On his death, A.D. 1517, it reverted to the Imâm of Saniia, and continued under that jurisdiction, though not without frequent intervals of independence, till the year 1728, when the chief of the Abdali tribe inhabiting the district threw off his allegiance to the Imâm, and subsequently succeeded in capturing Aden. His successors in the same family retained the government of both places until dispossessed of the latter by the British in 1839.

[1] I presume this to be the "Asas," or, according to his Arabic orthography, the "'Az'az," of Niebuhr, which he describes as a village on the confines of the domain belonging to Aden. As I have not met with the name in any of the Arabian authors within reach, I conclude it is a place of little note.

each other like dogs.¹ Let us return to the market, to which are brought many kinds of small spices, and a great quantity of stuffs, of wool, and of silk, and very excellent fruits, such as peaches, pomegranates, and quinces, figs, nuts, and good grapes. You must know that on each of these mountains there is a very strong fortress. Having beheld these things I departed thence and went to another city, which is distant from this two days' journey and is called Dante,² and is an extremely strong city, situated on the top of a very great mountain, and is inhabited by Arabs, who are poor, because the country is very barren.

THE CHAPTER CONCERNING ALMACARANA, A CITY OF ARABIA FELIX, AND OF ITS ABUNDANCE.

In order to follow out the desires after novel things already conceived in our minds we departed from that place, taking our way towards another city, distant two days' journey, which is called Almacarana,³ and is situated on the top of a

¹ That is, the northerners were *Sunnis*, and the southerners *Shiis*, or more probably *Zaidis*, the followers of Zaid, son of Ali, surnamed Zain el-'Âbidîn, which sect was very numerous in Yemen, and comprised the person and family of the Imâm. They held with the Shiis that Ali was unjustly superseded in the Khalîfate by Abubekr, 'Omar, and 'Othmân, and are represented as having no respect for the Twelve Imâms, and for omitting all mention of the saints in their devotions. These were the more salient points of antagonism between them and the Sunnis, which frequently led to bloody feuds. There were other differences of a more abstruse character respecting the Divine decrees, free will, and human responsibility. (See SALE's *Preliminary Discourse to the Korân*, p. 233, NIEBUHR, *Voy. en Arabie*, vol. iii. pp. 17, 18, and D'HERBELOT, sub voce *Zeidiah*, vol. iii. p. 734.)

² More correctly Damt. Niebuhr's orthography is worse than Varthema's: he writes it "Dimne," and describes it as a "bourg à foire au sud de mont Maharras," which mountain he says is very high and steep. It appears to have been an important stronghold, and will be found mentioned in the succeeding note.

³ El-Makrânah. It is surprising that Niebuhr has not enumerated

mountain, the ascent to which is seven miles, and to which only two persons can go abreast on account of the narrowness of the path. The city is level on the top of the mountain, and is very beautiful and good. Food enough for the whole city is collected here, and for this reason it appears to me to be the strongest city in the world. There is no want of water there nor of any other necessary of life, and, above all, there is a cistern there which would supply water

this place in his list of the towns and villages of Yemen. Arabs who have come to Aden from that and the adjoining districts have frequently dilated on the by-gone impregnability of its castle, and the extent of its great reservoir. The following extract, also, from the *Ruăh er-Ruăh*, recording the capture of the place from Sultân 'Âmir ibn Abd el-Wahhâb by the Egyptian army, strikingly corroborates several details contained in this chapter :—" Then the Ameer Bar-Sabbai [the Egyptian commander] deputed the Ameer Akbai over the affairs of Ta'ez, and went himself with his army towards El-Makrânah. On hearing this, Sultân Âmir hastened to the place, and took from thence his women [or wives], and as much treasure as he could conveniently remove, and departed towards El-Halkah, where he remained. Immediately after, the Egyptian army entered El-Makrânah and plundered it, taking therefrom the immense stores of wealth and provisions which it contained, and forcing some of the people to surrender the valuables which 'Âmir had deposited with them." Subsequently, a Fakîh named 'Amr el-Jabraty, who had acted as jester to the Sultan, disclosed to the Egyptian commander some treasures which were hidden in the castle, consisting of a vast amount of specie, jewels, and other valuables belonging to the royal family, all of which the captor seized and distributed among his soldiers.

Notwithstanding this spoliation, however, El-Makrânah was not plundered of all its wealth. Twelve years later, after the Imâm had succeeded in expelling the Egyptians from Sanăa, his son Mutahhir attacked them at El-Makrânah and Damt, and carried away considerable booty. The following narration of that event is from the author above quoted: —" Then Mutahhir proceeded to take Malikîah and all the intervening strongholds as far as Damt, which castle he captured, and proclaimed an amnesty to the inhabitants. Next he entered El-Makrânah, granting an amnesty to the Circassian [Mamlûk] garrison, and receiving the submission of the tribes. He then took all the arms and guns which he found there; also many copper utensils of *Ghassâni* manufacture inlaid with silver, and costly China ware, which had belonged to the Beni Dhâhir" [the Sultan's family].

for 100,000 persons. The Sultan keeps all his treasure in this city, because he derives his origin and descent from it. For this reason the Sultan always keeps one of his wives here. You must know that articles of every possible kind are brought here, and it has the best air of any place in the world. The inhabitants are more white than any other colour. In this city the Sultan keeps more gold than a hundred camels could carry, and I say this because I have seen it.

THE CHAPTER CONCERNING REAME, A CITY OF ARABIA FELIX, OF ITS AIR, AND OF THE CUSTOMS OF ITS INHABITANTS.

When I had rambled about the above-mentioned city, on parting thence I went to another place, distant from this one day's journey, which is called Reame,[1] and is for the most part inhabited by black people, who are very great merchants. This country is extremely fertile, excepting in firewood, and the city contains about two thousand families. On one side of this city there is a mountain, upon which stands a very strong castle. And here there is a kind of sheep, some of which I have seen, whose tails alone weigh forty-four pounds. They have no horns, and cannot walk on account of their size.[2] Here also is found a kind of white

[1] This is undoubtedly Yerim, which Niebuhr describes as "une petite ville mal bâtie, munie d'une forteresse sur un rocher escarpé; et située dans une plaine assez vaste, et à 4 licues d'Allemagne de Damâr;" nevertheless it was the residence of a *Dowla*, or governor, of the Imâm. He adds, that as the name of this town resembles that of the famous garden of *Irem* mentioned in the 89th chapter of the Korân, it is inferred by some that the terrestrial paradise stood in this region; but having himself travelled through the district, he considers that it is less fertile than many others in Yemen. It was at Yerim that one of his companions, the lamented Forskül, died on the 11th of July 1763, just a century ago. Niebuhr gives a view of the town in vol. i. of his *Voyage en Arabie*.

[2] This is generally a correct description, though I cannot vouch for the weight ascribed to the sheep's tails.

grape, which has no seeds within, than which I never tasted better.¹ Here also I found all kinds of fruit as I said above. The climate here is most perfect and singular. In this place I conversed with many persons who were more than one hundred and twenty-five years old, and were still very healthy. The people here go more naked than otherwise, but the men of good condition wear a shirt. The lower orders wear half a sheet crosswise, after the fashion of prelates.² Through the whole of this Arabia Felix the men wear horns made of their own hair, and the women wear loose trowsers, after the fashion of seamen.

THE CHAPTER CONCERNING SANA, A CITY OF ARABIA FELIX, AND OF THE STRENGTH AND CRUELTY OF THE KING'S SON.

Then I departed and took to a city named Sana,³ which is distant from the said city Reame three days' journey. It is

---

¹ These grapes are brought to Aden during the season in small baskets covered with wild sage. They resemble the *sultanas* which are imported from Smyrna.

² The original is: *Li altri di bassa conditione portano mezo un linzolo ad armacolla a la apostolicha*, the sense of which is very obscure. Perhaps it means that the cloth in question, which is oblong in shape, is worn like a pallium or a stole, sometimes thrown loosely round the neck, and sometimes over one shoulder, which is precisely the case. In addition to this, however, they generally wear a similar cloth round the loins. The uses of these simple garments are thus correctly described by Niebuhr:—" En déployant sa large ceinture il a un matelas, avec le linge d'épaule il couvre le corps et la tête, et c'est entre ces draps qu'il dort nud et content." *Voyage en Arabie*, vol. iii. p. 56.

³ Saná, the capital of Yemen and the residence of the Imâm, is situated *at the foot* of a high range of mountains called Jebal Nikam. With this exception, Varthema's notes, which are unusually brief on the subject, are generally correct. Edrîsi describes it as "abounding in good things, and full of buildings. It is the oldest, the largest, and most populous city of Yemen. It is in the centre of the first climate, has an even atmosphere, a fertile soil, and the heat and cold there are always

situated on the top of a very large mountain, and is extremely strong. The Sultan encamped before with 80,000 men for eight months in order to capture it, but could only gain it by capitulation.[1] The walls of this city are of earth, of the height of ten *braza*, and twenty *braza*

temperate." Ibn Batûta merely says "it is a large and well-built city." The Rev. Mr. Stern, who visited Saniia in 1856, estimates the population at about 40,000 inhabitants, of whom 20,000 are Muhammedans, and 18,000 Jews. Niebuhr gives a plan and a detailed description of the city in his *Voyage en Arabie*, vol. i. pp. 326-329.

[1] He should have said that the Sultan had utterly failed in capturing the place. The circumstances of the attempt referred to, which occurred two years before Varthema's visit, are thus narrated by the author of the *Kurrat el-Ayûn*:—"During this year [A.H. 907 = A.D. 1501] Sultan 'Amir besieged Saniia, and when the inhabitants were reduced to great straits, they wrote to Bahâl, offering him certain presents, together with the fortress of Dhamarmar, if he would come to their assistance. (Before their arrival, the Zaidich [Zaidis] abandoned the side of the Sultan.) They accordingly came in vast numbers, and a severe battle was fought between them and the Amir 'Ali el-Bâadâni, [one of the Sultan's generals,] in which neither party gained the advantage. Eventually, however, the Ameer's soldiers were overpowered; whereupon the Sultan collected all his forces, which were dispersed around Saniia, and formed them into one camp, in consequence of which movement the enemy were able to stop the road, and to cut off all his supplies. The Sultan then decided to return homewards, and to fall on the Zaidis who had gathered in strength to circumvent him; but God came to his relief. [Here, a different hand, probably a Zaidi, has added these words to the MS., 'had he remained he would have been caught.'] The Sultan, having collected his troops and equipage, retired from before Saniia on the 7th of Muharram, A.H. 908, followed by the Zaidis who harassed his rear; but his soldiers charged them like 'Antar and attacked them like 'Omar, and put them to an ignominious flight. Finally, he reached Dhamarmar in safety, ['and a fugitive,' adds the interpolator], losing nothing of any consequence, so that his safety was in effect a great victory to him and to those who were with him over the enemy, who were in such large numbers, and had succeeded in stopping all his supplies. This first siege lasted five months."

'Amir's second attack on Saniia was more successful. On that occasion, according to the author of the *Rûah er-Rûah*, his army consisted of 180,000 men, of which 3,000 were cavalry. When Varthema met him at Radâa, on his march towards Saniia, he witnessed a review of 80,000 (See p. 61 *ante* and note 2.)

wide. Think, that eight horses can go abreast on the top of it.[1] In this place many fruits grow the same as in our country, and there are many fountains. In this Sana there is a Sultan who has twelve sons, one of whom is called Mahometh. He is like a madman: he bites people and kills them, and then eats their flesh until his appetite is satisfied. He is four *braza* high, well proportioned, and of a dark brown colour.[2] In this city there are found some kinds of small spices which grow in the neighbourhood. This place contains about 4,000 hearths. The houses are very handsome and resemble ours. Within the city there are many vines and gardens as with us.

THE CHAPTER CONCERNING TAESA AND ZIBIT AND DAMAR, VERY LARGE CITIES OF ARABIA FELIX.

After seeing Sana I resumed my journey and went to another city called Taesa,[3] which is distant three days' jour-

---

[1] Niebuhr says that the walls are of earth, faced with unburnt brick and surmounted by a great many small turrets. According to the narrative of the French travellers who visited Sanäa in 1712, as given by De la Roque in his *Voyage de l'Arabie Heureuse*, the breadth of the walls is sufficient to admit of driving eight horses abreast.

[2] The then ruling Imâm was Ahmed ibn el-Imâm en-Nâsir, surnamed El-Mansûr, who was taken prisoner by Sultân 'Âmir when he captured Sanäa, and died at Ta'ez under suspicion of having been poisoned. I have not succeeded in discovering any notices corroborative of Varthema's statement respecting the cannibal propensities of one of his sons. Burton remarks on the passage: "This is a tale not unfamiliar to the western world. Louis XI. of France was supposed to drink the blood of babies,—'*pour rajeunir sa veine épuisée*.' The reasons in favour of such unnatural diet have been fully explained by the infamous M. de Sade." *Pilgrimage to El-Medinah and Meccah*, vol. ii. p. 352, n.

[3] Ta'ez is about one hundred and ten miles to the south of Sanäa. Abulfeda says that in his time (fourteenth century) it was the residence of the princes of Yemen, and describes it as "a fortress situated in the midst of the mountains which overlook the Tihâma [the sea coast], and the plain of Zebid. Above Ta'ez there is a pleasure-ground called Sahlah, to which spot the prince of Yemen has conducted a stream

ney from Sana aforesaid, and is situated in a mountain.
This city is very beautiful, and abounds in all kinds of
elegancies, and, above all, in a vast quantity of rose water,
which is distilled here. It is reported of this city that it is
extremely ancient: there is a temple there built like the
Santa Maria Rotonda of Rome, and many other very ancient
palaces. There are very great merchants here. These people
dress like those above mentioned. They are olive coloured.
Departing thence I went to another city, distant from this
three days' journey, which is called Zibit ;[1] a large and very

of water from the neighbouring heights. He has also erected several
large buildings in a garden, and, altogether, it is a most agreeable
place." Niebuhr, who gives a detailed account of the town together
with a view and plan, says it is situated at the foot of a fertile mountain called Jebel Sàbir, and is surrounded by a wall of crude bricks with
a slight *revêtement* of burnt bricks. Within the enceinte of the walls is
a steep rock four hundred feet high, on which the citadel El-Kâhirah
stands. Varthema's "temple" was probably the mosque of the renowned Mohammedan saint Isma'îl Mulk, which Niebuhr styles the
"Cathedral of Ta'ez." There are many mosques and other public buildings both within and without the city, but most of them are in a very
dilapidated condition. Baskets of rose-buds are brought from Ta'ez to
Aden during the season. The place was occupied by the Egyptian forces
on its evacuation by Sultàn 'Âmir ibn Abd el-Wahhâb, a few days
before his capture and death. At present, though nominally subject
to the Imâm of Sanäa, it is governed by the chief of the Sherjebi tribe
who inhabit the district.

[1] Zebîd, situated in one of the most fertile valleys of Yemen, was formerly the capital of the Tihâma, and a place of considerable importance;
but owing to the gradual filling-up of the old port of Ghâlifkah, much
of its trade was diverted to Mokha, Hodeidah, and Loheia, and it is now
reduced to a second-rate town. El-Edrîsi describes it in his time as
"a large city, its inhabitants are prosperous, being men of wealth and
substance, and the voyagers thereto are many. There assemble merchants from the Hijâz, and Abyssinia, and Egypt, who go up in Juddah
vessels. The Abyssinians bring their *(rakîk)* slaves thereto, and from
thence are exported different kinds of Indian aromatics, Chinese and other
commodities." (I was surprised to find that Gabriele Sionita, in his Latin
translation of El-Edrîsi, makes *merces* of the Arabic *rakîk*, which occurs
in this and in another extract which I have quoted in note 1, page 86.
Rakîk is a common word for slave in Yemen and in Egypt.) Abul-

excellent city, situated near the Red Sea, at half a day's journey. It is a place of very considerable extent by the Red Sea, and is supplied with an immense quantity of sugar, and has most excellent fruits; is situated on a plain between two mountains, and has no walls around it. A very great traffic is carried on here in spices of all kinds, which are brought from other countries. The dress and colour of these people is the same as of those before mentioned. Then I departed from this place and went to another city, distant one day's journey, called Damar,[1] inhabited by Moors, who are very great merchants. The said city is very fertile, and the manner of living and customs of the inhabitants are the same as of those before mentioned.

feda says Zebîd is "situated in a plain, somewhat less than a day's journey from the sea. Its water is derived from wells, and it abounds in palm-trees. It is surrounded by a wall, and has eight gates." As this latter observation contradicts the statement of Varthema, it must be borne in mind that Abulfeda wrote two centuries before his time, and the more recent account of Niebuhr is sufficient to establish our traveller's general veracity. Niebuhr states that "the wall of the town is almost entirely demolished to a level with the ground, and the poor people dig into the foundations to obtain stones wherewith to build their houses." Notwithstanding the existence of a river, which during the rainy season flows in a copious stream through the valley, the same author says that the inhabitants draw water from sunken wells, and that it is of an excellent quality. *Voy. en Arabie*, vol. i. pp. 261-264.

Zebîd was taken from 'Âmir ibn Abd el-Wahhâb by the combined Egyptian and Turkish armies on the 17th of Jumâd el-Awwal, 922 = 17th June, 1516. The excesses which they committed on the occasion, as recorded by the author of the *Kurrat el Ayán*, were atrocious in the extreme. It was wrested from the conquerors not long after by the Imâm of Saniia, and continued, nominally, a dependency of that principality until it finally fell into the hands of the Turks, together with several towns on the coast, about A.D. 1832.

[1] More correctly, Dhamâr, situated about sixty miles to the east of Zebîd,—a hard day's journey, but by no means an uncommon one with the Arabs, mounted on their fleet dromedaries. Abulfeda remarks that it is a well known city, and the birth-place of many authors on the Traditions. Niebuhr, who visited it, says that it is situated in a fertile territory, and is renowned for its breed of horses. The town, which is large and well built, has no wall, but is defended by a strong fortress

THE CHAPTER CONCERNING THE SULTAN OF ALL THE ABOVE-MENTIONED CITIES, AND WHEREFORE HE IS CALLED BY THE NAME SECHAMIR.

All these above-named cities are subject to the Sultan of the Amanni,[1] that is, the Sultan of Arabia Felix, who is called Sechamir.[2] *Secho* is the same as saint, *amir*, lord, and

adjoining. It contains a famous *Medresseh*, or College, belonging to the sect of the Zaidieh, which was frequented by five hundred students. *Voyage en Arabie*, vol. i. pp. 324-5.

[1] It now strikes me as most probable that Varthema's "Amauni" is merely his Italian way of writing "Yemen," which Gabriele Sionita, in his Latin version of El-Edrîsi, renders "Iaman." (For a different solution see note 2 on p. 57.)

[2] We have here another remarkable coincidence strikingly confirmative of Varthema's general correctness. The reigning prince at the time was 'Âmir ibn Abd el-Wahhâb ibn Daood ibn Dhâhir, etc., surnamed Edh-Dhâfir Salâh ed-Dîn, who succeeded his father Abd el-Wahhâb, generally styled El-Melck el-Mansûr, A.H. 894 = A.D. 1488. In the course of a few years he wrested the greater part of Yemen from the Imâm, and eventually occupied Sanäa. His career, indeed, was an unbroken series of victories until arrested, first by the Egyptian expedition in 1515, and then by the Turks, who invaded Yemen the year following. He was overtaken as a fugitive, on his way to seek shelter in the castle of Dhamarmar, by a detachment of the Egyptian army with which he had had a fierce engagement on the preceding day, and was murdered by them in cold blood on the 24th of Rabiäa el-Âkhir, 923 = 12th May, 1517. His head they carried to Sanäa, and exhibited it before the walls; whereupon the people surrendered at discretion, and opened the gates to the Egyptian commander.

The following account of the various public monuments erected by 'Âmir ibn Abd el-Wahhâb is from the *Kurrat el-Ayân*:—"He built the Great Mosque in the city of Zebid, which excels all others, and expended thereon enormous wealth. Also the Medresseh [College] called Edh-Dhâfirieh, opposite the Dâr el-Kebir, in the same city. Also the Medresseh of Sheikh Isma'îl ibn Ibrahîm el-Jabraty, and the tomb of the Fakîh Abi-bekr ibn 'Ali el-Haddâd, outside the town, near the Bâb el-Kartab. Also two Medressehs at Ta'ez, to which place he also brought a stream of water. Also the Great Mosque and a Masjid at El-Makrânah. Also a Medresseh at Radâä el-'Arsh. Also a Masjid at Aden, to which place he also conducted the water [from the country beyond] as far as the outer gate, and built a large reservoir in the town itself, and

the reason why they call him holy is this, that he never put
any one to death excepting in war. You must know that in
my time he had 15,000 or 16,000 men in chains, and to all
he gave two quattrini per man for their expenses daily, and
thus he left them to die in prison when they deserved death.
He also has 16,000 slaves whom he maintains, and they are
all black.

THE CHAPTER CONCERNING APES, AND SOME ANIMALS LIKE LIONS, VERY HOSTILE TO MAN.

Departing from this place I went to the above-mentioned
city of Aden for five days. In the middle of the route I
found a most terrible mountain, in which we saw more than

another at the village of 'Aik; besides innumerable other mosques, reservoirs, wells, and dams, wherever they were needed, and in detached hamlets. He it was who laid down the aqueduct to Aden from a distant place, which cost him immense treasures. Other pious acts without number are attributed to him,...and no passage of his life is censurable except his interference with the Fakihs and their endowments. And I think this was the cause of his downfal, and therefore counsel all sovereigns who may rule over the affairs of the Mussulmans, and all others who may have anything to do with them, not to meddle with the pious endowments, or with the Ulema, for I have never heard of any doing so who was not punished, either in his person, his property, or his family."

I find that 'Âmir ibn Abd el-Wahhâb was styled "Sheikh" prior to his succession to the principality, and although Arabian historians denominate him subsequently as "Sultân," it is highly probable that he continued to be styled, generally, "Sheikh 'Âmir." The word *Sheikh* means primarily an aged man, an elder; thence, a chief or ruler, a learned man, or one renowned for piety.

Varthema's statement that 'Âmir never put any one to death except in war, is contradicted by the narrative of his life contained in the *Kurrat el-Ayân;* though, as compared with his predecessors, and especially with the Egyptian and Turkish pashas who succeeded him, he was a remarkably lenient ruler. The "slaves" mentioned above were chiefly Abyssinians, and formed the principal part of the standing army.

10,000 apes,[1] amongst which were certain animals like lions, which do great injury to man when in their power to do so. On their account it is not possible to pass by that route excepting in companies of at least one hundred persons. We passed in very great danger, and with no little hunting of the said animals. However, we killed a great number of them with bows and slings and dogs, so that we passed in safety. As soon as I had arrived in Aden, I placed myself in the mosque pretending to be ill, and remained there all day. In the evening I went to find the captain of the ship, so that he put me on board secretly.

DISCOURSE TOUCHING SOME PLACES OF ETHIOPIA.

Having determined to see other countries we put to sea according to our intention; but as fortune is accustomed to exercise her unstable will on the water, equally unstable, we were turned somewhat from our design; for, six days from that time we took the route to Persia, sailing for seven days, and then an accident occurred which made us run as far as Ethiopia, together with twenty-five ships laden with madder to dye clothes; for every year they lade as many as twenty-five ships in Aden with it. This madder grows in Arabia Felix.[2] With extreme labour we entered into the port of a city named Zeila, and remained there five days, in order to see it and wait for favourable weather.

[1] In the original "gatti maimoni." Niebuhr states that he frequently saw hundreds of apes at a time in the woods of Yemen. *Voy. en Arabie*, vol. iii. p. 147.
Varthema's animal "something like a lion" was probably the hyena, which is not uncommon in the country. Some large apes still exist in the hills at Aden, and a hyena was killed there a few years ago.
[2] Arabicè, *Foowwah*. This root is still extensively exported from Aden and other ports of Yemen.

THE CHAPTER CONCERNING ZEILA, A CITY OF ETHIOPIA, AND OF THE ABUNDANCE OF IT, AND CONCERNING SOME ANIMALS OF THE SAID CITY, SUCH AS SHEEP AND COWS.

The beforenamed city of Zeila[1] is a place of immense traffic, especially in gold and elephants' teeth. Here also are sold a very great number of slaves, which are those people of Prester John whom the Moors take in battle, and from this place they are carried into Persia, Arabia Felix, and to Mecca, Cairo, and into India. In this city people live extremely well, and justice is excellently administered. Much grain grows here and much animal food, oil in great quantity, made not from olives but from *zerzalino*,[2] honey and

---

[1] Zaila, which Vincent identifies as the ancient Moondus, is situated on the north-east coast of Africa, opposite to Aden, and about sixty miles from the Straits of Bâb el-Mandeb. El-Edrisi, who calls it "Zalegh," says "it is a town small in size, but with many inhabitants; voyagers thereto also are numerous. Most of the ships of Kalzam come as far as this town, bringing various merchandise which is traded with in Abyssinia. Slaves and silver are taken from thence." (As silver does not appear among the exports from Abyssinia either in ancient or modern times, except in the shape of foreign coin which had previously been imported into the country, the Nubian geographer must have been misinformed in that particular.) Abulfeda correctly describes Zaila as "situated at the bottom of a bay, in a plain, and the heat of the place is excessive. The water is derived from wells, but is brackish. There are no gardens or fruits." Ibn Batûta says: "the stench of the country is extreme, as is also its filth, from the stink of the fish, and the blood of camels which are slaughtered in the streets." I may add, from personal experience, that it is a most wretched place in every respect; with a population of nearly a thousand souls, it can only boast of about a dozen houses built of madrepore, the remaining dwellings consisting of mats and reeds. Nevertheless, Zaila, as the principal seaport of Hurrur and southern Abyssinia, has still a considerable trade, of which gold dust and elephants' teeth form a part. Until within the last few years, also, it carried on a brisk traffic in slaves, who were exported to the places mentioned above by Varthema. It is now under the Ottoman Porte, but its customs are farmed by the Pasha of Hodeidah to a native.

[2] Eden, following the Latin version, has translated the passage thus:

wax in great abundance. Here is found a kind of sheep, the tail of which weighs fifteen or sixteen pounds, and with the head and neck quite black, but the whole of the rest of the body white.[1] There are also some other sheep, which have tails a *brazzo* long and twisted like vines, and they have the dewlap like that of a bull, which almost touches the ground. Also in this place I found a certain kind of cows, which had horns like a stag and were wild, which had been presented to the Sultan of the said city.[2] I also saw here other cows, which had a single horn in the forehead, which horn is a *palmo* and a half in length, and turns more towards the back of the cow than forwards.[3] The colour of these is red, that of the former is black. There is an abundance of provisions in this city, and there are many merchants here. The place has poor walls and a bad port,

"It hath also oyle, not of olyues, but of some other thyng, I knowe not what." The word "zerzalino" puzzled me till I remembered how frequently our author uses the letter *z* to express the sound of *j*, when I perceived at once that he meant *juljulán*, (Forskäl writes it "dsjildjylàri;" in India and farther east it is pronounced "jinjli" or "jirjili;" and Baretti gives "giuggiolana" as an Italian equivalent for *sesame*,) one of the Arabic names for the *Sesamum Indicum*, the oil of which is largely exported from Zaila. Honey and wax, also, are among its exports still.

[1] A correct description of the Berbera sheep generally. It is rare to see an entirely white one, or one marked otherwise than above stated; they have also a long dewlap. The other species mentioned is less common. The caudal extremity of the latter may be likened to an exaggerated pig's tail.

[2] Most probably the oryx, though Varthema would have been more correct had he represented the horns as similar to those of an *antelope*. The oryx abounds inland from Zaila, is often shot, but very rarely taken alive.

[3] We have here another *monoceros*, but it is quite clear that the animals described differed from the unicorns which Varthema saw at Meccah (see p. 47 *ante*.) He may have met with some specimens of the African rhinoceros at Zaila; but if so, they must have been brought thither from the distant interior, as the animal is not found in the neighbourhood; indeed, though the horns are frequently imported from thence to the Aden market, I have never heard of a live rhinoceros existing on that coast.

nevertheless it is situated on level ground and the mainland. The king of this Zeila is a Moor, and has many soldiers, both foot and horse. The people are warlike. Their dress consists of a shirt. They are olive-coloured. They go badly armed, and are all Mahommedans.[1]

THE CHAPTER CONCERNING BARBARA, AN ISLAND OF ETHIOPIA, AND OF ITS PEOPLE.

As soon as the weather became favourable, we set sail and arrived at an island which is called Barbara,[2] the lord of

[1] A tolerably accurate description of the *Somális*, so called from *Barr es-Sómál*, by which name the country from Ràs Hàfùn on the eastern coast of Africa as far as Zaila westward is designated. The inhabitants, according to Cruttenden, " are divided into two great nations, who, both tracing their origin from the Arab province of Hadhramaut, are yet at bitter and endless feud with each other. The principal of these two great families is that to the eastward, or windward, of Burnt Island. It is divided into four large and three smaller tribes....They claim as their common father Darrood, the son of Ishmail, the son of Okeil, the son of Arab, who came from Hadhramaut, and, marrying a daughter of the Haweea tribe residing on the north-east coast of Africa, became the first Muhammedan founder of the Somáli nation to the eastward...

"The second of these two nations extends from Burnt Island, or Bunder Jedid, to Zaila, and is divided into three great tribes, namely, the Haber-Gehajjis, the Haber-Awwal, and the Habert el-Jahlah, (*Haber* meaning the sons of), who were the children of Isaakh by three wives, the said Isaak having crossed over from Hadhramaut some time after his countrymen had founded the nation to the eastward, and settled at the town of Meyt, near Burnt Island, where his tomb exists to this day. Isaakh, finding his influence on the increase, owing to his intermarriage with a Galla tribe, made a sudden descent upon the neighbourhood of Berbera, then in the hands of a celebrated Galla chieftain, Sultan Harireh, and succeeded in obtaining possession of the country as far as Zaila...The patriarch Isaakh was gathered to his fathers at a very advanced age, and was buried at the town of Meyt, leaving behind him a name which is respected to this day." *Transactions of the Bombay Geographical Society*, vol. viii.

[2] This was undoubtedly Berbera, but it is not an island as Varthema

which with all the inhabitants are Moors. This island is small but good and very well peopled, and contains many

supposed. The name is generally applied to a deep and narrow inlet, forming a safe harbour during the north-east monsoon, and to the country in its neighbourhood. It is situated about one hundred and twenty miles to the south-east of Zaila.

Dr. Vincent identifies Berbera with the Mosullon of the author of the *Periplus*, and that it "has existed as a port of great trade for several centuries," writes Cruttenden, "I conceive to be almost sufficiently proved by the fact of its being an annual rendezvous for so many nations to the present day, and from the time for this great meeting having been chosen so as to suit the set of the Red Sea and Indian Monsoons... The annual fair is one of the most interesting sights on the coast, if only from the fact of so many different and distant tribes being drawn together for a short time, to be again scattered in all directions. From April to the early part of October the place is utterly deserted, not even a fisherman being found there; but no sooner does the season change, than the inland tribes commence moving down towards the coast, and preparing their huts for their expected visitors." It is estimated that as many as 20,000 natives assemble annually at this fair to barter their gums, resins, ostrich feathers, coffee, ghee, oil, cattle, and sheep, with merchants from the Red Sea, Muscat, Baharain, Basra, Porebunder, Mandavie, Bombay, and other Indian ports. A considerable quantity of these commodities is also brought over to the Aden market by the Sômâlis, and the town and garrison there are almost entirely supplied with butcher's meat from Berbera. Speaking of that country Cruttenden further says: "The number of sheep, goats, she-camels, etc., found on these plains is perfectly incredible, fully realizing the account given of the flocks and herds of the patriarchs of old; for many of the elders of these tribes own each more than 1,500 she-camels, and their flocks of sheep are literally uncounted." The territory is governed by the elders of the different tribes, but during the fair at Berbera no chief is acknowledged, the customs of by-gone years being the only recognized laws of the place.

As Berbera was inhabited when our traveller arrived there, it is obvious that his visit took place during the north-east monsoon, and that fact explains the circumstance of his having been driven back towards the African coast after sailing from Aden. The vessel probably encountered one of those strong north-westerly gales, called *Balát* by the Arabs, which occasionally occur during that season along the north-east coast of Arabia.

Although Varthema supplies us with few dates, we are enabled to verify this inference by several incidental remarks in the preceding nar-

animals of every kind. The people are for the most part black, and their wealth consists more in animals than in other things. We remained here one day, and then set sail and took the route towards Persia.

rative. He left Damascus on the 8th of April, reached Meccah in six weeks, and remained there several days at least. Was twelve days travelling to El-Medinah, where he also sojourned some time before starting for Juddah. He was detained a fortnight at the latter place, and was seventeen days more making the voyage to Aden. At Aden he was imprisoned for two months before being sent to Radāā, where he arrived during the hot weather, for grapes were in season, and on his release he travelled through a great part of Yemen, which occupied him not less than six weeks more. These periods combined make between seven and eight months, so that he probably left Aden about the middle of December, when the north-easterly monsoon was fully set in, and the fair at Berbera was at its height.

THE BOOK CONCERNING PERSIA.

THE CHAPTER CONCERNING DIUOBANDIERRUMI, AND GOA, AND GIULFAR, LANDS OF MESCHET, A PORT OF PERSIA.

WHEN we had sailed about twelve days we arrived at a city which is called Diuobandierrumi,[1] that is, " Diu, the port of

[1] Though Varthema heads this chapter as relating to Persia, the two places first named obviously belong to the Indian province of Guzerat, and the change in the course of the vessel in which he sailed, originally bound for the former country, may have been caused by the shipment of cargo for those places at Zaila and Berbera, between which and the Sômâli coast there is still considerable traffic.

Diu Bander er-Râm, which our traveller correctly renders "Diu the Port of the Turks" (or Greeks,) but which Eden, following the doubtful Latin version, mistranslates "The holy porte of Turkes," is undoubtedly the small island of Diu, situated in the Gulf of Cambay, at that period subject to Mahmûd Bigarrah, the reigning Sultân of Guzerat. I have sought in vain for the distinctive title which Varthema gives it, and which is Arabic in its form, in any other writer either before or after his time. The author of the *Kurrat el-'Ayûn* mentions a severe hurricane "at Bander Diu in the Indian Sea," in the month of January 1495, wherein many vessels were lost; and the *Ruâh er-Ruâh* records the death, five years later, of one 'Abdullah ibn Muhammed ibn 'Alowi, a famous Seyyed of Yemen, "at Bander Diu in India;" but the suffix "Er-Rûmi" never occurs in their works in connexion with the place. The following extract from the *Histoire des Voyages*, relating the events of 1530, though it fails to solve the difficulty, goes to prove that the name was familiar in those parts, and that foreigners styled " Rûmi" or " Rûm" resided at Diu about that period:—" Badur [Bahadur], qui avait succédé au tron de Cambaye, se crut redevable de son salut à Mustapha. Il lui accorda pour récompense le gouvernement de Baroche, avec le titre de *Rumi*,

the Turks," which city is situated a short distance from the
mainland. When the tide rises it is an island, and when
it falls you can pass over on foot. This city is subject to the
Sultan of Combeia, and the captain of this Diuo is one
named Menacheaz. We remained here two days. There is
an immense trade in this city. Four hundred Turkish merchants reside here constantly. This city is surrounded by
walls and contains much artillery within it. They have
certain vessels which are called Thalae, which are somewhat
less than galleys. We departed thence and went to a city
which is called Goa,[1] distant from the above about three

parce qu'il était Grec, et celui de *Kan*. Ainsi nous le verrons paroître
désormais sous le nom de Rumi-Kan." Vol. i. p. 118.

The town of Diu is situated at the eastern extremity of the island, and
is well fortified, being surrounded by a wall strengthened with towers at
regular intervals. The channel between the island and the mainland is
navigable only for fishing-boats and other small craft. Notwithstanding
the excellence of the harbour for ships of moderate draught, there is but
little traffic. (See Thornton's *Gazetteer of India*.) In this latter respect
the place must have fallen off considerably since Varthema's time.
M. Cæsar Fredericke, who visited it A.D. 1563, describes it as "a small
city, but of great trade, because there they lade very many great ships
for the straights of Mecca and Ormus with merchandise." (Hakluyt's
Voyages, vol. ii.) Diu was captured by the Portuguese in 1515, and
remains in their possession still. In 1539 they repelled an attack on
the place by the Turkish fleet under Suleiman Pasha, who was obliged
to return to Suez. On his way thither he remained some time at Zebîd,
exciting the people to revolt, with a view to extort money from the
Imâm. Such is the opinion of the author of the *Ruâh er-Ruâh*, who
adds:—"I have, moreover, heard from credible witnesses, that he accepted
rich gifts from the powers in India to induce him not to prosecute the war
in that quarter."

[1] This was unquestionably Goghâ, or, as it is now usually called, Gogo,
a town situate in the peninsula of Kattywar, on the western shore of the
Gulf of Cambay, about one hundred miles to the north-east of Diu.
Forbes describes it at present as "a neat and thriving seaport town,
containing upwards of eight thousand inhabitants, and possessing the
best roadstead in the Gulf of Cambay. Its seamen, called Goghârees,
partly of the Mohammedan faith, and partly Koolee or Hindoo, the
descendants of the navigators fostered by the kings of Unhilwâra, still
maintain their ancient reputation, and form the best and most trusted

days' journey. This Goa is a district of large extent and
great traffic, and is fat and wealthy. The inhabitants, however, are all Muhammedans. We quitted Goa and went to
another district called Guilfar, which is most excellent and
abounding in everything.[1] There is a good seaport there,
from which port setting sail with propitious winds we arrived
at another port which is called Meschet.[2]

portion of every Indian crew that sails the sea under the flag of England. On the south-west corner of the town, and outside the circuit of
the present wall, may, however, be observed the site of the ancient
citadel...The situation was admirably selected for defensive purposes,
being the highest in the neighbourhood, and commanding an extensive
view of the gulf and the island of Perumbh, or Peerum, on the one side,
and on the other of the whole country as far as the foot of the Khokurâ
hills." (*Râs Mâlâ*, vol. i. p. 318.) In Hamilton's time (1688-1723) Gogo
was "governed by an officer from the Great Mogul." It was taken from
the Mahrattas by the British in 1805, and now forms part of the district
of Ahmedabad.

[1] From Gogo, Varthema must have crossed the Indian Sea and
entered the Persian Gulf, for Julfâr is situated within the Gulf, on the
western side of Mussendom, about twenty miles to the south of that
cape. It is one of five towns belonging to the Shihiyyín Arabs, and its
inhabitants form the more stationary and civilized portion of that tribe,
being engaged chiefly in pearl-fishing, trade, and agriculture. Their
food consists of dates, wheat, barley, meat, and fish in abundance. The
remainder of the tribe is occupied in gaining a precarious livelihood by
fishing in the small bays on the coast, or in wandering over the arid rocks
of the interior, which supply a scanty vegetation for their flocks. The
male adults of the tribe are said to amount to 14,000.

Julfâr was captured by the Portuguese in the early part of the sixteenth century. They maintained an establishment there, protected by
a fort, for the purpose of pearl-fishing, until their expulsion from the
gulf, when it reverted to the Arabs. In 1819 the town and fort were
destroyed by a combined British and Máskat expedition, in retaliation
for several acts of piracy committed by vessels belonging to the tribe.

[2] Máskat (Muscat), the principal seaport town of the province of
Oman, or, more correctly, 'Ammán. As that place is situated on the
north-east coast of Arabia, bordering the Indian Sea, in lat. 23° 28′ N.,
long. 59° 19′ E., a retrograde voyage was made of two hundred miles.
The native vessel, however, does not appear to have had a fixed
course, although her destination on leaving Aden was the Persian Gulf;
but the Arab skipper was probably guided in his movements by the

THE CHAPTER CONCERNING ORMUS, A CITY AND ISLAND OF PERSIA, AND HOW THEY GET VERY LARGE PEARLS AT IT BY FISHING..

Pursuing our journey, we departed from Meschet and went to the noble city of Ormus,[1] which is extremely beautiful.

freights which he picked up here and there on the coast, and our traveller availed himself of the opportunities thus afforded to satisfy his desire for seeing new countries.

Máskat, at the period of Varthema's visit, was governed by a native sovereign who resided at Nezwa, two days' journey inland. It was captured by the Portuguese, together with several other places on the Bátinah coast, in the early part of the sixteenth century. They retained possession till 1640, when they were expelled from the country by Sultân Bin Seif, in whose family the sovereignty of Ammân remains to the present day.

[1] 'Abd er-Razzâk, who visited the island of Hormuz sixty years before Varthema, speaks in similar terms of its commercial prosperity. (See *India in the Fifteenth Century*, HAKLUYT SOCIETY's Publications, pp. 5, 6.) Ralph Fitch, in 1583, describes it as " an island in circuit about five and twenty or thirty miles, and the driest island in the world; for there is nothing growing in it but only salt; for the water, wood, or victuals, and all things necessary, come out of Persia, which is about twelve miles from thence. The Portuguese have a castle there, wherein there is a captain for the king of Portugal, having under him a convenient number of soldiers, whereof some part remain in the castle and some in the town. In this town are merchants of all nations, and many Moors and Gentiles. Here is a very great trade of all sorts of spices, drugs, silk, cloth of silk, fine tapestry of Persia, great store of pearls, which come from the isle of Baharim [Baharein], and are the best pearls of all others, and many horses of Persia, which serve all India. They have a Moor to their king, who is chosen and governed by the Portuguese." PINKERTON's *Voyages*, vol. ix. p. 407.

Hormuz was captured by the Portuguese under Alberquerque in 1508, who were expelled in turn by Shâh Abbâs, assisted by the British, in 1622, since which time it has been a dependency of Persia. Shâh Abbâs transferred its commerce to Gombrûn, or Gamrûn, situate on the continent, and styled after him Bander Abbâs. The island was a dependency of Persia when Marco Polo visited it towards the middle of the 13th century, and, although governed by an Arab ruler, it was tributary to that power when taken by the Portuguese, who allowed him to retain his dignity on payment of an annual tribute of 15,000 *ashrafi*, about

It is an island, and is the chief, that is, as a maritime place, and for merchandise. It is distant from the mainland ten or twelve miles. In this said island there is not sufficient water or food, but all comes from the mainland. Near this island, at a distance of three days' journey, they fish up the largest pearls which are found in the world, and the manner of fishing for them is as you shall hear. There are certain fishers with some little boats, who throw out a large stone attached to a thick rope, one from the stern and one from the prow, in order that the said boats may remain firm: they throw down another rope, also with a stone, to the bottom. In the middle of the boat is one of these fishers, who hangs a couple of bags round his neck, and ties a large stone to his feet, and goes fifteen paces under water, and remains there as long as he is able, in order to find the oysters in which are pearls. As he finds them he puts them into the bags, and then leaves the stone which he had at his feet, and comes up by one of the said ropes.[1] Sometimes, as many as three hundred vessels belonging to different countries are assembled at the said city, the Sultan of which is a Mahommedan.

£1,250 of our money. (*Histoire des Voyages*, vol. i. p. 110.) It is now farmed of the Persian Shah by the Sultan of Máskat, together with Bunder Abbás, Minau, and several other places on the mainland, for a yearly payment of 16,000 Toomans=£7,600; but it has lost all its former trade and prosperity, and its population consists of about four hundred inhabitants, mostly employed in the salt trade and as fishermen. The island has no water except what is saved in reservoirs during the rains. There are a number of these reservoirs in good repair, and the ruins of some hundreds, showing what the place was in former times. The old Portuguese lighthouse is still standing, though fast falling to decay. Large quantities of salt are exported from the island to all parts of the Persian Gulf and the coasts of Arabia. The fort is garrisoned by a hundred men belonging to the Sultan of Máskat. The channel between Hormuz and the mainland directly opposite is only four miles broad. Between the island and Bunder Abbás it averages between eleven and twelve.

[1] This is a correct description of the pearl fishery as it exists at the present day.

THE CHAPTER CONCERNING THE SULTAN OF ORMUS, AND OF THE CRUELTY OF THE SON AGAINST THE SULTAN HIS FATHER, HIS MOTHER, AND HIS BROTHERS.

At the time when I visited this country there happened that which you shall hear. The Sultan of Ormus had eleven male children. The youngest was considered to be simple, that is, half a fool: the eldest was looked upon as a devil unchained. Also the said Sultan had brought up two slaves, the sons of Christians, that is, of those of Prester John, whom he had purchased when quite young, and he loved them like his own children.[1] They were gallant cavaliers and lords of castles. One night, the eldest son of the Sultan put out the eyes of his father, mother, and all his brothers, excepting the half-witted one; then he carried them into the chamber of his father and mother, and put fire in the midst, and burnt the chamber with the bodies and all that was therein. Early in the morning what had taken place became known, and the city arose at the rumour, and he fortified himself in the palace, and proclaimed himself Sultan. The younger brother, who was considered a fool, did not, however, show himself to be such a fool as he was supposed to be; for, hearing what had taken place, he took refuge in a Moorish mosque, saying: "Vualla occuane saithan uchatelabu cculo cuane," that is, "O God, my brother is a devil; he has killed my father, my mother, and all my brothers, and after having killed them he has burnt them."[2] At the expiration of fifteen days the city became tranquil.

[1] *Habeshi*, or Abyssinian slaves, mostly of Christian parentage, were the most trusted and favourite soldiers of the sultans and other chiefs of Arabia at this period. They were also imported largely into India, and frequently acquired considerable influence in the courts of the native princes.

[2] *W'Allah, akhúna shaitán: hua kátel abáh, wa-kul akhwánana.* By God! our brother is a devil: he has killed his father, and all my brothers.

The Sultan sent for one of the slaves above mentioned and said to him: "Thale inte Mahometh." The slave, who was named Mahometh, answered: "Escult iasidi," that is, "What dost thou say, lord? Said the Sultan: "An ne Soldan?" that is, "Am I Sultan?" Mahometh replied: "Heu valla siti inte Soldan," that is, "Yes, by God, thou art Sultan."[1] Then the Sultan took him by the hand and made much of him, and said to him: "Roa chatel zaibei anneiati arba ochan sechala," that is, "Go and kill thy companion, and I will give thee five castles."[2] Mahometh replied: "Iasidi anue iacul menau men saibi theletin sane vualla sidi ancasent," that is, "O lord, I have eaten with my companion thirty years and acted with him, I cannot bring my mind to do such a thing."[3] Then said the Sultan: "Well, let it alone." Four days afterwards, the said Sultan sent for the other slave, who was named Caim, and made the same speech to him that he had made to his companion, that is, that he should go and kill. "Bizemele," Caim said at once, "erechman erachin Iasidi," that is, "So be it, lord, in the name of God;"[4] and then he armed himself secretly and went immediately to find Mahometh his companion. When Mahometh saw him, he looked him fixedly in the face, and said to him: "O traitor, thou canst not deny it, for I detect thee by thy countenance; but look now, for I will slay thee sooner than that thou slay me." Caim, who saw himself discovered and known, drew forth his dagger, and threw it at the feet of Mahometh, and falling

---

[1] *Taál anta, Muhammed.* Come hither, Muhammed. *Aish kult, ya sidi?* What do you say, sir? *Ana sultán?* Am I sultan? *Ay w'Allah, sidi, anta sultán.* Yes, sir, you are sultan.

[2] *Ruh aktal sáhibek, wa-ana 'aútík arbáa aw khams kaláa.* Go kill your comrade, and I will give you four or five castles.

[3] *Ya sidi, ána akált miia'u min sabi,—thláthín sana. W'Allah, sidi, ankássir.* Oh, sir, I have eaten with him from childhood,—thirty years. By God, sir, I shall fail.

[4] *B'ism-Illah, er-Rahmán, er-Rahím.* In the name of God, the Pitiful, the Compassionate. A formula frequently used to express assent.

on his knees before him said: " O, my lord, pardon me although I deserve death, and if it seem good to thee take these arms and kill me, for I came to kill thee." Mahometh replied: " It may be well said that thou art a traitor, having been with me, and acted with me, and eaten together with me for thirty years, and then at last to wish to put me to death in so vile a manner. Thou poor creature, dost thou not see that this man is a devil. Rise, however, for I pardon thee. But in order that thou mayest understand, know that this man urged me, three days ago, to kill thee, but I would not in any way consent. Now, leave all to God, but go and do as I shall tell thee. Go to the Sultan, and tell him that thou hast slain me." Caim replied: " I am content," and immediately went to the Sultan. When the Sultan saw him he said to him : " Well, hast thou slain thy friend ?" Caim answered : " Yes, sir, by God." Said the Sultan : " Come here," and he went close to the Sultan, who seized him by the breast and killed him by blows of his dagger. Three days afterwards Mahometh armed himself secretly and went to the Sultan's chamber, who, when he saw him, was disturbed and exclaimed : " O dog, son of a dog, art thou still alive ?" Said Mahometh : " I am alive, in spite of thee, and I will kill thee, for thou art worse than a dog or a devil ;" and in this way, with their arms in their hands, they fought awhile. At length Mahometh killed the Sultan, and then fortified himself in the palace. And because he was so much beloved in the city, the people all ran to the palace crying out: " Long live Mahometh the Sultan !" and he continued Sultan about twenty days. When these twenty days were passed, he sent for all the lords and merchants of the city, and spoke to them in this wise: " That that which he had done he had been obliged to do ; that he well knew that he had no right to the supreme power, and he entreated all the people that they would allow him to make king that son who was considered crazy ;"

and thus he was made king. It is true, however, that Mahometh governs everything. All the city said: "Surely this man must be the friend of God." Wherefore he was made governor of the city and of the Sultan, the Sultan being of the condition above mentioned.[1] You must know that there are generally in this city four hundred foreign merchants, who traffic in silks, pearls, jewels, and spices. The common food of this city consists more of rice than of bread, because corn does not grow in this place.

THE CHAPTER CONCERNING ERI IN CORAZANI OF PERSIA, AND OF ITS RICHES, AND OF THE ABUNDANCE OF MANY THINGS, AND ESPECIALLY OF RHUBARB.

Having heard this lamentable event, and seen the customs of the abovenamed city and island of Ormus, departing thence I passed into Persia, and travelling for twelve days I found a city called Eri,[2] and the country is called Cora-

---

[1] I have not succeeded in finding any historical notices corroborative of the events recorded in this chapter; but the following extract from the *Histoire des Voyages*, referring to the capture of the island by Albuquerque in 1508, four years subsequent to Varthema's visit, tends to confirm several of the principal facts narrated:—"Albuquerque trouva sur le trône Sayf Addin, jeune prince d'environ douze ans, dont les affaires étoient gouvernées par un esclave adroit et courageux." Vol. i. p. 109.

[2] Eri or Heri is the ancient name of Herât, and the question is, whether Varthema means that city, and, if so, whether he personally visited it. His description is sufficiently accurate to warrant an inference in the affirmative. Herât at the time was the capital of Khorassan, and the residence of Sultân Huseîn Mîrza, a descendant of Timour. Its commercial and general prosperity under that enlightened ruler has been perpetuated by the celebrated historian Khoudemir, and the natural resources of the country correspond with our traveller's account of them. Moreover, Varthema speaks as an eye-witness, and thus far I have not discovered a single instance inclining me to doubt his testimony as such. Besides, there appears no sufficient reason why, if he had not personally visited Herât, he should not have described it as he does

zani, which would be the same as to say "The Romagna." The king of Corazani dwells in this city, where there is great plenty, and an abundance of stuffs, and especially of silk, so that in one day you can purchase here three thousand or four thousand camel loads of silk. The district is most abundant in articles of food,[1] and there is also a great market for rhubarb.[2] I have seen it purchased at six pounds

---

Samarcand in a subsequent chapter, wherein he repeatedly states that his information is based on hearsay and the authority of others.

The only difficulty is the time occupied by our traveller in performing the journey. The distance between the coast opposite Hormuz and Herât is about six hundred miles, and, according to Abd-er-Razzâk's itinerary, he was twenty-two days on the road. True, Varthema says distinctly, that, after travelling twelve days, he reached Eri; but it is by no means clear that Hormuz or Bunder Abbâs was his starting-point, for he first "passed into Persia," from which we may infer that he had penetrated some way into the country before setting out for Herât.

In the following chapter Varthema gives an account of his route from Herât to Shirâz, which he accomplished in twenty or twenty-three days, the usual length of the caravan journey between the two places. That coincidence may be fairly considered as a corroborative proof of our traveller's personal visit to Herât.

[1] "Herât is the most fertile country in the whole of Khorassân. The suburbs are covered with rich and green orchards, producing considerable quantities of fruits. Silk is a native production of Herât. It is produced in great quantities, and is exported to many countries. The wheat is of many kinds....Cotton is abundantly cultivated in Herât, and sometimes is sent to Mashad. Mash, adas, nakhud, lemghash or muth, shamled or halbah, jawari and lobia, are also among its productions. Sebist and shaftal grōw exuberantly, and are given to horses. Opium is much grown here, and is transported to Bokhâra and other places." MOHUN LALL's *Travels*, pp. 272-275.

[2] Herât is styled by the natives the key of the commerce between Turkestân, Afghanistân, Persia, and India. It is much less so now than it was formerly. At the time of Varthema's visit it is highly probable that it was the principal highway between Mongolia and Thibet, the chief rhubarb-growing countries, and the West. That fact would account for the abundance of the drug found in the market of Herât. Tavernier mentions a northern road between Bhutân or Lassa and Câbul; and Bernier, writing in 1655, says: "It is not yet twenty years that there went caravans every year from Cashmere, which crossed all those mountains of the great Tibet, and arrived in about three

for the ducat, according to our use, that is, twelve ounces to the pound. This city contains about 6,000 or 7,000 hearths.[1] The inhabitants are all Mohammedans. I quitted this place and travelled twenty days on the mainland, finding cities and castles very well peopled.

THE CHAPTER CONCERNING THE RIVER EUFRA, WHICH I BELIEVE TO BE THE EUPHRATES.

I arrived at a large and fine river, which is called by the people there Eufra,[2] but, so far as I can judge, I believe that it is the Euphrates, on account of its great size. Travelling onwards for three days to the left hand, but following the river, I found a city which is named Schirazo, and this city receives its lord, who is a Persian and a Mahommedan, from the Persians. In this city there is a great abundance of jewels, that is, of turquoises,[3] and an infinite quantity of Balass rubies. It is true that they are not produced here,

months at Cataja...bringing back musk, cinnamon, rhubarb, and mamiron." (PINKERTON'S *Voyages*, vol. viii. p. 221.) I notice in the *Description of Persia*, contained in the same Collection, that "a kind of rhubarb, with which they purge their cattle," grows in that country; but the writer adds, "the best rhubarb comes from China, or rather from Eastern Tartary." *Ibid.* vol. ix. p. 181.

[1] Ferrier estimated the population of Herât in 1845 at from 20,000 to 22,000 souls. *Caravan Journeys*, p. 166.

[2] As there is no river between Herât and Shiráz bearing any resemblance in name to that above mentioned, I am inclined to think that if, as is very probable, his route was by Yezd, Varthema must have struck upon the Pulwân, near Merghâb, about eighty miles to the north-east of Shiráz, from which point there appears to be a highroad on the "left hand," or east, of that river, leading to the latter city by Istakâr. The Pulwân flows into the Bendemir, which is a rapid stream crossed by a bridge three hundred feet wide, and Varthema must have passed that also before reaching Shiráz.

[3] Shiráz is a great mart for turquoises. The best stones are found in the mountains near Nishapore in Khorassan. MALCOLM'S *History of Persia*, vol. ii. p. 515.

but come (as is reported) from a city which is called Balachsam. And in the said city there is a very large quantity of ultra marine, and much *tucia* and musk.[1] You must know that musk is rarely met with in our parts, which is not adulterated. The fact is this, for I have seen some experiments on this wise. Take a bladder of musk in the morning, fasting, and break it, and let three or four men in file smell it, and it will immediately make blood flow from the nose, and this happens because it is real musk and not adulterated. I asked how long its goodness continued. Some merchants answered me: "That if it were not adulterated it lasted ten years." Upon this it occurred to me that that which comes to our part is adulterated by the hands of these Persians, who are the most cunning men in intellect, and at falsifying things, of any nation in the world. And I likewise will say of them, that they are the best companions and the most liberal of any men who inhabit the earth. I say this because I have experienced it with a Persian merchant whom I met in this city of Schirazo. However, he was of the city of Eri above mentioned, in Corazani. This same merchant knew me two years previously in Mecca, and he said to me: "Iunus, what are you doing here? Are you not he who some time ago went to Mecca?" I answered

[1] Badakhshân, in the Khanât of Kunduz, is still famous for its lapis lazuli quarries and ruby mines. *Tucia*, spodium; or, more probably, *tátyá*, the Persian and Arabic name for antimony, which is used extensively in the preparation of the *kohl*, a collyrium. Antimony is said to abound in Persia. (PINKERTON's *Voyages*, vol. ix. p. 181.) Musk probably reached Badakhshân from Thibet and Tartary, where the best quality is found. Pigafetta writing in 1522 says : " The grains of musk brought to Europe are no other than small pieces of goat's flesh steeped in real musk." (PINKERTON, vol. xi. p. 378.) I am not able to vouch for the truth of Varthema's experiment, but it is well known that "some persons, from idiosyncrasy, cannot endure the remote odour of musk: it produces headache, giddiness, nausea, and fainting. Drowsiness and stupor have occasionally been induced by it when given in small medicinal doses." BRANDE, *Dictionary of Materia Medica*.

that I was, and that I was going about exploring the world. He answered me: "God be praised! for I shall have a companion who will explore the world with me." We remained fifteen days in the same city of Schirazo. And this merchant, who was called Cazazionor,[1] said: "Do not leave me, for we will explore a good part of the world." And thus we set ourselves together *en route* to go towards Sambragante.

THE CHAPTER CONCERNING SAMBRAGANTE, (AS IT IS CALLED), A VERY LARGE CITY, LIKE CAIRO, AND OF THE PERSECUTION BY THE SOFFI.

The merchants say that the present Sambragante[2] is a city as large as Cairo. The king of the said city is a Mohammedan. Some merchants say that he has sixty thousand horsemen, and they are all white people and warlike. We did not proceed farther; and the reason was, that the Soffi was going through this country putting everything to fire and flame; and especially he put to the sword all those who believed in Bubachar and Othman and Aumar, who are all companions of Mahomet; but he leaves unmolested those who believe in Mahomet and Ali, and protects them.[3] Then

[1] The first part of this word is undoubtedly *Khawája*, generally abbreviated into *Khôja*, equivalent to our English "Mister."

[2] Samarcand.

[3] The occurrence of these fierce religious dissensions between the two principal sects of Islâm at this period is corroborated by contemporaneous history. Shâh Isma'îl es-Sûfî, the founder of the Sufawîan dynasty, attained sovereign power over Persia and Khorassân about A.D. 1500. Deeply imbued with the Shiâh doctrines of his austere father, Haidar, who had endeavoured to revive the opinions of a famous *Sûfî* derwish, he put himself at the head of his adherents when only fourteen years old, and, taking advantage of the religious enthusiasm of his disciples, eventually succeeded in subjugating the whole country, and in converting the great mass of the people to the Shiâh creed. This was not effected without great strife and bloodshed, and Varthema's visit must have occurred when the contention between the rival factions was at its height. "The Persians dwell with rapture on the character of Isma'îl,

my companion said to me: "Come here, Iunus: in order that you may be certain that I wish you well, and that you may have reason to know that I mean to exercise good fellowship towards you, I will give you a niece of mine who is called Samis,[1] that is, the Sun. And truly she had a name which suited her, for she was extremely beautiful. And he said to me further: "You must know now that I do not travel about the world because I am in want of wealth; but I go for my pleasure, and in order to see and to know many things." And with this we set ourselves on our way, and returned towards Eri. When we had arrived at his house, he immediately shewed me his said niece, with whom I pretended to be greatly pleased, although my mind was intent on other things. We returned to the city of Ormus at the end of eight days, and embarked on board ship, and steered towards India, and arrived at a port which is called Cheo.[2]

---

whom they deem not only the founder of a great dynasty, but the person to whom that faith, in which they glory, owes its establishment as a national religion. He is styled in their histories Shah Shiân, or 'the King of the Sheahs.'" MALCOLM's *History of Persia*, vol. i. p. 505.

[1] *Shams*, the sun.

[2] As it is evident from the succeeding chapter that this place was in Scind, I find no difficulty in identifying it with Jooa (sometimes written Joah, Joaah, and Kow), one of the estuaries or creeks of the Indus. Dr. Heddle, in his memoirs of that river, describes the *raj* or village of Joah as four miles and a half from the sea by the winding of the stream. The largest sized native boats, which frequent this branch of the river for grain, are obliged to remain there, and their cargoes are brought down in flat-bottomed boats, called *doondies*." *Bombay Government Selections*, No. xvii. pp. 434-5.

THE FIRST BOOK CONCERNING INDIA.

THE CHAPTER CONCERNING COMBEIA, A CITY OF INDIA, ABOUNDING IN ALL THINGS.

HAVING promised at the commencement, if I remember rightly, to treat all subjects with brevity, in order that my narrative might not be wearisome, I will continue to relate concisely those things which appeared to me the most worthy to be known, and the most interesting.

We entered India where, near to the said port [Cheo], there is a very large river called the Indus, which Indus is near to a city called Combeia. This city is situated three miles inland, and to the south of the said Indus. You must know that you cannot go to the said city either with large or middling-sized ships, excepting at high water. There is a river which goes to the said city, and the tide flows up three or four miles.[1] You must know that the waters rise in the reverse

[1] Varthema appears to have had very confused notions respecting the relative positions of Cambay (more correctly, *Khumbáyut*) and the Indus. This is not surprising, since Philip Baldæus, writing a century and a half later, describes it as "situated at the entrance of one of the largest channels of that river." (COLLECTION OF VOYAGES, vol. iii. p. 566.) Nicolò de' Conti, who preceded our traveller by fifty years, places it more accurately "in the second gulf after having passed the mouth of the Indus." (*India in the Fifteenth Century*, iii. p. 19.) However, he correctly locates it to the south of the Indus, and near another river, which was undoubtedly the Myhee, and his description of that estuary is confirmed by the following extract from Horsburgh :—" Opposite the

way to ours; for with us they rise when the moon is at the full, but they increase here when the moon is on the wane.¹ This city of Combeia is walled, after our fashion; and truly it is a most excellent city, abounding in grain and very good fruits. In this district there are eight or nine kinds of small spices, that is to say, *turbidi, gallanga, spiconardo, saphetica,*

city of Cambay, seven or eight miles from the sea, the width is probably about three miles, and the water is so shallow from side to side, at low water spring tides, that the ground is left almost dry, and navigation is impracticable even for the smallest boats." *India Directory*, vol. i. p. 475.

¹ This is an error into which Varthema may have been led by the accounts which he heard, or by his own limited observation, of the peculiar and extraordinary tides in the Gulf of Cambay, called the *Bore*, which is thus described by the late Captain Ethersey of the Indian navy: "The eastern or principal Bore rises five miles to the W.S.W. of Cambay Creek, and is not perceptible on the neaps without the previous springs have been very high, when it may be observed slightly through the quarter. It generally commences when the springs begin to lift, the wave increasing daily in height as the tides gain strength, and is at its greatest height about two days after the new and full moon. Its height depends upon the position of the moon with respect to the earth, and consequently on the rise and strength of the tide; for at new moon, when she is in perigee, at which time the highest tides occur, the wave of the Bore will be the greatest; and at full moon, when she is in apogee, and the low tides lower than any other springs, it will be least. It also varies with the night and day tide, because the higher the tide the greater is its velocity; and as the two tides differ from six to eight feet, and still the flood of both runs the same length of time, the highest tide must have the greatest velocity; and hence the wave of the Bore will be highest with the greatest tide." (*Bombay Government Selections*, No. xvii. p. 87.) Dr. Vincent recognizes the *Bore* in the account which the author of the *Periplus* gives of the navigation of the Gulf of Cambay (*Commerce and Navigation of the Ancients*, etc., vol. ii. p. 396); and so imposing is its appearance, and so striking its effects, that we cannot be surprised at the notice which it attracted from the early travellers to India. Forbes says: "The first rush of the spring tide is irresistible in its force, and affords a scene which only an eyewitness can fully realize. A perpendicular wall of water, three or four feet in height, and extending across the Gulf as far as the eye can reach, approaches at the rate of twelve miles an hour in speed, and with an alarming noise, carrying certain destruction to the mariner whose ignorance or foolhardiness leads him to neglect its warning voice." *Rás Málá*, vol. i. p. 310.

and *lacra*,[1] with other spices, the names of which I do not
remember. An immense quantity of cotton is produced here,
so that every year forty or fifty vessels are laden with cotton
and silk stuffs, which stuffs are carried into different countries.
In this kingdom of Combeia also, about six days' journey,
there is the mountain whence cornelians are extracted, and
the mountain of chalcedonies. Nine days' journey from
Combeia there is another mountain in which diamonds are
found.[2]

THE CHAPTER CONCERNING THE ESTATE OF THE SULTAN OF THE VERY NOBLE CITY OF COMBEIA.

We will now declare the estate and condition of the sultan
of this Combeia, who is called the Sultan Machamuth. About

[1] The Latin version of Varthema omits all these names. The Italian
edition in *Ramusio* has " turbitti, galanga, spico nardo, assa fetida, e
lacca." The first is the well known drug *turbith*, the root of a species
of convolvulus (*C. Turpethum*, L.) which is found throughout India,
and also in the islands of the South Sea. I find it enumerated under
that name in a list of drugs purchased by Captain John Saris in 1612
from the captain of a native vessel which had arrived at Mokha from
Surat. *Galanga*, according to Baretti, is a kind of arrow-root used
medicinally. Spikenard and assafœtida are well known Indian drugs.
Lacca is, doubtless, the dye produced by the lac insect, of which Dr.
Buchanan gives a full account in his *Journey through Mysore, Canara,
and Malabar*. (See PINKERTON's *Voyages*, vol. viii. pp. 760-1.) Nicolò
de' Conti, writing of Cambay, says : "it abounds in spikenard, lac,
indigo, myrobalans, and silk ;" and Nikitin mentions "lek daakyk dalon"
as among its produce. These latter I take to be, lac ; *'akcek*, the Arabic
for agates; and *dàl*, the Hindostani for lentils, *phaseolus aconitifolius*.
(See *India in the Fifteenth Century*, ii. p. 20 ; iii. p. 19.)

[2] Cambay is still famous for agates, cornelians, and onyxes, which are
wrought into a great variety of ornaments. The best agates and cornelians are found in a peculiar stratum, about thirty feet below the surface, in a small tract among the Rajpeepla Hills, on the banks of the
Nerbudda, about seventy miles to the south-east of Cambay. I am not
aware of any diamond mines existing in or about Guzerat. Probably
those at Golconda are indicated.

forty years ago he captured this kingdom from a king of the
Guzerati, which Guzerati are a certain race which eats
nothing that has blood, and never kills any living thing. And
these same people are neither Moors nor heathens.[1] It is my

[1] The Sultan at the time was Fath Khân, entitled Mahmûd Bigarrah,
who began to reign A.D. 1459 and died in 1511; but our author is not
so correct in his history of the succession. Guzerat became independent
of Delhi under Dhûfir Khân, who assumed the sovereignty of the province in 1408. For obvious reasons that event does not tally with the
occurrence referred to by Varthema. The mention of "a king of the
Guzerattis", who was neither a Moor nor a Heathen, inclines me to
think that he distorted the accounts which he had heard of Mahmûd
Khân's successful wars with some of the native princes into the apocry-
phal statement respecting the time and manner of his accession to
supreme power. The most probable event in the history of that sovereign which may have led to this misapprehension, was his final capture
of the strong forts of Girnar and Janagarh from Rao Mandalik in 1472.
Those fortresses are in Kattywar, a province of Guzerat, and appear to
have been inhabited at the time chiefly by Jains. Writing of Girnar,
Postans says : " The whole of this extraordinary mount is invested with
peculiar sanctity, the origin of which would seem to be of high antiquity.
That the present system of worship would seem to be a graft of the
ancient Buddhist faith which obtained here, there can be no doubt.
The edicts of Pyadasi testify abundantly that the hill of Girinagar and
its neighbourhood was originally a stronghold of the Monotheists, whose
form of worship has now degenerated into the modern system of Jain-
ism." (*Notes on a Journey to Girnar*, p. 882.) I am the more inclined
to draw the foregoing inference from Varthema's description of the
creed and habits of the people to whom he refers; for the Jains generally,
who are numerous in and about Cambay, are very careful of animal life.
The Shravakas, one of the Jain castes, have many *Pinjreepols*, or hospitals for animals and reptiles, however vile. They have also another
peculiar establishment called a *Jevkotee*. This is a dome, with a door
large enough at the top for a man to creep in. In these repositories
wevils, and other insects which the Shravakas may find in their grain,
are provided with food by their charity and extraordinary protection
to everything containing life. Moreover, they profess to worship the
Supreme being alone, and wholly reject the agency of Devtas and the
Aryhuntas, or Gooroos. (See *Bombay Government Selections*, No. xxxix.
p. 342-5.) Fitch notices the *Pinjreepoles*. He says : " In Cambaia they
will kill nothing, nor have anything killed. In the town they have
hospitals to keep lame dogs and cats, and for birds. They will give
meat to the ants." PINKERTON's *Voyages*, vol. ix. p. 409.

opinion that if they were baptized, they would all be saved by virtue of their works, for they never do to others what they would not that others should do unto them. Their dress is this: some wear a shirt, and some go naked, with the exception of a piece of cloth about their middle, having nothing on their feet or on their legs. On their heads they wear a large red cloth; and they are of a tawny colour. And for this, their goodness, the aforesaid sultan took from them their kingdom.

You shall now hear the manner of living of this Sultan Machamuth. In the first place he is a Mohammedan, together with all his people. He has constantly twenty thousand horsemen. In the morning, when he rises, there come to his palace fifty elephants, on each of which a man sits astride; and the said elephants do reverence to the sultan, and they have nothing else to do. So in like manner when he has risen from his bed. And when he eats, there are fifty or sixty kinds of instruments, namely, trumpets, drums of several sorts, and flageolets, and fifes, with many others, which for the sake of brevity I forbear mentioning. When the sultan eats, the said elephants again do reverence to him. When the proper time shall come, I will tell you of the intelligence and understanding which these animals possess. The said sultan has mustachios under his nose so long that he ties them over his head as a woman would tie her tresses, and he has a white beard which reaches to his girdle.[1] Every day he eats poison. Do not, however, imagine that he fills his stomach with it; but he eats a certain quantity, so that when he wishes to destroy any great personage he makes him come before him stripped and naked, and then eats

---

[1] 'Ali Muhammed Khân, in his *History of Guzerat*, gives the following account of Sultan Mahmûd:—" Regarding his surname of Bigarrah, the people of Guzerat say, that each of his mustachios being large and twisted like a cow's horn, and such a cow being called Bigarrah, they thus obtained for him the name." BIRD's *Translation*, pp. 202-3.

certain fruits which are called *chofole*, which resemble a muscatel nut. He also eats certain leaves of herbs, which are like the leaves of the sour orange, called by some *tamboli;* and then he eats some lime of oyster shells, together with the above mentioned things. When he has masticated them well, and has his mouth full, he spurts it out upon that person whom he wishes to kill, so that in the space of half an hour he falls to the ground dead. This sultan has also three or four thousand women, and every night that he sleeps with one she is found dead in the morning.[1] Every time that he takes off his shirt, that shirt is never again touched by any one; and so of his other garments; and every day he chooses new garments. My companion asked how it was that this sultan eats poison in this manner. Certain merchants, who were older than the sultan, answered that his father had fed him upon poison from his childhood.

Let us leave the sultan, and return to our journey, that

[1] A similar account is repeated by Odoardo Barbosa, who appears to have visited Cambay shortly after Mahmûd Khân's death. He says: "I have heard that he was brought up from childhood to take poison; for his father fearing that, in accordance with the usage of the country, he might be killed by that means, took this precaution against such a catastrophe. He began to make him eat of it in small doses, gradually increasing them, until he could take a large quantity, whereby he became so poisonous, that if a fly lighted on his hand, it swelled and died incontinently, and many of the women with whom he slept died from the same cause." (RAMUSIO, vol. i. pp. 294-5.) Varthema seems to have believed further, that Mahmûd's spittle, after masticating the Betel leaf, in conjunction with the fruit of the Areca palm and fine lime, was fatal to any upon whom his Majesty might choose to eject it. Beyond the fact that he was an enormous eater, I can find nothing to substantiate these fabulous statements, which remind us of Mithridates, and of the Arabian Nights. The author of the *Miraüt Sikandari,* quoted by 'Ali Muhammed Khân, says: "Sultan Mahmûd was the best of all the Guzerat kings, on account of his great justice and beneficence, his honouring and observing all the Muhammedan laws, and for the solidity of his judgment, whether in great or small matters. He attained a great age, and was distinguished for strength, bravery, and liberality." BIRD's *Translation,* p. 203.

is, to the men of the said city, the greater part of whom go about in a shirt, and are very warlike and great merchants. It is impossible to describe the excellence of the country. About three hundred ships of different countries come and go here. This city, and another of which I will speak at the proper season, supply all Persia, Tartary, Turkey, Syria, Barbary, that is Africa, Arabia Felix, Ethiopia, India, and a multitude of inhabited islands, with silk and cotton stuffs. So that this sultan lives with vast riches, and fights with a neighbouring king, who is called king of the Ioghe, distant from this city fifteen days' journey.

THE CHAPTER CONCERNING THE MANNER OF LIVING AND CUSTOMS OF THE KING OF THE JOGHE.

This king of the Ioghe[1] is a man of great dignity, and has about thirty thousand people, and is a pagan, he and all his subjects; and by the pagan kings he and his people are considered to be saints, on account of their lives, which you shall hear. It is the custom of this king to go on a pilgrimage once in every three or four years, like a pilgrim, that is, at the expense of others, with three or four thousand of his people, and with his wife and children. And he takes

[1] I am unable to identify this "king of the Ioghe" (Joghees), with whom Sultan Mahmûd is said to have been at war. No dependance can be placed on Varthema's names and distances when given on the report of others. In this instance he probably indicates the Rajah of Eedur in the Myhee Kanta, against whom Mahmûd marched with a large force in 1494, and between the Koolee Rajahs of which place and the sovereigns of Guzerat there was a succession of fierce contests from A.D. 1400 till the latter country became a province of Akbar's empire in 1583. (See BIRD's *Translation* of the *Mirát Ahmadi*, pp. 121, 137, 222, 266, 325. Also FORBES's *Rás Mála*, vol. i. pp. 378, 381, 385, *et seq*.)

Perhaps the place of pilgrimage referred to by Varthema was the famous Buddhist shrine (Boodkhâna) at Perwuttum, which Nikitin describes as "the Jerusalem of the Hindoos, where people from all parts of India congregate." *India in the Fifteenth Century*, iii. p. 16.

four or five coursers, and civet-cats, apes, parrots, leopards, and falcons; and in this way he goes through the whole of India. His dress is a goat skin, that is, one before and one behind, with the hair outwards. His colour is dark tawny, for the people here begin to be more dark than white. They all wear a great quantity of jewels, and pearls, and other precious stones, in their ears, and they go dressed *à l'apostolica*,[1] and some wear shirts. The king and some of the more noble have the face and arms and the whole body powdered over with ground sandal-wood and other most excellent scents. Some of these people adopt as an act of devotion the custom of never sitting on any high seat; others, as an act of devotion, never sit on the ground; others adopt the custom of never lying at full length on the ground; others, again, that of never speaking. These always go about with three or four companions, who wait upon them. All generally carry a little horn at their neck; and when they go into a city they all in company sound the said little horns, and this they do when they wish alms to be given to them. When the king does not go, they go at least three or four hundred at a time, and remain in a city three days, in the manner of the Singani.[2] Some of them carry a stick with a ring of iron at the base. Others carry certain iron dishes which cut all round like razors, and they throw these with a sling when they wish to injure any person; and, therefore, when these people arrive at any city in India, every one tries to please them; for should they even kill the first nobleman of the land, they would not suffer any punishment because they say that they are saints.[3] The country of these people is not very fertile;

[1] We have here the same expression as in page 78. On second thoughts, I am inclined to think that Varthema borrows his figure from the Roman *toga*, in which the old Italian artists generally represent the Apostles. Not an inapt comparison with the manner in which the common people of India frequently wear the *langhûti*.

[2] *Zingani*, gipsies (?).

[3] By no means an exaggerated account of the austerities practised by

they even suffer from dearth of provisions. There are more
mountains than plains. Their habitations are very poor, and
they have no walled places.¹ Many jewels come into our
parts by the hands of these people, because through the
liberty they enjoy, and their sanctity, they go where jewels
are produced, and carry them into other countries without
any expense. Thus, having a strong country, they keep the
Sultan Machamuth at war.

THE CHAPTER CONCERNING THE CITY OF CEVUL, AND
ITS CUSTOMS, AND THE BRAVERY OF ITS PEOPLE.

Departing from the said city of Combeia, I travelled on
until I arrived at another city named Cevul,² which is distant

some of the Joghee Fakîrs, and of the estimation in which they were
held by their co-religionists. On this occasion, Varthema is more modest
in his description than either Bernier or Hamilton, who descend to the
most disgusting particulars in the habits of these filthy ascetics. See
PINKERTON's *Voyages*, vol. viii. pp. 180, 317-8.

¹ This description of the country inhabited by Varthema's "Ioghe"
confirms me in the impression that the Myhee Canta is indicated.

² Chaul, Choul, or Chowul, a town and seaport of the Northern Concan,
in the British district of Tannah, twenty-three miles south of Bombay.
It appears to have been a place of considerable trade in former times.
Nikitin, the Russian traveller, who calls it Chivil, visited it about thirty-
five years before Varthema, and describes the manners of the inhabitants
much as he does : " People go about naked, with their heads uncovered,
and bare breasts...Their *kniaz* [prince] wears a *fata* [a large silken gar-
ment] on the head, and another on the loins; the boyars wear it on the
shoulders and on the loins, [Varthema's *alla apostolicha*.] The servants
of the *kniaz* and of the boyars attach the *fata* round the loins, carrying
in the hand a shield and a sword, or a scimitar, or knives, or a sabre, or
a bow and arrows; but all naked and barefooted." (*India in the XVth.
Century*, iii. 8, 9.) Ralph Fitch, who was at Chaul in 1583, after its
capture by the Portuguese, says : " Here is great traffic for all sorts of
spices and drugs, silk and cloth of silk, saudals, and elephants' teeth."
The trade had fallen off considerably in Hamilton's time, for he says:
"the place is now miserably poor." PINKERTON's *Voyages*, ix. p. 408;
viii. p. 351.

from the above-mentioned city twelve days' journey, and
the country between the one and the other of these cities is
called Guzerati. The king of this Cevul is a pagan. The
people are of a dark tawny colour. As to their dress, with
the exception of some Moorish merchants, some wear a
shirt, and some go naked, with a cloth round their middle,
with nothing on their feet or head. The people are warlike: their arms are swords, bucklers, bows and spears made
of reeds and wood, and they possess artillery. This city is
extremely well walled, and is distant from the sea two miles.
It possesses an extremely beautiful river, by which a very
great number of foreign vessels go and return, because the
country abounds in everything excepting grapes, nuts, and
chestnuts. They collect here an immense quantity of grain,
of barley, and of vegetables of every description; and
cotton stuffs are manufactured here in great abundance. I
do not describe their faith here, because their creed is the
same as that of the king of Calicut, of which I will give
you an account when the proper time shall come. There
are in this city a very great number of Moorish merchants.
The atmosphere begins here to be more warm than cold.
Justice is extremely well administered here. This king has
not many fighting men. The inhabitants here have horses,
oxen, and cows, in great abundance.

THE CHAPTER CONCERNING DABULI, A CITY OF INDIA.

Having seen Cevul and its customs, departing thence, I
went to another city, distant from it two days' journey,
which is called Dabuli,[1] which city is situated on the bank of

[1] Situated in the British district of Rutnagherry, in lat. 17° 34' N.,
long. 73° 16' E., on the northern bank of the river Washishtee, (called
Halewacko and *Kalewacko* by the earlier navigators), and about two miles
from its mouth: apparently a place of little consequence now, as it is

a very great river. This city is surrounded by walls in our manner, and is extremely good. The country resembles that above described. There are Moorish merchants here in very great numbers. The king of this place [Dabuli] is a pagan, and possesses about thirty thousand fighting men, but according to the manner of Cevul before mentioned. This king is also a very great observer of justice. The country, the mode of living, the dress, and the customs, resemble those of the aforesaid city of Cevul.

THE CHAPTER CONCERNING GOGA, AN ISLAND OF INDIA, AND THE KING OF THE SAME.

I departed from the city of Dabuli aforesaid, and went to another island, which is about a mile distant from the mainland, and is called Goga,[1] and which pays annually to the king of Decan ten thousand golden ducats, called by them *pardai*. These *pardai* are smaller than the seraphim of Cairo, but thicker, and have two devils stamped upon one

not mentioned by Thornton, but formerly one of the principal seaports of Bijapûr. There 'Âdil Shâh landed from the island of Hormuz in 1458, and thither an ambassador from Persia was escorted from the capital, on his return homeward, in 1519. (SCOTT's *Ferishta*, vol. i. pp. 209, 258.) Nikitin describes it as a very large town and an extensive seaport, "the meeting-place for all nations navigating the coasts of India and Ethiopia." It was captured by the Portuguese under General Almeida in 1508. When Mandeslo visited it in 1639, its fortifications had been mostly demolished (lib. ii. p. 243); and fifty years later its importance as a seaport appears to have been a thing of the past; for Hamilton, after indicating its situation at the mouth of a large river, merely adds: "it was of old a place of trade, and where the English once had a factory." PINKERTON's *Voyages*, vol. viii. p. 350.

[1] The island of Goa, (Ibn Batûta writes it "Kâwah"), now belonging to the Portuguese, but at that time a dependency of the Muhammedan kingdom of the Deccan. The place was surprised and captured by the Portuguese under Albuquerque in 1510; but they were expelled shortly after by 'Âdil Shâh, the reigning sovereign. It was retaken by them, the

side of them, and certain letters on the other.¹ In this island there is a fortress near the sea, walled round after our manner, in which there is sometimes a captain, who is called Savain, who has four hundred Mamelukes, he himself being also a Mameluke. When the said captain can procure any white man, he gives him very great pay, allotting him at least fifteen or twenty *pardai* per month. Before he inscribes him in the list of able men, he sends for two tunics made of leather, one for himself and the other for him who wishes to enlist; each puts on his tunic, and they fall to blows. If he finds him to be strong, he puts him in the list of able men; if not, he sets him to some other work than that of fighting. This captain, with four hundred Mamelukes, wages a great war with the king of Narsinga,² of whom we will speak at the proper season. I departed thence, and, travelling for seven days on the mainland, I arrived at a city which is called Decan.

year following, from 'Ádil Sháh's successor, and has remained in their possession ever since. It does not appear to have been a great mart of trade prior to the Portuguese conquest, but its commerce increased considerably during the early period of their domination. Ralph Fitch, who visited Goa in 1583, says: "there are many merchants of all nations." It has now fallen into a hopeless state of decay.

¹ *Pardao* or *pertab*. The same coin appears to have been called also a *hun*. According to Prinsep, it generally bore the figures of Siva and Parbatí on one side, and a pyramidal temple on the others: hence its name of *pagoda* among Europeans; but among Marsden's *Coins of Southern India*, there is one on plate xlviii. No. MLXXII., which in size and superscription agrees with that mentioned by Varthema, having on the one side the double figure of Siva and Parbatí, and on the obverse a legend shewing it to have been struck by a female sovereign whose title was "Sri Sadà-Sivà." See Marsden's *Numismata Orientalia*, vol. ii. p. 738.

² The Rajah of Bijayanagar, then the metropolis of the famous Brahminical kingdom of the Carnatic, between which and the 'Ádil Sháhi realm of the Deccan there was constant war at this period. See Scott's *Ferishta*, vol. i. pp. 207-225 *et seq.*

THE CHAPTER CONCERNING DECAN, A VERY BEAUTIFUL CITY OF INDIA, AND OF ITS MANY AND VARIOUS RICHES AND JEWELS.

In the said city of Decan there reigns a king who is a Mohammedan. The above-mentioned captain is in his pay, together with the said Mamelukes. This city is extremely beautiful, and very fertile. The king of it, between the Mamelukes and others of his kingdom, has twenty-five thousand men horse and foot. There is a beautiful palace in this city, in which there are forty-four chambers before you arrive at that of the king. This city is walled after the manner of the Christians, and the houses are very beautiful.[1]

[1] This was unquestionably Bijapûr, now a ruined town in the Sattâra district, near the eastern frontier, towards Hydrabâd, but formerly the metropolis of the Muhammedan kingdom of the Deccan. Fitch, describing Goa in 1583, says: "It standeth in the country of Hidalcan [Ed-Deccan], which lieth in the country six or seven days' journey. Its chief city is called Bisapor" [Bîjapûr]. The reigning prince in Varthema's time was Yûsûf Khân, the reputed son of Murâd II. of Anatolia, who had been purchased as a slave for the body-guard of the King of Bidar (Ahmedabâd), but who subsequently raised himself to the highest offices of the state, and finally assumed independent sovereignty as 'Âdil Shâh in 1501. His resources must have been great, for he built the vast citadel of Bijapûr, which he made his capital. Our traveller's account of the magnificence and prosperity of the city, and of the gorgeous retinue of the king, as well as his military prowess, is attested by the noble remains which mark the site of the once famous Bijapûr, and by the full account given by Ferishta of the reign of 'Âdil Shâh. A traveller who visited the place in 1852, thus describes the ruins of the Pâdishah's palace: "It was magnificence, indeed; far surpassing, I could almost say, that of any ancient or modern European palace I ever beheld,—I mean as regards space and style of architecture. The bastioned walls which enclose the palace and its precincts are about a mile and a half in circumference, enclosing a space of about sixty-two acres. The broad moat without is shaded by large tamarind trees, and the courts within the citadel are also full of trees......As for Raglan Castle, it could be put away in one corner of the Beejapore palace, and Kenilworth in another." He estimates the present population at about eleven thousand souls. See *Bombay Quarterly Magazine*, July 1853; also SYDENHAM's *Account of Bîjapûr*.

The king of the said city lives in great pride and pomp. A great number of his servants wear on the insteps of their shoes rubies and diamonds, and other jewels; so you may imagine how many are worn on the fingers of the hand and in the ears. There is a mountain in his kingdom where they dig out diamonds, which mountain is a league distant from the city, and is surrounded by a wall, and is kept by a great guard.[1] This realm is most abundant in everything, like the above-mentioned cities. They are all Mohammedans. Their dress consists of robes, or very beautiful shirts of silk, and they wear on their feet shoes or boots, with breeches after the fashion of sailors. The ladies go with their faces quite covered, according to the custom of Damascus.

THE CHAPTER CONCERNING THE ACTIVITY OF THE KING IN MILITARY AFFAIRS.

The above-mentioned king of Decan is always at war with the king of Narsinga, and all his country is Mohammedan. The greater part of his soldiers are foreigners and white men.[2] The natives of the kingdom are of a tawny colour. This king is extremely powerful, and very rich, and most liberal. He also possesses many naval vessels, and is a very great enemy of the Christians.[3] Departing thence, we went to another city, called Bathacala.

[1] Probably the locality mentioned by Tavernier, who says: "The first of the mines I visited is situated in the territories of the King of Visapour (Bíjapûr), in the province of Carnatica. The place is called Raolconda. It is five days' journey from Golconda, and eight or nine from Visapour." PINKERTON's *Voyages*, vol. viii. p. 235.

[2] According to Ferishta, 'Âdil Shâh entertained a large number of foreign auxiliaries in his service, among whom were many Abyssinians. He also mentions that his successor, Ismâ'îl 'Âdil Shâh, "formed an army of 10,000 cavalry, consisting of Arabians, Persians, Turks, Usbecks, Koords, and other foreigners." SCOTT's *Translation*, vol. i. p. 245.

[3] 'Âdil Shâh expelled the Portuguese from Goa on their first capture

THE CHAPTER CONCERNING BATHACALA, A CITY OF INDIA, AND OF ITS FERTILITY IN MANY THINGS, AND ESPECIALLY IN RICE AND SUGAR.

Bathacala,[1] a very noble city of India, is distant from Decan five days' journey. The king thereof is a pagan. This city is walled, and very beautiful, and about a mile distant from the sea. The king is subject to the king of Narsinga. This city has no seaport, the only approach to it being by a small river. There are many Moorish merchants

of that place in 1510. He appears to have been an enthusiast in matters of faith chiefly on political grounds. After solemnly establishing the Shiäh creed as the national religion, he subsequently retracted his opinions and restored the Sunni rites, in order to allay the serious opposition which his apostasy had excited among the zealous adherents of 'Omar, Abubekr, and 'Othmân.

[1] I find no difficulty in identifying this place with the more modern Sedasevaghur, which Thornton describes as "a town in the British district of North Canara, on the north side of the Kála Nuddi, and a mile east of its mouth." It is just within the Karwar Head, where, in Hamilton's time, there was a British factory, and an adjacent cove was used by our vessels as a harbour of refuge and to careen. Karwar, he says, "has the advantage of a good harbour on the south side of a bay, and a river capable of receiving ships of three hundred tuns. The Rajah is tributary to the Mogul at present, but formerly it was a part of Visapore's dominions before Aurungzeb conquered that country." He styles the town Batcoal and adds: "the Portuguese have an island called Anjediva, about two miles from Batcoal." (PINKERTON's *Voyages*, vol. viii. pp. 361-2.) These indications are sufficiently explicit to prevent our confounding Varthema's "Bathacala" with Batcull, (Buchanan's "Batuculla" and Hamilton's "Batacola,") where the British had also a factory. The latter is in lat. 13° 59', or fifteen miles *south* of Honahwar, while Varthema, who is travelling southward, reaches Bathacala three days before arriving at Honahwar.

As an attempt is being made to restore and improve the old harbour, it is to be hoped that the more ancient, simple, and euphonious title of Bathcal or Bathcole will be given to the new settlement. That of "Sedashevagur," or "Sudaseoghur," as it is more generally written, appears to have originated with Sedashwa Rao, one of the Rajahs of Soonda, who built a fort at Bathcal, and grew into importance on the overthrow of the great kingdom of Bijayanagar in 1565.

here, for it is a district of great traffic. The above-named stream passes close to the walls of the city, in which there is a great quantity of rice, and a great abundance of sugar, and especially of sugar candied, according to our manner. We begin here to find nuts and figs, after the manner of Calicut. These people are idolaters, also after the manner of Calicut, excepting the Moors, who live according to the Mohammedan religion. Neither horses, nor mules, nor asses, are customary here, but there are cows, buffaloes, sheep, oxen, and goats. In this country no grain, barley, or vegetables are produced, but other most excellent fruits, usual in India. I quitted this place, and went to another island, which is called Anzediva,[1] and which is inhabited by a certain sort of people who are Moors and pagans. This island is distant from the mainland half a mile, and is about twenty miles in circumference. The air is not very good here, neither is the place very fertile. There is an excellent port between the island and the mainland, and very good water is found in the said island.

THE CHAPTER CONCERNING CENTACOLA, ONOR, AND MANGOLOR, EXCELLENT DISTRICTS OF INDIA.

Travelling for one day from the aforesaid island, I arrived at a place called Centacola,[2] the lord of which is not very

---

[1] An island two miles distant from the coast of North Canara. "It is about a mile in length, and possessed by the Portuguese. It appears on the outside rocky, but of a pleasant aspect on the opposite side next the main, where it is fortified by a wall and some towers." (HORSBURGH's *Directory*, vol. i. p. 507.) The island was captured by the Portuguese in 1505. Varthema greatly exaggerates its dimensions.

[2] Centacola I take to be Uncola, (the "Ankla" of Hamilton and "Ancola" of Buchanan,) "the principal place in the subdivision of the same name, in the British district of North Canara, a town two miles from the Arabian Sea or North Indian Ocean." (THORNTON's *Gazetteer*.) Varthema was one day reaching Centacola from Angediva, and Uncola

rich. A great quantity of cow beef is met with here, and much rice, and good fruits customary in India. In this city there are many Moorish merchants. The lord of it is a pagan. The people are of a tawny colour: they go naked and bare-footed, and wear nothing on the head. This lord is subject to the king of Bethacala. Travelling thence for two days, we went to another place called Onor,[1] the king of

being in lat. 14° 40′, is five geographical miles south of that island. Buchanan makes the distance eight *cosses* from Ancola to Sedasivaghur, and describes the former town as having a ruined fort and a bazaar, but few inhabitants, "as in this part of the country the population does not settle in numbers in any spot, but is dispersed in hamlets and farms. Midway between Gaukarna and Ancola, which are three *cosses* apart, is the Gangawali, an inlet of salt water...Its mouth toward the sea is narrow, but inwards it forms a lake, which is from one mile to half that extent in width...Boats of a considerable size (patemars) can come over the bar, and ascend the river for three *cosses*...The river has no trade, and the country on its banks, though very beautiful, seems rather barren." PINKERTON, vol. viii. 362, 756-7.

[1] Honahwar, (the "Hinaur" of Ibn Batûta, "Honawera" of Buchanan, "Honaver" of Wilks, and the "Onore" of the generality of British writers,) is a seaport town in the British district of North Canara. "It is situated on the north side of an extensive estuary, or rather inlet, of the sea, which at its south-eastern extremity receives the Sheravutty, a considerable river flowing from the western ghats...The lake abounds in fish, great quantities of which are taken and made an article of commerce. This port was formerly a place of great commerce, and still has a trade in pepper, cocoa-nuts, betel-nut, fish, and some other articles, especially the fragrant sandal-wood, which grows in great abundance on the rocky hills of the country." THORNTON'S *Gazetteer*.

Ibn Batûta, who visited Honahwar towards the middle of the fourteenth century, describes its local features in similar terms. "The women of this city," he adds, "and of all the Indian districts on the sea-shores, never dress in clothes that have been stitched, but the contrary. One of them, for example, will tie one part of a piece of cloth round her waist, while the remaining part will be placed upon her head and breast. ...The present king is Jamâl ed-Dîn Muhammed ibn Hasan. He is one of the best of princes, but is himself subject to an infidel king whose name is Horaib." (LEE'S *Translation*, pp. 165-6.) The Portuguese built a strong fort here in the sixteenth century, from which they were subsequently expelled by the Rajah of Canara. Hamilton describes a pagan temple at Honahwar, which was visited yearly by a great number

which is a pagan, and is subject to the king of Narsinga. This king is a good fellow, and has seven or eight ships, which are always cruising about. He is a great friend of the king of Portugal. As to his dress, he goes quite naked, with the exception of a cloth about his middle. There is a great deal of rice here, as is usual in India, and some kinds of animals are found here, viz., wild hogs, stags, wolves, lions, and a great number of birds, different from ours; there are also many peacocks and parrots there. They have beef of cows, that is, red cows, and sheep in great abundance. Roses, flowers, and fruits, are found here all through the year. The air of this place is most perfect, and the people here are longer lived than we are. Near the said district of Onor there is another place, called Mangolor,[1] in which fifty or sixty ships are laden with rice. The inhabitants are pagans and Moors. Their mode of living, their customs, and their dress, are like those above described. We departed thence, and went to another city, which is called Canonor.

of pilgrims. In Ibn Batûta's time the greater part of the inhabitants were Muhammedans, and had committed the Korân to memory!

[1] A town in the British district of South Canara, situate on the north side of the estuary formed by the junction of a river flowing from the north-east, and of the Naitravutty, a considerable river, but navigable only by small vessels...The town is large, and is washed on east and west by the two streams whose confluence forms the estuary. The houses are generally mean, and there are no public buildings worth notice. Mangalore, though a bad haven, was the principal seaport of the territory of Hyder Ali. (See THORNTON's *Gazetteer*.) It appears to have been so long before his time, for Ibn Batûta, who calls it Manjerûn, says: "in this place are some of the greatest merchants of Persia and Yemen... The king of this place is the greatest of the kings of Malabar, and in it are about four thousand Muhammedan merchants." (LEE's *Translation*, p. 169.) Hamilton also describes it as "the greatest mart for trade in all the Canary dominions."

THE CHAPTER CONCERNING CANONOR, A VERY GREAT CITY IN INDIA.

Canonor[1] is a fine and large city, in which the king of Portugal has a very strong castle. The king of this city is a great friend of the king of Portugal,[2] although he is a

[1] A seaport town in the British district of Malabar, situate on the north shore of a small bay, open to the south, but sheltered towards the Arabian Sea by a bluff headland, surrounded by a fort...It is a populous place, but very irregularly built; yet has many good houses, chiefly belonging to the Moplai or Mussulman family, proprietors of the town. ...It is a port of considerable trade, principally in pepper, grain, timber and cocoa-nuts." (THORNTON's *Gazetteer*.) Hamilton mentions the fort built by the Portuguese in 1507, who, however, did not seize the town till some time after. They were expelled by the Dutch about the year 1660, and they in turn sold it to the Moplai family. It subsequently fell into the hands of Tippoo Sultân, from whom it was finally captured by the British under Abercrombie in 1791.

The mention of the Moplahs in the foregoing paragraph induces me to suggest a different derivation of the word to that generally received. Duncan supposes it to be contracted from Mahapilla, or "child of Mocha," in Arabia, from which country they originally came, as, in the language of Malabar, *Maha* means Mocha, and *pilla*, child. (THORNTON's *Gazetteer*, sub voce *Malabar*.) I am inclined to think that the name is either a corruption of the Arabic *Múflih*, (from the root *fálaha*, to till the soil,) meaning prosperous or victorious,—in which sense it would apply to the successful establishments of these foreign Mussulmans on the western coast of India ; or, that it is a similar corruption of *Múflih*, (the active participial form of the same verb,) an agriculturist, —a still more appropriate designation of the Moplahs, who, according to Buchanan, are both traders and farmers. In the latter sense, the term, though not usually so applied among the Arabs, would be identical with *Felláh*, which is also a derivative from the triliteral root *fálaha*.

[2] The sequel will show that Varthema is here anticipating, in part, what did not actually take place till two or three years after his first visit, which must have occurred between 1504-5. The Portuguese under Pedro Alvarez Cabral made their first appearance at Cannanore on the 15th of January 1501. The second expedition, which was commanded by Juan de Nueva, followed in November of the same year, and on both occasions the foreigners were received and treated with the greatest consideration by the inhabitants, the Rajah himself offering to become their security for a large amount of produce rather than that their ships

pagan. This Canonor is the port at which the horses which come from Persia disembark. And you must know that every horse pays twenty-five ducats for customs duty, and then they proceed on the mainland towards Narsinga. There are many Moorish merchants in this city. No grain nor grapes grow here, nor any productions like ours, excepting cucumbers and melons. Bread is not eaten here, that is to say, by the natives of the country, but they eat rice, fish, flesh, and the nuts of the country. At the proper time we will speak of their religion and customs, for they live after the manner of those of Calicut. Here we begin to find a few spices, such as pepper, ginger, cardamums, mirabolans, and a little cassia. This place is not surrounded by a wall. The houses are very poor. Here also are found fruits different from ours, and which are also far superior to ours. I will make the comparison when the proper time comes. The country is well adapted for war, as it is full of hollow places artificially made. The king of this place has 50,000 Naeri,[1] that is, gentlemen who fight with swords, shields, lances and bows, and with artillery. And yet they go naked and unshod, with a cloth around them, without anything on their heads, excepting when they go to war, when they wear a turban of a red colour passed twice round the head, and they all have them tied in the same manner. They do not use here either horses, mules, camels, or asses. Elephants are sometimes used, but not for battle. At the proper time we will speak of the vigour exerted by the king

should return to Europe empty. In 1502 Vasco de Gama established a factory there, and the year following the Rajah gave him a house for the purpose, and entered into an offensive and defensive alliance with the Portuguese; but the fort does not appear to have existed till 1507, when Don Francisco de Almeyda, the first Viceroy, obtained permission to build it in the harbour, where he left Lorenzo de Britto with 150 men, and two vessels to cruise on the coast. See GREENE's *Collection of Voyages*, vol. i. pp. 48-60.

[1] Buchanan says: "the Nairs are the pure Súdras of Malayala, and all pretend to be born soldiers...They form the militia of Malayala, and their chief delight is in arms." PINKERTON's *Voyages*, viii. 735-6.

of Canonor against the Portuguese. There is much traffic in this place, to which two hundred ships come every year from different countries. Having spent some days here we took our way towards the kingdom of Narsinga, and travelled on the mainland for fifteen[1] days towards the east, and came to a city called Bisinegar.

THE CHAPTER CONCERNING BISINEGAR, A VERY FERTILE CITY OF NARSINGA IN INDIA.

The said city of Bisinegar[2] belongs to the king of Narsinga, and is very large and strongly walled. It is situated

[1] Abd er-Razzâk was eighteen days travelling between Bijayanagar and Maganor (Mangalore).

[2] Narsinga or Bijayanagar, (I believe that to be the correct orthography of the latter name, but it is spelt in a great variety of ways by modern as well as by earlier writers,) now a ruined city, was formerly the capital of the ancient Brahminical kingdom of the Carnatic, which before the conquests of the Muhammedans extended over the greater part of the peninsula between the Malabar and Coromandel coasts. It is situated on the western bank of the river Toongabudra, in lat. 15° 19', long. 76° 32'. It was visited by Abd er-Razzâk and by Nicolò de' Conti A.D. 1442-1445, and described about twenty-five years later by Nikitin, and their several narratives, contained in the volume entitled *India in the Fifteenth Century* of the HAKLUYT SOCIETY's Publications, concur in corroborating Varthema's brief sketch of the vastness and magnificence of this once famous metropolis, and the splendour of its court. The number of elephants, their strength and sagacity, and the large army of the Rajah, which Conti estimated at 90,000 men in the city alone, attracted the special attention of these early travellers. At the period of Varthema's visit, the administration of affairs was in the hands of Heemraj, one of the principal ministers of state, who on the death of See Rajah became regent on behalf of his son, a minor, who died shortly after, and Heemraj so disposed of his successors that he retained almost absolute sway for forty years, and was succeeded in office by his son Ramraj, during whose reign the power of the Bijayanagar state was broken by a confederacy of the Mussulman kings of the Deccan at the battle of Talikote in 1565. "Since that time," writes Ferishta, "the *raj* of Beejnugger has never recovered its ancient splendour; and the

on the side of a mountain, and is seven miles in circumference. It has a triple circle of walls. It is a place of great merchandise, is extremely fertile, and is endowed with all possible kinds of delicacies. It occupies the most beautiful site, and possesses the best air that were ever seen: with certain very beautiful places for hunting and the same for fowling, so that it appears to me to be a second paradise. The king of this city is a pagan, with all his kingdom, that is to say, idolaters. He is a very powerful king, and keeps up constantly 40,000 horsemen. And you must know that a horse is worth at least 300, 400, and 500 *pardai*, and some are purchased for 800 *pardai*, because horses are not produced there, neither are many mares found there, because those kings who hold the seaports do not allow them to be brought there. The said king also possesses 400 elephants and some dromedaries, which dromedaries run with great swiftness. It occurs to me here to touch upon a subject worthy of notice, viz., the discretion, the intelligence, and the strength of the elephant. We will first say in what manner he fights. When an elephant goes into battle he carries a saddle, in the same manner as they are borne by the mules of the kingdom of Naples, fastened underneath by two iron chains. On each side of the said saddle he carries a large and very strong wooden box, and in each box there go three men. On the neck of the elephant, between the boxes, they place a plank the size of half a span, and between the boxes and the plank a man sits astride who

city itself has been so destroyed, that it is now totally in ruins and uninhabited; while the country has been seized by the zemindars, each of whom hath assumed an independent power in his own district." After this disaster, the court was removed to Pennaconda, about ninety miles to the southward of Bellary, where the ruins of this once powerful dynasty continued to cast a lingering look at its former greatness till the country was subjected by Aurungzib in 1685. Bijayanagar, however, was still a large city when visited by Cæsar Fredericke in 1567. See Scott's *Ferishta*, vol. i. pp. 262, 295-298. Wilks's *Historical Sketches of the South of India*, Calcutta, pp. 4-15.

speaks to the elephant, for the said elephant possesses more intelligence than any other animal in the world; so that there are in all seven persons who go upon the said elephant; and they go armed with shirts of mail, and with bows and lances, swords and shields. And in like manner they arm the elephant with mail, especially the head and the trunk. They fasten to the trunk a sword two *braccia* long, as thick and as wide as the hand of a man. And in that way they fight.[1] And he who sits upon his neck orders him: " Go forward," or " Turn back," " Strike this one," " Strike that one," " Do not strike any more," and he understands as though he were a human being. But if at any time they are put to flight it is impossible to restrain them; for this race of people are great masters of the art of making fireworks, and these animals have a great dread of fire, and through this means they sometimes take to flight. But in every way this animal is the most discreet in the world and the most powerful. I have seen three elephants bring a ship from the sea to the land, in the manner as I will tell you. When I was in Canonor, some Moorish merchants brought a ship on shore in this manner, after the custom of Christians. They beach ships the prow foremost, but here they put the side of the vessel foremost, and under the said ship they put three pieces of wood, and on the side next the sea I saw three elephants kneel down and with their heads push the ship on to dry land.[2] Many say that the elephant has no joints, and I say that it is true that they have not the joints so high as other animals, but they have them low. I

---

[1] Nikitin's description is very similar. He says: "Elephants are greatly used in battle. Large scythes are attached to their trunks and tusks, and the animals are clad in ornamental plates of steel. They carry a citadel, and in the citadel twelve men in armour with guns and arrows." *India in the Fifteenth Century*, iii. p. 12.

[2] Turpin mentions that the Siamese make use of the elephant "to shove vessels into the water, which he does with his back." PINKERTON'S *Voyages*, vol. i. p. 615.

tell you, moreover, that the female elephant is stronger and more proud than the male, and some of the females are mad. The said elephants are as large as three buffaloes, and they have a skin like that of the buffalo, and eyes like those of a pig, and a trunk reaching to the ground, and with this they put their food into their mouth as also their drink; for their mouth is situated beneath their throat, and almost like a pig or a sturgeon. This trunk is hollow within, and I have many times seen them fish up a quattrino from the ground with it. And with this trunk I have seen them pull down a branch from a tree which twenty-four of our men could not pull to the ground with a rope, and the elephant tore it down with three pulls. The two teeth which are seen are in the upper jaw. The ears are two *palmi* every way, some more, some less. Their legs are almost as large at the lower extremity as at the upper. Their feet are round like a very large trencher for cutting meat on, and around the foot there are five nails as large as the shell of an oyster. The tail is as long as that of a buffalo, about three *palmi* long, and has a few scattered hairs. The female is smaller than the male. With respect to the height of the said elephant, I have seen a great many thirteen and fourteen *palmi* high, and I have ridden on some of that height; they say, moreover, that some are found fifteen *palmi* high. Their walk is very slow, and those who are not accustomed to it cannot ride them, because it upsets their stomach, just as it does in travelling by sea. The small elephants have a pace like that of a mule, and it is a pleasure to ride them. When the said elephants are to be ridden, the said elephant lowers one of the hind legs, and by that leg it is mounted; nevertheless, you must help yourself or be helped to mount. You must also know that the said elephants do not carry a bridle or halter, or anything bound on the head.

THE CHAPTER SHOWING HOW ELEPHANTS GENERATE.

The said elephant, when he wishes to generate, goes into a secret place, that is, into the water in certain marshes,[1] and they unite and generate like human beings. In some countries, I have seen that the finest present which can be made to a king is the parts of an elephant, which said king eats the said parts; for in some countries an elephant is worth fifty ducats, in some other countries it is worth one thousand and two thousand ducats. So that, in conclusion, I say that I have seen some elephants which have more understanding, and more discretion and intelligence, than any kind of people I have met with. This king of Narsinga is the richest king I have ever heard spoken of. This city is situated like Milan, but not in a plain. The residence of the king is here, and his realms are placed as it might be the realm of Naples and also Venice; so that he has the sea on both sides. His Brahmins, that is, his priests, say that he possesses a revenue of 12,000 *pardai* per day. He is constantly at war with several Moorish and pagan kings. His faith is idolatrous, and they worship the devil, as do those of Calicut. When the proper time comes we will state in what manner they worship him. They live like pagans. Their dress is this: the men of condition wear a short shirt, and on their head a cloth of gold and silk in the Moorish fashion, but nothing on the feet. The common people go quite naked, with the exception of a piece of cloth about their middle. The king wears a cap of gold brocade two spans long, and when he goes to war he wears a quilted dress of cotton, and over it he puts another garment full of golden piastres, and having all around it jewels of various kinds. His horse is worth more than some of our cities, on account of the ornaments which it wears. When he rides for his pleasure he is always accompanied by three

[1] This peculiarity is also noticed by Turpin. *Id*. p. 614.

K

or four kings, and many other lords, and five or six thousand horse. Wherefore he may be considered to be a very powerful lord. His money consists of a *pardao*, as I have said. He also coins a silver money called *tare*, and others of gold, twenty of which go to a *pardao*, and are called *fanom*. And of these small ones of silver, there go sixteen to a *fanom*. They also have another coin called *cas*, sixteen of which go to a *tare* of silver.[1] In this kingdom you can go

---

[1] The subjoined is a comparison of the Hindu coins current at Bijayanagar, and their relative value, as given by 'Abd er-Razzák and Varthema.

'ABD ER-RAZZAK, A.D. 1443. *Gold Coins* (with alloy).	VARTHEMA, A.D. 1504-5. *Gold Coins.*
Varáha = 2 Dinârs, *Kopcki.*	. . . .
Pertab = ½ a Varáha.	Pardao . . . . . .
Fanam = 1-10th of a Pertab.	Fanom = 1-20th of a Pardao.
Pure Silver.	*Silver.*
Tar = ⅙th of a Fanom.	Tare = 1-15th of a Fanom.
Copper.	*Copper.*
Djitel = ⅓rd of a Tar.	Cas = 1-16th of a silver Tare, (equal to a Venetian *quattrino*.)

The *Varáha* and the *Half Varáha*, called *Pertab* or *Pardao*, was the *Hun* of subsequent Mussulman writers and the *Pagoda* of Europeans, the latter a Portuguese appellation derived from the pyramidal temple generally depicted on one side of it. In 'Abd er-Razzák's *Varáha* and *Pertab* we have, consequently, the *Single* and *Double Pagoda* of after times. Varthema omits all mention of the *Varáha*, but as he gives twenty *Fanams* to the *Pardao*, while 'Abd er-Razzák allows only ten, his *Pardao* was probably identical with the *Varáha* or *Double Pagoda*. Hence, it appears that the gold coinage of the Bijayanagar state had undergone no material change in the half century intervening between the visits of the two travellers.

The silver coinage must have fluctuated considerably, for whereas 'Abd er-Razzák gives only six *Tars* to a *Fanam*, Varthema allows fifteen. Probably, the *Tar* of the latter was of a baser metal; that of the former is described particularly as being "cast in pure silver."

There is a still greater difference in the copper money of the two travellers, quite sufficient, indeed, to lead to the inference that the *Djitel* and the *Cas* were different coins; but as I am quite unlearned in Numismatics, I must leave these discrepancies to be solved by others. Prinsep

everywhere in safety. But it is necessary to be on your guard against some lions which are on the road. I will not speak of their food at the present time, because I wish to describe it when we shall be in Calicut, where there are the same customs and the same manner of living. This king is a very great friend of the Christians, especially of the king of Portugal, because he does not know much of any other Christians. When the Portuguese arrive in his territories they do them great honour. When we had seen this so noble city for some days we turned towards Canonor. And when we had arrived there, at the end of three days we took our way by land and went to a city called Tormapatani.

THE CHAPTER CONCERNING TORMAPATANI, A CITY OF INDIA; AND CONCERNING PANDARANI, A PLACE ONE DAY DISTANT; AND CONCERNING CAPOGATTO, A SIMILAR DISTRICT.

Tormapatani[1] is distant from Canonor twelve miles, and the lord of it is a Pagan. The land is not very rich, and is

affords but scanty assistance relative to the old Hindu coinage of the Carnatic.

It deserves to be noticed that neither 'Abd er-Razzâk nor Varthema mentions the *Cowrie* as forming part of the currency. Ibn Batûta specifies it under the Arabic name of *Wada'*, remarks that it was collected in the Maldive Islands where it passed for money, and was sent in large quantities to Bengal, where it was also current instead of coin. LEE's *Translation*, p. 178.

Nicolò de' Conti's account of the Indian currency in his time is very loose and unsatisfactory. He says: "In some parts of anterior India, Venetian ducats are in circulation. Some have golden coins, weighing more than double of our florin, and also less, and, moreover, silver and brass money. In some places pieces of gold worked to a certain weight are used as money." *India in the Fifteenth Century*, ii. p. 30.

[1] This is, undoubtedly, the *Dormapatam* of Hamilton, a harbour near the Tellicherry river, a little to the northward of that town, which latter I presume to be the place which Varthema indicates. Barbosa calls it

one mile from the sea, and it has a river not very large.
There are many vessels of Moorish merchants here. The
people of this country live miserably, and the greatest riches
here consist of Indian nuts, and these they eat there with a
little rice. They have plenty of timber here for building
ships. In this land there are about fifteen thousand Moors,
and they are subject to the Sultan or pagan lord. I do not
speak of their manner of living at present, because it will
be described in Calicut, inasmuch as they are all of one and
the same faith. The houses in this city are not too good,
for a house is worth half a ducat, as I will explain to you
further on. Here we remained two days, and then departed
and went to a place which is called Pandarani,[1] distant from

"Termapatani," and describes it as situated on a river with two outlets
to the sea, inhabited chiefly by *Mapuleres* (Moplahs,) who are great
merchants, and as the limit of the kingdom of Cannanore in the direction of Calicut. (*Ramusio*, vol. i. p. 335.) "The neighbouring country
is highly productive, the low lands producing annually two, and in some
places three, crops of rice in the year. The cocoa-nut tree also grows
in great abundance and perfection....The population is estimated at
twenty thousand, the majority of whom are Mussulman Moplahs."
(THORNTON's *Gazetteer*.) I am inclined to identify either Ibn Batûta's
"Jarafattan" or "Badafattan," both of which occur between his "Hîlî"
and "Kâlikût," with this Dormepatam, or, as Baldæus writes it, "Termapatan." Hîlî I take to be the Ulala of Buchanan, "a large town on the
south side of the lake of Mangalore, and formerly the residence of a
petty prince." PINKERTON's *Voyages*, vol. viii. p. 747.

[1] This name and that of Capogatto, the town next mentioned, have disappeared from the modern maps; but if not identical with Waddakarre and
Tikodi, they must be sought for in the vicinity of those places, which I
find spelt in a variety of ways by old travellers. Hamilton has "Burgara" and "Cottica," and off Cottica he says is "the Sacrifice Rock,
about eight miles in the sea," which is, doubtless, Varthema's "insula
deshabitata." D'Anville has "Bergare" and "Cotta": Buchanan writes
the former "Barrygurry" or "Vadacurry," and Arrowsmith makes
"Kotacull" of the latter; but the diversity is as endless as it is perplexing. Both places, however, are distinctly mentioned by Baldæus in
his account of the early proceedings of the Portuguese on the Malabar
coast:—"Between Cananor and Calecut lies the town of Panane seated
upon the seashore....In this place the Sammoryn kept his residence

this one day's journey, and which is subject to the king of
Calicut. This place is a wretched affair, and has no port.
Opposite to the said city, in the sea three leagues or thereabout, there is an uninhabited island. The manner of living
of this Pandarini, and their customs, are the same as those
of Calicut. This city is not level, and the land is high. We
departed hence and went to another place called Capogatto,
which is also subject to the king of Calicut. This place has

when Vasco de Gama came into those parts...The Sammoryn sent certain pilots to conduct the Portuguese fleet into the harbour of *Capogate*, where there was much better and safer anchorage." (CHURCHILL's *Collection of Voyages*, vol. iii. p. 625.) Another version of that visit, which occurred in 1498, describes De Gama's landing at *Padarane* and his progress towards *Kapokats*, where his attendants rested to refresh themselves. (GREENE's *Collection*, vol. i. pp. 30, 31.) This place, *Pandarani* or *Panane*, must not be confounded with Varthema's *Ponnani* to the south of Calicut, which Thornton writes " Ponany."

Barbosa also mentions a *Panderani* between Cannanore and Calicut, and describes it as inhabited by Moors, and as a great haven for ships; but he places it to the south of Capogatto, whereas Varthema's *Pandarani* occurs to the north of his Capogatto. I am of opinion that the seeming discrepancy arises from a similarity in the names of two different places. Barbosa's Capogatto he describes as situated about twelve miles up the river of *Tarmapatam*, whereas Varthema's Capogatto was evidently a seaport town, only four leagues distant from Calicut. Hence, I find no difficulty in identifying it with Barbosa's *Capucar*, which he locates six miles to the north of Calicut. He says : " Beyond this [Panderani] there is another place with a river, called Capucar, where there are many Moors, natives of the country, and many ships, and they carry on a large trade with the merchandize of the country, which is brought hither to be shipped...Six miles beyond this place is Calicut." (*Ramusio*, vol. i. p. 311.) There are several lacunæ in Barbosa's narrative of this part of the coast as given by Ramusio, owing apparently to a defect in the original MS. The following is his list of places as they occur consecutively between Cannanore and Calicut: CANANOR ; Crecate ; ...Tarmapatam ; Capogatto ;...Padripatam, the frontier of the kingdom of Calicut; Tircori ; Panderani ; Capucar ; CALICUT.

Though his description of the locality is widely different, I am nevertheless disposed to identify Varthema's *Pandarani* with Ibn Batûta's " Fandarainâ," where he landed before reaching Calicut from the northward. See LEE's *Translation*, p. 171.

*

a very beautiful palace, built in the ancient style, and there is a small river towards the south, and it is four leagues distant from Calicut. There is nothing to be said here, because they follow the manner and style of Calicut. We departed hence and went to the very noble city of Calicut. I have not written about the manner of living, the customs and faith, the administration of justice, dress, and country of Chiavul and of Dabul, of Bathacala, nor of the king of Onor, nor of Mangalor, nor of Canonor, nor, indeed, of the king of Cucin, nor of the king of Caicolone, nor of that of Colon, neither have I spoken of the king of Narsinga. Now I will speak of the king here in Calicut, because he is the most important king of all those before mentioned, and is called Samory,[1] which in the pagan language means God on earth.

[1] The English "Zamorin." According to some, this is a corruption of *Tamuri*, the name of the most exalted family of the Nair caste. Buchanan says: "The Tamuri pretends to be of a higher rank than the Brahmans, and to be inferior only to the invisible gods, a pretension that was acknowledged by his subjects, but which is held as absurd and abominable by the Brahmans, by whom he is only treated as a Súdra." (PINKERTON's *Voyages*, vol. viii. p. 735.) Others derive the title from *Zamoodin*, the sea; and the Zamorin of Calicut is so called from his being the Lord of the Sea.

THE SECOND BOOK CONCERNING INDIA.

Having nearly arrived at the head of India, that is to say, at the place in which the greatest dignity of India is centered, it has appeared to me fitting to bring the First book to an end and commence the Second; as, moreover, I have to lay before every kind reader matters of greater importance and comfort to the intellect, and of courage, so far as our favourite labour of travelling through the world may assist us and our intelligence may serve us, submitting, however, everything to the judgment of men who may, perhaps, have visited more countries than I have.

THE CHAPTER CONCERNING CALICUT, A VERY LARGE CITY OF INDIA.

Calicut[1] is on the mainland, the sea beats against the walls of the houses. There is no port here, but about a mile from

---

[1] Calicut, a seaport town in the British district of Malabar. "It is situate on the open beach, there being neither river nor haven; and ships must anchor in the open sea…The haven, said to have been once capacious, has been filled up with drifted sand…Forbes, who visited it in 1772, speaks of it as offering very little to interest a traveller, being chiefly composed of low huts shaded by cocoa-nut trees, on a sandy shore." (Thornton's *Gazetteer*.) Ibn Batûta describes Calicut as "one of the greatest ports in the district of Malabar;" Nicolò de' Conti as "a maritime city, eight miles in circumference, a noble emporium for all

the place towards the south there is a river, which is narrow at its embouchure and has not more than five or six spans of water. This stream flows through Calicut and has a great number of branches. This city has no wall around it, but the houses extend for about a mile, built close together, and then the wide houses, that is, the houses separate one from the other,[1] cover a space of about six miles. The houses are very poor. The walls are about as high as a man on horseback, and the greater part are covered with leaves, and without any upper room. The reason is this, that when they dig down four or five spans, water is found, and therefore they cannot build large houses.[2] However, the house of a merchant is worth fifteen or twenty ducats. Those of the common people are worth half a ducat each, or one or two ducats at the most.

THE CHAPTER CONCERNING THE KING OF CALICUT AND THE RELIGION OF THE PEOPLE.

The King of Calicut is a Pagan, and worships the devil in the manner you shall hear. They acknowledge that there is a God who has created the heaven and the earth and all

---

India ;" and 'Abd er-Razzák as " a perfectly secure harbour, which, like that of Hormuz, brings together merchants from every city, and from every country."

[1] That is, houses with *compounds*, as the open space around them is called by Anglo-Indians.

[2] In a subsequent chapter, Varthema alleges the same reason for the lowness and insignificance of the Zamorin's palace at Calicut. The following extract from Hamilton seems to corroborate his statement:—
" In anno 1703, about the middle of February, I called at Calecut on my way to Surat, and, standing into the road, I chanced to strike on some of the ruins of the sunken town built by the Portuguese in former times. Whether that town was swallowed up by an earthquake, as some affirm, or whether it was undermined by the sea, I will not determine." PINKERTON's *Voyages*, vol. viii. p. 378.

the world;[1] and they say that if he wished to judge you and
me, a third and a fourth, he would have no pleasure in being
Lord; but that he has sent this his spirit, that is the devil,
into this world to do justice: and to him who does good he does
good, and to him who does evil he does evil. Which devil
they call Deumo,[2] and God they call Tamerani.[3] And the
King of Calicut keeps this Deumo in his chapel in his
palace, in this wise: his chapel is two paces wide in each of
the four sides, and three paces high, with a wooden door
covered with devils carved in relief.[4] In the midst of this
chapel there is a devil made of metal, placed in a seat also
made of metal. The said devil has a crown made like that
of the papal kingdom, with three crowns; and it also has
four horns and four teeth, with a very large mouth, nose,
and most terrible eyes. The hands are made like those of a
flesh-hook, and the feet like those of a cock; so that he
is a fearful object to behold. All the pictures around the
said chapel are those of devils, and on each side of it there

[1] "They all believe in a great God, whose image they can neither fancy nor make." HAMILTON.

[2] "The word *Dev* means, indefinitely, a dweller in the upper worlds, and, more particularly, an inhabitant of Swerga, the paradise where Indra rules. Three hundred and thirty millions of Devs are spoken of in the Hindu scriptures; but, in its sense of God, the term can only apply to one being." (See FORBES's *Rás Málá*, vol. ii. pp. 423-442, for an able dissertation on this subject.) Varthema draws a distinction between a "Diavolo" and a "Sathanas," evidently making the latter the higher personage; but it is surprising that he gives so tolerably correct an account of the Hindu theogony and worship.

[3] *Tumbarán*, lord or master, is a common title of honour, throughout Malabar, among the higher classes of Nairs.

[4] "The great men of the clergy build temples, but they are neither large nor beautiful. Their images are all black and deformed, according as they fancy the infernal gods to be shaped, who, they believe, have some hand in governing the world, particularly about the benign and malignant seasons that happen in the productions or sterility of the earth, for which reason they pay a lateral adoration to them." (PINKERTON's *Voyages*, vol. viii. p. 376.) This quotation from Hamilton shows that, like Varthema, he understood the *Devs* to be devils.

is a Sathanas seated in a seat, which seat is placed in a flame of fire, wherein are a great number of souls, of the length of half a finger and a finger of the hand. And the said Sathanas holds a soul in his mouth with the right hand, and with the other seizes a soul under the waist. Every morning the Brahmins, that is the priests, go to wash the said idol all over with scented water, and then they perfume it;[1] and when it is perfumed they worship it; and some time in the course of the week they offer sacrifice to it in this manner: They have a certain small table, made and ornamented like an altar, three spans high from the ground, four spans wide, and five long; which table is extremely well adorned with roses, flowers, and other ornaments. Upon this table they have the blood of a cock and lighted coals in a vessel of silver, with many perfumes upon them. They also have a thurible, with which they scatter incense around the said altar. They have a little bell of silver which rings very frequently, and they have a silver knife with which they have killed the cock, and which they tinge with the blood, and sometimes place it upon the fire, and sometimes they take it and make motions similar to those which one makes who is about to fence; and finally, all that blood is burnt, the waxen tapers being kept lighted during the whole time. The priest who is about to perform this sacrifice puts upon his arms, hands, and feet some bracelets of silver, which make a very great noise like bells, and he wears on his neck an amulet (what it is I do not know); and when he has finished performing the sacrifice, he takes both his hands full of grain and retires from the said altar, walking backwards and always looking at the altar until he arrives at a certain tree. And when he has reached the tree, he throws the grain above his head as

[1] Forbes says: "The ordinary Hindu religious service consists in performing for the idol such acts as a menial servant performs for his human master." Among these, which are given in detail, he describes the anointing of the Dev with sandal-wood dust and water, and the burning of incense before him.

high as he can over the tree; he then returns and removes everything from the altar.¹

THE CHAPTER CONCERNING THE MANNER OF EATING OF THE KING OF CALICUT.

When the King of Calicut wishes to eat he uses the following customs: you must know that four of the principal Brahmins take the food which the king is to eat and carry it to the devil, and first they worship him in this manner: they raise their clasped hands over his head, and then draw their hands towards them, still clasped together, and the thumb raised upwards, and then they present to him the food which is to be given to the king, and stand in this manner as long as a person would require to eat it; and then the said Brahmins carry that food to the king. You must know that this is done only for the purpose of paying honour to that idol, in order that it may appear that the king will not eat unless the food has been first presented to Deumo.²

---

¹ I have not been able to verify this particular service; but it is generally known that animal sacrifices, propitiatory of the *Bhuta*, or wicked spirits, are offered by several sects of the Brahmins. Among the victims so offered by the Hindus of Mysore, the Abbé Dubois mentions buffaloes, hogs, rams, cocks, and the like. The amulet *(pentacola)* noticed by Varthema was probably the *poonool*, or Brahminical thread.

² An apt illustration of what St. Paul says (1 Cor. viii.) respecting meats offered to idols.

A Brahmin can only eat of what is prepared by one of his own caste. Buchanan states that the Kurūm, the highest order of Nairs in Malabar, act as cooks on all public occasions, which, among Hindus, is a sure mark of transcendent rank; for every person can eat the food prepared by one of higher birth than himself. Marco Polo notices the custom prevailing among the Brahmins of eating off leaves:—"Instead of dishes, they lay their victuals on dry leaves of the apples of Paradise," meaning, probably, the plantain. See Pinkerton's *Voyages*, vol. viii. pp. 735-6. Greene's *Collection*, vol. iv. p. 616.

The elaborate ceremonial of a Brahmin's repast is thus described by Forbes:—"The Brahmin, when his food is ready, before eating, performs

This food is in a wooden vessel, in which there is a very
large leaf of a tree, and upon this leaf is placed the said
food, which consists of rice and other things. The king eats
on the ground without any other thing. And when he eats,
the Brahmins stand around, three or four paces distant from
him, with great reverence, and remain bowed down with
their hands before their mouths, and their backs bent. No
one is allowed to speak while the king is speaking, and they
stand listening to his words with great reverence. When
the king has finished his meal, the said Brahmins take that
food which the king did not require and carry it into a court
yard and place it on the ground. And the said Brahmins
clap their hands three times, and at this clapping a very
great number of black crows come to this said food and eat
it.[1] These crows are used for this purpose, and they are free

Turpun, that is to say, he fills a copper with water, and puts therein a
few grains of barley, some sesamum, leaves of the sacred basil tree,
sandal, etc.; then, holding some sacrificial grass, he fills his joined
hands with water, which he pours back again into the cup, saying: 'I
offer this water to all the *Devs*.' He proceeds to make similar offerings
of water to men, animals, trees, rivers, seas, *Bhuts*, *Prets*, *Reeshees*, pro-
genitors, and others. Then he mentions the names, as many as he can
recollect, of his father's ancestors, his mother's ancestors, and his own
deceased friends. He now performs *hom*, or fire worship, by throwing a
portion of rice and clarified butter into a little copper or earthen vessel
containing fire, repeating, while so employed, the names of the *Devs*.
The Brahmin sets aside five portions of food for cows, beggars, dogs, ants,
and crows. He then takes a little of each dish, and offers it to the
Dev, in a vessel containing five divisions. He now sits down to breakfast." *Rás Málá*, vol. ii. p. 257.

[1] In Western India these birds do not generally wait to be summoned:
the difficulty is to scare them away when food is being served. Their
cunning, moreover, equals their pertinacity. I once saw a proof of this,
which I could hardly have believed on the testimony of another. A
flock of crows covered the branches of a tree, waiting for any offal from
a dinner which had just terminated. A dog brought out a bone into
the garden, and was quietly enjoying it, when the whole bevy alighted
and commenced an attack upon him in front. As often as they charged
in that direction the dog kept them at bay, until at length, as if by
concert among themselves, one of the assailants moved to the rear and

and go wherever they please, and no injury is done to them.

THE CHAPTER CONCERNING THE BRAHMINS, THAT IS THE PRIESTS OF CALICUT.

It is a proper, and at the same time a pleasant thing to know who these Brahmins are. You must know that they are the chief persons of the faith, as priests are among us. And when the king takes a wife he selects the most worthy and the most honoured of these Brahmins and makes him sleep the first night with his wife, in order that he may deflower her.[1] Do not imagine that the Brahmin goes willingly to perform this operation. The king is even obliged to pay him four hundred or five hundred ducats. The king only and no other person in Calicut adopts this practice. We will now describe what classes [or castes] of Pagans there are in Calicut.

THE CHAPTER CONCERNING THE PAGANS OF CALICUT, AND OF WHAT CLASSES THEY ARE.

The first class of Pagans in Calicut are called Brahmins. The second are Naeri, who are the same as the gentlefolks

quietly pecked at the dog's tail. While he savagely faced about to repel this unexpected assault, one of the enemy in front pounced upon the contested bone and carried it away in triumph.

[1] Hamilton says: "When the Samorin marries, he must not cohabit with his bride till the Nambourie, or chief priest, has enjoyed her, and, if he pleases, he may have three nights of her company, because the first-fruits of her nuptials must be an holy oblation to the god she worships." Buchanan confirms the statement:—"These ladies [of the Tamuri family] are generally impregnated by Namburis; although if they choose they may employ the higher ranks of Nairs; but the sacred character of the Namburis always procures them a preference." PINKERTON's *Voyages*, vol. viii. pp. 374, 734.

amongst us; and these are obliged to bear sword and shield or bows or lances. When they go through the street, if they did not carry arms they would no longer be gentlemen. The third class of Pagans are called Tiva, who are artizans. The fourth class are called Mechua, and these are fishermen. The fifth class are called Poliar, who collect pepper, wine, and nuts. The sixth class are called Hirava, and these plant and gather in rice. These two last classes of people, that is to say, the Poliar and Hirava, may not approach either the Naeri or the Brahmins within fifty paces, unless they have been called by them, and they always go by private ways through the marshes. And when they pass through the said places, they always go crying out with a loud voice, and this they do in order that they may not meet the Naeri or the Brahmins; for should they not be crying out, and any of the Narci should be going that way and see their fruits, or meet any of the said class, the above mentioned Naeri may kill them without incurring any punishment: and for this reason they always cry out. So now you have heard about these six classes of Pagans.[1]

[1] Hamilton's classification reads like a revised version of Varthema's:—"There are many degrees or dignities in the church as well as in the state. The *Nambouris* are first in both capacities. The *Brahmins* are the second in the church only. The *Buts*, or magicians, are next to them. The *Nayers*, or gentlemen, are next, and are very numerous. The *Teyvees* are the farmers of cocoa-nut trees, and are next to the gentry. The *Poulias* produce the labourers and mechanics. The *Muckwas*, or fishers, are I think a higher tribe than the Poulias, but the *Poulichees* are the lowest order of human creatures, and are excluded from the benefit of divine and human laws. If a Poulia or Teyvee meet a Nair on the road, he must go aside to let his worship pass, lest the air should be tainted, on pain of severe chastisement if not of death; but the Poulichees are in a much worse state...If accidentally they see any one coming towards them, they will howl like dogs, and run away, lest those of quality should take offence at their breathing in the same air that they do." The Poulichees seem to be the same people that Buchanan describes under the name of *Niadis*, and both bear a general resemblance to Varthema's "Hirava," though he describes them as cultivators of rice, whereas the former are not allowed to till the ground, but

THE CHAPTER CONCERNING THE DRESS OF THE KING AND QUEEN AND OTHERS OF CALICUT, AND OF THEIR FOOD.

The dress of the king and queen, and of all the others, that is to say, of the natives of the country, is this: they go naked and with bare feet, and wear a piece of cotton or of silk around their middle, and with nothing on their heads.[1] Some Moorish merchants, on the other hand, wear a short shirt extending to the waist; but all the Pagans go without a shirt. In like manner the women go naked like the men, and wear their hair long. With respect to the food of the king and the gentlemen, they do not eat flesh without the permission of the Brahmins. But the other classes of the people eat flesh of all kinds, with the exception of cow beef.[2] And these Hirava and Poliar eat mice and fish dried in the sun.

THE CHAPTER CONCERNING THE CEREMONIES WHICH THEY PERFORM AFTER THE DEATH OF THE KING.

The king being dead, and having male children, or brothers, or nephews on his brother's side, neither his sons, nor his brother, nor his nephews become king; but the heir of the king is the son of one of his sisters.[3] And if there be

---

dwell in woods and marshes, and subsist chiefly on hunting and begging. See PINKERTON'S *Voyages*, vol. viii. pp. 375, 738-9.

[1] As Ralph Fitch quaintly says: "The king goeth incached, as they do all."

[2] "None of the southern Brahmins can, without losing caste, taste animal food...The Nairs are permitted to eat venison, goats, fowls, and fish." BUCHANAN.

[3] Buchanan confirms this. He says: "The succession goes in the female line;" and adds, in speaking of a particular case wherein a nephew was heir to the rajahship: "his son will have no claim to it, and he will be succeeded by the son of his niece, who is the daughter of

no son of a said sister, the nearest [collateral] relation of the king succeeds him. And this custom prevails because the Brahmins have the virginity of the queen; and likewise when the king travels, one of these Brahmins, although he might be only twenty years of age, remains in the house with the queen, and the king would consider it to be the greatest favour that these Brahmins should be familiar with the queen, and on this account they say that it is certain that his sister and he were born of the same person, and that there is more certainty about her than of his own children, and therefore the inheritance falls to the sons of the sister. Also on the death of the king all the people of the kingdom shave their beards and their heads, with the exception of some part of the head, and also of the beard, according to the pleasure of each person. The fishermen also are not allowed to catch any fish for eight days. The same customs are observed when a near relative of the king dies. As an act of devotion, the king does not sleep with a woman or eat betel for a whole year. This betel resembles the leaves of the sour orange, and they are constantly eating it. It is the same to them that confections are to us, and they eat it more for sensuality than for any other purpose. When they eat the said leaves, they eat with them a certain fruit which is called *coffolo*, and the tree of the said *coffolo* is called *Areeha*,[1] and is formed like the stem of the date tree, and produces its fruit in the same manner. And they also eat with the said leaves a certain lime made from oyster shells, which they call *Cionama*.[2]

his sister." (PINKERTON's *Voyages*, vol. viii. p. 745.) It was the same in Ibn Batûta's time:—"Each of their kings succeeds to rule as being sister's son, not the son to the last." LEE's *Translation*, p. 167.

[1] The *Areca* palm.
[2] *Chunam*, the common Hindustani word for lime.

THE CHAPTER SHOWING HOW THE PAGANS SOMETIMES EXCHANGE THEIR WIVES.

The Pagan gentlemen and merchants have this custom amongst them. There will sometimes be two merchants who will be great friends, and each will have a wife; and one merchant will say to the other in this wise: " Langal perganal monaton ondo?"[1] that is, " So-and-so, have we been a long time friends?" The other will answer: " Hognan perga manaton ondo;" that is, " Yes, I have for a long time been your friend." The other says: " Nipatanga ciolli?" that is, " Do you speak the truth that you are my friend?" The other will answer, and say: " Ho;" that is, " Yes." Says the other one: " Tamarani?" that is, " By God?" The other replies: " Tamarani!" that is, " By God!" One

[1] I had hoped to have been able, by the assistance of others, to reduce this and the subsequent native words and phrases introduced by Varthema into readable Malayalim, in the same manner as I have treated his Arabic sentences; but the attempt has proved unsuccessful. Two Malayalim scholars, to whom they were submitted, concur in forming a very low estimate of our traveller's attainments in that language. One of the gentlemen states that "the majority of the words are not Malayalim, or, if they are, the writer has trusted to his ear, and made a marvellous confusion, which I defy anybody to unravel." This is not to be wondered at; on the contrary, there would have been reasonable ground for surprise if, under his peculiar circumstances, Varthema had succeeded in mastering, even to a tolerable extent, any one of the native languages. During his sojourn in the country, which was comparatively short, and seldom lasting more than a few days at each place, he must have heard several different dialects spoken, without any definite knowledge, perhaps, that they were such. Moreover, as his most intimate associates appear to have been the Arab traders, who, however long their intercourse with India, seldom speak any of the native languages correctly, he most probably acquired most of his vocabulary from them, jumbling that up with words and phrases which he had picked up here and there along the coast. The specimens of his Arabic are undoubtedly far superior to his essays in Malayalim, and, although strongly Italianized, by no means inferior to the colloquial of the majority of his countrymen at the present day after a much longer residence in the East where that is the vernacular language.

L.

says: "In penna tonda gnan penna cortu;" that is, "Let us exchange wives, give me your wife and I will give you mine." The other answers: "Ni pantagocciolli?" that is, "Do you speak from your heart?" The other says: "Tamarani!" that is, "Yes, by God!" His companion answers, and says: "Biti banno;" that is, "Come to my house." And when he has arrived at his house he calls his wife and says to her: "Penna, ingaba idocon dopoi;" that is, "Wife, come here, go with this man, for he is your husband." The wife answers: "E indi?" that is, "Wherefore? Dost thou speak the truth, by God, Tamarani?" The husband replies: "Ho gran patangociolli;" that is, "I speak the truth." Says the wife: "Perga manno;" that is, "It pleases me." "Gnan poi;" that is, "I go." And so she goes away with his companion to his house. The friend then tells his wife to go with the other, and in this manner they exchange their wives; but the sons of each remain with him. And amongst the other classes of Pagans above-mentioned, one woman has five, six, and seven husbands, and even eight.[1] And one sleeps with her one night, and another another night. And when the woman has children, she says

---

[1] The polyandria which prevailed at Calicut is also described by Nicolò de' Conti and 'Abd er-Razzâk. The three accounts vary in detail, and, as might be expected on a subject so intimately connected with the domestic life of the natives, involve several misconceptions. Dr. Buchanan's more accurate version of the custom is as follows:—"The Nairs marry before they are ten years of age;...but the husband never cohabits with his wife. Such a circumstance, indeed, would be considered very indecent. He allows her oil, clothing, ornaments, and food; but she lives in her mother's house, or, after her parents' death, with her brother, and cohabits with any person she chooses of an equal or higher rank than her own...It is no kind of reflection on a woman's character to say that she has formed the closest intimacy with many persons; on the contrary, the Nair women are proud of reckoning among their favoured lovers many Brahmins, Rajahs, or other persons of high birth...In consequence of this strange manner of propagating the species, no Nair knows his father, and every man looks on his sisters' children as his heirs." PINKERTON'S *Voyages*, vol. viii. p. 737.

it is the child of this husband or of that husband, and thus the children go according to the word of the woman.

THE CHAPTER CONCERNING THE MANNER OF LIVING, AND OF THE ADMINISTRATION OF JUSTICE, AMONG THE PAGANS.

The said Pagans eat on the ground in a metal basin, and for a spoon make use of the leaf of a tree, and they always eat rice and fish, and spices and fruits. The two classes of peasants eat with the hand from a pipkin; and when they take the rice from the pipkin, they hold the hand over the said pipkin and make a ball of the rice, and then put it into their mouths. With respect to the laws which are in use among these people:—If one kills another, the king causes a stake to be taken four paces long and well pointed at one end, and has two sticks fixed across the said stake two spans from the top, and then the said wood is fixed in the middle of the back of the malefactor and passes through his body, and in this way he dies. And this torture they call *uncalvet*. And if there be any one who inflicts wounds or bastinadoes, the king makes him pay money, and in this manner he is absolved. And when any one ought to receive money from another merchant, there appearing any writing of the scribes of the king,(who has at least a hundred of them,) they observe this practice:—Let us suppose the case that some one has to pay me twenty-five ducats, and the debtor promises me to pay them many times, and does not pay them; I, not being willing to wait any longer, nor to give him any indulgence, shall take a green branch in my hand, shall go softly behind the debtor, and with the said branch shall draw a circle on the ground surrounding him, and if I can enclose him in the circle, I shall say to him these words three times: "Bramini raza pertha polle;" that is, "I command you by the head of the Brahmins and of the king, that you do not depart hence until you have paid me and satisfied me as much as I ought to have from thee." And he will satisfy me, or truly he will die there without any other guard. And should he quit the said circle and not pay me, the king would put him to death.[1]

[1] It is remarkable that the administration of justice in India has been the theme of general admiration from the earliest times. Greek and Roman writers, from Diodorus Siculus downward, have eulogized it, Marco Polo witnesses on the same side, and later Arabian authors confirm their favourable testimony. El-Edrîsi says : " Justice is a natural instinct among the inhabitants of India, and they hold nothing in equal estimation. It is stated that their numbers and prosperity are due to their integrity, their fidelity in fulfilling engagements, and to the general uprightness of their conduct. It is, moreover, on this account that visitors to their country have increased, that the country flourishes, and that the people thrive in plenty and in peace. As a proof of their adherence to what is right and their abhorrence of what is wrong may be instanced the following usage : if one man owes another money, the creditor finding him anywhere draws a line in the shape of a ring around him. This the creditor enters, and also the debtor of his own free will, and the latter cannot go beyond it until he has satisfied the claimant ; but should the creditor decline to force him, or chooses to forgive him, he, the creditor, steps out of the ring." 'Abd er-Razzâk also, speaking of Calicut, says : " Security and justice are so firmly established in this city, that the most wealthy merchants bring thither from maritime countries considerable cargoes, which they unload, and unhesitatingly send into the market and bazaars, without thinking in the meantime of any necessity of checking the account, or of keeping watch over the goods." *India in the Fifteenth Century*, i. p. 14.

The mode of procedure against debtors, as described by El-Edrîsi and Varthema, and which Marco Polo, before them, states to have seen carried out against the person of the king of Malabar, is confirmed by Hamilton with slight variation :—" They have a good way of arresting people for debt, viz. there is a proper person sent with a small stick from the judge, who is generally a Brahmin, and when that person finds the debtor, he draws a circle round him with that stick, and charges him in the king and judge's name not to stir out of it till the creditor is satisfied either by payment or surety ; and it is no less than death for the debtor to break prison by going out of the circle." PINKERTON'S *Voyages*, vol. viii. p. 377.

Diodorus Siculus mentions the punishment by impaling as existing in India. Lib. ii. 18.

THE CHAPTER CONCERNING THE MODE OF WORSHIP OF THE PAGANS.

Early in the morning these Pagans go to wash at a tank, which tank is a pond of still water. And when they are washed, they may not touch any person until they have said their prayers, and this in their house.[1] And they say their prayers in this manner :—They lie with their body extended on the ground and very secret, and they perform certain diabolical actions [or motions] with their eyes, and with their mouths they perform certain fearful actions [or motions]; and this lasts for a quarter of an hour, and then comes the hour for eating. And they cannot eat unless the cooking is performed by the hands of a gentleman, for the ladies only cook for themselves. And this is the custom among the gentlemen. The ladies wait to wash and perfume themselves. And every time that a man wishes to associate with his wife, she washes and perfumes herself very delicately; but, under any circumstances, they always go scented and covered with jewels, that is to say, on their hands and in their ears, on their feet and on their arms.

THE CHAPTER CONCERNING THE FIGHTING OF THESE PEOPLE OF CALICUT.

In general they practise every day with swords, shields, and lances. And when they go to war, the king of Calicut maintains constantly one hundred thousand people on foot, because they do not make use of horses, only of some ele-

---

[1] Brahmins are obliged to wash the whole body before eating. Some are under a vow to bathe before sun-rise, which they do either in warm water at home, or in a tank or river. After dressing, the Brahmin sits down to eat, but must preserve himself from numerous accidents which would render him impure, and compel him to desist from his meal. See FORBES's *Rás Málá*, vol. ii. pp. 255-8.

phants for the person of the king. And all the people wear a cloth bound round the head, made of silk and of a vermilion colour, and they carry swords, shields, lances, and bows. The king carries an umbrella[1] instead of a standard, made like the stem of a boot: it is formed of the leaves of a tree, and is fixed on the end of a cane, and made to keep off the sun from the king. And when they are in battle, and one army is distant from the other two ranges of a crossbow, the king says to the Brahmins: "Go into the camp of the enemy, and tell the king to let one hundred of his Nacri come, and I will go with a hundred of mine. And thus they both go to the middle of the space, and begin to fight in this manner. Although they should fight for three days, they always give two direct blows at the head and one at the legs. And when four or six on either side are killed, the Brahmins enter into the midst of them, and make both parties return to their camp. And the said Brahmins immediately go to the armies on both sides, and say: "Nur manczar hanno." The king answers: "Matile?" that is, "Do you not wish for any more?" The Brahmin says: "No." And the adverse party does the same. And in this manner they fight, one

---

[1] The *chattra*, or black Chinese umbrella, commonly used in India, when folded up, looks something like the leg of a boot. It is one of the insignia of royalty throughout India, as it is with several other eastern nations. Malcolm supposes the word "satrap" to be a corruption of *chattrapa*, lord of the umbrella of state, which, it is probable, those provincial rulers only were allowed to bear. He adds: "The distinction of carrying an umbrella is common to many countries of Asia; and that it was known in Persia, there can be no better evidence than the sculpture of Persepolis, where the umbrella often marks the prince, or chief, of the group of figures. *Chattra*, which signifies umbrella, is a term common to Persian and Sanscrit. *Pa*, a contraction of *pati*, i.e. lord, is now lost in the former though preserved in the latter language. The name, or rather title, of *Chattra pati*, or "lord of the umbrella," distinguishes one of the highest officers of the federal government of the Mahratta state." (*History of Persia*, vol. i. p. 271, *n.*) Within my own recollection, no person was allowed to pass before the Sultan's palace on the Bosphorus without lowering his umbrella.

hundred against one hundred. And this is their mode of fighting. Sometimes the king rides on an elephant, and sometimes the Naeri carry him. And when they carry him they always run. And many instruments sounding always accompany the said king. To the said Naeri he gives as pay to each four carlini the month, and in time of war he gives half a ducat. And they live on this pay. The beforementioned race have black teeth, on account of the leaves which I have already told you they eat. When the Naeri die they are burnt with very great solemnity, and some preserve their ashes. But with respect to the common people, after death some bury them within the door of their house; others, again, in their garden.[1] The money of the said city is struck here, as I have already told you in Narsinga. And inasmuch as, at the time when I was in Calicut, there were a very large number of merchants there from different countries and nations, I being desirous of knowing who these persons were, so different one from the other, asked, and was informed that there were here very many Moorish merchants, many from Mecca, a part from Banghella, some from Ternasseri, some from Pego, very many from Ciormandel, in great abundance from Zailani, a great quantity from Sumatra, not a few from Colon and Caicolon, a very great number from Bathacala, from Dabuli, from Chievuli, from Combeia, from Guzerati, and from Ormus. There were also some there from Persia and from Arabia Felix, part from Syria, from Turkey, and some from Ethiopia and Narsinga. There were merchants from all these realms in my time. It must be known that the Pagans do not navigate much, but it is the Moors who carry the merchandize; for in Calicut there are at least fifteen thousand Moors, who are for the greater part natives of the country.[2]

[1] This is confirmed by Buchanan, who says that the Nairs burn their dead, but most of the inferior castes bury.

[2] That the Hindoos have never been *seamen* may be inferred from the

THE CHAPTER CONCERNING THE MANNER OF NAVIGATING IN CALICUT.

It appears to me very suitable and to the purpose, that I should explain to you how these people navigate along the coast of Calicut, and at what time, and how they build their vessels. First, they make their vessels, such as are open, each of three hundred or four hundred butts. And when they build the said vessels they do not put any oakum between one plank and another in any way whatever, but they join the planks so well that they keep out the water most excellently. And then they lay on pitch outside, and put in an immense quantity of iron nails. Do not imagine, however, that they have not any oakum, for it comes there in great abundance from other countries, but they are not accustomed to use it for ships.[1] They also possess as good

almost universal silence of ancient writers on India regarding their maritime affairs, whereas most of them describe the constitution of an Indian army in detail. It seems highly probable, indeed, that the laws of Manu, which mention bottomry, and which led Sir William Jones to infer that the Hindoos must have been navigators in the age of that work, referred primarily to river navigation, the superintendence of which was committed to water-bailiffs, whose business, besides, it was to keep the boundaries of the fields, to take care that each derived benefit from the conduits and canals, etc. (See *Manu*, viii. 408-9.) Arrian states expressly that sea-voyages were forbidden, and Pliny, that Indians never emigrate (vi. 20); and although it may be conceded that their navigation was not absolutely confined to rivers, nevertheless the weight of testimony is decidedly against the idea that they were mariners in the ordinary sense of the word.

It was undoubtedly the natural or religious antipathy of the Hindoos for the sea, or a combination of both sentiments, which threw the navigation of the Indian ocean, from the earliest ages, into the hands of the more nautical Arabs, who thereby succeeded eventually in acquiring a predominating influence on the western coast. The same aversion, proceeding from religious prejudice, is noticed by Marco Polo, who in describing the customs of the Malabarians remarks, that the testimony of one who sails by sea was not admissible, because such men were regarded as desperate. See PINKERTON'S *Voyages*, vol. vii. p. 163.

[1] This description coincides generally with the existing mode of ship-

timber as ourselves, and in greater quantity than with us.[1] The sails of these ships of theirs are made of cotton, and at the foot of the said sails they carry another sail, and they spread this when they are sailing in order to catch more wind; so that they carry two sails where we carry only one. They also carry anchors made of marble, that is to say, a piece of marble eight *palmi* long and two *palmi* every other way. The said marble has two large ropes attached to it; and these are their anchors. The time of their navigation is this: from Persia to the Cape of Cumerin, which is distant from Calicut eight days' journey by sea towards the south. You can navigate through eight months in the year, that is to say, September to all April; then, from the first of May to the middle of August it is necessary to avoid this coast because the sea is very stormy and tempestuous. And you must know that during the months of May, June, July, and August, it rains constantly night and day; it does not merely rain continually, but every night and every day it rains, and but little sun is seen during this time. During the other eight months it never rains.[2] At the end of April they depart from the coast of Calicut, and pass the Cape of Cumerin, and enter into another course of navigation, which is safe during these four months, and go for small spices.[3] As

building on the Malabar coast. Marco Polo states, however, that the vessels which were constructed there in his time were well caulked with oakum. A mistake on his part, or, perhaps, of his English translator.

[1] In a Report published by the *Royal Asiatic Society*, (No. iv. 350-369,) one hundred and twenty valuable sorts of timber are enumerated as produced in Malabar.

[2] A generally correct statement of the prevailing winds and weather during the two monsoons.

[3] Many vessels quit the Malabar coast at that season of the year for the Indian Archipelago, and return thither, or proceed to the Persian Gulf or the Red Sea, at the opening of the north-east monsoon; "for the south-west monsoon, which prevails outside of Achin-head, from April to October, seldom blows far into the strait, particularly near the Sumatra side, for the force of the monsoon being repelled by the mountains and

to the names of their ships, some are called *Sambuchi* and these are flat-bottomed. Some others which are made like ours, that is in the bottom, they call *Capel*. Some other small ships are called *Parao*, and they are boats of ten paces each, and are all of one piece, and go with oars made of cane, and the mast also is made of cane. There is another kind of small bark called *Almadia*, which is all of one piece. There is also another kind of vessel which goes with a sail and oars. These are all made of one piece, of the length of twelve or thirteen paces each. The opening is so narrow that one man cannot sit by the side of the other, but one is obliged to go before the other. They are sharp at both ends. These ships are called *Chaturi*, and go either with a sail or oars more swiftly than any galley, *fusta*, or brigantine.[1] There are corsairs of the sea, and these *Chaturi* are made at an island which is near, called Porcai.[2]

high land, stretching from Achin along the coast of Pedri, it is succeeded by light variable winds and calms, with sometimes land breezes or hard squalls from the Sumatra coast at night." HORSBURG's *Directory*, Part ii.

[1] These names of ships and boats furnish another indirect proof against the notion that the early Hindoos were navigators; for with one exception, viz., that of *Capel* or *Kapal*, which Crawfurd says is of Telugu or Telinga origin, the remainder are derived from foreign sources. *Prau* belongs equally to the Malay and Javanese languages. *Sambuch* is from the Arabic *Sanbûk*. *Almadia* is the Arabic *El-Miiadiah*, a ferry. And *Chaturi* I take to be a corruption of *Shakhtûr*, the ordinary name for a boat on the coast of Syria, and one not unknown in the Red Sea and the Persian Gulf. *Fusta* is the Italian for a kind of light galley.

[2] As there is no island so called in the vicinity of Calicut, I presume Varthema refers to the town of that name, situated on the coast, about two degrees farther south. "It has no haven or port of any kind, and ships trading there anchor in the open sea off the town in two fathoms water, one and a half or two miles from shore. It was formerly a place of much greater importance than it is at present, and was the principal place of a small *raj* or state, which was subverted in the year 1746 by the rajah of Travancore." (THORNTON's *Gazetteer*.) Barbosa gives the following description of the place:—" Porca has a lord of its own. Here many Gentile fishermen reside who do nothing, and have no other occupation than that of fishing during the winter, and of plundering on the

THE CHAPTER CONCERNING THE PALACE OF THE KING OF CALICUT.

The palace of the king is about a mile in circumference. The walls are low, as I have mentioned above, with very beautiful divisions of wood, with devils carved in relief. The floor of the house is all adorned with cow dung.[1] The said house is worth two hundred ducats or thereabouts. I

sea during summer such as fall in their way. They possess certain small boats, like brigantines, which they row skilfully, and collecting many of these together, they themselves being armed with bows and arrows, they surround any ship that is becalmed, and after forcing it to surrender by means of their arrows, they proceed to plunder the crew and the ship, casting the men naked on the ground. The booty they divide with the lord of the country, who countenances them. This kind of boat they call *Caturi*." (RAMUSIO, vol. i. p. 312.) These piracies appear to have declined in Hamilton's time. He says: " Porcat or Porkah is of small extent, reaching not above four leagues along the seacoast. The prince is poor, having but little trade in his country, though it was a free port for pirates when Evory and Kid robbed along the coast of India ; but since then the pirates infest the northern coasts, finding the richest prizes amongst the Mocha and Persia traders." (PINKERTON'S *Voyages*, vol. viii. p. 383.) Baldæus calls the place *Percatti*, and in Keith Johnston's superb new atlas it is written *Parrakad*.

Query? Is the whole or any part of the territory which formerly constituted the small state of Porca ever insulated by the " Backwater of Cochin ?" Horsburgh does not enable me to decide the question, but judging from the maps it seems highly probable.

[1] A solution of cow dung (*gobar*) is in general use among the natives throughout India for anointing the walls and floors of their mud huts, on account of its binding and supposed purifying properties. Buchanan says: " It is also much used as fuel, even where wood is abundant, especially by men of rank, as, from the veneration paid to the cow, it is considered as by far the most pure substance that can be employed. Every herd of cattle, when at pasture, is attended by women, and those often of high caste, who with their hands gather the dung, and carry it home in baskets. They then form it into cakes, about half an inch thick, and nine in diameter, and stick them on the walls to dry. So different, indeed, are Hindu notions of cleanliness from ours, that the walls of their best houses are frequently bedaubed with these cakes." PINKERTON'S *Voyages*, vol. viii. p. 612.

now saw the reason why they could not dig foundations, on account of the water, which is close to them.¹ It would be impossible to estimate the jewels which the king wears, although in my time he was not in very good humour, in consequence of his being at war with the king of Portugal, and also because he had the French disease,² and had it in the throat. Nevertheless, he wore so many jewels in his ears, on his hands, on his arms, on his feet, and on his legs, that it was a wonder to behold.³ His treasure consists of two magazines of ingots of gold, and stamped golden money, which many Brahmins said that a hundred mules could not carry. And they say, that this treasure has been left by ten or twelve previous kings, who have left it for the wants of the republic. This king of Calicut also possesses a casket three spans long and one and a half span high, filled with jewels of every description.

[1] See note on p. 136 *ante*.

[2] *Frang* or *Frank* is the common name among Arabs for the disease referred to.

[3] The following is a description of the Zamorin's dress when he gave audience to Pedro Alvarez Cabral in 1500 :—" He had only a piece of white cloth, embroidered with gold, about his middle ; all the rest of his body being naked. On his head was a cap of cloth of gold. At his ears hung jewels, composed of diamonds, sapphires, and pearls, two of which were larger than walnuts. His arms, from the elbow to the wrist, and his legs, from the knees downwards, were loaded with bracelets, set with infinite precious stones of great value. His fingers and toes were covered with rings. In that of his great toe was a large ruby of surprising lustre. Among the rest was a diamond bigger than a large bean. But all this was as nothing compared with the richness of his girdle, made with precious stones set in gold, which cast a lustre which dazzled everybody's eyes. Near the Zamorin stood a chair of state and his litter, all of gold and silver, curiously made, and adorned with precious stones. There were three trumpets of gold and seventeen of silver, whose mouths were set with stones also ; not to mention the silver lamps and censers smoking with perfumes, and his golden spitting-basin." GREENE's *Collection*, vol. i. p. 43.

THE CHAPTER CONCERNING THE SPICES WHICH GROW IN THAT COUNTRY OF CALICUT.

Many pepper trees are found in the territory of Calicut: there are also some within the city, but not in large quantities. Its stem is like that of a vine, that is to say, it is planted near to some other tree, because, like the vine, it cannot stand erect. This tree grows like the ivy, which embraces and climbs as high as the wood or tree which it can grasp. The said plant throws out a great number of branches, which branches are from two to three *palmi* long. The leaves of these branches resemble those of the sour orange, but are more dry, and on the underneath part they are full of minute veins. From each of these branches there grow five, six, and eight clusters, a little longer than a man's finger, and they are like small raisins, but more regularly arranged, and are as green as unripe grapes. They gather them in this green state in the month of October and even in November, and then they lay them in the sun on certain mats, and leave them in the sun for three or four days, when they become as black as they are seen amongst us without doing anything else to them. And you must know that these people neither prune nor hoe this tree which produces the pepper.[1]

[1] " Pepper is proverbially styled the money of Malabar...The trailing plant which produces pepper is propagated by planting a cutting at the root of the jak, the mango, or other trees having rough bark, up which the vine climbs. After it has been planted it requires no great trouble or attention, the cultivator having little more to do than to collect the produce in the proper season. When the fruit is intended for black pepper, it is not allowed to ripen, but is collected green, and becomes black on drying. That which is intended for white pepper is left to ripen thoroughly, in which state the berries are covered with a red pulp, which being washed off, leaves the peppercorn white, and requiring merely to be dried to be fit for the market." (THORNTON'S *Gazetteer*.) Fitch says : " The shrub is like unto our ivy tree, and if it did not run about some tree or pole, it would fall down and rot. When first they

In this place ginger also grows, which is a root, and of these same roots some are found of four, eight, and twelve ounces each. When they dig it, the stem of the said root is about three or four spans long, and is formed like some reeds [cannuze]. And when they gather the said ginger, in that same place they take an eye of the said root, which is like an eye of the cane, and plant it in the hole whence they have dug that root, and cover it up with the same earth. At the end of a year they return to gather it, and plant it in the aforesaid manner.[1] This root grows in red soil, and on the mountain, and in the plain, as the mirabolans grow, every kind of which is found here.[2] Their stem is like that of a middle-sized pear tree, and they bear like the pepper tree.

gather it, it is green; and then they lay it in the sun and it becometh black." (PINKERTON's *Voyages*, vol. ix. p. 425.) Barbosa gives a detailed account of the plant, and also of the pepper trade shortly after the arrival of the Portuguese in India. RAMUSIO, vol. i. p. 322.

[1] Hieronimo di Santo Stefano, who visited Calicut some years prior to Varthema, describes the pepper-vine and ginger-shrub in similar terms. Of the latter, he says: "For the propagation of ginger, they plant the piece of a small fresh root, about the size of a small nut, which at the end of a month grows large. The leaf resembles that of a wild lilly." (*India in the Fifteenth Century*, iv. p. 4, 5.) Fitch likens the plant to "our garlic, and the root is the ginger." Dr. Buchanan states that the cuttings of ginger are planted between the months of April and May, and that between December and January the roots are fit for pulling. Those intended for replanting are mixed with a little mud, and immediately buried in a pit. See *A Journey from Madras through Mysore*, &c., vol. ii. p. 469.

[2] "Of *Terminalia*, the genus to which the Myrobalans belong, Wright and Arnott, in their *Prodromus Floræ Peninsulæ Indiæ Orientalis*, vol. i, p. 312 *et seq.*, enumerate eleven species; but probably only five of them have edible fruits, viz.:

    1. *Terminalia Angustifolia*, Jacq.
    2.   ,,   *Catappe*, L.
    3.   ,,   *Bellerica*, Roxb.
    4.   ,,   *Chebula*, Roxb.
    5.   ,,   *Travancorensis*, W. & A." J. J. Bennett.

THE CHAPTER CONCERNING SOME FRUITS OF CALICUT.

I found in Calicut a kind of fruit which is called *Ciccara*. Its stem is like that of a large pear tree. The fruit is two or two and a half *palmi* long, and is as thick as a man's thigh. This fruit grows on the trunk of the tree, that is to say, under the boughs, and partly on the middle of the stem. The colour of the said fruit is green, and it is formed like the pine, but the work is more minute. When it begins to ripen, the skin becomes black and appears rotten. This fruit is gathered in the month of December, and when it is eaten it seems as though you were eating musk melons, and it appears to resemble a very ripe Persian quince. It appears also, as though you were eating a preparation of honey, and it also has the taste of a sweet orange. Within the said fruit there are some pellicles like the pomegranate. And within the said pellicles there is another fruit which, if placed on the embers of the fire and then eaten, you would say that they were most excellent chestnuts. So that this appears to me to be the best and the most excellent fruit I ever ate.[1] Another fruit is also found here, which is called *Amba*,

---

[1] The fruit here described is obviously the Jack (*Artocarpus integrifolia*), the large seeds of which, when roasted, are frequently eaten. They were a favourite dish with my late lamented friend Sir James Outram, who used to say they were equal to chestnuts. Though the taste of the pulp is sweet, the smell is very disagreeable to Europeans. Varthema, who seems to affix the odour to the skin, is the only one of the old travellers who appears to have noticed this peculiarity. I cannot discover the origin of the name *Ciccara* which he gives to the fruit, unless it be a corruption of the Malayalim *Tsjaka* or *Tuca*. Ibn Batûta mentious two species of the Jack, *Esh-Shaki* and *El-Barki*, and, in describing the fruit, says: "When it grows yellow in the autumn, they gather and divide it: and in the inside of each is from one to two hundred seeds. Its seed resembles that of a cucumber, and has a stone something like a large bean. When the stone is roasted, it tastes like a dried bean." (LEE's *Translation*, p. 105.) The distinction thus drawn between the seed and the stones of the Jack seems to justify Varthema

the stem of which is called *Manga*. This tree is like a pear tree, and bears like the pear. This *Amba* is made like one of our walnuts in the month of August, and has that form; and when it is ripe it is yellow and shining. This fruit has a stone within like a dry almond, and is much better than the Damascus plum. A preserve is made of this fruit, such as we make of olives, but they are much superior.[1] Another

in calling the latter "another fruit;" and I am gratified to find that this inference is in a measure confirmed by the following valuable remarks communicated to me by John J. Bennett, Esq., of the British Museum, to whose kindness I am also indebted for several subsequent notes on the different fruits mentioned in this chapter:—

"The fruit of the Jack is compound, and made up of a number of single-seeded fruits cohering together. It is singular that this fact, which is not very obvious at first sight, should have been partially noticed by these old writers. Roxburgh's description of it is as follows: 'Fruit compound, oblong, murexed (muricate), from twelve to twenty inches long, from six to twelve in diameter, weighing from ten to sixty pounds. Seeds uniform, one in each germ, were all to come to maturity, which can never happen. They are about the size of a nutmeg, enveloped in a thin, smooth, leathery sheath, lodged within the fleshy edible part of the fruit, which formed the exterior coverings of the germ, already noticed...The fruit of this tree is so universally known that it is unnecessary for me to say anything respecting its excellence, as well as that the seeds, when roasted, are not inferior to the best chestnuts. In Ceylon, where the tree grows most plentifully, and where the fruit attains to its greatest size, the inhabitants make them a very considerable article of their diet.' *Flora Indica*, vol. iii. p. 532."

[1] Though he misapplies their import, it is remarkable that Varthema uses these two names in connexion with this fruit. *Am*, *Amb*, *Amba* or *Anba*, appears to be derived from the Sanscrit *Amrá*; but, as written by Ibn Batûta, '*Anbâ*, it resembles so closely the collective form '*Anab*, and the singular '*Anbah*, the Arabic for *grape*, that I scarcely wonder at Professor Lee translating it by that word, more especially as there is no original name for the Mango in the Arabic language. The fruit is not indigenous to any part of Arabia, though a very inferior quality is now to be found in the southern parts of Yemen, and in the province of 'Ammân (Oman). I am able to fix the date of its introduction into the latter country (but, unfortunately, not the place from whence it was imported, though in all probability it was from India), by the following extract from a manuscript history of 'Ammân in my possession, entitled *El-Fath el-Mubin*. The author, writing of El-Fellâh ibn el-Muhsin,

fruit is found here resembling a melon, and it has similar divisions, and when it is cut, three or four grains, which look like grapes or sour cherries, are found inside. The tree which bears this fruit is of the height of a quince tree, and forms its leaves in the same manner. This fruit is called *Corcopal ;* it is extremely good for eating, and excellent as a medicine.[1] I also found there another fruit, which is exactly like the medlar, but it is white like an apple. I do not remember by what name it was called.[2] Again, I saw another kind of fruit which resembled a pumpkin in colour, is two spans in length, and has more than three fingers of pulp, and is much better than a gourd (zuccha) for confections, and it is a very curious thing, and it is called *Comolanga*, and grows on the ground like melons.[3] This country also pro-

who ruled over a portion of that country towards the end of the fifteenth century, says : " It was he who planted the '*Amba* at Makniyât, and it increased in 'Ammân where before it was unknown. It had been sent to him as a rarity, and described as an excellent fruit, so he caused a great many of those trees to be planted."

The word *Mango*, according to Crawfurd, is a corruption of *Mangga* which, though used by Malays, he says was picked up by our traders at Bantam, on the coast of Sumatra. (*Hist. of the Indian Archipelago*, vol. i. p. 425.) The seafaring Arabs of Malabar probably borrowed it from the same source.

[1] The names given by Varthema to the fruits mentioned in this chapter do not appear to be in use at the present day, and Malayalim scholars fail to recognize them as belonging to that language. With regard to the *Corcopal*, Mr. Bennett remarks : " I can hardly give a guess. It might be the *Papau*, but differs in the character of the leaves, and in the number of seeds. Or, it might be a species of *Diospyros*."

[2] " The medlar-like fruit here described may be either the Rose-apple or the Guava, of both of which there are white-fruited varieties. The large open calyx in either may have suggested the comparison to a medlar." BENNETT.

[3] " Probably nearly allied to, if not identical with, the Water melon." With regard to the *Corcopal* and *Comolanga*, Mr. Bennett observes : " I find that Julius Cæsar Scaliger has been poaching in Varthema, whom he translates somewhat differently, not naming the source of his information. The following are his chapters with their headings : —

" ' *Melo Corcopali et Mespilum.* Corcopal Indiæ provincia est : in qua

duces another very singular fruit, which fruit is called *Malapolanda.* The tree which bears this fruit is as high as a man or a little more, and it produces four or five leaves which are branches and leaves. Each of these covers a man against rain and sun. In the middle of this it throws out a certain branch which produces flowers in the same manner as the stalk of a bean, and afterwards it produces some fruits which are half a *palmo* and a *palmo* in length, and they are as thick as the staff of a spear. And when they wish to gather the said fruit they do not wait until it is ripe, because it ripens in the house. One branch will produce two hundred or thereabouts of these fruits, and they all touch one against the other. Of these fruits there are found three sorts. The first sort is called *Cianchapalon;* these are very restorative things to eat. Their colour is somewhat yellow, and the bark is very thin. The second sort is called *Cadelapalon,* and they are much superior to the others. The third sort are bitter. The two kinds above mentioned are good like our figs, but superior. The tree of this fruit produces once and then no more. The said tree always has at its stem fifty or sixty shoots (figlioli), and the owners remove these shoots by the hand and transplant them, and at the end of a year they produce their fruit. And if the said branches are too green when they cut them, they put a little lime upon the said fruits to make them ripen quickly. You must know that a

cydonii magnitudine et foliis arbor prægrandem gerit fructum, melonis figura, eodemque sulcatum modo. Intra quem terna quaternave grana, acinorum uvæ facie, acore cerasi. Ubi est adversus tuam subtilitatem naturæ simplicitas. Non enim granorum numerus, uti tu volebas in Punicis, certus est: sicuti neque in Cicçara. Melonem hanc et edendo esse, et ad medicinas utilem. Ibi Mespilum colore albo, Malo magnitudine.'

"'*Comolanga.* In eadem Corcopal Comolanga fructus esitatur, sesquipede major, curcubitæ colore. Humi jacet, ut melo. Pulpæ plurimum. Condimenta ex ea, vel cucurbitinis, quas Carabassades Hispani vocant, vel citriis meliora, atque sapidiora.' EXERCITATIO clxxxi. *cap.* 13, 15." *Idem.*

very large quantity of such fruits is found at all times of the year, and twenty are given for a quattrino.[1] In like manner, roses and most singular flowers are found here on all the days of the year.

THE CHAPTER CONCERNING THE MOST FRUITFUL TREE IN THE WORLD.

I will describe another tree to you, the best in all the world, which is called *Tenga*,[2] and is formed like the trunk

---

[1] "This is certainly the Plantain, in its several varieties, and very well described. With respect to its dying off after producing its fruit, I need only quote what Roxburgh says : 'They blossom at all seasons, though generally during the rains, and ripen their seed in five or six months afterwards. The plant then perishes down to the root, which long before this time has produced other shoots : these continue to grow up, blossom, etc., in succession for several years. *Flora Indica*, i. p. 663." *Idem.*

Malapolanda may be a corruption of *Valei pullum*, which, according to Ainslie, is the Tamil name for Plantain. See his *Materia Indica*, vol. i. sub voce *Plantain*.

[2] This is, obviously, the Cocoa-nut tree, the Malayalim name of which, according to Ainslie, is *Tǎnghǎ*. I am aware of none among the earlier travellers who has so thoroughly described this palm, and the several uses to which it is applied, as Varthema; and the accuracy of his details may be tested by the following quotation from Seemann:—"The cocoa-nut tree attains a height of from sixty to one hundred feet, and a diameter of one or two feet....It flourishes best in a sandy soil...The wood is devoted to various purposes. The leaves are from eighteen to twenty feet long : the Cingalese split them in halves, and plait the segments so as to form baskets. Under the denomination of *cadjans*, they form the usual covering of their huts, as well as of the European bungalows. The midribs of the leaves, when tied together, form brooms for the decks of ships...There is one portion of the tree which attracts much the attention of the observer,—it is a kind of net-work at the base of the petiole. It is stripped off in large pieces, and used in Ceylon as strainers, particularly for the toddy. A tree produces several bunches of nuts, and from twelve to twenty large nuts, besides several small unproductive ones, may be seen on each bunch. In good situations the fruit is gathered four or five times in the course of the year. The latter

of a date tree. Ten useful things are derived from this tree. The first utility is wood to burn; nuts to eat; ropes for maritime navigation; thin stuffs which, when they are dyed, appear to be made of silk; charcoal in the greatest perfection; wine; water; oil; and sugar: and with its leaves which fall, that is, when a branch falls, they cover the houses. And these ward off water for half a year. Were I to declare to you in what manner it accomplishes so many things you would not believe it, neither could you understand it. The said tree produces the above-named nuts in the same manner as the branch of a date tree; and each tree

is much used as an article of food, both meat and drink, when green or young: in that state it yields an abundance of a delicious cooling beverage. The water, beautifully clear, has a sweetness, with a slight degree of astringency, which renders it agreeable...From the flower spathes, before the flowers are expanded, toddy or palm-wine is made. To procure the toddy, the spathe is tied with strips of the young leaves to prevent its expansion. It is cut a little transversely from the top, and beaten either with the handle of the toddy-knife, or a small piece of ebony or iron-wood: this process having been continued morning and evening, (at dawn of day, and just as the sun declines below the horizon,) for five or six successive days, the under part of the spathe is taken off, so as to permit of its being gradually bent, when the toddy-drawers, for the purpose of keeping it in that position, attach it to some neighbouring leaf-stalk. After a further period of five days, an earthen *chatty* or calabash is hung to the spathe, so as to receive the toddy that exudes, which is collected every morning and evening, and the spathe cut a little every day: the quantity collected varies much.

"Fermentation takes place in a few hours after the toddy has been collected, when it is used by the bakers as yeast...Arrack is distilled from toddy, which also yields abundance of *jaggery* or sugar...The rind or husk of the cocoa-nut is very fibrous, and when ripe is the *Koya* or Coir of commerce...Another valuable production of the nut is the oil... The Malabar method of extracting it is by dividing the kernels into two equal parts, which are ranged on shelves made of the laths of the Betel-nut palm, or split bamboo, spaces being left between each lath of half an inch wide: under them a charcoal fire is then made, and kept up for two or three days, in order to dry them. After this process they are exposed to the sun on mats, and when thoroughly dried (then called *Koppera*) are placed in an oil-press or *siccoor*." *Popular History of the Palms and their Allies,* pp. 146-175.

will produce from one hundred to two hundred of these nuts,
the outer part of which is taken off and used as firewood.
And then, next to the second bark, there is taken off a
certain substance like cotton or linen flax, and this is given
to workmen to beat, and from the flower, stuffs which
appear like silken stuffs are made. And the coarse part
they spin, and make of it small cords, and of the small they
make large cords, and these they use for the sea. Of the
other bark of the said nut excellent charcoal is made. After
the second bark the nut is good to eat. The size of the said
fruit is [at first] that of the little finger of the hand. When
the said nut begins to grow, water begins to be produced
within; and when the nut has arrived at perfection, it is full
of water, so that there are some nuts which will contain four
and five goblets of water, which water is a most excellent
thing to drink, and is also like rose-water, and extremely
sweet. Most excellent oil is made from the said nut, and
thus you have eight utilities from it. Another branch of
the said tree they do not allow to produce nuts, but they cut
it in the middle and give it a certain inclination; and in the
morning and evening they make an opening with a knife,
and then they apply a certain fluid and that fluid draws out
a certain juice. And these men set a pot underneath and
collect that juice, of which one tree will produce as much as
half a jug between the day and the night. This they
place over the fire and boil it one, two, and three times,
so that it appears like brandy, and will affect a man's
head by merely smelling it, to say nothing of drinking it.
This is the wine which is drunk in these countries. From
another branch of the said tree they produce in a similar
manner this juice, and convert it into sugar by means of
fire; but it is not very good. The said tree always has fruit
either green or dry, and it produces fruit in five years.
These trees are found over two hundred miles of country,
and all have owners. As to the goodness of this tree, when

the kings are at enmity one with another, and kill each other's children, they nevertheless sometimes make peace. But if one king cut down any of these trees belonging to another king, peace will never be granted to all eternity.[1] You must know that the said tree lives for twenty or five and twenty years, and grows in sandy places. And when these nuts are planted to produce these trees, and until they begin to germinate, or that the tree begins to grow from them, it is necessary that the men who plant them should go every evening to uncover them, in order that the cool night air may blow over them; and early in the morning they return to cover them up, in order that the sun may not find them thus uncovered. And in this manner does this tree generate and grow. In this country of Calicut, there is found a great quantity of *zerzalino*,[2] from which they make very excellent oil.

THE CHAPTER CONCERNING THE PRACTICE THEY FOLLOW IN SOWING RICE.

The men of Calicut, when they wish to sow rice, observe this practice. First, they plough the land with oxen as we do, and when they sow the rice in the field they have all the instruments of the city continually sounding and making merry. They also have ten or twelve men clothed like

---

[1] The Israelites were expressly forbidden to cut down food-bearing trees even in an enemy's country. (Deut. xx. 19.) To injure trees, according to Manu, was an offence proportioned to the value of the tree. (viii. 285.) Quintus Curtius was correct when he said of the ancient Hindus that they deified certain trees, which it was a capital crime to destroy. (Lib. viii. cap. 9.) "The *ficus religiosa*, and other trees, are never injured by the Hindus. Ward mentions a tree which was so much reverenced that not even its withered branches were permitted to be cut." *Bombay Quarterly Magazine*, October 1850.

[2] *Sesame*, see note 2, p. 86 *ante*.

devils, and these unite in making great rejoicing with the players on the instruments, in order that the devil may make that rice very productive.

THE CHAPTER CONCERNING THE PHYSICIANS WHO VISIT THE SICK IN CALICUT.

When a merchant, that is, a Pagan, is sick and in great danger, the abovementioned instruments and the aforesaid men dressed like devils go to visit the sick man; and they go at two or three o'clock in the morning; and the said men so dressed carry fire in their mouths; and in each of their hands and on their feet they wear two crutches of wood, which are one pace (*passo*) high, and in this manner they go shouting and sounding the instruments, so that truly if the person were not ill, he would fall to the ground from terror at seeing these ugly beasts. And these are the physicians who go to see and to visit the sick man. And although they should fill the stomach full up to the mouth, they pound three roots of ginger and make a cup of juice, and this they drink, and in three days they no longer have any illness, so that they live exactly like beasts.[1]

[1] Hindus generally attribute all disease to malignant spiritual agency, which must be either propitiated or exorcised; and although this notion does not wholly prevent their seeking relief from dietetics and physic, their chief reliance, nevertheless, is placed on medical thaumaturgy. The practitioners are men of low caste, who pretend to effect great cures by amulets, philtres, and various incantations, not unfrequently associated with a noisy display similar to that above described by Varthema. Buchanan mentions a tribe of Telinga origin, called the Pacanet Joghis, which is scattered over the peninsula, whose business consists in collecting and exhibiting the plants used in medicine. He says: "Their virtuous men, after death, are supposed to become a kind of gods, and frequently to inspire the living, which makes them speak incoherently, and enables them to foretel the event of diseases;" and then adds: "Medicine in this country has, indeed, fallen into the hands of charlatans equally impudent and ignorant." (PINKERTON's *Voyages*, vol. viii.

THE CHAPTER CONCERNING THE BANKERS AND MONEY-CHANGERS.

The money-changers and bankers of Calicut have some weights, that is, balances, which are so small that the box in which they stand and the weights together do not weigh half an ounce; and they are so true that they will turn by a hair of the head. And when they wish to test any piece of gold, they have carats of gold as we have; and they have the touchstone like us. And they test after our manner. When the touchstone is full of gold, they have a ball, of a certain composition which resembles wax, and with this ball, when they wish to see if the gold be good or poor, they press on the touchstone and take away some gold from the said touchstone, and then they see in the ball the goodness of the gold, and they say: "Idu mannu, Idu aga," that is, "this is good, and this is poor." And when that ball is full of gold they melt it, and take out all the gold which they have tested by the touchstone. The said money-changers are extremely acute in their business. The merchants have this custom when they wish to sell or to purchase their merchandise, that is, wholesale:—They always sell by the hands of the *Cortor* or of the *Lella*,[1] that is, of the broker. And when the purchaser and the seller wish to make an agreement, they all stand in a circle, and the Cortor takes a cloth and holds it there openly with one hand, and with the other hand he takes the right hand of the seller, that is, the two fingers next to the thumb, and then he covers with the said cloth his hand and that of the seller, and touching each other with these two fingers, they count from one ducat up

---

p. 669.) For some valuable remarks on Medical Thaumaturgy in India, see the *Bombay Quarterly Magazine* for October 1850, and FORBES's Chapter on *Bhoots, Rás Málá*, vol. ii. pp. 379-400.

[1] *Cortor* is probably a contraction of the Portuguese *Mercador*. *Lella* is doubtless a corruption of the Arabic *Dallál*, a go-between, a broker.

to one hundred thousand secretly, without saying " I will have so much" or "so much." But in merely touching the joints of the fingers they understand the price and say: " Yes" or " No." And the Cortor answers " No" or " Yes." And when the Cortor has understood the will of the seller, he goes to the buyer with the said cloth, and takes his hand in the manner above mentioned, and by the said touching he tells him he wants so much. The buyer takes the finger of the Cortor, and by the said touches says to him : " I will give him so much."[1] And in this manner they fix the price.

[1] This method of transacting business prevails among the Arabs in the Red Sea and along the north-eastern coast of Arabia. Dr. Beke also noticed it at the market of Baso in Abyssinia, and describes it thus :— " The principals or their brokers, seated on the ground, take each other's hand,—the hands being covered with their clothes so that they may not be seen,—and then by a peculiar grasping or pressing of the fingers they make known the price which they are respectively willing to give or accept. A few examples will best explain this : Having first settled between themselves whether the price in question is to be in gold (ounces,) in silver (dollars,) or in salt (ámoles,) they then, if the price is in *ámoles*, for fifty grasp the whole five fingers; for forty, only four. For sixty they first grasp the whole five, and then say 'this,' and then, after a momentary pause, add 'and this,' accompanying the latter words with the pressure of one finger only. One hundred *ámoles* would be five fingers and then again five, or simply a single finger ; 110, one finger alone, say 'this'—'and this,' and pressing it twice ; 120 would, of course, be first one finger and then two. If the price is settled in silver or gold, then it will be two, three, or four fingers, according to their value ; and subdivisions of the *wokíet* [ounces] are made known by pressing the nail of the forefinger on the forefinger of the other party, the end joint being $\frac{1}{4}$, the second joint or middle of the finger $\frac{1}{2}$, and the middle of the first phalanx $\frac{3}{4}$. As it mostly happens that several persons are interested,— or, if not so, at all events take part in the transaction as friends or advisers,—its progress is communicated to them by the principals through their other hands, which are in like manner hidden under their clothes ; and thus the price can be passed on in succession to an indefinite number of individuals, without its being once openly named. When any of these think the amount offered sufficient, they cry out 'sell, sell;' and should the conclusion of the bargain be long delayed, this cry is repeated, making a curious impression on a bystander, who may not happen to be aware what is going on." *Letters on the Commerce and Politics of Abyssinia*, p. 19.

If the merchandise about which they treat be spices, they deal by the *bahar*, which *bahar* weighs three of our *cantari*. If they be stuffs, they deal by *curia*, and in like manner if they be jewels. By a *curia* is understood twenty; or, indeed, they deal by *farasola*, which *farasola* weighs about twenty-five of our *lire*.[1]

[1] The names of these weights and measures, I am informed, are not Malayalim, though I think it highly probable that they are still used by the Arabs who frequent the Malabar coast. *Buhár* is an Arabic word, indicating usually a weight of three hundred pounds. By some Arabian lexicographers it is supposed to be of Coptic origin, and Prinsep seems to regard it as a term " properly Hindu," a corruption either of *bhára* or *báha*. (See LANE's *Arabic-English Lexicon*, sub voce *Buhár*, and PRINSEP's *Useful Tables*, part i. p. 76. *Calcutta*, 1834.) Crawfurd says it is the only weight introduced into the Archipelago by the Arabs, and was in use even as far as the Moluccas when the Portuguese first arrived. (*Descriptive Dictionary of the Indian Islands*, sub voce *Weights*.) Hamilton mentions the " Bahaar" as a weight used in several parts of the East Indies in his time. PINKERTON's *Voyages*, vol. viii. p. 518.

Curia stands undoubtedly for *kóraja*, and *Farasola* is the plural of *fársala*, both words being still in ordinary use among the Arabs of the Red Sea and Persian Gulf; but I am unable to verify their origin. The latter seems identical with *ferrah*, a corruption of *parah*, the name of an old Hindu weight, which is known throughout India, and used in measuring lime, etc.; and the former may be derived from the Sanscrit *kauri*, a score. (PRINSEP's *Tables*, id.) *Kóraja* means twenty, and is applied to bales of hides, piece-goods, etc., containing that number. It is written " Gorjes" in the bill of goods purchased at Mokha in 1612 by Captain John Saris from a native merchant of Surat, and Saris also enumerates it among the weights and measures known at Java and other islands of the Indian Archipelago, e. g. " TAFFATA, in Boults, an hundred and twelve yards the Piece, forty-six Ryals of Eight the *Gorj*, or twenty Pieces." GREENE's *Collection of Voyages*, vol. i. pp. 466, 504.

The present weight of a *fársala* at Aden is 28 lbs. Hamilton, who calls it " Frasella," and places it among the *Banyan Weights*, reckoned it in his time at 29½ lbs. avoirdupois; and Niebuhr, who names it among the weights of Mokha, makes it 30 *livres*. See PINKERTON's *Voyages*, vol. viii. p. 518; *Voyage en Arabie*, vol. iii. p. 192.

THE CHAPTER SHOWING HOW THE POLIARI AND HIRAVA FEED THEIR CHILDREN.

The women of these two classes of people, that is, the Poliari and Hirava, suckle their children for about three months, and then they feed them upon cow's milk or goat's milk. And when they have crammed them, without washing either their faces or their bodies, they throw them into the sand, in which they remain covered up from the morning until the evening, and as they are more black than any other colour, they cannot be distinguished from little buffalos or little bears; so that they appear misshapen things, and it seems as though they were fed by the devil. Their mothers give them food again in the evening. These people are the most agile leapers and runners in the world.[1] I

[1] See note on p. 142 *ante*. That this is not an exaggerated picture of the mode in which the offspring of these wretched outcasts are nurtured, may be fairly inferred from the following description of the class which they compose:—" The creatures in human form, who constitute the number of 100,000, the agrestic slave population of Malabar, are distinguishable, like the savage tribes still to be found in some of the forests in India, from the rest of the human race by their degraded, diminutive, squalid appearance, their dropsical pot-bellies contrasting horribly with their skeleton arms and legs, half-starved, hardly clothed children, and in a condition scarcely superior to the cattle that they follow at the plough." (THORNTON'S *Gazetteer*, sub voce *Malabar*.) Buchanan says: " The only means they employ to procure a subsistence is by watching the crops, to drive away wild hogs and birds. Hunters also employ them to rouse game; and the *Achumars*, who hunt by profession, give them one-fourth part of what they kill. They gather a few wild roots, but can neither catch fish, nor any kind of game. They sometimes procure a tortoise, and are able, by means of hooks, to kill a crocodile. Both these amphibious animals they reckon delicious food. All these resources, however, are inadequate to their support, and they subsist chiefly by begging. They have scarcely any clothing, and every thing about them discloses want and misery. They have some wretched huts built under trees in remote places; but they generally wander about in companies of ten or twelve persons, keeping at a little distance from the road; and when they see any passenger they set up a howl, like so many hungry dogs."

think I ought not to omit explaining to you the many kinds of animals and birds which are found in Calicut, and especially about the lions, wild hogs, goats, wolves, kine, buffalos, goats, and elephants (which, however, are not produced here, but come from other places),[1] great numbers of wild peacocks, and green parrots in immense quantities; also a kind of red parrot. And there are so many of these parrots, that it is necessary to watch the rice in order that the said birds may not eat it. One of these parrots is worth four *quattrini*, and they sing extremely well. I also saw here another kind of bird, which is called *saru*.[2] They sing better than the parrots, but are smaller. There are many other kinds of birds here different from ours. I must inform you, that during one hour in the morning and one hour in the evening there is no pleasure in the world equal to that of listening to the song of these birds, so much so that it is like being in paradise, in consequence of there being such a multitude of trees and perpetual verdure, which arises from the circumstance that cold is unknown here, neither is there excessive heat. In this country a great number of apes are produced, one of which is worth four *casse*, and one *casse* is worth a *quattrino*. They do immense damage to those poor men who make wine.[3] These apes mount on the top of those nuts and drink that same liquor, and then

Hamilton's account is somewhat different. He says: "they are cunning in catching wild beasts and birds;" and strikingly corroborates Varthema by remarking that "they are very swift in running." PINKERTON's *Voyages*, vol. viii. pp. 375-6, 729.

[1] Wild elephants, inferior in size to none in India, exist in the jungles and forests of Malabar. Varthema probably meant that they were not bred in the immediate vicinity of Calicut. All the other quadrupeds and birds which he enumerates, and a great many besides, abound in the country.

[2] *Saru* is probably from the Persian *sar*, a starling. Shakespeare, however, gives *saro* as an Hindostani name for that bird. He seems, moreover, to make it identical with the *mainá* (*Gracula religiosa*).

[3] That is, cocoa-nut wine, or toddy.

they overturn the vessel and throw away all the liquor they cannot drink.

THE CHAPTER CONCERNING THE SERPENTS WHICH ARE FOUND IN CALICUT.

There is found in this Calicut a kind of serpent which is as large as a great pig, and which has a head much larger than that of a pig, and it has four feet, and is four *braza* long.[1] These serpents are produced in certain marshes. The people of the country say that they have no venom, but that they are evil animals, and do injury to people by means of their teeth. Three other kinds of serpents are found here which, if they strike a person a little, that is, drawing blood, he immediately falls to the ground dead. And it has often happened here in my time that there have been many persons struck by these animals, of which animals there are three kinds. The first resemble deaf adders; the next are scorpions; the third are thrice as large as scorpions. Of these three kinds there are immense numbers. And you must know that when the king of Calicut learns where the nest of any of these brutal animals is, he has made over it a little house, on account of the water.[2] And if any person should kill one of these animals

[1] Crocodiles, the animals here indicated, swarm in the rivers of Malabar. "Of other reptiles, there are the skink, a large lizard about four feet long, the salamander, tortoise, snakes of various kinds, as the cobra de capello, the bite of which results in inevitable death, and many other venomous kinds, as also the boa constrictor, generally swept down by torrents from the jungly valleys of the Ghats." THORNTON's *Gazetteer*, sub voce *Malabar*.

[2] I visited one of these retreats for serpents at Kolapore in the Southern Mahratta country, and witnessed them feasting on milk which had been prepared for them by the guardians of the shrine; nevertheless, on two different occasions I have seen Hindus join heartily in killing a cobra de capello.

Baldæus, speaking of the cobras at Negapatam, says: "They are in

the king would immediately put him to death. In like manner, if any one kill a cow, he would also put that person to death. They say that these serpents are spirits of God, and that if they were not his spirits, God would not have given them such a power, that biting a person a little he would immediately fall dead. And it is from this circumstance that there are such numbers of these animals who know the Pagans and do not avoid them. In my time one of these serpents entered into a house during the night and bit nine persons, and in the morning they were all found dead and swollen. And when the said Pagans go on a journey, if they meet any of these animals they receive it as a good augury.

THE CHAPTER CONCERNING THE LIGHTS OF THE KING OF CALICUT.

In the house of the king of Calicut there are many chambers, in which as soon as evening comes they have ten or twelve vases made in the form of a fountain, which are composed of cast metal, and are as high as a man. Each of these vases has three hollow places for holding oil, about two spans high from the ground. And, first, there is a vase in which is oil with cotton wicks lighted all round. And above this there is another vase more narrow, but with the same kind of lights, and on the top of the second vase there stands another yet smaller, but with oil and lights ignited. The foot of this vase is formed in a triangle, and on each of the faces of the foot there are three devils in relief, and they are very fearful to behold. These are the squires who hold

such reverence among these Pagans, that if they should happen to kill one of them, they will look upon it as an expiable [inexpiable ?] crime, and to forbode some great misfortune." CHURCHILL's *Collection*, vol. iii. p. 651.

the lights before the king. This king also makes use of
another custom. When one of his relations dies, as soon as
the year of mourning is accomplished, he sends an invita-
tion to all the principal Brahmins who are in his own kingdom, and he also invites some from other countries. And
when they are arrived, they make great feastings for three
days. Their food consists of rice dressed in various ways,
the flesh of wild hogs, and a great deal of venison, for they
are great hunters. At the end of the three days, the said
king gives to each of the principal Brahmins three, four, and
five *pardai*, and then everyone returns to his house. And
all the people of the kingdom of the king shave their beards
for joy.

THE CHAPTER SHOWING HOW A GREAT NUMBER OF
PEOPLE CAME TO CALICUT ON THE 25TH OF
DECEMBER TO RECEIVE THEIR PARDON.

Near to Calicut there is a temple in the midst of a tank,
that is, in the midst of a pond of water: which temple is
made in antique style with two rows of columns, like San
Giovanni in Fonte at Rome.[1] In the middle of that temple

[1] This was probably the temple which De Gama and his companions
visited on their way from Padarane to Calicut about six years previously,
and where some of them, wittingly or unwittingly, took part in the
heathen services. "The temple was as large as a great monastery. It
was built of freestone, and covered with tiles. Over the front door there
hung seven bells; and before it stood a pillar as high as the mast of a
ship, made of wire, with a weathercock of the same at top. Within, it
was full of images: this made De Gama and the rest take it for a Christian church. Entering it, they were met by certain men, naked from
the waist upwards, and from thence to the knees covered with calico.
They wore pieces of calico also under the armpits, with certain threads,
which were hung over their left shoulder, and passed under the right arm,
just as the Romish priests used to wear their stoles formerly. These
men, with a sponge dipped in a fountain, sprinkled their visitants; and
then gave each of them some Sanders [sandal-wood] pulverized to strew

there is an altar, made of stone, where sacrifices are performed. And between each of the columns of the lower circle there stand some little ships made of stone, which are two paces long, and are full of a certain oil, which is called *Enna*.[1] Around the margin of the said tank there is an immense number of trees all of one kind, on which trees there are lights so numerous that it would be impossible to count them. And in like manner around the said temple there are oil lights in the greatest abundance. When the 25th day of the month of December arrives, all the people for fifteen days' journey around, that is to say, the Naeri and Brahmins, come to this sacrifice. And before performing the said sacrifice, they all wash in the said tank. Then the principal Brahmins of the king mount astride of the little vessels above-mentioned where the oil is, and all these people come to the said Brahmins, who anoint the head of each of them with that oil, and then they perform the sacrifice on that altar before-mentioned. At the end of one side of this altar there is a very large Sathanas, which they all go to worship, and then each returns on his way. At this season the land is free and frank for three days, that is, they cannot exercise

upon their heads, (as the Papists do ashes,) and on their arms. The Portuguese did one, but not the other, because their clothes were on. On the walls of the temple were many images painted, some with great teeth sticking above an inch out of their mouth ; others with four arms, and such frightful faces that the Portuguese began to doubt whether it was a Christian church or not. Upon the top of the chapel, which stood in the middle of the temple, was a fort, or freestone tower, with a little wire door, and stone stairs on the outside. In the wall of this tower was an image, on sight whereof the Malabars called out ' Mary !' [Probably some native word of similar sound forbidding the strangers to approach any nearer, or inviting them to worship.] Whereupon De Gama and the rest, taking it for an image of the Virgin, fell on their knees and prayed. Only one, Juan de Sala, who had some doubt of the matter, in making his genuflexions, said : ' If this be the devil, I worship God ;' which made De Gama smile." GREENE's *Collection*, vol. i. p. 51.

[1] Probably from *Neh*, one of the Sanscrit names for oil, with the Arabic article *el-* or *en-* prefixed.

vengeance one against another. In truth, I never saw so many people together at one time, excepting when I was at Mecca.[1] It appears to me that I have sufficiently explained to you the customs and manner of living, the religion and the sacrifices, of Calicut. Wherefore departing thence, I will recount to you step by step the rest of my journey, together with all the events which happened to me in the course of it.

[1] I am unable to determine the precise festival here described, and which in the year of Varthema's visit (probably 1505) fell on the 25th of December. In many respects it resembles the festival at Bijayanagar, which was also of three days' duration, described in detail by 'Abd er-Razzák, and called by him "Mahanadi." (See *India in the XVth Century*, i. pp. 35-39.) Perhaps it was the *Navarátra*, or Hindu New Year; but it would not be difficult for those skilled in comparative chronology to identify it.

THE THIRD BOOK CONCERNING INDIA.

My companion, who was called Cogiazenor,[1] seeing that he could not sell his merchandize because Calicut was ruined by the king of Portugal, for the merchants who used to come there were not there, neither did they come.—And the reason why they did not come was that the [king of Calicut] consented that the Moors should kill forty-eight Portuguese, whom I saw put to death. And on this account the king of Portugal is always at war, and he has killed, and every day kills, great numbers. And therefore the said city is ruined, for in every way it is at war.[2]—And so we departed, and took

[1] This appears to be the same person that Varthema picked up as a companion at Shiráz. See p. 103 *ante*.

[2] Although Vasco de Gama's first reception by the Zamorin was friendly, the resident Muhammedans generally, and more especially the foreign Arabs, who possessed great influence at the court, and who seem to have feared a rivalry in their trade, did all in their power to thwart his views. In consequence of this opposition, De Gama left India without establishing commercial relations with Calicut. Two years later, Pedro Alvarez Cabral succeeded in settling a factory there, but the Mekkah merchants prevented their getting any cargoes, and instigated an attack on the factory, which was completely destroyed, and many Portuguese killed. In revenge for this outrage, Cabral bombarded the town, and in the course of the following year the Zamorin's fleet was defeated by Juan de Nueva. Between 1502-3 De Gama again appeared before Calicut, and having seized fifty Malabarians at sea caused them to be hung on board his ships, and then ordered their amputated hands and feet to be sent on shore in a *prau*. After this, he cannonaded the place for several hours, demolishing many houses, and among them the Zamorin's palace. Then in 1505 Lope

our road by a river,[1] which is the most beautiful I ever saw, and arrived at a city which is called Cacolon, distant from

Soarez came to Calicut with a fleet of thirteen ships, on which occasion certain prisoners who had been taken in the former wars were delivered up to him ; but as some were detained, he battered the city for two days, ruining a great part of it, and killing three hundred of the inhabitants. Calculating that Varthema must have been at Calicut about this time, I think it highly probable that the forty-eight Portuguese whom he saw dead were the individuals who had not been surrendered to Soarez. (See GREENE's *Collection of Voyages*, vol. i. pp. 29-57, whose account of the early voyages of the Portuguese to India is extracted from Casteuheda, De Barros, and De Faria y Souza.)

[1] The maps, unfortunately, do not enable me to decide whether inland navigation is practicable to the southward *beginning* at Calicut, and Horsburgh is silent on that particular point ; but if the hydrography of Keith Johnston's Atlas is correct, there is a continuous water communication, formed by the different rivers and estuaries, and running parallel with the coast, extending from Panane, (Thornton's *Ponany*, and Keith Johnston's *Ponani*,) twenty-eight miles south of Calicut, as far as Quilon, which is nearly two degrees to the southward of Panane. This fact would partially justify Varthema in saying that he proceeded on his journey from Calicut " by a river ;" but I am inclined to think that, with the exception, perhaps, of an occasional very brief run at sea, from one estuary to another, his statement, on a more thorough investigation than I have the means of giving it, will be verified in its entirety, especially as I find that Ibn Batûta appears to have travelled by the same route; for he says : " I proceeded, therefore, [from Calicut] to that place [Kâwlam=Quilon] by river. It is situated at a distance of ten days from Calicut ;" meaning, of course, that the river journey occupied that time. See LEE's *Translation*, p. 174.

The following quotations illustrate the subject generally :—" Many of these rivers [of Malabar] during the monsoon have inland communications, by which navigation is practicable, from stream to stream and estuary to estuary, in a direction parallel to the shore. Of these waters, the most remarkable is that of Chowgaut, a fine sheet on the south-eastern frontier towards Cochin, twenty miles in length and eight in breadth, having numerous islands, coves, and inlets, and characterized by Buchanan as ' one of the finest inland navigations imaginable.' " (THORNTON's *Gazetteer*, sub voce *Malabar*.) Of the river of Cochin, which is forty-nine miles to the south of Panane or Ponani, Horsburgh says : " It may be considered as an arm of the sea, for it extends to the southward parallel to the line of coast, and a very little distant from it, communicating with Iviker inlet or river, which falls into the sea to the

Calicut fifty leagues.¹ The king of this city is a pagan and is not very rich. The manner of living, the dress, and the customs, are after the manner of Calicut. Many merchants arrived here, because a great deal of pepper grows in this country, and in perfection. In this city we found some Christians of those of Saint Thomas, some of whom are merchants, and believe in Christ, as we do. These say that every three years a priest comes there to baptize them, and that he comes to them from Babylon. These Christians keep Lent longer than we do; but they keep Easter like ourselves, and they all observe the same solemnities that we do. But they say mass like the Greeks. The names of whom are four, that is to say, John, James, Matthew, and Thomas.² The country, the air, and the situation, resemble

northward of Quilon, forming islands by the various inlets." (*Directory*, vol. i p. 508.) These salt-water inlets, and the estuaries communicating with them, form what is technically called by seamen the *Backwater of Cochin*.

The foregoing extract from Horsburgh convinces me that Porca or Parrakad, which lies between Cochin and Quilon, is sometimes, if not always, insulated by the rivers and estuaries in its neighbourhood. Varthema is therefore justified in calling that place an island. See p. 154, and note 2.

¹ I have looked in vain for this place in Thornton's *Gazetteer*. It is written *Kayan Kulam* in Keith Johnston's Atlas, but the same designation is incorrectly given to Quilon also. The two places are distinct, and appear always to have had distinct names. Barbosa, a few years after Varthema, says : " After passing the aforesaid place [Porca,] the kingdom of *Coulan* commences, and the first place is called *Caincoulan*, inhabited by many Gentiles, Moors, and Christians of the doctrine of Saint Thomas, many of whom, in the interior, live among the Gentiles. Much pepper grows in this place, with which many vessels are loaded." (RAMUSIO, vol. i. p. 312.) Baldæus, nearly a century and a half later, describes Kayan Kulam thus :—"The next adjoining kingdom [to Percatti or Porca] is *Calecoulany*, of no great extent. Here the Dutch had a factory." (CHURCHILL's *Collection of Voyages*, vol. iii. p. 643.) Hamilton, who writes it *Coilcoloan*, says it is "a little principality contiguous to Porkah." (PINKERTON's *Voyages*, vol. viii. p. 383.) The two last mentioned authors mention Quilon also, the former calling it *Coulany*, and the latter *Coiloan*.

² Varthema would have been more correct if he had merely adduced

those of Calicut. At the end of three days we departed the above names as examples of those borne by these Christians; but that may be his meaning.

It is difficult to decide, from the imperfect and prejudiced accounts of the early Portuguese, to what rite these Christians belonged at this period, or whether they belonged to more rites than one. Varthema's notice of them is very brief, and what he does say would apply equally either to the Syrian Jacobite or to the Nestorian community, with the exception of his remark about Babylon, which, if reliable, (and he was less likely to err in the name of a place than in the definition of a doctrine,) undoubtedly connects the Christians whom he met at Cacolon with the latter. *Catholic* or Patriarch of Babylon is the vague title which has been applied to the Primate of the Nestorians while located successively at the royal seats of Seleucia, Ctesiphon, and Baghdad, and at the time referred to, the Nestorian patriarchate was established at Baghdad, whereas the Jacobite Patriarch resided then, as he does still, at Mardin in Mesopotamia. Be that as it may, at the present day the Christians of Malabar, as they are generally called, are divided into two distinct communities, one nominally subject to the spiritual primacy of the Chaldean Patriarch at Mosul, (*Chaldeans* is the name assumed by the Nestorians in Turkey and Persia who have submitted to the Church of Rome,) and the other recognizing the Syrian Jacobite Patriarch at Mardin. On the demise of the Malabar bishop of the latter body, a successor, in the person of a native priest, was sent to Mardin, where he was consecrated to the episcopate under the name of Mar Athanasius; but on returning to India the validity of his priesthood was questioned by some of the community, who asserted that he had been ordained by the laying-on of the bishop's hands after the death of the latter. This and some other objections induced the Jacobite Patriarch to send one Bishop Kirillos (Cyril,) a native of Mesopotamia, to Malabar, which gave rise to new contentions among the Jacobites of that country, who, from all the accounts that have reached me, appear to be involved in an uninterrupted succession of ecclesiastical squabbles.

The Malabar Christians who composed the Nestorian section have as a body conformed to Rome, preserving, however, their own Syriac rituals, and such other ecclesiastical customs and observances, of eastern origin, as were not considered heterodox by the Latin Church. At what precise period they ceased their connexion with the Nestorian Patriarchate at Baghdad is uncertain. Efforts were certainly made by Roman missionaries as early as the fourteenth century to induce the Malabar Christians generally to abjure their alleged schism, and some valuable notices of their proceedings at that epoch will be found in Colonel Yule's Preface to his translation of the *Mirabilia Descripta*, written by Friar Jordanus, who was Bishop of Columbum (Quilon) *circa* A.D. 1330;

from this place, and went to another city called Colon,[1] distant from that above mentioned twenty miles. The king of this city is a Pagan, and extremely powerful, and he has 20,000 horsemen, and many archers, and is constantly at war

but it seems most probable that the separation was not consummated prior to the settlement of the Portuguese in India, through whose instrumentality the Nestorians were brought into communion with the See of Rome, when, of course, their relations with the Patriarch at Baghdad ceased, and their priests received ordination through the Latin bishops located in the country. Recently, however, they appear to have become dissatisfied with that arrangement, and decided to have a bishop of their own. Accordingly, about four years ago, they deputed twelve of their number, several of whom had been ordained to the minor orders, to Mar Yûsuf, the Chaldean Patriarch at Mosul, desiring that one of them should be raised to the Episcopate. Mar Yûsuf, acting on instructions from Rome, declined to comply with this very natural request, and persisted in his refusal notwithstanding the urgent solicitations of the Chaldeans in favour of the Malabarians. Resolved not to be frustrated, the latter proceeded from Mosul to Mar Shimôn, the Nestorian Patriarch residing at Julamerk in Kurdistan, who readily consecrated the episcopal candidate; whereupon the deputation returned to India. It remains to be seen what will be the result of this step as regards the native Christian community in Malabar.

[1] The modern town of Quilon, "situated in the native state of Travancore, on the seacoast, in a bight where ships may anchor under shelter at about two and a half or three miles from the fort...The vegetable productions are timber, cocoa-nuts, pepper, cardamums, ginger, betel-nuts, and coffee. The population is stated to be about 20,000." (See THORNTON's *Gazetteer*, whose account of the place is very meagre.) Quilon, under different modifications of that name, is mentioned by the earliest Arabian and European travellers to India, and appears to have been a considerable mart in those days. It is unquestionably the *Kaukammali* of the Two Muhammedan travellers of the ninth century, who describe it as the first place which vessels touch at proceeding to India from Máskat, and a month's sail from that port with a fair wind. (PINKERTON, vol. vii. p. 185.) Any doubt which may arise on this point from the difference in the name is removed by Lee's note on Ibn Batúta's *Káwlam*, wherein he says: "In our MS., as well as in that of Mr. Apetz, it often appears thus: *Kawkam*." (p. 169.) El-Edrísi also mentions *Kawlam Meli*, in the viith. Chapter of the 2nd. Climate; but erroneously places it, I think, too far north. (Vincent attempts to reconcile the difference between *Káwkam* and *Káwlam* by supposing the translator to have been misled by the want of diacritical points in the

with other kings. This country has a good port near to the sea-coast. No grain grows here, but fruits, as at Calicut,

original, which was certainly not the case in this instance, for neither word in Arabic has any such points ; but he very judiciously recognises in the suffix *Mali* a reference to *Malè*, or Malabar. (*Com. and Nav. of the Ancients*, vol. ii. p. 477.) I am very much disposed, however, after a careful analysis of the original, to regard El-Edrisi's viiith. Chapter as, in part, a recapitulation of the viith., and to identify another place mentioned in the latter, or rather the same place under the name of *Kalkiyán*, which he locates six days from Fandaraina (see note on p. 113 *ante*,) and six or seven days from Serindíb (Ceylon,) and describes as growing much brazil-wood, with the town of Quilon.

That Quilon is identical with Marco Polo's *Coulam* is obvious from his description of the people and productions of the latter place. He says : " Here, among the idolaters, dwell Jews and Christians, who have a language of their own. The produce are pepper, brazil, indigo, black lions, and white parrots of divers sorts…They are very libidinous, and marry their sisters." (GREENE'S *Collection*, vol. iv. p. 616.) His statement that *Coulam* is situated five hundred miles north-west from Malabar (in *Pinkerton* it is south-west !) may be an error ; but whether it is so or not depends on the limits which he allows to that country. It is clear that he extended them as far as Cape Comorin on the south, and carried them a considerable distance up the coast trending to the north-east, for he writes :—" Sailing sixty miles west from Zeilan (Ceylon) is the great province of Maabar…In this kingdom is a pearl-fishery between the coast of Zeilan, in a bay where is not twelve fathom water," (*Id.* p. 614,) which was probably Tuticorin. Now, that district which Marco Polo thus includes within " the great province of Maabar," Barbosa in the sixteenth century comprehends within the kingdom of *Coulam*, the boundaries of which he prolongs still further in the same direction :—" Leaving this island of *Zeilan*, and returning to the continent where it bends by *Cape Cumeri*, we come at once upon the country of the king of *Coulam*, and of other kings who are subject to him and reside therein, which is called *Quilicare*" [Killakarai.] And, again :— " After passing the province of *Quilacare*, onward by the coast, towards the north-east wind, there is another town called *Cael*, also belonging to the king of *Coulam*." (RAMUSIO, vol. i. p. 313.) From which it is evident that the *Malabar* of these writers comprehended, *at least*, the entire line of coast between Cape Comorin and the Palk Strait, and although that distance is scarcely more than half the five hundred miles which Marco Polo places between Quilon and Malabar, it is, nevertheless, quite as near a guess as his saying that *Maabar* is only " sixty miles west from Zeilan." Vincent comes to a similar conclusion, though I do not per-

and pepper in great quantities. The colour of this people, their dress, manner of living, and customs, are the same as at Calicut. At that time, the king of this city was the friend of the king of Portugal, but being at war with others, it did not appear to us well to remain here. Wherefore, we took our way by sea, aforesaid, and went to a city which is called Chayl,[1] belonging to the same king, opposite from Colon fifty

ceive on what ground he draws a distinction between *Mahabar* and *Malabar*. He says: "The Mahabar of Marco Polo is written Malabar by some of his translators; but his *Mahabar* is the Coast of Coromandel." (*Periplus*, vol. ii. p. 520 *n*.) And the same terminology appears to have obtained at a much later date, for Hamilton writes:—"Having thus run along the seacoast of Malabar from Decully to Negapatam," etc., thereby giving to Malabar an extension of nearly six hundred miles. PINKERTON, vol. viii. p. 389.

The following is Barbosa's account of Quilon:—"Proceeding onward [from Caincoulan] by the same coast towards the south, there is another principal seaport, with a town which is called *Coulam*, where many Moors, Pagans, and Christians reside, who are great merchants, and own many ships with which they traffic with the country of Coromandel, the island of Zeilan, Bengala, Malacha, Sumatra, and Pegu; but these do not trade with Cambaia. Here much pepper is grown. The king is a Pagan, and a great lord over an extensive territory, is very rich, and has many warriors who for the most part are expert archers." RAMUSIO, vol. i, p. 312.

The Portuguese were well received at *Coulan* on their first arrival in India, and Albuquerque settled a factory there in 1503. Its political and commercial importance seem to have greatly declined during the succeeding century and a half, for Baldæus, who styles it *Coulang*, describes it as the least among the Malabar kingdoms, (see CHURCHILL's *Collection of Voyages*, vol. iii. p. 643;) and Hamilton, in whose time it was still in the hands of the Dutch, and who writes it *Coiloan*, calls it a small principality, and says that its trade was inconsiderable. See PINKERTON, vol. viii. p. 383.

[1] This name has also disappeared from the maps, but collating Barbosa with Varthema, I conclude that it is identical with Hamilton's "Coil," which he places to the north-east of *Tutecareen* on the "promontory that sends over a reef of rocks to the island of *Zeilan*, called commonly Adam's Bridge." (PINKERTON, vol. viii. p. 384.) Tuticorin, formerly famous for its pearl-fishery, is ninety miles nearly due east of Quilon, and was probably the spot where our traveller witnessed the fishing for pearls while on the voyage to *Chayl*, and which he loosely

miles. We saw those pearls fished for [here] in the sea, in the same manner as I have already described to you in Ormus.

located at a distance of fifty miles opposite to *Colon*." Chayl seems, moreover, to be identical with Marco Polo's *Cael* or *Kael*, which he mentions before enumerating Coulam and other regions to the westward, and describes as "a great city, governed by Astiar...who is very rich, and uses merchants kindly." (GREENE, vol. iv. p. 616.) Barbosa's account of it is as follows :—" After passing the province of Quilacare, [*Killakarai* of Keith Johnston's Atlas,] onward by the coast, towards the northeast wind, there is another city called *Cael*, belonging to the king of Coulam, inhabited by Pagans and Moors, who are great merchants, and there is a seaport where many ships from Malabar, Coromandel and Bengala come every year. Here traffic is carried on by all sorts of merchants from every quarter. The people of this city are expert jewellers, who trade in small pearls, for here great quantities thereof are taken ; and this fishery belongs to the king of Coulam, and for many years past has been farmed to a very rich Moorish merchant." RAMUSIO, vol. i. p. 313.

I am surprised that Dr. Vincent, who was well acquainted with Ramusio's Collection, has made no reference to this *Cael* or *Coil* in his identification of the *Kolkhi* of the author of the *Periplus* with the *Kôru* and *Calligicum* of Ptolemy and the *Kôlis* of Dionysius, as the existence of a town of that name, and in the locality occupied by *Cael*, seems to supply the only desideratum for removing the doubt which attaches to his deductions. I quote his argument in full, leaving the reader to form his own judgment on my suggestion :—" Ptolemy has still another particular which is very remarkable ; for as he places the northern point of his Tapróbane opposite to a promontory named Kôru, so he has an island Kôru between the two, and a Tala-Côri on Ceylon ; and Kôry, he says, is the same as Calligicum...The expedition of Ram to Ceylon, and his victory over Rhavan or Rhabau, king of that island, is one of the wildest fables of Hindoo mythology, but he passed into the island at the strait, since called, by the Mohamedans, Adam's Bridge. The whole country round, in consequence of this, preserves the memorial of his conquest. There is a Ramanad-buram on the continent close to the bridge ; a Rami-Ceram, or country of Ram, the island close to the continent ; [*Rameswaram*, called *Rammanana Kojel* by Baldæus, and *Ramonan Coil* by D'Anville ;] and a Point Rama on the continent. The bridge itself, formed by the shoals between Rami-ceram and Mannar, is Rama's Bridge ; and in Rami-ceram is Raman-Koil, the temple of Ram. This Koil or temple [*Koil* means a temple in Malayalim] is undoubtedly the origin of Kôru ; and the repetition of it three times in Ptolemy is in perfect correspondence with the various allusions to Ram at the present

THE CHAPTER CONCERNING CIOROMANDEL, A CITY OF INDIA.

We then passed further onwards, and arrived at a city which is called Cioromandel,[1] which is a marine district, and

day. Kôru is likewise written Kôlis by Dionysius, and the natives called Kóniaki, Koliki, and Koliaki, by different writers. This fluctuation of orthography will naturally suggest a connection with the Kolkhi of Ptolemy and the Periplus, which both of them make the seat of the Pearl Fishery; and if Sosikoorè be Tuta-corin, as D'Anville supposes, the relation of Kolkhi to that place will lead us naturally to the vicinity of Ramana-Koil; for Tuta-corin was the point where the Dutch presided over the fishery while it was in their hands, and maintains the same privilege now under the power of the English. But Koil, whether we consider it, with Ptolemy, as the point of the continent, or seek for it on the island of Ramiscram, is so near, and so intimately connected with Manaar, the principal seat of the fishery, that there can be little hesitation in assigning it to the Kolkhi of the ancients. Whether there be now a town of consequence either on the continent or on the island, I am not informed; but that Koil, and Kôlis, and Kolkhi, and Kalligicum, (for Kállígicum, Salmasius reads Κωλιακόν,) are related, I have no doubt." *Commerce and Navigation of the Ancients*, vol. ii. pp. 501-503.

[1] I am not aware that a city so called has ever existed on the coast referred to, and am therefore led to conclude that in this instance, as in the case of Bîjapûr which Varthema styled "Decan," he gives to one of the principal towns the name of the district in which it was located. The alleged vicinity of St. Thomas's tomb points to the neighbourhood of Maliapur; but as that position is irreconcileable with the other indications supplied, I am inclined to infer either that our author was misinformed in that particular, or that an error in the numerals recording the distance has crept into the existing versions of his travels. His "Cioromandel" I take to be Negapatam, "a town on the western coast of the Bay of Bengal. Here is a diminutive estuary of the Cauvery, capable of receiving small coasting-vessels, which carry on a considerable trade...The inhabitants have also considerable traffic with Ceylon, and the lands and islands lying eastward." (THORNTON'S *Gazetteer*.) It appears to have been the principal town on that part of the coast, for Ralph Fitch nearly a century after Varthema does not mention the name of Coromandel, but describes it as "the mainland of Negapatan." (PINKERTON, vol. ix. p. 424.) Its situation about three hundred miles, by the coast, from Quilon would make the interval be-

distant from Colon seven days' journey by sea, more or less, according to the wind. This city is very large, and is not surrounded by walls, and is subject to the king of Narsinga. The said city is situated opposite to the island of Zeilon, when you have passed the Cape of Cumerin. In this district they gather a great quantity of rice, and it is the route to very large countries. There are many Moorish merchants here who go and come for their merchandize. No spices of any description grow here, but plenty of fruits, as at Calicut. I found some Christians in this district who told me that the body of St. Thomas was twelve miles distant from that place, and that it was under the guard of some Christians. They also told me that Christians could not live in that country after the king of Portugal had come there, because the said king had put to death many Moors of that country, which trembled throughout from fear of the Portuguese. And, therefore, the said poor Christians cannot live here any longer, but are driven away and killed secretly, in order that it may not come to the ears of the king of Narsinga, who is a very great friend of the Christians, and especially of the Portuguese. One of these Christians also told me a very great miracle which his priest had told him, that forty-five years ago the Moors had a dispute with the Christians, and there were wounded on both sides; but one Christian, among the rest, was much wounded in the arm, and he went to the tomb of St. Thomas and touched the tomb of St. Thomas with that wounded arm, and immediately he was

tween the two places a seven days' voyage "more or less, according to the wind;" and the actual distance which separates it from the nearest point of Ceylon being one degree of latitude, corresponds approximately with the twelve or fifteen leagues which Varthema subsequently places between his *Cioromandel* and that island. The shoals and rocks in the Palk Strait render navigation difficult at all times, and his notice of them as endangering the passage from the mainland is an additional argument in favour of the foregoing identification, proving, at least, that his *Cioromandel* was to the northward of Calimere Point.

cured.¹ And that from that time henceforward, the king of Narsinga has always wished well to the Christians. My companion disposed of some of his merchandize here, and inasmuch as they were at war with the king of Tarnassari we remained here only a few days, and then we took a ship with some other merchants, which ships are called *Ciampane*,² for they are flat-bottomed, and require little water and carry much goods. We passed a gulf of twelve or fifteen leagues where we had incurred great peril because there are many shoals and rocks there; however, we arrived at an island called Zailon,³ which is about 1000 miles in circumference, according to the report of the inhabitants thereof.

THE CHAPTER CONCERNING ZAILANI, WHERE JEWELS ARE PRODUCED.

In this island of Zailon there are four kings,⁴ all Pagans.

¹ A very insignificant miracle compared with many others attributed to the sepulchre of St. Thomas. Barbosa piously records a tradition that the right arm of the Apostle protruded from his tomb at Maliapur, and for a long time resisted every attempt to cover it.

² *Sampan*, the common name for a canoe or skiff in Malay and Javanese.

³ Ceylon. Our traveller's informants were better acquainted with the extent of the island than Marco Polo, who made it 2,400 miles in circuit, and says that "anciently it was 3,600 miles, as is seen in the maps of the mariners of those places; but the north winds have made a great part of it sea." (PINKERTON, vii. p. 161.) Nicolò de' Conti estimated its circumference at 3,000 miles. "The extreme length of the island is about 270 miles; its breadth varies greatly, but the average is about 100 miles." THORNTON's *Gazetteer*.

From the description which Varthema gives of the locality,—the large river, the adjacent mountains, and the cinnamon cultivation,—I conclude that he landed at Colombo on the western coast; for it is by no means a necessary inference that because he mentions the width of the passage between the mainland and the island that the voyage was limited to that extent.

⁴ Marco Polo gives the same number of kings in his time. Varthema's brief description of the political condition of the island at the period of

I do not describe to you all the things of the said island, because these kings being in fierce war with each other, we could not remain there long, neither could we see or hear the things thereof; however, having remained there some few days, we saw that which you shall hear. And first, an immense quantity of elephants which are produced there.[1]

his visit is fully confirmed by Sir J. E. Tennent. Writing of A.D. 1505, he says: " The seaports on all parts of the coast were virtually in the hands of the Moors: the north was in the possession of the Malabars, whose seat of government was at Jaffna-patam ; and the great central region, (since known as the Wanny,) and Neuera-kalawa, were formed into petty chiefships, each governed by a *Wanniya*, calling himself a vassal, but virtually uncontrolled by any paramount authority. In the south the nominal sovereign Dharma Prakrama Bahu IX. had his capital at Cotta, near Colombo, whilst minor kings held mimic courts at Badulla, Gampola, Peradenia, Kandy, and Mahagam, and caused repeated commotions by their intrigues and insurrections. The rulers had long ceased to busy themselves with the endowment of temples, and the construction of works for irrigation; so that already in the fourteenth century, Ceylon had become dependent upon India for supplies of food, and annually imported rice from the Dekkan." (*Ceylon*, vol. ii. p. 7.) The same author, in a note on the above passage from Varthema, remarks:—" These conflicts and the actors in them are described in the Singhalese chronicle called the *Rajavali*." I could not find Upham's translation of that work in the British Museum ; but the following extract from Knighton is, I presume, partly based on its authority:—"We have already explained that on the arrival of Almeida, Ceylon was divided into three distinct principalities, of which Dharma Pakramabahu IX., who then resided at Cotta was king of the larger and more important one, the other two being the territory of the Malabars in the north and the wild Veddahs on the north and east. Europeans have frequently been misled into the idea that the island was divided into a vast number of petty kingdoms, each independent of the other. Such, however, was not the case. Sub-kings, or, as we should call them, lieutenants, subject to the Emperor of Cotta, were appointed in many places, who frequently endeavoured to play upon western visitors, by representing themselves as independent princes." *History of Ceylon*, pp. 222-3.

[1] " The elephant, the lord paramount of the Ceylon forests, is to be met with in every district, on the confines of the woods...In recent years there is reason to believe that their numbers have become considerably reduced." TENNENT's *Ceylon*, vol. i. p. 158.

We also saw rubies found there, at a distance of two miles from the sea shore, where there is an extremely large and very long mountain, at the foot of which the said rubies are found.[1] And when a merchant wishes to find these jewels, he is obliged first to speak to the king and to purchase a *braza* of the said land in every direction, (which *braza* is called a *molan*,)[2] and to purchase it for five ducats. And then when he digs the said land, a man always remains there on the part of the king. And if any jewel be found which exceeds ten carats, the king claims it for himself, and leaves all the rest free. There is also produced near to the said mountain, where there is a very large river,[3] a great quantity of garnets, sapphires, jacinths, and topazes.[4] In this island there grow the best fruits I have ever seen, and especially certain artichokes (carzofoli) better than ours.[5] Sweet oranges, (melangoli,) the best, I believe, in the world, and many other fruits like those of Calicut, but much superior.

[1] "The extent to which gems are still found is sufficient to account for the early traditions of their splendour and profusion, and fabulous as the story of the ruby of the Khandyan king may be, [which according to Marco Polo was a span in length, and without a flaw,] the abundance of gems in Saffragam has given the capital of the district the name of *Ratnapoora*, which means literally the City of Rubies. They are not, however, confined to this quarter alone, but quantities are still found on the western plains, between Adam's Peak and the sea." *Id.* p. 33.

[2] Perhaps for *Ammonan*, which according to Pridham was equal to 2 acres, 2 square roods, $37\frac{1}{2}$ square inches. *Ceylon and its Dependencies*, vol. ii. p. 853.

[3] This was most probably the Kalané-ganga, which Pridham describes as "the chief river of the island in importance...It is formed by the union of several torrents which have their source in the western division of the mountainous range of Saffragam, connected with Adam's Peak... It debouches at Modera, about four miles to the north of the fort of Colombo." (*Id.* p. 635.) The river is navigable for a considerable distance from its mouth.

[4] These and many other precious stones are enumerated and described in Tennent's *Ceylon*, vol. i. pp. 33-38.

[5] Probably the Custard Apple, which in outer form is not unlike an artichoke.

THE CHAPTER CONCERNING THE TREE OF THE *CANELLA*.

The tree of the *Canella* is the same as the laurel, especially the leaves; and it produces some berries like the laurel, but they are smaller and more white. The said *Canella*, or *Cinnamon*, is the bark of the said tree, in this wise: Every three years they cut the branches of the said tree, and then take off the bark of them; but they do not cut the stem on any account. There are great numbers of these trees. When they collect that cinnamon it has not the excellence which it possesses a month afterwards.[1] A Moorish merchant told me that at the top of that very large mountain there is a cavern to which the men of that country go once in the year to pray, because, as they say, Adam was up there praying and doing penance, and that the impressions of his feet are seen to this day, and that they are about two spans long.[2] Rice does not

[1] If this is true, the cultivation and preparation of cinnamon must have been very backward in Varthema's time, as at present it appears to be gathered twice a-year.—"The best cinnamon is obtained from the twigs or shoots, which spring almost perpendicularly from the roots after the parent bush or tree has been cut down; but great care is requisite both as to the exact size and age...The rods cut for peeling are of various sizes and lengths, depending on the texture of the bark: these are first peeled, then scraped on the outside, and while drying cut up into long narrow rolls called *quills*, then stuck into one another, so as to form pipes about three feet long, which are then made up in round bundles. There are two regular seasons for taking cinnamon, one from April to August, another from to November to January; but considerable quantities are gathered at other times as the spice attains maturity." PRIDHAM, *Ceylon and its Dependencies*, p. 387.

[2] "Adam's Peak is 7,420 feet above the level of the sea, and its summit, of an elliptic form, 72 feet in length by 34 in breadth, is surrounded by a wall five feet high. Immediately within this, a level space of irregular breadth runs all the way round, and the centre is occupied by the apex of the mountain, a solid granite rock about nine feet high at the highest part. On this is the *Sree Pada*, or Sacred Footstep. Whether this much cherished memorial is rightfully attached to Saman by a prior claim (whence Samanala, Hamallel, or Samantakuta,) the Sree Pada is now

grow in this country, but it comes there from the main land. The kings of this island are tributaries of the king of Narsinga, on account of the rice which comes there from the main land.[1] The air in this island is extremely good, and

<small>held by the Buddhists to be a memorial of Gautama Buddha; by the Mohammedans it is claimed for Adam, and called Baba-Aadamlai; and the Malabars and other Hindoos maintain that it was Siva who left the impression of a monster footstep, and call it Sivanolipadam." *Id.*, ii. p. 614-5.

Sale has the following respecting the Mussulman tradition above alluded to:—" The Mohamedans say, that when they were cast down from paradise, Adam fell on the island of Ceylon, or Serindib, and Eve near Juddah, the port of Meccah, in Arabia; and that after a separation of two hundred years, Adam was, on his repentance, conducted by the angel Gabriel to a mountain near Mekkah, where he found and knew his wife, the mountain being thence named Arafàt; and that he afterwards retired with her to Ceylon, where they continued to propagate their species.

" It may not be improper here to mention another tradition concerning the gigantic stature of our first parents. Their prophet, they say, affirmed Adam to be as tall as a high palm-tree; but this would be too much in proportion, if that were really the print of his foot, which is pretended to be such, on the top of a mountain in the isle of Ceylon, thence named *Pico di Adam*, and by the Arab writers *Rahûn*, being somewhat about two spans long; though others say it is seventy cubits long, and that when Adam set one foot here, he had the other in the sea;—and too little, if Eve were of so enormous a size, that when her head lay on one hill near Meccah, her knees rested on two others in the plain, about two musket-shots asunder." *Note* on chapter ii. of the *Korán*.

Ibn Batûta mentions " a cave known by the name of Istà Mahmûd," also "a place called the seven caves," and again " the ridge of Alexander, in which is a cave and a well of water," on his pious pilgrimage to Adam's Foot, (LEE's *Translation*, p. 187-9;) but I find no mention of any locality corresponding with Varthema's " cavern" in the modern descriptions of the route up to the Peak.

[1] On this statement Sir J. E. Tennent remarks:—" There can be little doubt that it applied chiefly to the southern parts of the island, and that the north was still able to produce food sufficient for the wants of the inhabitants." Rice appears to have been extensively cultivated in many parts of Ceylon, but probably not in the maritime district visited by Varthema. "The soil near the coast is light and sandy, but in the great central districts of Neuera-kalawa and the Wanny, there is found</small>

the people are of a dark tawny colour. And here it is neither too hot nor too cold. Their dress is *alla apostolica*; they wear certain stuffs of cotton or silk, and go bare-footed. This island is placed under the equinoctial line, and the inhabitants of it are not very warlike. Artillery is not used here; but they have some lances and swords, which lances are of cane, and with these they fight amongst each other; but they do not kill each other overmuch, because they are cowardly fellows.[1] Here there are roses and flowers of every kind,[2] and the people live longer than we do. Being in our ship one evening, a man came on the part of the king to

in the midst of the forests a dark vegetable mould, in which in former times rice was abundantly grown by the aid of prodigious artificial works for irrigation, the ruins of which still form one of the wonders of the island. Even after centuries of neglect, the beds of many of these tanks cover areas of from ten to fifteen miles in circumference. They are now generally broken and decayed; the waters which would fertilise a province are allowed to waste themselves in the sands, and hundreds of square miles capable of furnishing food for all the inhabitants of Ceylon are abandoned to solitude and malaria, whilst rice for the support of the non-agricultural population is annually imported from the opposite coast of India." *Ceylon*, vol. i. pp. 27, 639.

[1] Fire-arms appear to have been unknown in Ceylon at this period. Referring to the introduction of them into the island by the Portuguese, Sir J. E. Tennent quotes the following passage from the *Rajavali*:—"And now it came to pass that in the Christian year 1522 [1507?], a ship from Portugal arrived at Colombo, and information was brought to the king, that there were in the harbour a race of very white and beautiful people who wear boots and shoes, and never stop in any place. They eat a sort of white stone, and drink blood; and if they get a fish they give two or three *ridé* in gold for it; and, besides, they have guns with a noise like thunder, and a ball shot from one of them, after traversing a league, will break a castle of marble." (*Ceylon*, vol. i. p. 418.) Marco Polo says of the Singhalese: "the men are unfit for soldiers, and hire others when they have occasion." PINKERTON, vol. vii. p. 162.

[2] "The indigenous phænogamic plants described up to August 1856 was 26,700...When it is considered that this is nearly double the indigenous flora of England, and little under *one-thirtieth* of the entire number of plants hitherto described over the world, the botanical richness of Ceylon, in proportion to its area, must be regarded as equal to that of any portion of the globe." TENNENT'S *Ceylon*, vol. i. p. 83 n.

my companion, and told him that he should carry to him his corals and saffron; for he had a great quantity of both. A merchant of the said island, who was a Moor, hearing these words, said to him secretly: "Do not go to the king, for he will pay you for your goods after his own fashion." And this he said out of cunning, in order that my companion might go away, because he himself had the same kind of merchandize. However, answer was given to the message of the king, that on the following day he would go to his lord. And when morning came, he took a vessel and rowed over to the mainland.

THE CHAPTER CONCERNING PALEACHET, A COUNTRY OF INDIA.

We arrived in the course of three days at a place which is called Paleachet,[1] which is subject to the king of Narsinga.

[1] Pulicat: "a town in the British district of Chingleput, about twenty-two miles north of Madras, situated on an extensive inlet of the sea, or salt water lake, of the same name...From one to two miles off shore is the road called Pulicat Anchorage, where there are six or seven fathoms water." (THORNTON's *Gazetteer*.) Pulicat appears to have been a place of considerable trade at this period. Barbosa describes it a few years after Varthema as having a good port, which was frequented by "an infinite number" of Moorish vessels from all quarters. In his time it was governed by a deputy appointed by the Narsinga, or Rajah of Bijayanagar, who appears to have retained possession of a great part of the sea-coast for more than half a century after the destruction of his capital by the confederate Mussulman kings of the Deccan in 1565; for in 1611, when Pulicat was visited by Captain Anthony Hippon, being the seventh voyage set forth by the East India Company, the administration was in the hands of "the Governess Konda Maa, on the part of Wankapati Raja, king of Narsinga." (GREENE's *Collection*, vol. i. p. 436.) But the coast to the north of Pulicat, including Masulipatam, became tributary to Bijapúr during the reign of Muhammed Sháh Bhamâni, about A.D. 1480, and formed subsequently a part of the kingdom of Golconda, including Telingana, which in Fitch's time, 1583-91, was ruled by "Cutub de lashah," (Muhammed Kúli Kutb Sháh,) who

This district is one of immense traffic in merchandize, and especially in jewels, for they come here from Zailon and from Pego. There are also here many great Moorish merchants of all kinds of spices. We lodged in the house of a Moorish merchant, and we told him where we came from, and that we had many corals to sell, and saffron, and much figured velvet, and many knives. The said merchant, understanding that we had this kind of merchandize, was greatly pleased. This country is most abundant in everything which is produced in India, but no grain grows there. They have rice here in great abundance. Their laws, manner of living, dress, and customs, are the same as at Calicut, and they are a warlike people, although they have no artillery. As this country was at fierce war with the king of Tarnassari, we could not remain here a very long time. But after remaining here a few days we took our route towards the city of Tarnassari, which is distant a thousand miles from here. At which city we arrived in fourteen days by sea.

built Bhajnugger, which name he afterwards changed to Hydrabad. On his death, which occurred in 1586, there appears to have been a break in the Kutb-Shâhi dynasty, for Abdallah Kutb Shâh, who became tributary to the Emperor Shâh Jehân, did not commence his reign till 1611, and must have succeeded "Kotobara of Badaya or Lollongana [Bhajuugger or Telingana?] and of Masulipatam," who, according to Floris's account, died on the 20th of January of that year while he was with Captain Hippon at the latter place. Abdallah Kutb Shâh still reigned over Golconda and Telingana in 1639 (MANDELSLO, p. 289,) but in 1672 it was incorporated into the empire of Arungzib.

I infer from De Faria y Souza that the Portuguese established a colony at Pulicat as early as A.D. 1522, but I do not find the name in the list of their *forts* on the Coromandel coast. They were succeeded in 1600 by the Dutch, who built a fort there called Geldria, and made it their chief settlement after the loss of Negapatam. PINKERTON, vol. xi, p. 203 n.

THE CHAPTER CONCERNING TARNASSARI, A CITY OF INDIA.

The city of Tarnassari[1] is situated near to the sea: it is a

[1] Dr. Vincent, in his Dissertation on the Sequel to the *Periplus*, appears to have identified this town with Masulipatam; or, as he did not find the name in the modern maps, he concluded that "it might lie between Pulcachat and Bengal." The inference is totally inadmissible; for in the first place Varthema interposes one thousand miles between Pulcachet and *Tarnassari*, and in a subsequent chapter makes the latter seven hundred miles from *Banghella*; whilst the distance between Pulicat and Masulipatam is only 220, and between Masulipatam and the mouths of the Ganges somewhat under 500 miles. Moreover, the branch of the Kistnah runs to the *south* of Masulipatam, but the river of *Tarnassari* was on the *north* of that town. The fauna and flora of the country, as also several of its other productions, as described by our traveller, are equally irreconcilable with the south of India; whereas, taking his *Tarnassari* to be identical with Tenasserim on the eastern coast of the ancient kingdom of Siam, and of which at the time it formed a part, these inconsistencies disappear, and his conjectural distances and other data are approximately correct. The only point which I have been unable to clear up, either from a want of historical records of the period, or from my own unacquaintance with them, is Varthema's twice repeated statement that there was continual war between the king of *Tarnassari* and the Narsinga, with the latter of whom, in this chapter, he couples the king of *Banghella*.

Like Dr. Vincent, I long searched in vain for a *Tarnassari* on the southern coast of India, but ultimately found one in Baldæus's map placed some distance inland on the south side of the branch of the Kistnah which debouches at Masulipatam. As he gives no account of the place, I presume that he borrowed the name directly from Varthema, or from some subsequent geographers who drew the same erroneous inference respecting its locality as Dr. Vincent. In fact, I found the following description of the town, under the heading of "*Narsingæ Regnum*," in the Geography of Io. Ant. Magino Patavino, printed at Bologna, A.D. 1597, which is evidently compiled from this and the two chapters succeeding the next of Varthema's narrative:—"*Tarnassari* urbs ad hoc regnum pertinet, quæ olim proprium agnoscebat regem idololatram, valdè potentem, qui ad bellum mittere solebat centum elephantes armatos, et centum millia milites, tum equites tum pedestres. Incolæ hujus urbis uxores suas deflorandas albicantis coloris hominibus tradunt, sive Christianis, sive Mahumetanis; quæ quidem uxores ornatæ accomptæ post mariti obitum honoris ac fidelitatis ergò vivæ construuntur unà

level place and well watered, and has a good port, that is, a river on the side towards the north. The king of the city

cum viri cadavere, aliter perpetua infamiæ nota laborarent: quem morem in universo quoq; Narsingæ regno observant." *Geographiæ Universæ tum Veteris tum Novæ absolutissimum Opus*, etc., p. 258.

As far as I know, Varthema's is the first authentic account which we possess of the province of Tenasserim, with the exception of the following brief notice by Conti about A.D. 1440 :—" Leaving the island of Taprobane [Sumatra], he arrived, after a stormy voyage of seventeen days, at the city of *Ternassari*, which is situated on the mouth of a river of the same name. The land around abounds in elephants and produces much brazil-wood." (*Ramusio*, vol. i, p. 339.) Barbosa, a few years after our traveller, gives us some additional particulars respecting its government, from which we learn that it was then a province of Siam, but ruled by an almost independent viceroy :—" Immediately on leaving the kingdom of Pegu, there is another called *Ternassari*, where are many Moorish and Gentile merchants, who trade in all kinds of wares. They have vessels with which they navigate towards Bengala, and Malaca, and other parts. Very excellent benzoin, which is the juice of certain trees, is grown in the interior, and the Moors call it *lubaniabi* [*lubán Jáwi*, Java frankincense ?]. In this port of *Ternassari* there are many Moors from different parts." And in the *Summary of Kingdoms* we read :—" The Siamese trade on the *Tenacerim* side with Pacem, Pedir, Queda, Pegu, Bengala, and Guzerat. The king [of Siam] is called *Perchoara*, which means the lord of all. With the king is Aiam Campetit, who is viceroy on the side of Pegu, and makes war with Brema [Burmah] and Iamgoma...The second, who is viceroy of Longor, is called *Peraia*... The other is the *Aia Chatoteri*, who is the viceroy on the side of Queda and *Tenacerin:* he is a chief person, and has power over all. He is perpetual captain of *Tenacerin*, is lord over many people, and of a country abounding in all kinds of provisions." (*Ramusio*, vol. i. p. 330.) Ralph Fitch, A.D. 1583-91, merely mentions that he passed by *Tenasseri* on his way from Pegu to Malacca. In 1600, Master John Davis touched at " the city of *Tanassarin*," which he styles " a place of great trade." (GREENE, vol. i. p. 261.) He was followed in 1612 by Captain John Floris, who states that it was then tributary to Pegu, (*Id.* p. 439,) by which power the province had been conquered in 1568, but was recovered by the black king of Siam, aided by the Portuguese, in 1603. (*Mod. Univ. History*, vol. vi. p. 259.) *Purchas* records that " in the year 1606 Balthasar Sequerius, a Jesuit, landing at *Tanassery*, passed from thence, partly by good rivers, partly over cragged and rough hills and forests stored with rhinoceros, elephants, and tigers, into Odia" [the capital of Siam.] (Vol. i. p. 491.) Master William Methold, about A.D. 1619, describes

is a Pagan, and is a very powerful lord. He is constantly fighting with the king of Narsinga and the king of Banghella. He has a hundred armed elephants, which are larger than any I ever saw. He always maintains 100,000 men for war, part infantry and part cavalry. Their arms consist of small swords and some sort of shields, some of which are made of tortoise-shell, and some like those of Calicut; and they have a great quantity of bows, and lances of cane, and some also of wood. When they go to war they wear a dress stuffed very full of cotton. The houses of this city are well surrounded by walls. Its situation is extremely good, after the manner of Christians, and good grain and cotton also grow there. Silk is also made there in large quantities.[1] A

the province as follows:—"*Tanassery* lyeth next to Pegu, a small kingdom and tributary to Syam, from which place this is but the port, and that only to the inhabitants of this gulf [Bengal;] for we find a way with our shipping into the river of Syam." (*Id.* vol. v. p. 993.) Mandelslo, twenty years later, reckons *Tanacerim* among the principal tributary cities of Siam. (*Voyages*, p. 334.) The English had a factory at Mergui on the Tenasserim river about this time, but in 1687 the settlers were nearly all massacred by the Siamese. (See PINKERTON, vol. viii. p. 429-30.) Turpin describes the province in 1770 as producing "an abundance of rice and excellent fruits. It is in its safe and commodious port that vessels of all nations arrive, and the people find more means of subsisting there than in the other parts of the kingdom." (*Id.* vol. ix. p. 578.) From that period, however, Tenasserim appears to have declined in importance, chiefly by the removal of its trade to Mergui. (*Mod. Univ. Hist.*, vol. vi. p. 267.) In 1793 the entire province was ceded to Ava, and in 1826 it became a British possession by the Treaty of Yandaboo. The old town is now a place of no importance, containing only one hundred houses and four hundred inhabitants. It is situate on the river of the same name, at the confluence of the Little Tenasserim. The river is navigable up to the town for vessels of one hundred and twenty tons burthen. The town was once surrounded by a brick wall, which is now so much in ruins that its remains can be traced only at intervals." The trade of the province is as yet comparatively insignificant, but the population, since the British domination, has increased from 90,000 to 191,476. See THORNTON's *Gazetteer*.

[1] "Cotton is grown to a small extent in the province of Tenasserim, but it is not indigenous, and was probably introduced from the continent

great deal of brazil-wood is found there, fruits in great abundance, and some which resemble our apples and pears, some oranges, lemons, and citrons, and gourds in great abundance.[1] And here are seen very beautiful gardens, with many delicate things in them.

THE CHAPTER CONCERNING THE DOMESTIC AND WILD ANIMALS OF TARNASSARI.

In this country of Tarnassari there are oxen, cows, sheep, and goats in great quantities,[2] wild hogs, stags, roebucks, wolves, cats which produce the civet, lions, peacocks in great multitudes, falcons, goss-hawks, white parrots, and also

of India." (THORNTON's *Gazetteer.*) I find no mention of silk as a natural production of the country; but Yule calls it "the staple of the import trade" into Burmah, "and is said to come from a city called *Tsa-chöë-Sing,* eighty-three days' journey from Bamó, and fifty days beyond the city of Yunan." He estimates the value of silk imported in 1854 at £120,000, and states that the weaving of the raw material gives employment to a large body of the population." (*Narrative of a Mission to the Court of Ava,* pp. 149-53.) Varthema probably alludes to this manufacture, for he does not say that the country produces silk, but merely "*se fa quivi* seta in grandissima quantità."

[1] "The fruits are the pineapple, mango, orange, shaddock, lime, citron, melon, gourd, guava, and darian." THORNTON's *Gazetteer.*

[2] Captain Low, writing of the provinces of Tenasserim and Mergui, says: "goats are scarce, and there are no sheep!" In like manner, Cæsar Fredericke, sixty years after Varthema, states that at all the villages on his route "hennes, pigeons, eggs, milk, rice, and other things, be very good and cheape;" whereon Colonel Yule remarks:— "a very different state of things from the present, when our hungry Surveyors complain that they can get neither 'hennes' nor eggs, let alone 'other things,' for love or money." Allowing for exaggeration in the accounts of the old travellers, it seems evident that the agricultural and other productions of Pegu, as well as its population and trade, have greatly fallen off since their time, the consequence, doubtless, of the intestine and foreign wars which for upwards of a century subsequent to their visits devastated the country, and of the misrule which succeeded. See *Narrative of a Mission to the Court of Ava,* pp. 211-2.

other kinds which are of seven very beautiful colours. Here there are hares and partridges, but not like ours. There is also here another kind of bird, one of prey, much larger than an eagle, of the beak of which, that is, of the upper part, they make sword-hilts, which beak is yellow and red, a thing very beautiful to behold. The colour of the said bird is black, red, and some feathers are white.[1] There are produced here hens and cocks, the largest I ever saw, so much so that one of these hens is larger than three of ours. In this country in a few days we had great pleasure from some things which we saw, and especially that every day in the street where the Moorish merchants abide they make some cocks fight, and the owners of these cocks bet as much as a hundred ducats on the one which will fight best. And we saw two fight for five hours continuously, so that at the last both remained dead.[2] Here also is a sort of goat, much larger than ours, and which is much more handsome, and which always has four kids at a birth. Ten and twelve large and good sheep are sold here for a ducat. And there is another kind of sheep, which has horns like a deer:[3] these

[1] I am indebted to the kindness of Professor Owen of the British Museum for the following interesting note:—"This coloured bill applies to the Helmet-Hornbill, (*Buceros galeatus,*) of which the bowl of a jewelled ladle, for sherbet, which was sent from Constantinople for my inspection, was formed. The tradition of this sherbet-ladle, which is part of the crown-jewels of the Sultan, is that the bowl was made from the beak of the Phœnix. *Buceros galeatus*, however, is not known to exist, as an indigenous bird, out of the islands of the Indian Archipelago. Its plumage agrees, in a general way, with that ascribed to a bird with the parti-coloured bill in the text."

[2] According to Turpin, "cock-fighting in Siam attracts multitudes, as the field is always stained by the death of one of the combatants." (PINKERTON, vol. ix. p. 598.) Low also, in his *History of Tenasserim*, says: "they fight cocks with artificial spurs, but these are generally made of bone, or of an alligator's tooth, or even of a human bone, if the parties are of royal extraction, and so shaped as to resemble the natural spur." *Journal of the Royal Asiatic Society*, vol. ii. p. 272.

[3] "More probably like an ox. It may refer to the huge horns of the male of *Ovis ammon*." PROFESSOR OWEN.

are larger than ours, and fight most terribly. There are buffalos here, much more misshapen than ours. There are also great numbers of fish like ours. I saw here, however, a bone of a fish which weighed more than ten *cantari*.[1] With respect to the manner of living of this city, the Pagans eat all kinds of flesh excepting that of oxen,[2] and they eat on the ground, without a cloth, in some very beautiful vessels of wood. Their drink is water, sweetened where possible. They sleep high from the ground, in good beds of cotton, and covered with silk or cotton. Then, as to their dress, they go *alla apostolica*,[3] with a quilted cloth of cotton or silk. Some merchants wear very beautiful shirts of silk or cotton: in general, they do not wear anything on their feet, excepting the Brahmins, who also wear on the head a cap of silk or camelot, which is two spans long. In the said cap they wear on the top a thing made like a hazel-nut, which is worked all round in gold. They also wear two strings of silk, more than two fingers wide, which they hang round the neck. They wear their ears full of jewels and none on their fingers.[4] The colour of the said race is semi-white,

---

[1] Turpin says: "The rivers and sea coasts of this kingdom [Siam] abound more with fish than elsewhere: the reason doubtless is, because the rivers for six months in the year overflow the sown grounds, and then the fish find plenty of food, and do not prey on one another." (PINKERTON, vol. ix. p. 632.) The bone which Varthema describes may have been that of a stray whale, as, according to Crawfurd, whales are only found in this region on the shores of some of the more easterly islands of the Archipelago. The Italian *cantaro* varies in different provinces and according to the article weighed. Its average is about a cwt. English.

[2] "The people live on rice, fish, venison, pork, and in general on the flesh of almost every sort of animal and reptile; but they seldom use beef or poultry, and do not make butter." *Journ. of R. A. Soc.*, vol. ii. p. 266.

[3] See note on p. 112 *ante*.

[4] A similar dress is described by Colonel Symes as worn by the Burmese gentry:—"It consists of a long robe, either of flowered satin or velvet, reaching to the ancles, with an open collar and loose sleeves;

because the air here is cooler than it is in Calicut, and the seasons are the same as with us, and also the harvests.[1]

THE CHAPTER SHOWING HOW THE KING CAUSES HIS WIFE TO BE DEFLOWERED, AND SO ALSO THE OTHER PAGANS OF THE CITY.

The king of the said city does not cause his wife's virginity to be taken by the Brahmins as the king of Calicut does, but he causes her to be deflowered by white men, whether Christians or Moors, provided they be not Pagans. Which Pagans also, before they conduct their wives to their house, find a white man, of whatever country he may be, and take him to their house for this particular purpose, to make him deflower the wife. And this happened to us when we arrived in the said city. We met by chance three or four merchants, who began to speak to my companion in this wise: "Langalli ni pardesi," that is, "Friend, are you strangers?" He answered: "Yes." Said the merchants: "Ethera nali ni banno," that is, "How many days have you been in this country?" We replied: "Mun nal gnad banno," that is, "It is four days since we arrived." Another

over this there is a scarf, or flowing mantle, that hangs from the shoulders; and on their heads they wear high caps made of velvet, either plain or of silk embroidered with flowers of gold, according to the rank of the wearer. Earrings are a part of male dress: persons of condition use tubes of gold about three inches long, and as thick as a large quill, which expands at one end like the mouth of a speaking-trumpet; others wear a heavy mass of gold beaten into a plate, and rolled up; this lump of metal forms a large orifice in the lobe of the ear, and drags it down by the weight, to the extent sometimes of two inches." PINKERTON, vol. ix. p. 496.

[1] "The natives on the coast divide the year into three seasons, viz., the hot, the rainy, and the cold; the temperature, however, hardly varies sufficiently to justify the adoption of this division. THORNTON'S *Gazetteer*.

one of the said merchants said: "Biti banno gnan pigamanathon ondo," that is, "Come to my house, for we are great friends of strangers;" and we, hearing this, went with him. When we had arrived at his house, he gave us a collation, and then he said to us: "My friends, Patanci nale banno gnan penna periti in penna orangono panna panni cortu," that is, "Fifteen days hence I wish to bring home my wife, and one of you shall sleep with her the first night, and shall deflower her for me." We remained quite ashamed at hearing such a thing. Then our interpreter said: "Do not be ashamed, for this is the custom of the country." Then my companion hearing this said: "Let them not do us any other mischief, for we will satisfy you in this;" but we thought that they were mocking us. The merchant saw that we remained undecided, and said: "O langal limaranconia ille ocha manezar irichenu," that is, "Do not be dispirited, for all this country follows this custom." Finding at last that such was the custom in all this country, as one who was in our company affirmed to us, and said that we need have no fear, my companion said to the merchant that he was content to go through this fatigue. The merchant then said: "I wish you to remain in my house, and that you, your companions and goods, be lodged here with me until I bring the lady home." Finally, after refusing, we were obliged to yield to his caresses, and all of us, five in number, together with all our things, were lodged in his house. Fifteen days from that time this merchant brought home his wife, and my companion slept with her the first night. She was a young girl of fifteen years, and he did for the merchant all that he had asked of him. But after the first night, it would have been at the peril of his life if he had returned again, although truly the lady would have desired that the first night had lasted a month. The merchants, having received such a service from some of us, would gladly have retained us four or five months at their own expense, for all kinds of wares cost very little money, and also because they are most liberal and very agreeable men.[1]

THE CHAPTER SHOWING HOW THE DEAD BODIES ARE PRESERVED IN THIS CITY.

All the Brahmins and the king are burnt after death, and at that time a solemn sacrifice is made to the devil. And then they preserve the ashes in certain vases made of baked earth, vitrified like glass, which vases have the mouth narrow like a small *scutella*.[2] They then bury this vase with the ashes of the burnt body within their houses. When they make the said sacrifice, they make it under some trees,

[1] I find nothing to confirm the flagrant profligacy described in this chapter, either as regards Tenasserim or Siam; on the contrary, Turpin states that "the nuptial couch is seldom polluted by adultery...There is a whimsical custom, however, which deranges all matrimonial agreements. Sometimes the monarch bestows a wife, of whom he is tired, on one of his favourites: it is a flattering distinction, which often constrains the inclination." (PINKERTON, vol. ix. p. 585.) Nevertheless, revolting as the custom must appear to us, and difficult as it may be to account for so strange an illustration of human depravity, I see no reason to doubt the veracity of Varthema's narrative, more especially as Richard describes a similar usage as prevailing in the neighbouring country of Aracan:—"Virginity is not an esteemed virtue with them. Husbands prefer running the risk of fathering the children of others, rather than marry a novice. It is generally Dutch sailors, who are liberally paid for this infamous prostitution." *Id.* pp. 760-1.

The colloquy between Varthema's party and the Tenasserim merchants was carried on through an interpreter, who appears to have communicated with the former in a corrupt Malayalim, as the specimens of the native dialect introduced bear a close affinity to those given in one of the preceding chapters on Calicut.

[2] Or *scodella*. This word, which is nearly obsolete except in some of the Italian dialects, signifies a bowl or basin, and according to Alberti is a diminutive form of *scudo*, a shield. Not an inappropriate name for the *chatties* common throughout India, the lower part of which is round and convex. The upper part is generally drawn into a narrow mouth.

after the manner of Calicut. And for burning the dead body they light a fire of the most odoriferous things that can be found, such as aloes-wood, benzoin, sandal-wood, brazil-wood,[1] storax and amber, incense, and some beautiful

[1] In the original, "verzino ;" but I am at a loss to account for the etymology of the word. It cannot be a corruption of "Brazil," for Conti uses it half a century before the discovery of that country in his brief description of *Ternasseri:*—"Tutto il paese ch'è al'intorno è copioso di elephanti, e vi nasco molto *verzino.*" (*Ramusio*, vol. i. p. 332.) The Latin original has *verzano*, which by a mistake, such as the most careful translators sometimes fall into, is rendered "a species of thrush" in the translation of De' Conti's travels contained in *India in the Fifteenth Century*, ii. p. 9. The wood indicated is doubtless the Sappan, (*Cæsalpina sappan*,) which abounds in this quarter. Mr. O'Riley, in his *Vegetable Products of the Tenasserim Provinces*, writes :—"For many years past a trade from Mergui to Dacca in Sapan wood has been prosecuted by the native boats, the article being obtained from the Sapan-wood forests lying near the frontier hills, from the eastern side of which large supplies are annually imported through Bangkok into Singapore. It is also found throughout the valley of the Great Tenasserim river." (*Journal of the Indian Archipelago*, vol. iv. p. 60.) With regard to the dye-wood in question, Crawfurd says : " It has, like many indigenous products, a distinct name in the different languages, the only agreement, and this not perfect, being between the Malay and Javanese, in the first of which it is called *Sápang*, the origin of the European commercial and scientific names, and in Javanese *Sáchang*. In one language of the true Moluccas we have it as *Samya*, and in another as *Roro*, while in Amboynese it is *Lolan*, and in the Tagala of the Philippines *Sibukao*," (*Dictionary of the Indian Islands*, p. 376 ;) and I may add that the Arabic name is *Bákkam*. None of these, however, afford any clue to the Italian word *verzino*. If the latter has any relationship with the term "Brazil," is it not possible that that name was a corruption of the earlier *verzino*, and was given to the country so called on account of the quantity of Sappan-wood found there ?

Since writing the above, I have lighted on the following interesting note by Mr. J. Winter Jones, which places the subject beyond dispute : —"The name given to this country [Brazil] by the discoverers was Santa Cruz, which was afterwards changed to Brazil, from the immense quantity of the wood so called found there. There is early evidence to prove that the wood gave the name to the country and not the country to the wood. The following passage occurs in the *Liber Radicum* of the Rabbi Kimchi, a Spaniard who lived in the thirteenth century :— 'Algummin (2 Chron. ix. 10) alias Almugim (1 Kings, x. 12 ;) both

branches of coral,[1] which things they place upon the body, and while it is burning all the instruments of the city are sounding. In like manner, fifteen or twenty men, dressed like devils, stand there and make great rejoicing. And his wife is always present, making most exceedingly great lamentations, and no other woman. And this is done at one or two o'clock of the night.[2]

THE CHAPTER SHOWING HOW THE WIFE IS BURNT ALIVE AFTER THE DEATH OF HER HUSBAND.

In this city of Tarnassari, when fifteen days have passed after the death of the husband, the wife makes a banquet for

stand for the same, and in common language it is called Corallo; but some persons declare it to be a sort of wood used for dying, called in Arabic, *Albakam*, and in common language *Brazil*." HAKL. SOC. PUBS., *Divers Voyages touching the Disc. of America*, p. 46, *n*.

[1] *Grampa de coralli.* "CORAL, in large Branches, five and six Ryals the *Mallaya Tael*," is enumerated in Captain Saris's list among the articles most vendible in the Indian Archipelago. GREENE, vol. i. p. 503.

[2] Ferdinand Mendez Pinto, (if he is to be believed,) witnessed the funeral of the king of Siam, which he describes as follows :—" A mighty great pile was forthwith erected, made of sandal, aloes, calembas, and benjamin; on the which the body of the deceased king being laid, fire was put to it; with a strange ceremony: during all the time the body was a burning, the people did nothing but wail and lament beyond all expression; but in the end, it being consumed to ashes, they put them into a silver shrine, which they imbarqued in a *Laulea* very richly equipped, that was accompanied with forty *Seroos* full of *Talagrepos*, which are the highest dignity of their Gentile Priests, and a great number of other vessels, wherein there was a world of people...All these vessels got to land at a *Pagode*, called *Quiay Poutor*, where the silver shrine, in which the king's ashes were, was placed." (*Voyages and Adventures*, p. 276.) Captain Low says that the Burmans and Peguers of the Tenasserim provinces generally burn their dead, but that all under fifteen years of age are buried. He adds : " The body of the high priest also, who died at Martaban, just after its capture, was burned in the way which is described in Symes's *Ava*." *Journal of the R. A. Society*, vol. ii. p. 274.

all her relations and all those of her husband. And then they
go with all the relations to the place where the husband was
burnt, and at the same hour of the night. The said woman
puts on all her jewels and other objects in gold, all that she
possesses. And then her relations cause a hole to be made
of the height of a human being, and around the hole they
put four or five canes, around which they place a silken
cloth, and in the said hole they make a fire of the abovementioned things, such as were used for the husband. And
then the said wife, when the feast is prepared, eats a great
deal of betel, and eats so much that she loses her wits, and
the instruments of the city are constantly sounding, together
with the abovementioned men clothed like devils, who carry
fire in their mouths, as I have already told you in Calicut.
They also offer a sacrifice to *Deumo*.[1] And the said wife goes
many times up and down that place, dancing with the other
women. And she goes many times to the said men clothed
like devils, to entreat and tell them to pray the *Deumo* that
he will be pleased to accept her as his own. And there are
always present here a great many women who are her relations. Do not imagine, however, that she is unwilling to do
this; she even imagines that she shall be carried forthwith
into heaven. And thus running violently of her own free
will, she seizes the abovementioned cloth with her hands,
and throws herself into the midst of the fire. And immediately her relations and those most nearly allied to her fall
upon her with sticks and with balls of pitch, and this they
do only that she may die the sooner. And if the said wife
were not to do this, she would be held in like estimation as
a public prostitute is among us, and her relations would put
her to death. When such an event takes place in this
country the king is always present. However, those who
undergo such a death are the most noble of the land: all, in

---

[1] See note 2 on p. 137 *ante*.

general, do not do thus.[1] I have seen in this city of Tarnassari another custom, somewhat less horrible than the beforementioned. There will be a young man who will speak to a lady of love, and will wish to give her to understand that he really is fond of her, and that there is nothing he would not do for her. And, discoursing with her in this wise, he will take a piece of rag well saturated with oil, and will set fire to it, and place it on his arm on the naked flesh, and whilst it is burning he will stand speaking with that lady, not caring about his arm being burnt, in order to show that he loves her, and that for her he is willing to do every great thing.[2]

---

[1] It would appear from the foregoing narrative that the practice of *Sati* at Tenasserim was confined to a particular sect, which did not include the royal family of Siam; for Pinto relates that the widow of the king, whose funeral he describes, subsequently " married Uquumcheuiraa, who had been one of the purveyors of her house, and caused him to be crowned king in the city of Odiaa, the eleventh of November, 1545." *Voyages and Adventures*, p. 278.

[2] The proof by fire, in default of written or testimonial evidence, appears to have formed part of the judiciary system of Siam; but I have met with nothing to corroborate its use in the wooing of Tenasserim lovers. Captain Low describes the modern ceremony of marriage, omitting all mention of the fiery ordeal :—" The Elder now gives the bride a nosegay, and makes her repeat some Bali sentences, first directed to her father, again to her mother, next to the parents of the bridegroom, and lastly to her husband. The bridegroom goes through the same ceremony, beginning with his parents and relatives, but does not address the bride. The Elder then takes the flower from the bride, and places it on the wall of the house; she takes a little rolled-up betel-leaf and presents it to the bridegroom, who exchanges the flower for it. They then both sit on one mat, the bridegroom on the right; a feast ensues, and they finish the ceremonies by eating out of the same dish." *Journ. Roy. As. Soc.*, vol. ii. p. 270.

THE CHAPTER CONCERNING THE ADMINISTRATION OF JUSTICE WHICH IS OBSERVED IN TARNASSARI.

He who kills another in this country is put to death, the same as in Calicut.[1] With respect to conveying and holding, it is necessary that it should appear by writing or by witnesses. Their writing is on paper like ours, not on the leaves of a tree like that of Calicut. And then they go to a governor of the city, who administers justice for them summarily. However, when any foreign merchant dies who has no wife or children, he cannot leave his property to whomsoever he pleases, because the king wills to be his heir. And in this country, that is, the natives, commencing from the king, after his death his son remains king.[2] And when any Moorish merchant dies, very great expense is incurred in odoriferous substances to preserve the body, which they put into wooden boxes and then bury it, placing the head towards the city of Mecca, which comes to be towards the north.[3] If the deceased have children, they are his heirs.

[1] That is, by impalement; see p. 147 *ante*. Turpin, in his *History of Siam*, describes the horrible process as follows:—"The criminal is made to lie down on his belly, and after being securely tied, a stake of wood is forced up his fundament by the blows of a club, and it is driven till it comes out, either through the stomach or through the shoulders: they afterwards raise this stake, and fix it in the earth. It often happens that the sufferer dies under the operation, but sometimes the stake passes through the body without injuring any of the noble parts, and then the poor wretch endures for several days the most agonizing torments." PINKERTON, vol. ix. p. 594.

[2] I infer from Pinto, who states that the son of the king, whose death he records, succeeded his father, though he was shortly after poisoned by the queen mother, that the sovereignty of Siam was hereditary. The same order of succession probably prevailed as regards the Viceroys of the principal provinces. See note on p. 197 *ante*, where the ruler of the dependency of Tenasserim is styled "perpetual Captain."

[3] This is another incidental proof that Varthema's *Tarnassari* was not on the coast of Bengal, which is nearly in the same latitude as Meccah.

THE CHAPTER CONCERNING THE SHIPS WHICH ARE USED IN TARNASSARI.

These people make use of very large ships and of various kinds, some of which are made flat bottomed, because such can enter into places where there is not much water. Another kind are made with prows before and behind, and they carry two helms and two masts, and are uncovered. There is also another kind of large ship which is called Giunchi,[1] and each of these is of the tonnage of one thousand butts, on which they carry some little vessels to a city called Melacha,[2] and from thence they go with these little vessels for small spices to a place which you shall know when the proper time comes.

THE CHAPTER CONCERNING THE CITY OF BANGHELLA, AND OF ITS DISTANCE FROM TARNASSARI.

Let us return to my companion, for he and I had a desire to see farther on. After we had been some days in this said city, and being, indeed, tired of that same service of which you have heard above, and having sold some of our merchandise we took the route towards the city of Banghella,[3]

---

[1] "The name for a large trading vessel in Malay and Javanese is *jung*, which the Portuguese converted into *junco*, and we, improving on this corruption, into *junk*." CRAWFURD's *Desc. Dict. of the Indian Islands.*

[2] Malacca.

[3] *Gour* was undoubtedly the capital of Bengal at this period, but it appears that the name of the province was very commonly applied to the city, more especially by foreigners. The following is from Barbosa: —"Beyond the Ganges, onward towards the East, is the kingdom of *Bengala*, wherein there are many places and cities, as well inland as on the sea-coast. Those in the interior are inhabited by Gentiles, who are subject to the king of *Bengala*, who is a Moor; and the stations on the coast are full of Moors and Gentiles, among whom are many merchants and traders to all parts. For this sea forms a gulf which bends towards the north, at the head of which is situated a great city inhabited

which is distant from Tarnassari seven hundred miles, at which we arrived in eleven days by sea. This city was one of the best that I had hitherto seen, and has a very great realm. The sultan of this place is a Moor, and maintains two hundred thousand men for battle on foot and on horse; and they are all Mohammedans; and he is constantly at war

by Moors, which is called *Bengala*." (RAMUSIO, vol. i. p. 330.) In 1537, during the viceroyalty of Nunno de Cunna, when the Portuguese first attempted to establish a fort in Bengal, "*Gouro*, the capital city, extended three leagues in length along the Ganges, and contained 1,200,000 families." (GREENE, vol. i. p. 84.) In Ralph Fitch's time, 1583-1591, Tanda appears to have succeeded *Gour* as the capital of the kingdom, which had then become tributary to the Moghul Emperor:— "From Patanau [Patna] I went to Tanda, which is in the land of *Gouren*. It hath in times past been a kingdom, but is now subdued by Zelabdim Echebar [Jalál ed-Dín, Akbar.] Great trade and traffic is here of cotton and cloth of cotton...It standeth in the country of Bengala...Tanda standeth from the Ganges a league, because in times past the river flowing over the banks in time of rain drowned the country and many villages, and so they remain. And the old way which the river Ganges was wont to run remaineth dry, which is the occasion that the city standeth so far from the water." (PINKERTON, ix. p. 414.) I conclude, therefore, that Mandelslo errs in enumerating Bengal as a city of that province distinct from Gour and Tanda. He says: "En tirant vers le septentrional on trouve le royaume de Bengala, qui donne le nom au golfe que les anciens appellent *Sinus Gangeticus*...On trouve plusieurs belles villes dans ce royaume, comme sont celles de *Gouro*, d'Ougely, de Chatigan, de *Bengala*, de *Tanda*, de Daca, de Patana, de Banares, d'Elabas, et de Ragmehela." (*Voyages*, p. 290.) The following is from Major Rennell on this subject:—" Gour, called also Lucknouti, the ancient capital of Bengal, and supposed to be the *Gangia regia* of Ptolemy, stood on the left bank of the Ganges, about twenty-five miles below Rajemal. It was the capital of Bengal 730 years B.C., and was repaired and beautified by Homayoon, who gave it the name of Jennutcabad, which name a part of the *circar*, in which it was situated, still bears. According to Ferishta's account, the unwholesomeness of its air occasioned it to be deserted soon after, and the seat of government was removed to Tandah or Taurah, a few miles higher up the river. No part of the site of ancient Gour is nearer to the present bank of the Ganges than four miles and a half, and some parts of it which were regularly washed by that river are now twelve miles from it." *Mem. of a Map of Hindostan*, quoted in STEWART's *Hist. of Bengal*, p. 44.

with the king of Narsingha.¹ This country abounds more in grain, flesh of every kind, in great quantity of sugar, also of ginger, and of great abundance of cotton, than any country in the world. And here there are the richest merchants I ever met with. Fifty ships are laden every year in this place with cotton and silk stuffs, which stuffs are these, that is to say, *bairam, namone, lizati, ciantar, doazar,* and *sinabaff*. These same stuffs go through all Turkey, through Syria, through Persia, through Arabia Felix, through Ethiopia, and through all India.² There are also here very great merchants in jewels, which come from other countries.

THE CHAPTER CONCERNING SOME CHRISTIAN MERCHANTS IN BANGHELLA.

We also found some Christian merchants here. They said that they were from a city called Sarnau, and had brought for sale silken stuffs, and aloes-wood, and benzoin, and musk. Which Christians said that in their country there were many lords also Christians, but they are subject to the great Khan [of] Cathai.³ As to the dress of these

---

¹ I have failed to discover any historical notices confirmatory of this remark, though it is highly probable that the Sultans of Bengal cooperated generally with the Mussulman powers of the Deccan at this period against the great Brahminical kingdom of Bijayanagar. (See note 2, on p. 125 *ante*.) The reigning sovereign at the time of Varthema's visit must have been the Patan Sultan 'Âla ed-Din Husein Shâh bin Seyyed Ashraf.

² These names are mostly of Arabic or Persian derivation, and several of them are still in use among the Arabs, while similar technical terms, which obtained among British traders in the time of Captain Saris, such as *Sayes, Rashes, Bourats, Caniant, Juwart,* etc., have disappeared from our modern commercial vocabulary. In Varthema's *sinabaff*, I recognize *Sina baft*, China woven-cloth.

³ From the description of the manners of these Christians, I should have inferred that they were Armenians, but as they wrote contrary to us, that is, from right to left, they were most probably Nestorians. (I

Christians, they were clothed in a *xebec*[1] made with folds, and the sleeves were quilted with cotton. And on their heads they wore a cap a palm and a half long, made of red cloth. These same men are as white as we are, and confess that they are Christians, and believe in the Trinity, and likewise in the Twelve Apostles, in the four Evangelists, and they also have baptism with water. But they write in the contrary way to us, that is, after the manner of Armenia. And they say that they keep the Nativity and the Passion of Christ, and observe our Lent and other vigils in the course of the year. These Christians do not wear shoes, but they wear a kind of breeches made of silk, similar to those

need hardly remark that Varthema is wrong in stating that the Armenians write in that way, for they write as we do from left to right.) Assemanni, indeed, concludes that all the Christians formerly in Tartary and China were Nestorians, quoting Marco Polo, among others, as his authority:—" Christianos in Sinarum regno Nestorianos fuisse, non Armenios, neque ex Armenia, sed partim ex Assyria et Mesopotamia, partim ex Sogdiana, Bactriana et India illuc convolasse, eo maxime tempore, quo Tartari in illud regnum invaserunt, ipse Marcus Paulus Venetus, qui a Trigautio citatur, pluribus in locis affirmat, ubi quoties Christianorum in Sinis meminit, eos Nestorianos vocat." The same author defines the limits of the ancient kingdom of Cathay as follows:— " Cataja Sinam borealem significat, quam orientalis Sinæ nomine appellant: habet autem Turchestanam ad occasum ; Sinam ad austrum ; terram et mare Esonis, vulgò de Jesso, ad ortum ; et Tartariam veram ad septentrionem. Sericæ antiquæ pars est, ut ex Ptolemæo scribit Cellarius ;" but I have perused the interesting section from which this quotation is made, (*Biblioth. Orient.*, vol. iv. § vi.), and every other available author from Marco Polo downwards, without discovering any clue to Varthema's city of *Sarnau*. The only additional information which his book affords respecting its locality is given in a subsequent chapter, and while he was at Sumatra, from which island his Christian companions told him it was 3,000 miles distant.

I note, as a mere coincidence, that Ferdinand Mendez Pinto designates the kingdom of Siam " The Empire of Sornau." (*Voyages and Adventures*, p. 284.) Whether he had any better authority than that of his own fertile imagination for the name, I cannot say ; but I do not find it applied to that country by any other author. Gasparo Balbi and some of the early Portuguese writers calls it " Silon."

[1] A jerkin.

worn by mariners, which breeches are all full of jewels, and
their heads are covered with jewels. And they eat at a table
after our fashion, and they eat every kind of flesh. These
people also said that they knew that on the confines of the
Rumi, that is, of the Grand Turk, there are very great
Christian kings. After a great deal of conversation with
these men, my companion at last showed them his merchandise, amongst which there were certain beautiful branches
of large coral. When they had seen these branches they
said to us, that if we would go to a city where they would
conduct us, that they were prepared to secure for us as
much as 10,000 ducats for them, or as many rubies as in
Turkey would be worth 100,000.[1] My companion replied
that he was well pleased, and that they should depart immediately thence. The Christians said: "In two days' time
from this a ship will sail which goes towards Pego, and we
have to go with it; if you are willing to come we will go
together." Hearing this we set ourselves in order, and embarked with the said Christians and with some other Persian
merchants. And as we had been informed in this city that
these Christians were most faithful, we formed a very great
friendship with them. But before our departure from
Banghella, we sold all the rest of the merchandise, with the
exception of the corals, the saffron, and two pieces of rose-
coloured cloth of Florence. We left this city, which I
believe is the best in the world, that is, for living in. In
which city the kinds of stuffs you have heard of before are
not woven by women, but the men weave them. We departed thence with the said Christians, and went towards a
city which is called Pego, distant from Banghella about a
thousand miles. On which voyage we passed a gulf towards
the south, and so arrived at the city of Pego.

[1] See note 1 on p. 206 *ante*.

THE CHAPTER CONCERNING PEGO,[1] A CITY OF INDIA.

The city of Pego is on the mainland, and is near to the sea. On the left hand of this, that is, towards the east, there

[1] In chapter viii. of his *Narrative of a Mission to the Court of Ava*, Colonel Yule has arranged in chronological order a valuable collection of *Notes on the Intercourse of the Burmese countries with Western nations up to the peace of Yandabo*, comprising all the information available respecting Pegu and the adjacent kingdoms at this period. These notes, with his own interspersed commentary, form the most authentic history of those kingdoms extant, and the four sketch maps representing the historical geography of the Burmese countries at several epochs, convey at a glance the principal political and territorial changes which have successively taken place in that empire since A.D. 1500. With regard to the map illustrative of that date, I perceive that Tavoy is apparently described as an independent state embracing the entire seabord between the tenth and fifteenth degrees of latitude, whereas in a preceding note on pp. 197-8, I have implied that Tenasserim, which is included within those limits, was the principal kingdom on that part of the coast at the period indicated, but subordinate, nevertheless, to the suzerainty of Siam. (Towards the end of that century Tenasserim became tributary to Pegu, and a few years later, *cir.* A.D. 1619, judging from the extract quoted from Master William Methold's *Relations of the Kingdome of Golchonda, and other Neighbouring Nations within the Gulf of Bengale*, in the note last referred to, it appears to have reverted, for a time at least, to the authority of Siam.) I notice this discrepancy rather by way of suggesting a doubt as to the correctness of my own inference, than with the idea of questioning the accuracy of my learned friend Colonel Yule.

The following chapter from the Geography of Patavino, evidently compiled from the travels of Nicolo de' Conti, Varthema, Cæsar Fredericke, and the best authorities who succeeded them, contains so admirable an account of Pegu at the date when the work was published (1597), and when the kingdom was at the zenith of its glory, that I deem it worthy of quotation in full :—" PEGU regnum occupat littoris spatium 300 milliarium iuxta Occidentalem oram sinus Bengalici, ab urbe scilicet *Tauay* ad caput usque *Nigraes* ; in Mediterraneis verò valdè extenditur. Optimos habet portus, ex quibus præcipuus est *Martabane*, in quo onerantur circiter 40 naues ex oryza, quæ in insulam Sumatram comportantur. Ager huius regni pinguis ac fertilissimus est, et rei frumentariæ ut plurimum admodum accommodus ; animalia innumera nutrit, inter

is a very beautiful river, by which many ships go and come.[1] The king of this city is a Pagan. Their faith, customs, manner of living and dress, are after the manner of Tarnassari; but with respect to their colour, they are somewhat more white. And here, also, the air is somewhat more cold. Their seasons are like ours. This city is walled, and has

quæ sunt equi pusilli, ad ferendum tamen idonei, quorum ingens est numerus, sicut etiam eliphantorum, qui in altissimis quibusdam montibus capiuntur, ac ad belli usum adseruantur. Psittaci etiam vocaliores quàm usquam alibi, et pulchriores reperiuntur, atque etiam feles, qui zibettum gignunt: arundines hîc excrescunt ad crassitiem unius dolij: nascuntur quoque hîc rubini. Unde regnum ipsum opulentissimum est et mercatoribus frequentissimum, qui commercijs plurimum operam nauant, et in ipsis portubus plures sunt mercatores Mauri ac gentiles. Deferunt autem ex hoc Regno ad Malacam oryzam, laccam, benzuinum, muscum, lapillos preciosos, argentum, batyrum, oleum, sal, cepas, et alia huius generis comestibilia: contra verò ex Malaca istuc ferunt porcellanas, colores, argentum vivum, æs, cinnabarim, Damascum floribus contextum, stannum, et alia. Ciuitas Regia est PEGU, clarissima totius Indiæ, mœnibus munita, et ædibus elegantissimus ornata, quæ à mari ciciter 25 milliaribus abest, quam fluuius eiusdem nominis maximus abluit, quæ etiam per totum regnum percurrens intumescit interdum adeò, ut magnum terræ tradum inundet: unde ab hoc incolæ oryzam copiosissimè colligunt. Præter hanc sunt insignes *Tauay*, *Martabane*, et *Losmin* emporium celebre. Sunt autem Peguini mediocris staturæ, magis ad crassitiem accedentes, agiles, et viribus præditi, ad bellum tamen inepti: nudi incedunt præter pudenda, capita tegunt albicantis pannis ad instar mitræ: luxuriæ præterea valde dediti sunt, qui in mulierum gratiam ad virile membrum tintinabula aurea vel argentea appensa gestant ut sonum reddant dum per ciuitatem deambulant. Sunt verò super mortales omnes superstitiosissimi, et vanissimas habent circa religionem opiniones, ac ab omni veritate alienas. Rex PEGU multa hodie possidit regna, nempe *Tangù*, *Prom*, *Melintay*, *Calam*, *Bacam*, *Mirandù*, *Aua*, *Brema* [Burmah?] ad Septentrionem exposita; deinde regnum *Siam*, et portus *Martabanæ* ac *Ternasseri*, et *Aracam*, ac *Macin* regna: et appellari quoque consueuit à scriptoribus nonnullis Rex Bremæ, seu Barmæ." p. 260.

[1] Symes says: "The Pegue river is called by the natives *Bayoo Kioup*, or Pegue rivulet, to distinguish it from *Mioup*, or river. It is navigable but a very few miles to the northward of the city of Pegue, and for this it is indebted wholly to the action of the tide." PINKERTON, vol. ix., p. 446.

good houses and palaces built of stone, with lime.¹ The king is extremely powerful in men, both foot and horse, and has with him more than a thousand Christians of the country which has been above mentioned to you.² And he

¹ So Ralph Fitch eighty years after Varthema :—" Pegu is a city very great, strong, and very fair, with walls of stone, and great ditches round about it. There are two towns, the old and the new. In the old town are all the merchants strangers, and very many merchants of the country. All the goods are sold in the old town, which is very great, and hath many suburbs round about it, and all the houses are made of canes, which they call *bambos,* and are covered with straw." (*Id.,* pp. 416-7.) Symes says : " The extent of ancient Pegue may still be accurately traced by the ruins of the ditch and wall that surrounded it : from this it appears to have been a quadrangle, each side measuring nearly a mile and a half. In several places the ditch is filled up with rubbish that has been cast into it, and the falling of its own banks ; sufficient, however, still remains to show that it was no contemptible defence." He describes the streets of the new town as well paved with the bricks brought from the old city, but all the houses of the former as being made of mats, or sheathing boards, supported on bamboos or posts, " the king having prohibited the use of brick or stone in private buildings, from the apprehension that if people got leave to build brick houses, they might erect brick fortifications." *Id.,* pp. 436-8.

² We have Colonel Yule's authority for believing that Armenians, who were most probably petty merchants like their representatives there at the present day, have long frequented the Burmese court and capital; but the existence of a regiment of Armenians or Nestorians in the service of an Indian potentate at this period may be set down as a fable, and I read of no native Christians in Pegu prior to the advent of the Portuguese a few years later. Conti, who visited several parts of the country in 1444, states that the people turned towards the East every morning, and with clasped hands said : " God in Trinity and His Law defend us !" Varthema probably heard that a similar belief was professed by a portion of the Pegu army, and forthwith christianized them. Yule makes the following remark on the Burmese prayer above quoted :—" This, which at first sight looks like fiction, is really an evidence of Conti's veracity. He had doubtless heard of the 'Three Precious Ones,' the Triad of *Buddha, Dharma,* and *Sanga,* the Buddha, the Law, and the Clergy." And he adds in a foot-note, that " in a letter which the King of Ava wrote to the Governor-General of India, in 1830, his majesty speaks of his 'observing the three objects of worship, namely, God, his Precepts, and his Attendants or Priests.'" *Mission to the Court of Ava,* p. 208.

gives to each, for pay, six golden *pardai* per month and his expenses. In this country there is a great abundance of grain, of flesh of every kind, and of fruits of the same as at Calicut. These people have not many elephants, but they possess great numbers of all other animals; they also have all the kinds of birds which are found at Calicut. But there are here the most beautiful and the best parrots I had ever seen. Timber grows here in great quantities, long, and I think the thickest that can possibly be found. In like manner I do not know if there can be found in the world such thick canes as I found here, of which I saw some which were really as thick as a barrel. Civet-cats are found in this country in great numbers, three or four of which are sold for a ducat. The sole merchandise of these people is jewels, that is, rubies, which come from another city called Capellan,[1] which is distant from this thirty days' journey; not that I have seen it, but by what I have heard from merchants. You must know that in the said city, a large pearl and diamond are worth more here than with us, and also an emerald. When we arrived in this country, the king was fifteen days' journey distant, fighting with another who was called king of Ava.[2] Seeing this, we determined to

[1] Fitch mentions the same locality:—"Caplan is the place where they find the rubies, saphires, and the spinelles: it standeth six days' journey from Ava, in the kingdom of Pegu. There are many great hills out of which they dig them." (PINKERTON, vol. ix. p. 421.) Tavernier, "that rambling jeweller, who had read nothing, but had seen so much and so well," as Gibbon describes him, has the following on the same subject:— "There are but two places in the east in which coloured stones are found, that is, the kingdom of Pegu and the island of Ceylon. The first is a mountain about a dozen days' journey from Siren [Sirian], on the north-east, and is called Capelan. This is the mine which produces the greatest quantity of rubies and spinels, otherwise called the mother of rubies, yellow topazes, jacinths, amethysts, and other stones of different colours." *Id.* vol. viii. p. 250.

[2] Pegu was also at war with Ava when visited by Hieronimo di San Stephano in 1496. In 1544, and again in 1552, it was subjected by the neighbouring King of Toungoo, called by Portuguese writers " King of

go and find the king where he was, in order to give him
these corals. And so we departed thence in a ship made all
of one piece,[1] and more than fifteen or sixteen paces long.
The oars of this vessel were made of cane. Understand well
in what manner : where the oar takes the water it was cloven,
and they insert a flat piece of board fastened by cords, so
that the said vessel went with more power than a brigantine.
The mast of it was a cane as thick as a barrel where they
put in the provisions. In three days we arrived at a village
where we found certain merchants, who had not been able
to enter into the said city of Ava on account of the war.
Hearing this, we returned with them to Pego, and five days
afterwards the king returned to the said city, who had
gained a very great victory over his enemy. On the second
day after the return of the king, our Christian companions
took us to speak with him.

THE CHAPTER CONCERNING THE DRESS OF THE KING OF PEGO ABOVE MENTIONED.

Do not imagine that the king of Pego enjoys as great a
reputation as the king of Calicut, although he is so humane
and domestic that an infant might speak to him, and he

the Burmas," who extended his conquests over Ava, Magoung, Jangomai (Zimmé), the west of Yunan, and other adjoining states. This monarch appears to have been still on the throne when Cæsar Fredericke was at Pegu in 1586, and the extract from Patavino's Geography, quoted on pp. 215-6, gives an apparently authentic account of the different dependencies of the kingdom towards the end of that century. About that time, however, the empire began to decline, and its fall was as rapid as its rise : in 1600, Pegu was besieged by the kings of Aracan and Toungoo, and its sovereign put to death ; and thirteen years later the King of Ava was crowned at Pegu, from which period may be dated the dominance of the Avan monarchy over the lower provinces. See YULE's *Narrative of a Mission to the Court of Ava*, pp. 208-213.

[1] The μονοξύλα of the author of the *Periplus*. See VINCENT's *Com. and Nav. of the Ancients*, vol. ii. p. 521.

wears more rubies on him than the value of a very large
city, and he wears them on all his toes. And on his legs he
wears certain great rings of gold, all full of the most beautiful rubies; also his arms and his fingers all full. His ears
hang down half a palm, through the great weight of the
many jewels he wears there, so that seeing the person of the
king by a light at night, he shines so much that he appears
to be a sun.[1] The said Christians spoke with him, and told
him of our merchandise. The king replied: " That we
should return to him the day after the next, because on the
next day he had to sacrifice to the devil for the victory
which he had gained." When the time mentioned was past,
the king, as soon as he had eaten, sent for the said Christians, and for my companion, in order that he might carry to
him his merchandise. When the king saw such beautiful
corals he was quite astonished and greatly pleased; for, in
truth, among the other corals there were two branches, the
like of which had never before entered India. This king
asked what people we were. The Christians answered:
" Sir, these are Persians." Said the king to the interpreter:
" Ask them if they are willing to sell these things." My
companions answered : " That the articles were at the service
of his highness." Then the king began to say: "'That he had
been at war with the king of Ava for two years, and on that

---

[1] Both Gasparo Balbi and Ralph Fitch describe the richness of the
King of Pegu's dress and the splendour of his court retinue in their
time. The former saw him start on a war expedition against the King
of Ava "all over covered with gold and jewels;" and the latter says :
" When the king rideth abroad, he rideth with a great guard, and many
noblemen, often on an elephant with a fine castle upon him, very fairly
gilded with gold, and sometimes in a great frame like a horse litter,
which hath a little house upon it covered overhead, but open on the sides,
which is all gilded with gold, and set with many rubies and saphires,
whereof he hath infinite store in his country, and is carried on sixteen
or eighteen men's shoulders....He hath also houses full of gold and silver,
and bringing in often, but *spendeth very little*." PINKERTON, vol. ix.
pp. 404, 418.

account he had no money; but that if we were willing to barter for so many rubies, he would amply satisfy us." We caused him to be told by these Christians that we desired nothing further from him than his friendship,—that he should take the commodities and do whatever he pleased.[1] The Christians repeated to him what my companion had charged them to say, by telling the king that he might take the corals without money or jewels. He hearing this liberality answered: "I know that the Persians are very liberal, but I never saw one so liberal as this man;" and he swore by God and by the devil that he would see which would be the more liberal, he or a Persian. And then he desired one of his confidential servants to bring him a certain little box which was two palms in length, worked all round in gold, and was full of rubies, within and without. And when he had opened it, there were six separate divisions, all full of different rubies; and he placed it before us, telling us we should take what we wished. My companion answered: "O, sir, you show me so much kindness, that by the faith which I bear to Mahomet I make you a present of all these things. And know, sir, that I do not travel about the world to collect property, but only to see different people and different customs." The king answered: "I cannot conquer you in liberality, but take this which I give you." And so he took a good handful of rubies from each of the divisions of the said casket, and gave them to him. These rubies might be about two hundred, and in giving them he said: "Take these for the liberality you have exercised towards

---

[1] A thoroughly oriental way of driving a good bargain, though extensively copied by tradesmen on the continent of Europe. The artifice is as old as the days of Abraham, who was a long time in getting the children of Heth to name the price of Machpelah. At length Ephron, overcoming his modesty, ventured to say: "My lord, the land is worth four hundred shekels of silver," (which was most probably ten times its value,) but politely added: "What is that betwixt me and thee?" *Genesis*, chap. xxiii.

me." And in like manner he gave to the said Christians two rubies each, which were estimated at a thousand ducats, and those of my companions were estimated at about one hundred thousand ducats. Wherefore by this he may be considered to be the most liberal king in the world, and every year he has an income of about one million in gold. And this because in his country there is found much *lacca*,[1] a good deal of sandal-wood, very much brazil-wood, cotton and silk[2] in great quantities, and he gives all his income to his soldiers. The people in this country are very sensual. After some days, the said Christians took leave for themselves and for us. The king ordered a room to be given to us, furnished with all that was requisite for so long as we wished to remain there; and so it was done. We remained in the said room five days. At this time there arrived news that the king of Ava was coming with a great army to make war upon him, on hearing which, this one [of Pego] went to meet him half way with a great many men, horse and foot. The next day we saw two women burnt alive voluntarily, in the manner as I have described it in Tarnassari.

[1] This I take to be the colouring matter produced by the lac insect, or *coccus ficus*, which is abundant throughout the Burmese provinces. Barbosa speaks of it as one of the principal exports from Martaban, and says that the Indians and Persians called it *Laco Martabani*. He does not seem, however, to have been aware how it was produced :—" They say this *lacca* is the gum of trees ; others state that it is produced on the branches of trees, just as the *grane* grow in our parts, and this account seems more natural and probable. They carry it in small vases, because they may not gather too much of it." (RAMUSIO, vol. i. p. 317.) Alberti, in his definition of *grane*, says :—" Sono coccole d'un albero, simili quasi alle coccole dell' ellera, colle quali si tingono i panni in rosso o paonazzo ed è preziosa tinta. Oggidì si potrebbe anche dire *Cochenille*." The early Italian travellers appear to have used the same word, *lacca*, to describe both the lac and the lacca-wood.

[2] See note 1 on p. 198 *ante*.

THE CHAPTER CONCERNING THE CITY MELACHA, AND THE RIVER GAZA, OTHERWISE GANGE AS I THINK, AND OF THE INHUMANITY OF THE MEN.

The next day we embarked on board a ship and went to a city called Melacha,[1] which is situated towards the west, at which we arrived in eight days. Near to the said city we found an extremely great *fiumara*, as large as any we had ever seen, which they call Gaza,[2] which is evidently more than twenty-five miles wide. And opposite to the said river there is a very large island, which is called Sumatra. The inhabitants of it say that the circumference of it is four thousand five hundred miles. I will tell you about the said island at the proper time. When we had arrived at the city of Melacha, we were immediately presented to the Sultan, who is a Moor, as is also all his kingdom.[3] The said city is

[1] Malacca, or, more correctly, Málaca, the well-known town on the western side of the Malay peninsula. Our traveller was the first to make Europe acquainted with its name and situation.

[2] By "fiumara" Varthema undoubtedly means the Straits, which are about twenty-five miles broad opposite Malacca. "Gaza," I take to be a contraction of *Boghǎz*, the Arabic for a strait. The Arabs of the present day use the same word to denote the passage between the island of Sumatra and the Malay peninsula, calling it *Boghǎz Málaca*, or *Boghǎz Singafûra*. I notice that Crawfurd, in his *Descriptive Dictionary*, sub voce *Archipelago*, remarks that Varthema underrates the breadth of the Strait; but he quotes our traveller from *Ramusio* as describing the *fiumara* to be only "about *fifteen* miles broad." (*Id.* sub voce *Malacca Straits*.) Crawfurd himself says in one place, that the town of Malacca is "washed by the Straits which bear its name, and which are here about five-and-twenty miles broad;" and in another, that "the town of Malacca is distant from the nearest shore of Sumatra about forty-five miles," (*Id.* sub voce *Malacca*, pp. 238, 249;) the approximate measurements being apparently given, in the one case, between Malacca and the island of Rupat directly opposite, and in the other between Malacca and the *mainland* of Sumatra.

[3] "Of the time in which the Muhammedan religion was embraced by the people of Malacca, there is no precise statement. The Malay account assigns the event to the reign of a prince called Sultan Muham-

on the mainland and pays tribute to the king of Cini,[1] who caused this place to be built about eighty years ago, because there is a good port there, which is the principal port of the main ocean. And, truly I believe, that more ships arrive here than in any other place in the world,[2] and especially there come here all sorts of spices and an immense quantity

med Shâh, who ascended the throne in 1276...The statement of De Barros respecting the conversion is as follows :—' The greatness of Malacca induced the kings who followed Xaquem Darsa [Sekandar Shâh,] to throw off their dependency on the kings of Siam, and this chiefly, since the time when induced by the Persians and Gujrati Moors, who came to Malacca and resided there, for the purpose of trade, from Gentiles to become converts to the sect of Muhammed.'" CRAWFURD's *Descriptive Dictionary of the Indian Islands*, etc., p. 245.

[1] If by *Cini* is meant Siam, the statement is corroborated, generally, by the learned researches of Mr. Crawfurd, who writes :—"The subjection of Malacca to Siam seems, indeed, to be admitted by all parties. Four of the most northerly of the States of the Peninsula are still subject to it; while a claim of supremacy is made for, at least, three more. The author of the Commentaries of Albuquerque, giving a greater extension to Malacca than De Barros, thus describes it and its subjection to Siam :—' The kingdom of Malacca on one side borders on Queda; and on the other, Pam [Pahang]. It has one hundred leagues of coast, and inland extends to a chain of mountains where it is parted from Siam, a breadth of ten leagues. All this land was anciently subject to Siam.'" *Id.*, p. 244-5.

"The port is an open road, but, notwithstanding, safe at all seasons, not being within the latitude of hurricanes, nor within the influence of either monsoons; or, as the Commentaries of Albuquerque express it :— 'it is the beginning of one monsoon, and the end of another.'" *Id.*, p. 249.

[2] "The flourishing condition of Malacca, at the time it was attacked by the Portuguese, [five years after Varthema's visit,] has no doubt been much exaggerated; but making every abatement, enough will remain to show that it was a place of considerable commercial importance, judging it by the ideas of the beginning of the 16th century, and by the peculiar value then attached to some of the commodities of which its trade consisted. ' In matters of trade,' says De Barros, ' the people [the Malays] are artful and expert, for, in general, they have to deal with such nations as the Javanese, the Siamese, the Peguans, the Bengallis, the Quelijo [Chulias or Talugus,] Malabaris, Gujratis, Persians, and Arabians, with many other people, whose residence here has made

of other merchandise. This country is not very fertile,[1] yet
there is produced there grain, a little animal food, wood,
birds like those of Calicut, excepting the parrots, which are
better here than in Calicut. A great quantity of sandal-
wood and of tin is found here.[2] There are also a great many
elephants, horses, sheep, cows and buffalos, leopards and
peacocks, in great abundance. A few fruits like those in
Zeilan. It is not necessary to trade here in anything excepting in spices and silken stuffs.[3] These people are olive-

them very sagacious. Moreover, the city is also populous, owing to the
ships which resort to it from the country of the Chijs [Chinese], the
Lequios [Japanese], the Luçoes [people of Luzon in the Philippines],
and other nations of the Orient. All these people bring so much wealth,
both of the East and the West, that Malacca seems a centre at which
are assembled all the natural productions of the earth, and all the artificial ones of man. On this account, although situated in a barren land,
it is, through an interchange of commodities, more amply supplied with
everything than the countries themselves from which they come.'" *Id.*
p. 245.

[1] Varthema's remark respecting the comparative infertility of the
country, is confirmed by De Barros in the preceding note, and fully corroborated by Crawfurd, who says :—" It is in vain to plead for the un-
productiveness of Malacca the maladministration of former national
adminstrations, for Malacca has been, with little interruption, nearly
sixty years under British rule, while Arracan, in less than half the
time, under the same government, competing with its immediate neigh-
bour Bengal, has become one of the principal granaries of India."
Id., p. 239

[2] I infer from Crawfurd that sandal-wood, if it exists there at all, is
produced in very small quantities in the territory of Malacca, the chief
places of its growth being several of the islands of the Malay Archipelago, but more especially Timur and Sumba, which latter takes its
European name of Sandal-wood Island from it.

In 1847, the quantity of tin obtained from the mines in the Malacca
territory was about five thousand cwts., and it is yearly increasing. *Id.*
p. 240.

[3] Meaning, I presume, that these were the most marketable commodities. With regard to silk, Crawfurd says : " It may probably have been
first made known to the inhabitants of the Indian Islands by the Hindus, if we are to judge from its Sauscrit name ; but in all times known
to us, they have been supplied with this article raw and wrought by the

Q

coloured, with long hair. Their dress is after the fashion
of Cairo. They have the visage broad, the eye round, the
nose compressed. It is not possible to go about the place
here when it is dark, because people are killed like dogs,[1]
and all the merchants who arrive here go to sleep in their
ships. The inhabitants of this city are of the nation of
Giavai. The king keeps a governor to administer justice
for foreigners, but those of the country take the law into
their own hands, and they are the worst race that was ever

Chinese, the original inventors of silk;"...nevertheless, he adds:—"that
from the raw silk of China, the Malays and Javanese always wove, and
still continue to do so, some strong and often rich domestic fabrics suited
to their own peculiar tastes. *Id.*, p. 394.

[1] Crawfurd describes the Malays as a brown-complexioned, lank-
haired people, of a squat form, with high cheek-bones, large mouth,
and flattened nose. With regard to costume, I had frequent opportunities, during my long residence at Aden, of seeing many Malay merchants on their way to Meccah, who were generally dressed like the
same class in Syria and Egypt. As to character, the Malays in general
bear a very questionable one, and are notorious for their vindictiveness.
Barbosa describes them as "very skilful and exquisite workmen; but
very malevolent and treacherous, rarely speaking the truth, and ready
to commit any outrage and to die...There are some of them also, if attacked with any serious illness, make a vow to God that if restored to
health, they will voluntarily select a more honourable death in His
service. On recovery, they leave their houses with a dagger in hand,
and rush through the streets, where they kill as many persons as they
can, men, women, and children, insomuch that they seem like mad dogs.
These are called *Amulos*, and when seen in this frenzy, all begin to
cry out, *Amulos! Amulos!* in order that the people may be on their
guard, who with knives and lances immediately put them to death."
(RAMUSIO, vol. i. p. 318.) *Amulos*, I take to be a corruption of the
native *amuk*, and the origin of our "running a-muck," which, according
to Crawfurd, is a phrase introduced into our language from the Malay,
the latter word signifying a furious and reckless onset.—"Running
a-muck with private parties is often the result of a restless determina-
tion to exact revenge for some injury or insult; but it also results, not less
frequently, from a monomania taking this particular form, and originat-
ing in disorders of the digestive organs. The word and the practice are
not confined to the Malays, but extend to all the people and languages
of the Archipelago that have obtained a certain amount of civilization."
Desc. Dict., p. 12.

created on earth. When the king wishes to interfere with them, they say that they will disinhabit the land, because they are men of the sea.[1] The air here is very temper-

[1] Considering that Varthema was the first European to describe Malacca, and that his stay there did not extend beyond a few days, it is surprising to find how strikingly correct his brief remarks are, not only as regards the natural objects which were open to his inspection, but others also which were less obvious, connected with the past history of the people and their actual civil condition at the period of his visit. The statement that Malacca was inhabited by a nation of Javanese is corroborated by the learned researches of Crawfurd, who says: "On one point, all parties seem to agree, that not only the founders of Malacca, but even of Singapore, were Javanese and not Malays; for even the Malayan account is substantially to this effect, since it brings the emigrants who established themselves at Singapore from Palembang, which was a Javanese settlement." *Id.* p. 243.

Equally remarkable is our traveller's notice of two distinct classes among the Malays, one given to trade and agriculture and subject to an organized government, the other a wild race acknowledging no superior authority, and who either felt themselves strong enough to resist any attempt to impose it by expelling the more civilized community from the country, or who did not care to reside on land because they were "men of the sea;" for Varthema's words—"Et quando il re si vol mettere fra loro, essi dicono che deshabitarauno la terra perche sono homini de mare,"—will bear both interpretations. How surprisingly this account is corroborated by Crawfurd, except that the latter makes three sections of the Malays, will be seen by the following extract:— "The Malay nation may be divided naturally into three classes: *the civilized Malays*, or those who possess a written language, and have made a decent progress in the useful arts; *the gipsy-like fishermen*, called the *Sea People;* and *the rude half savages*, who, for the most part, live precariously on the produce of the forests. The civilized Malays consist of the inhabitants of the eastern side of Sumatra, of much of the interior of that island, and of those of the sea-boards of Borneo and the Malay Peninsula. The sea-gipsies are to be found sojourning from Sumatra to the Moluccas...The only habitations of this people are their boats, and they live exclusively by the produce of the sea, or by the robberies they commit on it. The most usual name by which they are known is *orang-laut*, literally, 'men of the sea'...The rude wandering class, speaking the Malay language, is found in the interior of the Malay Peninsula, in Sumatra, and in the islands lying between them, but in no other part of the Archipelago."...These three classes of Malays existed near three centuries and a half ago, when the

ate.¹ The Christians who were in our company gave us to understand that we ought not to remain long here because they are an evil race. Wherefore we took a junk and went towards Sumatra to a city called Pider, which is distant from the mainland eighty leagues, or thereabouts.

THE CHAPTER CONCERNING THE ISLAND OF SUMATRA,² AND CONCERNING PIDER, A CITY IN SUMATRA.

They say that in this district there is the best port of the whole island, which I have already told you is in circum-

Portuguese first arrived in the waters of the Archipelago, just as they do at the present day. That people describes them as having existed also for two centuries and a half before that event, as without doubt they did in times far earlier. Thus De Barros describes the first class of Malays as ' men living by trade, and the most cultivated of these parts;' the second as 'a vile people,' whose ' dwelling was more on the sea than the land,' and who 'lived by fishing and robbery ;' and the third as ' half savages' (quasi meios salvages,) while the Malay language was common to all of them." *Id.*, p. 250.

¹ "The climate of Malacca, as to temperature, is such as might be expected in a country not more than one hundred miles from the equator, lying along the sea shore,—hot and moist. The thermometer in the shade ranges from 72° to 84° of Fahrenheit, seldom being so low as the first of these, and not often higher than the last. The range of the barometer is only from 29.8 to 30.3 inches. Notwithstanding constant heat, much moisture, and many swamps, the town at least is remarkable for its salubrity." *Id.*, p. 239.

² Mr. Crawfurd makes Varthema "the first writer who gives the name [of this island] as we now write it," which remark is only correct if restricted to the modern orthography of the word ; for Sumatra is undoubtedly the island where Nicolò de' Conti was detained a year, and which he calls *Sciamuthera*. But although Conti was most probably the first to make known the name to our continent, I deem it tolerably certain that it was the island visited by Ibn Batûta about A.D. 1330, which he designates *Jâwah*, but the capital of which, situated four miles from the coast, he calls *Shumatrah* or *Sumatrah*. Our Java, to which he subsequently proceeded, he distinguishes by the name of *Mul-Jâwah*. This inference is corroborated by the fact that the former place was then under a Muhammedan king called Ez-Zâhir Jamâl ed-Dín, whereas, according

ference 4,500 miles. In my opinion, which agrees also with what many say, I think that it is Taprobana, in which there

to Crawfurd, though several attempts had been made between 1358 and 1460 to convert the Javanese, it was not till 1478 that the Muhammedans succeeded in capturing the capital, and establishing their own power and faith ;" which further agrees with Ibn Batûta's account of *Mul-Jáwah*, who calls it " the first part of the territory of the infidels." (See LEE's *Translation*, pp. 199-205 ; and CRAWFURD's *Desc. Dict.*, p. 185.) As Ibn Batûta was proceeding from Bengal to China, and appears to have touched at the Andaman or Nicobar Islands on his voyage from the former coast, I think it highly probable that the present Achin was the place which he visited in the island of Sumatra; for that town lies about two miles from the shore, and the Achinese are stated to have been converted to Islâm as early as the year 1204 And if Achin was also the city where Conti was detained, which is not unlikely, his designation of it strikingly accords with Ibn Batûta, for he applies that of *Sciamuthera* to the *city* as well as to the island, describing the former as " a very noble emporium." Coupling these ideas with the following quotation from Crawfurd, I think it by no means improbable that *Shumatrah*, or some modification of that word, was the prevailing name of Achin (and, perhaps, of the island also,) in Ibn Batûta's time, and that its present name is of more recent date :—" The native name is correctly Acheh ; but this word, which means a ' wood-leech,' *does not, although naturalized, belong to any of the Malayan languages, but to the Telinga or Telugu of the Coromandel coast.*" (*Id.*, p. 2.) I note, however, that the same author conjectures that the word *Sumatra* is of Sanscrit or Hindu origin, probably from *Samudra*, the sea or ocean (*Id.*, p. 414.)

Respecting Marco Polo's visit, Mr. Crawfurd has the following observations :—" It is remarkable that the name of Sumatra had not reached Marco Polo, although he was six months wind-bound at the island, and in communication with the natives. That of Java, the only large territory of the Archipelago, familiarly called an island, by the natives, had done so ; and he called Sumatra, knowing it to be an island but ignorant of its relative extent, Java Minor." (*Id.*, p. 414.) Whereon I venture to suggest, that although Marco Polo designates Sumatra, the compass of which he approximately estimated at 2,000 miles, by the name of Java the Less, he nevertheless describes it as comprising eight kingdoms, six of which he visited, and one of these latter, namely, that where he was detained for several months, he calls *Samara*. That word, as it stands, approaches very nearly the orthography of the present name, and by the simple addition of the letter *t*, which may have been omitted by an oversight in the original manuscript or in the first copies, we have *Samatra* in full. It is further deserving of notice that the same traveller apparently makes

are three crowned kings who are Pagans, and their faith, their
manner of living, dress, and customs, are the same as in Tar-

Samara the chief kingdom in the island, for he says of its people :—
" Hauno re grande e potente, e chiamansi per il Gran Can." RAMUSIO,
vol. ii, p. 52.

Varthema greatly exaggerates the extent of the island, which is
" about 1,000 miles in length, its extreme ends being its narrowest parts,
and its centre its broadest. Its area is reckoned at 128,560 geographical
square miles." (*Desc. Dict.*, p. 414.) Prior to the publication of his book,
our traveller appears to have had some discussions with the learned men
of Europe, consequent on his own discovery, respecting the ancient
geography of the island, which led him, as it did many others, to identify
it with the Taprobana of Ptolemy. The locality of that famous island
was a vexed question at the end of the sixteenth century, for Patavino
in describing Sumatra writes :—" Hanc Insulam antiquorum Taprobanam
fuisse omnes penè auctores sentiunt, licet aliqui magnæ eruditionis viri
ipsam Auream fuisse Chersonesum putent, ac ob id antiquis ceu penin-
sulam creditam fuisse." And, again, under the head of Ceylon :—
" ZEILAN verò insula præstantissima est, quæ...antiquam fuisse Ptolemæi Taprobanam Andreas Corsalus et Joannes Barrius cum plerisque alijs
censent; Mercator verò, cui magis in hac re fidem præstamus, putat esse
Ptolemæi Nanigerim." *Geographia*, pp. 26.

With respect to the government of Sumatra, it has been already mentioned that Marco Polo divided the island into eight kingdoms, one of
which was Felich, where the inhabitants of the coast had embraced
Muhammedanism, " by frequent trade with the Saracens; but those who
dwelt in the mountains were still like beasts." Varthema diminished
the number to " iii Re di corona," which probably comprised only those
of the principal states on the eastern side; Odoardo Barbosa says the island has " molti regni di quali il principal è Pedir della banda di tramontana ;" while De Barros enumerates no less than twenty-nine on the
sea-board alone, of which Pedir, then an independent sovereignty, is one.
Patavino sums up the information acquired on this subject up to the
end of the sixteenth century in those words :—" Scribunt quidam univer-
sam hanc insulam in quatuor regna esse divisam : alii in decem, alii
autem in 29. ex quibus nota sunt tantummodo decem: nempe Regnum
Pedir, quod cæteris præstat ; *Pazem* seu *Pacem* ; *Achem* seu *Acem* ;
Campar ; *Menancabo*, quod est fundamentum divitiarum, universæ insulæ, cùm in eo sint mineræ auri opulentissimæ ; et regnum *Zunde* : et
hæc quidem sex regna sunt circa littus ipsius insulæ, ac à Mauris occu-
pata olim fuère." (*Id.*, p. 265.) The last remark agrees with De Barros
as quoted by Crawfurd :—" The inhabitants of the coast follow the sect
of Muhammed ;" nevertheless, Varthema's account, which makes some

nassari, and the wives also are burnt alive. The colour of these inhabitants is almost white, and they have the face broad, and the eyes round and green.[1] Their hair is long, the nose broad and flat, and they are of small stature. Here justice is strictly administered, as in Calicut.[2] Their money is gold, and silver, and tin, all stamped. Their golden money has on one side a devil, on the other there is something resembling a chariot drawn by elephants: the same on the silver

of the sovereigns Hindu by religion, and more especially the reigning king of Pedir, is too circumstantial to be set aside by any *general* descriptions of an island of such vast extent, and comparatively so little known to the best Portuguese historians of that age. Moreover, Varthema had become well versed in the externals, at least, of Muhammedanism, and was not likely to confound the observances of Paganism with those of Islàm. In the absence, therefore, of any definite proof to the contrary, I see no reason to discredit this part of his narrative, more especially as we have Crawfurd's authority for believing that "the people of Sumatra had certainly adopted a kind of Hinduism, and this is sufficiently attested by an examination of their languages, and even by a few monuments and inscriptions." *Desc. Dict.*, p. 419.

[1] De Barros, as quoted by Crawfurd, says : " The people of the coast, as well as of the interior of the island, are all of a yellowish-brown colour (baço), having flowing hair, are well made, of a goodly aspect, and do not resemble the Javanese, although so near to them." *Id.*, p. 419. He does not mention the "*green* eyes."

[2] The same remark is made of the country by Hamilton :—" No place in the world punishes theft with greater severity than Atcheen, and yet robberies and murders are more frequent there than in any other place. For the first fault, if the theft does not amount to a *tayel* value, it is but the loss of a hand or a foot, and the criminal may choose which he will part with ; and, if caught a second time, the same punishment and loss is used ; but the third time, or if they steal five *tayel* in value, that crime entitles them to souling or impaling alive. When their hand or foot is to be cut off, they have a block with a broad hatchet fixed in it, with the edge upwards, on which the limb is laid, and struck on with a wooden mallet, till the amputation is made, and they have a hollow bamboo, or Indian cane, ready to put the stump in, and stopped about with rags or moss, to keep the blood from coming out, and are set in a conspicuous place for travellers to gaze on, who generally bestow a little spittle in a pot, being what is produced by the mastication of beetel, and that serves them instead of salve to cure their wounds." PINKERTON, vol. viii. p. 446.

and tin money.[1] Of the silver coin ten go to a ducat, and of those of tin, twenty-five. Elephants in immense quantities are produced here, which are the largest I ever saw. These people are not warlike, but attend to their merchandise, and are very great friends of foreigners.

[1] Crawfurd says that prior to the arrival of the Europeans, the natives of the Archipelago generally had no other coin than small bits of copper, brass, tin, or zinc, though he subjoins that "the Javanese appear to have coined some of their own money, as we find from many examples excavated from their own temples and other places. These contain impressions of scenic figures, such as are still represented in their dramas, called *wayang* or shadows, but having no date, and, indeed, no written characters, until after their adoption of Mahommedanism," which was not till towards the end of the fifteenth century. He further excepts Achin, the state adjoining, (which probably comprised Pedir in Varthema's time,) and remarks as follows :—" The only native country of the Archipelago in which a coin of the precious metals seems ever to have been coined is Achin. This is of gold, of the weight of nine grains, and of about the value of 14*d.* sterling...All the coins of this description which have been made are inscribed with Arabic characters, and bear the names of the sovereigns under whom they were struck, so that they are comparatively modern." (*Desc. Dict.,* p. 286.) As a Muhammedan king was reigning in Sumatra when Ibn Batûta visited that island, similar coins may have been current then ; but, be that as it may, Varthema's account fully proves that such "stamped" money existed at the time of his visit, and I see no reason for doubting that it comprised, as he states, coins of silver and of tin, as well as of gold. It is by no means improbable, however, that some of the coined money at Achin was imported, through the ordinary transactions of trade, from different parts of India ; but I have searched Marsden's *Numismata Orientalia* in vain for a counterpart of the Sumatran device—a chariot drawn by elephants—on any of the early Indian coinage. That Indian coins had obtained a certain degree of circulation in the Archipelago at this period, may be inferred from Varthema's statement regarding Banda, one of the Nutmeg Islands : —" La moneta corre qui *alla usanza di Calicut.*" See the chapter " Concerning the Islands of Bandan."

THE CHAPTER CONCERNING ANOTHER SORT OF PEPPER, AND CONCERNING SILK, AND BENZOIN, WHICH ARE PRODUCED IN THE SAID CITY OF PIDER.

In this country of Pider[1] there grows a very great quantity of pepper, and of long pepper which is called *Molaga*. This said kind of pepper is larger than that which comes here to us, and is very much whiter, and within it is hollow, and is not so biting as that of ours, and weighs very little, and is sold here in the same manner as cereals are sold with us.[2] And you must know that in this port there are laden with it every year eighteen or twenty ships, all of which go

---

[1] Pider, or "Pedir, is the name of a Malay state on the eastern side of Sumatra, and comprising that portion of the sea-board of the island which extends from Diamond Point, the Tanjung-pârlak of the Malays, to Achin...It was the first spot in the Archipelago at which the Portuguese touched, and they found it carrying on some foreign trade, being frequented by ships from different parts of the continent of India. At present it is a place of no moment, except for its export of the areca-nut and a little pepper which is carried to the British settlement of Penang. The principal town, bearing the same name, is situated on a small river, a little east of a headland, which is in north latitude 5° 29' and east longitude 96°." *Id.*, 330-1.

[2] Being uncertain whether this was the *Piper longum* of botanists, I consulted Mr. Bennett of the British Museum, whose kindness I have already had occasion to acknowledge, and append his note in reply:—"There can be no doubt that the second kind of pepper referred to by Varthema is the same as that which we now call *long pepper*. His account exactly tallies with it in every respect, and is singularly correct, as indeed most of his descriptions are." Crawfurd says: "This commodity is probably a native of Java, although now grown in other countries of the Archipelago," and then remarks: "it is singular that it is not named by Barbosa, but there can be little doubt but that it must have been an article of trade in his time." (*Desc. Dict.*, p. 335.) It is mentioned by Pigafetta, Barbosa's companion, as growing in one of the Banda islands, and he describes it thus:—"The long pepper grows on a plant or tree like the ivy, that is, it is flexible, and rests on other trees, the fruit hangs on the stem, and the leaf is like that of the mulberry. It is called *luli*." (RAMUSIO, vol. i. p. 368.) Conti also enumerates *pepe lungo* among the productions of Sumatra. *Id.*, p. 339.

to Cathai, because they say that the extreme cold begins there. The tree which produces this pepper produces it long, but its vine is larger, and the leaf broader and softer, than that which grows in Calicut. An immense quantity of silk is produced in this country, a great deal is also made in the forests without being cultivated by any one. This, it is true, is not very good.[1] A great quantity of benzoin is also produced here, which is the gum of a tree.[2] Some say, for I have not seen it myself, that it grows at a considerable distance from the sea, on the mainland.

THE CHAPTER CONCERNING THREE SORTS OF ALOES-WOOD.

Inasmuch as it is the variety of objects which most delights and invites man, as well to read as to understand, it has therefore appeared to me well to add that of which I

---

[1] It is singular that a similar statement is made by De Barros, who in describing the productions of Sumatra says: "It produces also silk in such quantity that there are cargoes of it sent to many parts of India;" whereon Crawfurd remarks:—"This is probably an error on the part of that usually reliable writer. I am not even aware that wild silk is produced in any of the insular forests such as it is found to be in many of those of Hindustan." The same author asserts, indeed, that "the culture of the mulberry and the rearing of the silk-worm have never been practised by the natives of the Archipelago, whether from the unsuitableness of this branch of industry to the climate, or to the state of society, is not ascertained." (*Desc. Dict.*, p. 394.) The discrepancy is a wide one, and I can suggest nothing to reconcile the contradictory statements. It is noticeable, however, that Odoardo Barbosa does not enumerate silk among his list of the productions of Sumatra.

[2] "Benzoin, the resin of the *Styrax benzoni*, obtained by wounding the bark. The plant, which is of moderate size, is an object of cultivation, the manner of culture being from the seed. The trees are ripe for the production of the resin at about seven years old, and the plant is the peculiar product of the islands of Borneo and Sumatra." Crawfurd thinks that it may be the *malabathrum* of the ancients. (*Id.*, p. 50.) Benzoin is called by the Arabs *Bakh-khûr Jâwî*, Java incense.

have real certainty by my own experience. Wherefore
you must know that neither benzoin nor aloes-wood comes
much into Christian ports, and therefore you must understand that there are three sorts of aloes-wood. The first
and most perfect sort is called *Calampat*, and which does
not grow in this island, but comes from a city called Sarnau,
which (as the Christians our companions said) is near to
their city, and here this first sort grows. The second sort is
called *Loban*, which comes from a river. The name of the
third sort is called *Bochor*.[1] The said Christians also said

[1] The *Lignum aloes* or *Agila*, the Eagle-wood of commerce. Barbosa
mentions it under the two former names, and Crawfurd in describing it
says : " There can be no doubt but that the perfumed wood is the result
of disease in the tree that yields it, produced by the thickening of its
sap into a gum or resin...It is found in the greatest perfection in the
mountainous country to the east of the Gulf of Siam, including Camboja and Cochin-China. It is found, however, although of inferior
quality, as far north as Sylhet, in Bengal, and as far south as the Malay
Peninsula and Sumatra." (*Desc. Dict.*, p. 6, 7.) In his earlier *History
of the Indian Archipelago*, (vol. i. p. 519,) he had remarked of the wood
in question that " if it be a native of the Indian islands, the countries
which produce it have not been ascertained ;" but his later researches
corroborate Varthema both as regards the existence of the tree in Sumatra, and his other statement that the best quality of the perfumed
wood, the *Calamput* or *Kalambak*, was of foreign growth. The latter I
take to be the *'Ood el-Kumârî* of the *Two Muhammedan Travellers*,
(PINKERTON," vol. vii. p. 208,) and of Ibn Batûta, (LEE's *Translation*,
p. 201,) who both make that quality to come from Komâri in China.
I notice, however, that Castenheda, as quoted by Crawfurd, describes
the *Kalambak* as indigenous to Sumatra. He writes :—" It [Campar,
on the eastern side of the island,] has nothing but forests which yield
aloes-wood, called in India *Calambuco*. The trees which produce it are
large, and when they are old they are cut down, and the *aloes-wood*
taken from them, which is the heart of the tree, and the outer part is
agila. Both these woods are of great price, but especially the *Calambuco*, which is rubbed in the hands, yielding an agreeable fragrance ;
the *agila* does so *when burned*." *Desc. Dict.*, p. 7.

The names of the other two qualities mentioned by Varthema are
Arabic, and merely conventional, for *lubán* means frankincense, and
bakh-khár incense generally. Ibn Batûta apparently specifies the same
inferior kinds, and uses the word *lubán*, in describing the aromatic pro-

that the reason the said *Calampat* does not come to us is
this, that in Gran Cathai, and in the kingdom of Cini and
Macini,[1] and Sarnau and Giava, they have a much greater

ducts of Java :—"There is only the *lubán* of Java, camphor, cloves, and
'*Ood Hindi*," Indian aloes-wood. (LEE's *Trans.*, pp. 201-2.)

From Castanheda's account of the *Kalambak*, and the experiment of
its fragrance when simply held in the warm hand, as described by Varthema in the next chapter, I am inclined to infer with him that that
quality seldom finds its way to the westward. The '*Ood* is generally
used as a *pastille* by the Arabs, and their poets, ancient and modern,
who are fond of dilating on the excellency of the wood, and ransack
their imaginations to multiply its suggestive imagery, mostly associate
the perfume with the action of fire. The following is nearly a literal
translation of an Arabic couplet which I found on the fireplace of an
old khân in the district of Aleppo. For the English versification I am
indebted to the kindness of my friend the Rev. P. G. Hill, rector of
St. Edmund the King and Martyr :—

> " When God would bring man's virtue to the light,
> He sets against him Envy's tongue of spite :
> Just as the flames the Aloës-wood surround,
> Ere its delicious fragrance can be found."

The same pretty idea, clothed in similar language, occurs in Gregory
the Great's *Morals on the Book of Job* :—" For as unguents, unless they
be stirred, are never smelt far off, and as aromatic scents spread not
their fragrance except they be burned, so the Saints in their tribulations make known all the sweetness that they have of their virtues."
Library of the Fathers, vol. xviii. p. 18.

[1] *Sín Máchín*, or *Sín wa-Máchín*, and sometimes the word *Sín* alone,
with the prefixed article, *Es-Sín*, are used synonymously by the Arabs
of the present day to signify the Empire of China generally. I have
frequently endeavoured to ascertain from masters of Arab ships whether
they attached any definite limits to the country or countries designated
by the double name, but the result was unsatisfactory : some maintained that it indicated the entire territory to the north of Siam ; others
that *Sín* was specially applicable to Siam and Cochin-China, and *Máchín*
to China including Tartary ; and others, again, that *Máchín* was Siam,
and *Sín*, China. Conti, who most probably derived his nomenclature
from native traders, does not mention either *Sín* or China, but says that
the province of Ava was called *Macinus* by the inhabitants, and styles
the country beyond, towards the north, Cathay. Nikitin, who wrote by
report only, speaks of the seaports of *Cheen* and *Machin* as very large,
and supplies a few notices rendering it probable that Siam and China

abundance of gold than we have. They also say that there
are much greater lords there than there are in our parts,
and that they delight more than we do in those two sorts of
perfumes, and that after their death a very great quantity
of gold is expended in these perfumes; and for this reason
these excellent sorts do not come into our parts. In Sarnau
they are worth ten ducats per pound, because there is very
little of them.

are meant, but nothing further. D'Herbelot gives a clue to the origin
of the conjoined names, and notices the contradictory opinions, much as
I have stated them, which had obtained regarding the countries which
they respectively indicated. After remarking that *Sin* or *Chin*, (China,)
according to the Persians and other Orientals, took its name from the
eldest son of Japhet, he adds:—" Tchin eut pour fils aîné Matchin, et il
suffira de dire icy, que les Orientaux, en parlant de la Chine en general, l'appellent *Tchin et Matchin*, de même que pour exprimer la Tartarie entière,
ils se servent des termes d'Jagioug' et Magioug', qui sont le Gog et Magog
de l'Ecriture Sainte. Il y a pourtant des Geographes qui prétendent,
qu'il faut entendre par le mot *Tchin*, la Chine Septentrionale, que
plusieurs croyent être la même que la Khatha ou Kathaï, et par celuy de
Matchin, la Chine Meridionale, en y comprenant la Cochin-Chine, la
Tunquin, e la Royaume d'Anau avec ceux de Siam et la Pegu." (*Bib.
Orient.* sub voce SIN.) This is satisfactory as far as it goes, but it leaves
untouched another point suggested by the two names as used by the
early European travellers above quoted, and their prevalence among the
Arabs and Persians at the present day. Neither Suleimân in the ninth
century, nor Edrîsi in the twelfth, nor Marco Polo in the thirteenth, nor
Ibn Batûta before the middle of the fourteenth, all of whom describe
China as *Sin*, ever mention the word *Matchin*. There must be some
reason for this singular fact, though I am unable to suggest any. I
note, however, that D'Herbelot, in his article on SIN, remarks that
"the author of the Humaioun Naméh, which is the book of Kalilah and
Dimnah, says that Homaïounfal was formerly a powerful king of *Tchin*
and *Matchin*." I have searched carefully through De Sacy's Arabic
version of those famous fables without discovering the latter word, and
conclude, therefore, that the reference is to some annotations of Ali
Chélebi, who translated the *Kalilah wa-Dimnah* into Turkish in the
beginning of the tenth century, and dedicated it to Suleiman I., under
the title of *Humayân-Naméh*.

THE CHAPTER CONCERNING THE EXPERIMENT WITH THE SAID ALOES-WOOD AND BENZOIN.

The aforesaid Christians made us see an experiment with the two kinds of perfume. One of them had a little of both sorts. The *Calampat* was about two ounces, and he made my companion hold it in his hand as long as he could say four times, "Miserere mei, Deus," holding it firmly in his closed hand. Then he made him open his hand. Truly, I never smelt such an odour as that was, which exceeded all our perfumes. Then he took a piece of benzoin as large as a walnut, and he took of that [the Calampat] which grows in Sarnau about half a pound, and had it placed in two chambers in vases with fire within. In truth I tell you, that that little produced more odour, and a greater softness and sweetness, than two pounds of any other kind would have done. It is impossible to describe the excellence of those two kinds of scents and perfumes. So that you have now heard the reason why these said things do not come to our parts. There also grows here a very great quantity of *lacca*[1] for making red colour, and the tree of this is formed like our trees which produce walnuts.

THE CHAPTER CONCERNING THE VARIETY OF DEALERS IN THE SAID ISLAND OF SUMATRA.

In this country I saw the most beautiful works of art I ever saw in my life, that is, some boxes worked in gold, which they gave for two ducats each, which, in truth, with us, would be valued at one hundred ducats.[2] Again, I saw

---

[1] "Lacca, in Malay, *Laka*, the *Tanarius major*, a tree with a rose-coloured wood, a native of Sumatra, used in dyeing and pharmacy. It is an article of considerable native trade, and is chiefly exported to China." CRAWFURD'S *Disc. Dict.*, p. 204.

[2] "Gold ornaments of considerable beauty are made by most of the

here in one street about five hundred money-changers, and these because a very great number of merchants come to this city, where they carry on a very extensive traffic.[1] For the sleeping of these people, there are good beds of cotton, covered with silk and cotton sheets. In this island they have an extreme abundance of timber, and they make here great ships which they call *giunchi*, which carry three masts, and have a prow before and behind, with two rudders before and two behind. And when they navigate through any archipelago, (for here there is a great sea like a canal,) while sailing, the wind will sometimes come in their face, they immediately lower the sail, and quickly, without turning, hoist sail on the other mast, and turn back. And you must know that they are the most active men I have ever met with. They are also very great swimmers, and excellent masters of the art of making fire-works.[2]

---

civilized nations of the Archipelago. The neck-chains of Manilla are examples of very delicate workmanship, and the filagree work of the Malays of Sumatra is still more remarkable. In all these cases, what is most striking is the beauty of the work compared with the rudeness and simplicity of the workmen and their tools." *Id.*, p. 145.

[1] This remark undesignedly confirms Varthema's former statement respecting the coins which were current at Sumatra. (See note on p. 232 *ante*.) The money-changers were probably foreigners, natives of India, like those at Malacca, where Crawfurd says "a colony of the Hindus of Telingana still exists, whose profession it is to try gold by the touch and to refine it." *Id.*, p. 287.

[2] "Fuochi artificiati." Crawfurd has collected abundant evidence to prove that fire-arms were in use among the more advanced Malay nations when the Portuguese first arrived in the Archipelago, and he concludes that their knowledge of artillery was communicated by the Arabs, who had acquired it from the Christians. If such was the case, it must have been from the Arabs of the Persian Gulf, for, as has been shown in a former note, (p. 65,) those of Yemen were generally unacquainted with fire-arms when the Egyptians invaded that country in 1515. I think Mr. Crawfurd's conclusion very probable, but I venture to question one of the premises as contained in the following quotation:—"The name by which fire-arms are usually called [among the Malays] is *bádil*, a general one for any missile, and *mariam*, which is Arabic, and

THE CHAPTER CONCERNING THE HOUSES, AND HOW THEY ARE COVERED, IN THE SAID ISLAND OF SUMATRA.

The habitations of the said place consist of walled houses of stone, and they are not very high, and a great many of them are covered with the shells of sea turtles,[1] because they

in that language signifies 'the Virgin Mary,' which would seem to imply that the knowledge of artillery was derived by the Arabs themselves from the Christians, as without doubt it was." *Mariam* does, indeed, mean Mary, not in Arabic only, but in several other Oriental languages, and Mussulmans are as familiar with the name through the Korân as Christians are through the Bible. Moreover, as the word is certainly never used by the Arabs in Arabia or Egypt to designate fire-arms, I can only suppose it to be a conventional term confined to those residing in the Archipelago, and, as such, can hardly be adduced in support of Mr. Crawfurd's hypothesis. Varthema's notice of the skill displayed by the people of Sumatra in the preparation of "fuochi artificiati" at this early period is corroborated by the same learned author's remarks on that subject:—"A knowledge of gunpowder must have been, at least, as early in the Indian islands as that of cannon. It is not improbable that it may have been even earlier known through the Chinese, for the manufacture of fire-works [is] known to the Malays under the name of *Màrchàn*, a word of which the origin is not traceable. The principal ingredients of gunpowder are sufficiently abundant over many parts of the Archipelago, and known by native names, *sandâwa* being the name of saltpetre, and *bâlirang* or *walirang*, of sulphur." *Desc. Dict.*, p. 22.

[1] Conti merely describes the houses at Sumatra as being very low, but Barbosa says that all the cities of the kingdoms in the island were built of straw, which contradicts Varthema, unless the latter refers to some locality unknown to Barbosa. I have discovered nothing in the accounts of the early European travellers to confirm the use made of the shell as mentioned in the text; but it is a well known fact that turtles measuring from five to six feet are found in the seas of the Indian Archipelago, and Conti had heard that some of the churches belonging to the Christians at Cathay were constructed entirely of tortoise-shell. (See *India in the Fifteenth Cent.*, ii. 33.) There is nothing improbable, however, in Varthema's statement, and its coincidence with the accounts of the ancient Greek and Roman authors is most striking. Mr. R. H. Major's learned researches on this subject deserve to be quoted in full. Referring to the enormous tortoise described by Sinbad in the *Arabian Nights* as measuring twenty cubits

are found here in great quantities, and in my time I saw one weighed which weighed one hundred and three pounds. I also saw two elephants' teeth which weighed three hundred and thirty-five pounds. And I saw, moreover, in this island, serpents very much larger than those of Calicut. Let us revert to our Christian companions, who were desirous of returning to their country: wherefore they asked us what was our intention, whether we wished to remain here, or to go farther on, or to return back. My companion answered them: "Since I am brought where the spices grow, I should like to see some kinds before I return back." They said to him: "No other spices grow here excepting those which you have seen." And he asked them where the nutmegs and the cloves grew. They answered: "That the nutmegs and mace grew in an island which was distant from there three hundred miles." We then asked them if we could go to that island in safety, that is, secure from robbers or corsairs. The Christians answered: "That secure from robbers we might go, but not from the chances of the sea;" and they said that we could not go to the said island with that large ship. My companion said: "What means then

in length and breadth, he remarks :—"The account of these animals is not to be attributed to a licentious exuberance of fancy in the Arabian author. He might have seen in Ælian (*De Naturâ Anim.*, l. xvi. c. xvii.) that the tortoises, whose shells were fifteen cubits in length, and sufficiently large to cover a house, were found near the island of Taprobane. Pliny and Strabo mention the same circumstance (*Nat. Hist.*, l. ix. c. 10): they likewise turn them upside down, and say that men used to row in them as in a boat. (*Geog.*, l. xvi. 6.) Diodorus Siculus adds to their testimony, and assures us, on the faith of an historian, that the *chelonophagi* (shell-fish eaters, L. iv. c. 1) derived a threefold advantage from the tortoise, which occasionally supplied them with a roof to their houses, a boat, and a dinner." Mr. Major then proceeds to identify this colossal tortoise with the *Colossochelys Atlas*, the first fossil remains of which were discovered in the sub-Himalayahs by Dr. Falconer and Major Cautley in 1835, an idea of the vast size of which is afforded by the cast in the upper galleries of the British Museum. See *Introduction* to *India in the Fifteenth Cent.*, pp. xliii-v.

R

might there be for going to this island?" "They answered:
"That it was necessary to purchase a *Chiampana*,"[1] that is,
a small vessel, of which many are found there. My companion begged them to send for two, which he would buy.
The Christians immediately found two, furnished with people whom they had there to manage them, with all things
necessary and proper for such a voyage; and they bargained
for the said vessels, men, and necessary things, for four hundred *pardai*, which were paid down by my companion, who
then began to say to the Christians: "O my very dear
friends, although we are not of your race, we are all sons of
Adam and Eve, will you abandon me and this other my companion who is born in your faith?" "How in our faith? This
companion of yours, is he not a Persian?" He replied: "He
is a Persian now, because he was purchased in the city of
Jerusalem." The Christians hearing Jerusalem mentioned,
immediately raised their hands to heaven, and then kissed the
earth three times, and asked at what time it was that I was
sold in Jerusalem. We replied: "That I was about fifteen
years old." Then said they: "He ought to remember his
country." Said my companion: "Truly he does recollect
it, for I have had no other pleasure for many months but
that of hearing of the things of his country, and he has
taught me [the names of] all the members of the body and
the names of the things to eat." Hearing this, the Christians
said: "Our wish was to return to our country, which is
distant from here three thousand miles; for your sake and
for that of your companion we are willing to come where
you shall go; and if your companion is willing to remain
with us, we will make him rich, and if he shall desire to
observe the Persian law, he shall be at liberty to do so." My
companion replied: "I am much pleased with your company, but it is out of order for him to remain with you,
because I have given him a niece of mine to be his wife for

---

[1] See note 2 on p. 188 *ante*.

the love which I bear him.¹ So that, if you are willing to come in company with us, I wish that you first take this present which I give you, otherwise I should never be satisfied." The good Christians answered : " That he might do as he pleased, for they were satisfied with everything." And so he gave them half a *curia*² of rubies, which were ten, of the value of five hundred *pardai*.³ Two days afterwards the said *Chiampane* were ready, and we put on board many articles of food, especially the best fruits I ever tasted, and thus took our way towards the island called Bandan.

THE CHAPTER CONCERNING THE ISLAND OF BANDAN,⁴ WHERE NUTMEGS AND MACE GROW.

In the course of the said journey we found about twenty islands, part inhabited and part not, and in the space of

¹ See p. 104 *ante*. ² See note on p. 170 *ante*.
³ See note on p. 130 *ante*.
⁴ Bàndan, the modern Banda, one of "the Banda or Nutmeg Islands, which consist of a group of mere islets, said to be five in number, like the Clove Islands, but really amounting to ten, although some of them be uninhabited." (*Desc. Dict.*, p. 33.) Barbosa makes the population Moors and Pagans, and Pigafetta speaks of them as being Moors only. (RAMUSIO, vol. i. pp. 319, 368.) De Barros, as quoted by Crawfurd, gives the following description of the inhabitants and produce of the Banda Islands, which on most points strikingly confirms Varthema's account :—" The people of these islands are robust, with a tawny complexion and lank hair, and are of the worst repute in these parts. They follow the Mohammedan sect, and are much addicted to trade, their women performing the labours of the field. They have neither king nor lord, and all their government depends on the advice of their elders; and as these are often at variance, they quarrel among themselves. The land has no other export than the nutmeg. This tree is in such abundance that the land is full of it, without its being planted by any one, for the earth yields it without culture. The forests which produce it belong to no one by inheritance, but to the people in common. When June and September come, which are the months for gathering the crop, the nutmeg woods are allotted, and he who gathers most has most profit." *Desc. Dict.*, p. 35.

fifteen days we arrived at the said island, which is very ugly and gloomy, and is about one hundred miles in circumference, and is a very low and flat country. There is no king here, nor even a governor, but there are some peasants, like beasts, without understanding. The houses of this island are of timber, very gloomy, and low. Their dress consists of a shirt; they go barefooted, with nothing on their heads; their hair long, the face broad and round, their colour is white, and they are small of stature. Their faith is Pagan, but they are of that most gloomy class of Calicut called *Poliar* and *Hirava*;[2] they are very weak of understanding, and in strength they have no vigour, but live like beasts. Nothing grows here but nutmegs and some fruits. The trunk of the nutmeg is formed like a peach tree, and produces its leaves in like manner; but the branches are more close, and before the nut arrives at perfection the mace stands round it like an open rose, and when the nut is ripe the mace clasps it, and so they gather it in the month of September; for in this island the seasons go as with us, and every man gathers as much as he can, for all are common, and no labour is bestowed upon the said trees, but nature is left to do her own work. These nuts are sold by a measure, which weighs twenty-six pounds, for the price of half a *carlino*. Money circulates here as in Calicut. It is not necessary to administer justice here, for the people are so stupid, that if they wished to do evil they would not know how to accomplish it. At the end of two days my companion said to the Christians: "Where do the cloves grow?" They answered: "That they grew six days' journey hence, in an island called Monoch, and that the people of that island are beastly, and more vile and worthless than those of Bandan. At last we determined to go to that island be the people what they might, and so we set sail, and in twelve days arrived at the said island.

[1] See p. 171 and *note*.

THE CHAPTER CONCERNING THE ISLAND OF MONOCH,[1] WHERE THE CLOVES GROW.

We disembarked in this island of Monoch, which is much smaller than Bandan; but the people are worse than those

[1] Varthema here applies the collective name to one of the five islands forming the proper *Moluccas*, but affords no indication enabling us to identify the island where he landed, which was probably either Ternaté or Tidor. With regard to the collective appellative, Mr. Crawfurd remarks:—" The collective name, which the Portuguese write *Maluca*, and is correctly *Maluka*, is equally unknown, although said to be that of a place and people of the island of Gilolo. No such name is, at present, known to exist in that island. There can be no doubt, however, but that this word was used by the Malays and Javanese, who conducted the spice trade, before it fell into the hands of the Portuguese; for it is employed by Barbosa, who visited the Archipelago before the conquest of Malacca; and again in 1521 by Pigafetta, who writes the word *Malucco*." (*Desc. Dict.*, p. 283.) It is clear that Gilolo was not Varthema's *Monoch*, for he describes the latter as much smaller than *Bandan*. Pigafetta gives a circumstantial account of the group, but Barbosa's briefer narrative comprises the most important particulars respecting their condition at this period:—"In advance of these islands, [Ambon = Amboyna,] towards the north, are the five islands of *Maluco*, in all of which cloves grow, and they belong to Pagans and Muhammedans, and the kings are Muhammedans. The first is called *Bachan*; the second, *Machian*, which has a good harbour; the third, *Motel*; the fourth, *Tidoro*; the fifth, *Terenati*, in which there is a Muhammedan king called Sultan Heraram Corala, [the second word is probably a corruption of *Khair-Allah*; I can make nothing of the first,] who used to rule over all the said Clove islands, but four were taken from him, and each has a king of its own. The mountains of these five islands are all full of cloves, which grow on certain trees like the laurel, which has a leaf like the *comari* [?] and grows like the flower of an orange. In the beginning it [the clove] is green, then it becomes white, and when ripe is red. The people then gather it with the hand, climbing on the trees, and place it to dry in the sun, which makes it black; and if there is no sun, they dry it in smoke, and when it is well dried, they sprinkle it with *acqua salsa* [this may mean salt water] that it may not break, and that it may retain its virtue. Of these cloves, the quantity is so great that they can never wholly gather them, so that much of them is left to go to the bad. Those trees from which fruit is not collected for three years remain in a wild state, and those cloves are worthless. These islands are frequented every year by those from *Malaca* and *Giava* who come to load with cloves, and bring to buy with, quicksilver, cinnaber, cloths from *Cambaia*,

of Bandan, but live in the same manner, and are a little more white, and the air is a little more cold. Here the cloves grow, and in many other neighbouring islands, but they are small and uninhabited. The tree of the cloves is exactly like the box tree, that is, thick, and the leaf is like that of the cinnamon, but it is a little more round, and is of that colour which I have already mentioned to you in Zeilan, [Ceylon,] which is almost like the leaf of the laurel. When these cloves are ripe, the said men beat them down with canes, and place some mats under the said tree to catch them. The place where these trees are is like sand, that is, it is of the same colour, not that it is sand. The country is very low,[1] and the north star is not seen from it. When we had seen this island and these people, we asked the Christians if there was anything else to see. They replied: "Let us see a little how they sell these cloves." We found that they were sold for twice as much as the nutmegs, but by measure, because these people do not understand weights.

THE CHAPTER CONCERNING THE ISLAND OF BORNEI.

We were now desirous of changing countries, in order to

Bengala, and *Paleacate*, drugs of *Cambaia*, some pepper, porcelain vases, large metal bells which are made in *Giava*, and brass and tin basins. The cloves here are so cheap, that they get them almost for nothing. This king of *Maluco* is a Muhammedan, and almost a Pagan, for he has a Muhammedan wife, and keeps in his house between three and four hundred beautiful girls who are Pagans, of whom he has sons and daughters, and only the sons of the Muhammedan women become Muhammedans. Besides, he has always in his service many hunchbacked women, whose shoulders and backs he causes to be broken in infancy, and this he does for the sake of show and reputation. He has between eighty and a hundred of these, who always stand around and near him, and serve him instead of pages, for one hands him betel-leaf, and another his sword, and in like manner they perform all other offices." RAMUSIO, vol. i. p. 319.

[1] Meaning, perhaps, as to latitude.

learn new things in every way. Then said the Christians:
"O dear companion, since God has conducted us so far in
safety, if it please you, we will go to see the largest island in the
world,[1] and the most rich, and you will see a thing which you
have never seen before. But we must first go to another island
which is called Bornei, where we must take a large ship, for

[1] By "the greatest island in the world" the Christians appear to have meant Java, showing how ignorant they were of the comparative size of Borneo. At what point of the latter island the party landed is uncertain, but it was undoubtedly on the southern part, for our author says: "pigliammo il camino verso la detta isola, alla qual sempre si va *al mezzo giorno*." And yet, if this inference is correct, one fails to perceive the necessity of the precaution suggested by the Christians, that they must first go to Borneo, and take a larger vessel there, because the sea on the way was rougher; since, from the southern part of that island, their route to Java would have been much the same as that by which they had sailed from Sumatra to the Banda Islands, except, indeed, that in the one case they probably hugged the coast of Java, (Varthema tells us that they found about twenty islands on the way,) and in the other would have to cross the Java sea. Unfortunately, the approximate measurement given of the distance between the Moluccas and Borneo affords no aid in settling either the course pursued or the point of disembarcation, as the nearest extremities of the two places are 450 miles apart, which leads to the conjecture that by some mischance "200 *miles*" may have been substituted for "200 *leagues*" in the original MS., or in the first copies. Further, it is open to question whether the mainland of Borneo was the locality visited: Varthema's description of the island as being "*alquanto maggiore* che la sopradetta [referring to his *Maluch*,] e molto più bassa," would rather indicate one of the islets on the south-eastern side of Borneo, though perhaps by "bassa" he refers to latitude; otherwise we must pronounce his usual accuracy greatly at fault in this instance, or infer that his informants were as unacquainted as himself with the real size of *Bornei*. However this may be, his statement respecting the large export of camphor warrants the inference that the place was situated in the highway of the trade of that period, and his account of the inhabitants shows that they had attained a degree of civilization far beyond that of the aboriginal Dayaks. These latter, according to Crawfurd, rarely reach the sea-coast, which is in the occupation of foreign settlers, whom he considers to be generally of Malay descent, and Varthema's brief description of those whom he met at *Bornei* coincides with that opinion.

For further information respecting Borneo, I refer the reader to the

the sea is more rough." He replied: "I am well pleased to do that which you wish." And so we took our way towards the said island, the route to which is constantly to the southward. While on our way the said Christians had no other pleasure, night and day, than that of conversing with me upon subjects relating to the Christians and about our faith. And when I told them of the Volto Santo which is in St. Peter's, and of the heads of St. Peter and St. Paul, and of many other saints, they told me secretly that if I would go with them I should be a very great lord, for having seen these things. I doubted that after they had conducted me there I should ever have been able to return to my country, and therefore I abstained from going. When we had arrived in the island of Bornei, which is distant from Monoch about two hundred miles, we found it to be somewhat larger than the abovementioned, and much lower. The people of this island are Pagans, and are good people. Their colour is more white than otherwise. Their dress consists of a cotton shirt, and some go clothed in camelots. Some wear red caps. In this island justice is strictly administered, and every year a very great quantity of camphor is shipped, which they say grows there, and which is the gum of a tree. If it be so, I have not seen it, and therefore I do not affirm it. Here my companion chartered a vessel for one hundred ducats.

THE CHAPTER SHOWING HOW THE MARINERS MANAGE THE NAVIGATION TOWARDS THE ISLAND OF GIAVA.

When the chartered vessel was supplied with provisions, we took our way towards the beautiful island called Giava,

able article under that head in Mr. Crawfurd's *Descriptive Dictionary*, where he has collected together all the available authorities on the early history of the island, and the first attempts made by Europeans to open commercial relations with the inhabitants.

at which we arrived in five days, sailing towards the south. The captain of the said ship carried the compass with the magnet after our manner, and had a chart which was all marked with lines, perpendicular and across. My companion asked the Christians: " Now that we have lost the north star, how does he steer us? Is there any other north star than this by which we steer?" The Christians asked the captain of the ship this same thing, and he showed us four or five stars, among which there was one which he said was *contrario della* (opposite to) our north star,[1] and that he sailed by the north because the magnet was adjusted[2] and subjected to our north. He also told us that on the other side of the said island, towards the south, there are some other races, who navigate by the said four or five stars opposite to ours ;[3]

[1] In Varthema's Travels as contained in the edition of *Ramusio* of 1613, the words are : " ch'era incontro della." The meaning doubtless is, over against, opposite to.

[2] In the original " acconcia," *i.e.* conformed to, adjusted to.

[3] Being but very imperfectly acquainted with nautical astronomy, I submitted this chapter to my friend C. R. Markham, Esq., the Honorary Secretary of the Hakluyt Society, and also to R. H. Major, Esq., of the British Museum, whose able Introduction to the *Early Voyages to Terra Australis, now called Australia*, is a sufficient warranty of his qualifications to give an opinion on any subject connected with the infancy of navigation in that part of the globe. I append their respective notes, with the initials of their names attached.

" These four or five stars are the constellation of the Southern Cross. When the Southern Cross is vertical, a line drawn through the upper and lower stars passes through the South Pole, and meets a star called *B. Hydrus*, which is about twice as far from the South Pole as the star which we call the Pole Star is from the North Pole. This, no doubt, is the star alluded to by Varthema as being ' contrary to our North Star.' The skipper navigated by the North, because his compass was of European manufacture[?], its index pointing to the North, and not like that of the Chinese pointing to the South." C. R. M.

Andrea Corsalis, a century after Varthema, gives the following interesting account and diagram of the Southern Cross, which he also describes as being " opposta alla nostra Tramontana :"—" After passing the equinoctial line, we were in an altitude of 37°, in the other hemisphere, opposite the Cape of Good Hope,—a stormy and cold climate,

and, moreover, they gave us to understand that beyond the
the sun being at this season in the northern constellations, and we found
the night fourteen hours long. Here we saw a wonderful order of
the stars, which, in the part of the sky opposite to our north, revolve in
infinite numbers. Wherever the Antarctic Pole might be, for the degrees
of altitude we took the day by the Sun, and we reconnoitred the night by
the astrolabe, and they made manifest two nebulæ [or clouds] of tolerable
size, which, alternately falling and rising, continually moved round it, [this
order of the stars,] having a star always in the centre, which, with them,
revolved about eleven degrees from the Pole. Above these, there appeared a wonderful Cross in the midst of five stars which surround it,
(as the Wain does the North [Star],) with other stars which, therewith,
go round the Pole, revolving round it at a distance of about 30°, and
performed the circuit in twenty-four hours; and it [the Cross] is so
beautiful, that in my opinion none of the celestial constellations can be
compared to it, as will be seen by the annexed figure. And, unless I
am mistaken, I believe this to be the *Crusero* of which Dante, with a
spirit of prophecy, speaks in the beginning of his *Purgatory*."

[Reference is here made to the opening part of Canto I :—

"Io mi volsi a man destra, e posi mente
All' altro polo, e vidi quattro stelle
Non viste mai, fuor ch' alla prima gente.
Goder pareva 'l Ciel di lor fiamelle.
O settentrional vedovo sito,
Poi che privato se' di mirar quelle!"

We may fairly question Dante's prophetical powers, but if the Southern
Cross is indicated in these lines, whence did he obtain his knowledge?]

"A. ANTARCTIC POLE.   B. *CRUSERO*."   (RAMUSIO, vol. i. p. 177.)

said island the day does not last more than four hours, and that there it was colder than in any other part of the world. Hearing this we were much pleased and satisfied.[1]

THE CHAPTER CONCERNING THE ISLAND OF GIAVA, OF ITS FAITH, MANNER OF LIVING AND CUSTOMS, AND OF THE THINGS WHICH GROW IN THE SAID ISLAND.

Following then our route, in five days we arrived at this island of Giava, in which there are many kingdoms, the kings of which are Pagans. Their faith is this: some adore idols as they do in Calicut, and there are some who worship the sun, others the moon; many worship the ox; a great many the first thing they meet in the morning; and others

---

[1] "This sentence is very important if it should point to latitudes on a line with or south of Australia. The point where the shortest day would only last four hours would be 15° south of the southern point of Van Diemen's Land. It is most improbable that the Malay skipper should have been so far south; yet his statements indicate a knowledge of countries as far south, at least, as Australia." C. R. M.

"Vague as this sentence is, it either means nothing, or it contains information of very great importance. It is difficult to suppose that the Malay skipper should have been so far south as the great Southern Continent; yet it is more difficult to believe him capable of describing a phenomenon natural to these high latitudes, except from his own observation, or that of other navigators of that early period. But even should we feel disposed to withhold our belief in the probability of an event so astonishing as this would be, there yet remains the almost unavoidable conclusion that Australians are alluded to in the description of people to the south of Java who navigated by the four or five stars, doubtless the constellation of the Southern Cross. This reference to Australia is the more remarkable, that it precedes, in time, even those early indications of the discovery of that country which I have shown to exist on manuscript maps of the first half of the sixteenth century, although the discoverers' names, most probably Portuguese, and the date of the discovery, as yet remain a mystery." R. H. M.

worship the devil in the manner I have already told you.[1] This island produces an immense quantity of silk,[2] part in our manner and part wild, and the best emeralds[3] in the

[1] Java was unknown, even by name, to the civilized nations of Europe before Marco Polo's time, and his account of the island was founded on the report of others. Of the government, he merely remarks that the king was independent. Ibn Batûta, who visited Java *circa* A.D. 1330, says that the king was an infidel. Varthema places the country under many rulers, and makes all the rulers and people Pagans. The first statement is confirmed by De Barros, who says: " The island of Java is divided into many kingdoms ;" the second is modified by Barbosa, who describes Java Major as " inhabited by many Pagans, and in the seaports by Moors, wherein there are many villages and localities containing very many dwellings of Moors and of Moorish kings, who, however, are all subject to the king of the island, who is a Pagan, and resides inland. He is a very great lord, and is called *Pate udora*. Sometimes they rebel against him, but he immediately reduces them again." (RAMUSIO, vol. i. p. 319.) This appears to be the most probable account of the government and religion of the Javanese at the period referred to, though Crawfurd says: " All authorities are agreed in assigning the year of Christ 1478 as that in which Majapait [the capital of the principal Hindu state] was overthrown." I am unable to adjust the discrepancy, which, after all, is not a wide one ; but that Islamism had not absorbed the population generally till long after is evident, for Crawfurd himself, quoting from De Barros, writes :—" When Henrique Lemé visited the country of the Sundas in 1522, forty-four years after the supposed final conversion of the Javanese, he found idolatrous temples, nunneries, and the practice of concremation, still existing ;" (*Descr. Dict.*, pp. 185-6 ;) and Hamilton describes the religion of Java at the beginning of the last century as partly Muhammedan and partly Pagan. See PINKERTON, vol. viii. p. 455.

[2] I find nothing to corroborate this statement about the growth of silk at Java, on the contrary, Crawfurd's account entirely contradicts it : —" The only material, besides cotton, from which cloth is made by the Javanese is silk, and as the art of rearing the silk-worm has never been introduced into Java, with any effectual result, the raw material has always been imported." *Id.*, p. 178.

[3] If emeralds were found at Java, they must have been imported from some other quarter. These stones appear to have been very scarce even in India at this period, for Andrea Corsali, writing of that country, says : " I do not know where emeralds are produced : here they are in greater estimation than any other stone." (RAMUSIO, vol. i. p. 180.) Varthema himself says the same of Pegu. See p. 218 *ante*.

world are found here, and gold and copper in great quantity;[1] very much grain, like ours, and excellent fruits like those of Calicut. Animal food of all kinds, like ours, is found in this country. I believe that these inhabitants are the most trustworthy men in the world: they are white and of about our stature, but they have the face much broader than ours, their eyes large and green, the nose much depressed, and the hair long.[2] The birds here are in great multitudes, and all different from ours excepting the peacocks, turtle-doves, and black crows, which three kinds are like ours. The strictest justice is administered among these people, and they go clothed *all' apostolica* in stuffs of silk, camelot, and cotton, and they do not use many arms, be-

---

[1] I infer from Crawfurd that gold is found in its native state in Java, where also "massive ornaments of this metal, with images of the same, are frequently discovered." (*Hist. of the Ind. Archp.*, vol. i. p. 183.) With regard to copper, the same author says: "Ores of this metal have been found in Sumatra, Celebes, and Timur...In Sumatra, mines of it are said to be worked, but if such be the case, even their locality has certainly never been shown. The probability is, that this metal has always been, as it now is, imported...The use of copper in Java, chiefly in the formation, with tin and zinc, of alloys, is attested to have been of considerable antiquity by the discovery in old ruins of many statues and utensils of bronze, and even of copper itself. *Desc. Dict.*, pp. 116-7.

[2] "Java, whether the inhabitants be of the Javanese or Sunda nation, is peopled by the same race, the Malayan. This is characterised by a short and squat person,...the face is round, the mouth wide, the cheekbones high, the nose short, small, never prominent as with the European, and never flat as with the African negro. The eyes are always black, small, and deep-seated. The complexion is brown, with a shade of yellow, not so dark as with the majority of Hindus, and never black as with some of them." As to the moral character of the Javanese, Mr. Crawfurd fully coincides with Varthema, in which respect, however, both are decidedly at issue with Barbosa, who calls them, by report, "genti molto superbe, bugiarde, e traditori." Crawfurd, on the contrary, says they are "a peaceable, docile, sober, simple, and industrious people;" and adds:—"from my own experience of them, I have no difficulty in pronouncing them the most straightforward and truthful people that I have met with." *Desc. Dict*, pp. 173-4.

cause those only fight who go to sea.¹ These carry bows, and the greater part darts of cane. Some also use *zarabottane*² (blow-pipes), with which they throw poisoned darts; and they throw them with the mouth, and, however little they draw blood, the [wounded] person dies. No artillery of any kind is used here, nor do they know at all how to make it.³ These people eat bread made of corn; some also

¹ Barbosa speaks of the Javanese as being "gran corsari, perchè vanno travagliando per mare;" and Crawfurd says that boat-building is still an art extensively practised all along the northern coast of Java. Their maritime propensities may be inferred also from the fact that they have no fewer than four generic names for a ship or vessel: *prau, jong, biïita*, and *palwa*,—all native words." See *Desc. Dict.*, p. 176.

² This weapon is thus described by Crawfurd :—" The chief missile in use before the introduction of fire-arms, was a small arrow ejected from a blow-pipe by the breath, called a *Sumpitan*, meaning the object blown through. This instrument is at present in general use by most of the wild tribes of Sumatra, Borneo, and Celebes. The bow for discharging arrows is well known to all the more advanced nations of the Archipelago, but does not seem, at any time, to have been generally employed, the blow-pipe probably superseding its use, although a far less effectual weapon. It is found represented on the sculptures of some of the monuments of Java of the twelfth and thirteenth centuries." *Id.*, p. 21.

³ Barbosa, in describing the Javanese by report from four to nine years subsequent to Varthema, says : " they are great masters in casting artillery. They make here many *spingarde*, [one-pounders?] muskets, and fire-works, and in every place are considered excellent in casting artillery, and in the knowledge of discharging it. (RAMUSIO, vol. i. p. 319.) Crawfurd also adduces satisfactory evidence to prove that fire-arms were used by the natives of Malacca when that place was assaulted by Albuquerque in 1511, and sums up his researches into the subject with this inference :—that although there is no record of the actual year in which fire-arms were first made known to the inhabitants of the Archipelago, yet, considering the frequent intercourse which subsisted between them and the maritime parts of Western India, " we may safely conclude that the event did not take place earlier than fifty years before the arrival of the Portuguese, that is, about the middle of the fifteenth century, or about a century after they had been in common use in Europe." (*Id.*, p. 23.) Varthema's contrary statement cannot stand against this weight of authority; nevertheless, I venture to suggest in his behalf, what I am disposed to consider very probable, especially from the subject of the next chapter, whereon he is again in

eat the flesh of sheep, or of stags, or, indeed, of wild hogs, and some others eat fish and fruits.

THE CHAPTER SHOWING HOW IN THIS ISLAND THE OLD PEOPLE ARE SOLD BY THEIR CHILDREN OR THEIR RELATIONS, AND AFTERWARDS ARE EATEN.

The people in this island who eat flesh, when their fathers become so old that they can no longer do any work, their children or relations set them up in the market-place for sale, and those who purchase them kill them and eat them cooked.[1] And if any young man should be attacked by any

antagonism with Mr. Crawfurd, that our traveller may have landed at some out-of-the-way place in the island, where the people were comparatively uncivilized, and that he drew his general inferences from what he saw in that restricted locality. Under any circumstances, the introduction of fire-arms into Java at this period was recent, and their use at the outset was most likely confined to the people of the more advanced maritime districts, whilst those residing in less frequented parts, and in the interior, would not have adopted them till some time after. In support of the plausibility of this suggestion, I submit the two following considerations:—1st., that the Arabs of Yemen were unacquainted with fire-arms in 1515, although the Egyptians, who invaded their coast in that year, had long possessed them, (see note on p. 65 *ante*;) and, 2ndly., that notwithstanding the contiguity of the two countries, and the frequent intercourse which had for centuries subsisted between them, the inhabitants of Ceylon appear to have been ignorant of artillery in 1507 when Don Lorenzo De Almeyda first discovered that island, whereas those of Western India had certainly used it at least twenty-five years before. See p. 193 *ante*, and *note*.

[1] Mr. Crawfurd remarks on Varthema's description of Java generally, and on this statement in particular, that "his account is obviously false or worthless, for he describes parents as selling their children to be eaten by the purchasers, and himself as quitting the island in haste for fear of being made a meal of." (*Desc. Dict.*, pp. 165-6.) Now, it is evident that our traveller is speaking of a class quite distinct from the more civilized community of the place, for these latter he had designated as "the most trustworthy men in the world;" hence, the question arises whether among the rude aborigines of the island at that period, (and I have already conjectured that Varthema may have visited

great sickness, and that it should appear to the skilful that he might die of it, the father or the brother of the sick man kills him, and they do not wait for him to die. And when they have killed him they sell him to others to be eaten. We, being astonished at such a thing, some merchants of the country said to us: "O you poor Persians, why do you

a part where such were likely to be found,) there were not some addicted to the practice of eating human flesh. *Non nobis tantas componere lites;* nevertheless, I would submit the following independent testimony as to the prevalence of cannibalism in the Malayan Peninsula and the Archipelago at this period, leaving the reader to form his own judgment on Varthema's credibility. Premising as possible, that the credulity and fears of the party may have been imposed upon in this instance, such a supposition is inadmissible in the case of Nicolò de' Conti, who resided in Sumatra a whole year, and who describes the custom as prevailing there in his time :—" In one part of the island called Batech, the inhabitants eat human flesh, and are in a state of constant warfare with their neighbours. They keep human heads as valuable property, for when they have captured an enemy they cut off his head, and, having eaten the flesh, store up the skull and use it for money." To which quotation the editor appends the following note :—" *Batech*=Batta ; a district extending from the river Singkell to the Tabooyong, and inland to the back of Ayer Bañgis. Marsden, in his *History of Sumatra* (p. 390, 3rd edit.) gives instances of cannibalism among this people as late as the year 1780." (*India in the Fifteenth Century*, ii. p. 9.) Pigafetta also, describing *Sulacho*, fifty miles distant from the Moluccas, says : " The men of this island are Pagans, and eat human flesh ;" and he subsequently attributes the same practice to one of the Ladrone or Marian Islands, which he calls *Maulla*, stating that " its inhabitants are savages and bestial, and eat human flesh." (RAMUSIO, vol. i. p. 368.) I note that Mr. Crawfurd must have used a different edition of Pigafetta's Voyages from that given in *Ramusio*, for this passage does not appear in his long quotation from that author. (*Desc. Dict.*, pp. 268-9.) Lastly, De Faria y Souza, in his account of the territory of Siam, says : " It contains much mountain and plain, and in both sundry sorts of people, some most barbarous and cruel, who feed on human flesh, as the *Guei*, who for ornament make figures on their bodies with hot irons." *Portuguese Asia*, translated by STEVENS, vol. i. p. 223.

On the whole, although Varthema's account of Java is certainly less accurate than his descriptions in general, I hardly think it merits the epithets of being " obviously false or worthless" which Mr. Crawfurd casts upon it.

leave such charming flesh to be eaten by the worms?" My companion hearing this immediately exclaimed: "Quick, quick, let us go to our ship, for these people shall never more come near me on land."

THE CHAPTER WHERE, AT MID-DAY, THE SUN CASTS A SHADOW[1] IN THE ISLAND OF GIAVA.

The Christians said to my companion: "O my friend, take this news to your country, and take this other also which we will show you. Look there, now that it is midday, turn your eyes towards where the sun sets." And raising our eyes we saw that the sun cast a shadow to the left more than a *palmo*.[2] And by this we understood that we were far distant from our country, at which we remained exceedingly astonished. And, according to what my companion said, I think that this was the month of June; for I had lost our months, and sometimes the name of the day. You must know that there is little difference between the cold with us and here. Having seen the customs of this island, it appeared to us that there was not much reason to remain in it, because it was necessary to be all night on guard for fear some wretch should come and carry us off to eat us. Wherefore, having called the Christians, we told them that, as soon as they could, we would return to our country. Before we departed, however, my companion

[1] In the original, "fa spera," but in the edition of *Ramusio* of 1613 it is rendered "faceva ombra." This is undoubtedly a gloss, but the meaning is preserved.

[2] I am indebted to my friend Mr. Markham for the following note on this passage:—"The equator bisects the island of Borneo, therefore, in the month of June, when Varthema was navigating, his vessel on the way to Java would have crossed the sun's path, and, as he so concisely observes, when he looked to the west the sun would be to his north, and the shadow or reflection would be cast on his left hand."

bought two emeralds for a thousand *pardai*, and he purchased for two hundred *pardai* two little children who had no sexual organs; for in this island there are a kind of merchants, who follow no other trade excepting that of purchasing little children, from whom they cut off in their childhood everything, and they remain like women.[1]

THE CHAPTER CONCERNING OUR RETURN.

Having remained in this island of Giava altogether fourteen days, we determined to return back, because, partly through the fear of their cruelty in eating men, partly also through the extreme cold, we did not dare to proceed farther, and also because there was hardly any other place known to them [the Christians]. Wherefore we chartered a large vessel, that is, a *giunco*, and took our way outside the islands towards the east; because on this side there is no archipelago, and the navigation is more safe. We sailed for fifteen days and arrived at the city of Malacha, and here we stopped for three days, where our Christian companions remained, whose bewailings and lamentations it would be impossible shortly to describe; so that, truly, if I had not

---

[1] Barbosa attributes a similar inhuman practice to the Mussulmans of Bengal :—"Li Mori mercatanti di questa città vanno fra terra a comprar garzoni piccolini dalli lor padri e madri gentili, e da altri, che gli rubbano, e li castrano, levandogli via il tutto, di sorte che restano rasi, come la palma della mano : e alcuni di questi moiono, ma quelli che scampano, gli allevano molto bene, e poi li vendono per cento e ducento ducati l'uno alli Mori di Persia, che gli apprezzano molto, per tenerli in guardia delle lor donne, e della lor robba, e per altre dishonestà." Pigafetta also mentions the kingdom of *Cirote* in Burmah as the place "dove si fanno tutti li Ennuchi che sono condotti di Levante." (RAMUSIO, vol. i. pp. 316, 391.) It is a well known fact, that the excision described was at one time extensively practised in Upper Egypt, and that rumour, whether true or false I know not, attributed the horrible operation to certain Coptic monks.

had a wife and children, I would have gone with them. And likewise they said, that if they had known how to come in safety, they would have accompanied us. And I believe also that my companion comforted them for not coming, because they would not be obliged to give an account to the Christians of so many lords who are in their country, who are also Christians and possess immense riches. So that they remained, saying that they would return to Sarnau,[1] and we went with our ship to Cioromandel. The captain of the ship said that around the island of Giava, and around the island of Sumatra, there were more than eight thousand islands. Wherefore my companion bought in Malacha five thousand *pardai* worth of small spices, and silk stuffs, and odoriferous things. We sailed for fifteen days, and arrived at the said city of Cioromandel, and here the ship chartered in Giava was unladen. We remained in this country about twenty days, and then took a ship, that is to say, a *Ciampana*, and went to Colon,[2] where I found twenty-two Portuguese Christians. On which account I had a very great desire to escape, but I remained, because they were few, and I was afraid of the Moors; for there were some merchants with us who knew that I had been at Mecha and to the body of Mahomet, and I was afraid that they might imagine that I should discover their hypocrisies, wherefore I abstained from running away. Twelve days afterwards we took our route towards Calicut, that is, by the river,[3] and arrived there in the space of ten days.

Now it will be an easy thing for every kind reader to perceive, by the long discourse concerning various countries contained in the above written books, that my companion and myself having become wearied, partly by the different temperatures of the air as may be imagined, partly by the

---

[1] See note 3 on p. 212 *ante*.
[2] Colon=Quilon. See note on pp. 182-4 *ante*.
[3] See note on pp. 179-80 *ante*.

different customs we met with at every step as has been described, and especially by the inhuman men not unlike beasts, determined to return. I will now recount shortly, (in order that my narrative may not be wearisome,) what happened to me on our return, because it will be useful to some either in restraining their too eager appetite for seeing the inestimable greatness of the world, or, being on their road, in knowing how to regulate themselves and use their understanding in sudden emergencies. Being then arrived in Calicut on our return, as I have shortly before written, we found two Christians who were Milanese. One was called Ioan-Maria, and the other Piero Antonio, who had arrived from Portugal with the ships of the Portuguese, and had come to purchase jewels on the part of the king.[1] And when they had arrived in Cocin,[2] they fled to Calicut. Truly I never had greater pleasure than in seeing these two Christians. They and I went naked after the custom of the country. I asked them if they were Christians. Ioan-Maria answered: "Yes, truly we are." And then Piero Antonio asked me if I was a Christian. I answered: "Yes, God be praised." Then he took me by the hand, and led me into his house. And when we had arrived at the house, we

[1] Don Emanuel of Portugal, surnamed the Fortunate.

[2] Cochin:—"a town which, though giving name to a small *ráj* or native state, belongs to the British, and is included within the district of Malabar, under the presidency of Madras. Lat. 9° 8′, long. 76° 18′." (THORNTON's *Gazetteer*.) When the Portuguese first arrived in India, Cochin was governed by a Rajah called Triumpara or Trimunpara, who appears to have been subject to the Zamorin of Calicut. Pedro Alvarez Cabral was well received by this sovereign, and established a factory in the town as early as 1500. In 1502, the Zamorin endeavoured to detach Triumpara from the Portuguese, but without effect, and the latter on their part engaged to support him against his suzerain, who in the following year attacked and defeated him. He was subsequently restored by the Portuguese, on which occasion they received permission to build a fort and church at Cochin, and became virtually masters of the place. It was taken from them by the Dutch in 1662. This is the first time that Varthema mentions Cochin.

began to embrace and kiss each other, and to weep. Truly, I could not speak like a Christian: it appeared as though my tongue were large and hampered, for I had been four years without speaking with Christians.[1] The night following I remained with them; and neither of them, nor could I, either eat or sleep solely for the great joy we had. You may imagine that we could have wished that that night might have lasted for a year, that we might talk together of various things, amongst which I asked them if they were friends of the king of Calicut. They replied that they were his chief men, and that they spoke with him every day. I asked them also what was their intention. They told me that they would willingly have returned to their country, but that they did not know by what way. I answered them: "Return by the way you came." They said that that was not possible, because they had escaped from the Portuguese, and that the king of Calicut had obliged them to make a great quantity of artillery against their will,[2] and on this account they did not wish to return by that route; and they said that they expected the fleet of the king of Portugal very soon. I answered them, that if God granted me so much grace that I might be able to escape to Cananor when the fleet had arrived, I would so act that the captain of the Christians should pardon them; and I told them that it was not possible for them to escape by any other way, because it was known through many nations that they made artillery. And many kings had wished to have them in their hands on

[1] Meaning, Europeans or European Christians.

[2] Most of the cannoniers in the service of the Indian states at this period appear to have been either Franks or Turks; and a knowledge of artillery was evidently much prized, for Varthema professed himself capable of making the largest mortars in the world in order to escape from his Mamlûk companions at Meccah. (See p. 50 *ante*.) De Faria y Souza mentions incidentally, that in 1507 a renegade Christian directed the assault against the fort which the Portuguese had then recently built on the island of Angediva. STEVENS's *Portuguese Asia*, vol. i. p. 108.

account of their skill, and therefore it was not possible to
escape in any other manner. And you must know that they
had made between four and five hundred pieces of ordnance
large and small, so that in short they had very great fear of
the Portuguese; and in truth there was reason to be afraid,
for not only did they make the artillery themselves, but they
also taught the Pagans to make it; and they told me, moreover, that they had taught fifteen servants of the king to
fire *spingarde*. And during the time I was here, they gave
to a Pagan the design and form of a mortar, which weighed
one hundred and five *cantara*, and was made of metal.
There was also a Jew here who had built a very beautiful
galley, and had made four mortars of iron. The said Jew,
going to wash himself in a pond of water, was drowned.
Let us return to the said Christians: God knows what I said
to them, exhorting them not to commit such an act against
Christians. Piero Antonio wept incessantly, and Ioan-
Maria said it was the same to him whether he died in Calicut
or in Rome, and that God had ordained what was to be.

The next morning I returned to find my companion,
who was making great lamentation, for he thought that I
had been killed. I told him, in order to excuse myself,
that I had been to sleep in a Moorish mosque to render
thanks to God and to Mahomet for the benefit received in
that we had returned in safety, and with this he was much
pleased. And in order that I might be able to know what
was going on in the country, I told him that I would
continue to sleep in the mosque, and that I did not want
any goods, but that I wished always to be poor. And
wishing to escape from them, I thought that I could only
deceive them by hypocrisy; for the Moors are the most
stupid people in the world, so that he was satisfied. And
this I did in order that I might be able to talk frequently
with the Christians, because they knew everything, from
day to day, from the court of the king. I began to put my

hypocrisy in practice, and pretended to be a Moorish saint, and never would eat flesh excepting in the house of Ioan-Maria, where every night we ate two brace of fowls. And I would no longer associate with merchants, neither did any man ever see me smile, and all day I remained in the mosque excepting when he [my companion] sent for me to go and eat; and he scolded me because I would not eat flesh. I replied: "That too much eating leads man to many sins." And in this manner, I began to be a Moorish saint, and happy was he who could kiss my hand and some my knees.

THE CHAPTER SHOWING HOW I MADE MYSELF A PHYSICIAN IN CALICUT.

It happening that a Moorish merchant fell sick of a very great malady, and could not by any means get natural relief, he sent to my companion, who was a great friend of his, to know if he or any one in his house could give him any remedy. He answered that I would go to visit him; and so he and I together went to the house of the sick man and questioned him about his illness. He said to us: "I feel very bad in my stomach and bowels." I asked him if he had had any cold by which this illness might have been caused? The sick man replied: "That it could not be cold, for he did not know what that was." Then my companion turned to me and asked me: "O Iunus, dost thou know any remedy for this my friend?" I replied: "That my father was a physician in my country, and that that which I knew, I knew by the practice which he had taught me." My companion said: "Well, then, let us see if by any remedy this merchant, my very dear friend, can be relieved." Then I said: "Bizmilei creehman crathin!"[1] and then I took his hand, and, feeling his pulse, found that he had a great

---

[1] See note 1 on p. 41 *ante*.

deal of fever, and I asked him if his head ached. He replied: "Yes, it aches very much." Then I asked him if his bowels were relieved. He answered: "They had not been relieved for three days." I immediately thought to myself, this man has an overloaded stomach, and to assist him he requires an injection; and saying so to my companion he replied: "Do what you like, so that he be cured." Then I made preparation for the injection in this wise: I took sugar, eggs, and salt, and for the decoction I took certain herbs, which did more harm than good: the said herbs were such as leaves of walnuts. And in this way, in the course of a day and a night, I administered five injections to him; and it did him no good on account of the herbs, which produced a contrary effect, so that I should have been glad had I not been involved in such a task. At length, seeing that he could not obtain relief on account of the wretched herbs, I took a good bunch of purslain, and made about half a jug of liquor, and put in it the same quantity of oil, and a good deal of salt and sugar, and then strained it all well. And here I committed another blunder, for I forgot to warm it, and administered it cold as it was. As soon as the injection was administered, I tied a cord to his feet, and we hoisted him up until he touched the ground with his hands and head, and we held him up thus high for the space of half a quarter of an hour. My companion said: "O Iunus, is it the custom to do thus in your country?" I replied: "Yes, when the sick man is *in extremis*." He said that that was a good reason, for in that position the mixture would penetrate better. The poor sick man cried out and said: "Matile, Matile, gnancia tu poi, gnancia tu poi!" that is, "No more, no more, for I am killed; I am killed!" and so we standing there to comfort him, whether it were God or nature, his bowels began to act like a fountain, and we immediately let him down; and truly he was relieved to the extent of half a vat full, and he was well pleased. On the following day he had neither fever nor pain in his head or stomach, and, after that, he was relieved several times.

The next morning, he said that he felt pain in his side. I made him take cow or buffalo butter and anoint himself and bind himself up with hemp tow, and then I told him that if he wished to be cured he must eat twice a day, and before eating, I wished him to walk a mile on foot. He replied: " O nonal irami tino biria biria gnancia tu poi," that is, " If you do not wish me to eat more than twice in the day, I shall be dead very soon ;" for they eat eight or ten times a day. This order appeared to him very severe. However, at last he was very well cured, and this gained great credit for my hypocrisy. They said that I was the friend of God. This merchant wished to give me ten ducats, but I would not receive anything. I even gave three ducats which I had to the poor, and this I did publicly in order that they might know that I did not want any property or money. From this time forward happy was he who could take me to his house to eat, happy was he who kissed my hands and feet; and when anyone kissed my hands, I kept my ground steadily, giving him to understand that he did an act which I deserved, as being a saint. But it was my companion above all who procured me credit, because he also believed me, and said that I did not eat flesh, and that he had seen me at Mecca, and at the body of Mahomet, and that I had always travelled in his company, and that he knew my manners, and that I was truly a saint, and that, knowing me to be of a good and holy life, he had given me one of his nieces for my wife, so that, in this way every man wished me well, and every night I went secretly to talk with the Christians, who told me, on one occasion, that twelve Portuguese ships had come to Canonor. Then I said, now is the time for me to escape from the hands of dogs, and we considered together for eight days in what manner I could

escape. They advised me to escape by land, but I had not
the courage, through the fear that I might be killed by the
Moors, I being white and they black.

THE CHAPTER CONCERNING THE NEWS OF THE SHIPS OF THE PORTUGUESE WHICH CAME IN TO CALICUT.

One day, while eating with my companion, two Persian
merchants of Canonor arrived, whom he immediately called
to eat with him. They answered: "We have no wish to
eat and bring bad news." We asked them: "What words
are these which you utter?" They said: "Twelve ships
of the Portuguese have arrived, which we have seen with
our eyes." My companion asked: "What people are they?"
The Persians replied: "They are Christians, and are all
armed in white arms, and they have commenced building a
very strong castle in Canonor."[1] My companion turned to
me and asked me: "O Iunus, what people are these Portuguese?" I answered him: "Do not speak to me of such a
race, for they are all thieves and corsairs of the sea, and I
should like to see them all of our Mohammedan faith."
Hearing this he became very malignant, and I rejoiced
much in my heart.

[1] This must have been towards the end of 1506, and that inference is
confirmed by the date, 3rd December, given in the chapter succeeding
the next. In note 2 on pp. 123-4 *ante*, I have delayed the building of
the fort at Cannanore till 1507: it was not probably completed till the
beginning of that year, for when he reached that place Varthema says:
"il castello *si faceva*." The ships mentioned in the text were undoubtedly part of the fleet of Don Francisco de Almeyda, who arrived
at Cannanore about this time, and received the Rajah's permission to
erect the fort in the harbour.

THE CHAPTER SHOWING HOW THE MOORS SUMMON TO THE CHURCH THOSE WHO ARE OF THEIR SECT AND FAITH.

On the following day all the Moors, having heard the news, went to the mosque to say their prayers. But first some, deputed to this office, mounted the tower of their church, as is the custom amongst them three or four times a day, and, instead of bells, began with a loud voice to call the others to this same prayer, keeping one finger constantly in their ear and saying: "Alla u eccubar, Alla u eccubar, aialassale aialassale aialalfale aialalfale Alla u eccubar lcilla illala esciadu ana Mahometh resullala,"[1] that is, "God is great, God is great, come to the church, come to the church, come to praise God, come to praise God, God is great, God is great, God was, God will be, Mahometh the messenger of God will rise again." And they took me also with them, saying to me that they wished to pray to God for the Moors; and so they set me publicly to make the prayer, which you shall hear, which prayer is as common with them as the Pater Noster is with us, and the Ave Maria. The Moors stand all in a row; but there are many rows, and they have a priest as we have, who, after they have well washed, begins to pronounce the prayer in this manner, saying: "Un gibilci nimi saithan e regin bizimilci crachman crachinal hamdulile ara blaharami crachman crachin malichi iaum edmi iachie nabudu hiachie nesta himi edina sarathel mostachina ledina ana antha alyhin gayril magdubin alchy-

---

[1] *Allâhu âkbar! Allâhu âkbar! Hie 'ala 's-salâ! Hie 'ala 's-salâ! Hie 'ala 'l-falâh! Hie 'ala 'l-falâh! Allâhu âkbar! La ilâh illa Allâh; wa-ash-hadna Muhammed rasûl Allâh.* God is most Great! God is most Great! Come to prayer! Come to prayer! Come to security! Come to security! There is no god but the God, and I testify that Muhammed is God's Apostle! This is the ordinary *adhân* or call to prayer, chaunted by the *muâdh-dhin* from the minaret of the mosque.

himu ualla da lim amin alla u eccubar."[1] And so I pronounced the prayer in the presence of all the people, and then I returned home with my companion. On the next day I pretended to be very ill, and remained about eight days wherein I would not eat with him, but every night I went to eat with the two Christians. He [my companion] was very much surprised, and asked me why I would not eat. I replied: "That I felt very ill, and my head felt as though it were very large and full; and I said to him that it appeared to me that it proceeded from that air, that it was not good for me." He, for the singular affection which he bore me, would have done everything to please me; wherefore, hearing that the air of Calicut was injurious to me, he said to me: "Go and stay in Canonor until we return to Persia, and I will direct you to a friend of mine, who will give you all that you require." I answered him: "That I would gladly go to Canonor, but I hesitated because of those Christians." "Do not hesitate," said he, "nor have any fear of them, for you shall remain constantly in the city." Finally, having well seen all the fleet which was preparing in Calicut, and all the artillery, and the army which had been raised against the Christians, I set out on my journey to give them notice of it, and to save myself from the hands of dogs.

THE CHAPTER CONCERNING THE FLIGHT FROM CALICUT.

One day, before I set out, I arranged all that I had to do with the two Christians, and then my companion placed me in the company of those two Persians who carried the news

[1] This is a tolerably correct wording, very badly spelt, of the *Fátihah*, or opening chapter of the Korân, preceded by the common formula of renunciation, "I abhor the lapidated Devil." (See note 2 on p. 45 *ante*.) Varthema, on this occasion, appears to have acted the part of *Imám* and led the prayers of the congregation.

of the Portuguese, and we took a little bark. Now, you will understand in what danger I placed myself, because there were twenty-four Persian, Syrian, and Turkish merchants, all of whom knew me, and bore me great affection, and knew well what the genius of Christians was. I feared that if I took leave of them, they would think that I wanted to escape to the Portuguese. If I departed without speaking with them, and I was by chance discovered, they would have said to me: "Why did you not speak to us?" And this I balanced in my mind. However, I determined to go without speaking to any one excepting my companion. On Thursday morning, the third of September, I set out with the two Persians by sea, and when we had got about a bow-shot in the sea, four Naeri came to the sea-shore, who called the captain of the vessel, and we immediately returned to land. The Naeri said to the captain: "Why do you carry away this man without leave of the king?" The Persians answered: "This man is a Moorish saint, and we are going to Canonor." "We know well," said the Naeri, "that he is a Moorish saint, but he understands the language of the Portuguese, and will tell them all that we are doing here, because a great fleet is being got ready;" and they ordered the captain of the ship that he should not take me away on any account, and he acted accordingly. We remained on the sea-shore, and the Naeri returned to the king's house. One of the Persians said: "Let us go to our house," that is, to Calicut. I answered: "Do not go, for you will lose these fine *sinabaph*[1] (which were pieces of cloth we carried), because you have not paid the king's dues." The other Persians said: "O sir, what shall we do?" I replied: "Let us go along this shore until we find a *parao*," that is, a small bark; and they were pleased so to do, and we took our way for twelve miles, always by land, laden with the said goods. You may imagine how my heart felt,

[1] See note 2 on p. 212 *ante*.

seeing myself in such danger. At length we found a *parao* which carried us to Canonor. We arrived at Canonor on Saturday evening, and I immediately carried a letter which my companion had written for me to a merchant his friend; the tenor of which letter stated that he should do as much for me as for his own person until he came; and he told him about my being a saint, and of the relationship there was between him and me. The merchant, as soon as he had read the letter, laid it on his head and said, that he would answer for me with his head; and immediately had an excellent supper prepared, with many chickens and pigeons. When the two Persians saw the chickens come, they exclaimed: "Alas, what do you do?" Colli tinu ille," that is, " This man does not eat flesh;" and other things came immediately. When we had finished eating, the said Persians said to me: " Let us go a little to the sea to amuse ourselves;" and so we went where the Portuguese fleet was. Imagine, O reader, the joy I felt. Going a little farther, I saw before a certain low house three empty casks, from which I imagined that the factory of the Christians was there. Then, being somewhat cheered up, I felt a desire to escape within the said gate; but I considered that, if I did so in their presence, the whole country would be in an uproar. And I, not being able to fly in safety, noted the place where the castle of the Christians was being made, and determined to wait until the following day.

THE CHAPTER SHOWING HOW I ESCAPED FROM CANONOR TO THE PORTUGUESE.

On Sunday morning I rose early, and said that I would go to amuse myself a little. My companions answered: "Go where you please;" and so I took my way according to my fancy, and went where the castle of the Christians was being built; and when I was a little distant from my companions, coming to the sea-shore I met two Portuguese Christians, and said to them: "O sirs, where is the fortress of the Portuguese?" These two Christians said: "Are you a Christian?" I answered; "Yes, sir, praised be God." And they said to me: "Where do you come from." I answered them: "I come from Calicut." Then said the one to the other of the two companions: "Go you to the factory, and I will take this man to Don Lorenzo," that is, the son of the Viceroy.[1] And so he conducted me to the said castle, which is distant from the beach half a mile. And when we arrived at the said castle, the Señor Don Lorenzo was at breakfast. I immediately fell on my knees at the feet of his lordship and said: "Sir, I commend myself to you to save me, for I am a Christian." At this juncture, we heard a great uproar in the neighbourhood because I had escaped. The bombardiers were immediately summoned, who loaded all the artillery, fearing that those of the city might come to the castle to fight. Then the captain, seeing that those of the place did not do any harm, took me by the hand and conducted me into a chamber to interrogate me concerning the affairs of Calicut, and kept me three days to talk with me; and I, being desirous of the victory of the Christians, gave them all the particulars about the fleet preparing in Calicut. These conversations being concluded,

[1] After garrisoning the new fort at Cannanore, Don Francisco de Almeyda proceeded to Cochin, but hearing there that the factor at Quilon and all his men had been murdered by the Mussulmans, "he sent his son Don Lorenzo with three ships and three caravels, with orders to procure lading, without taking notice of what had passed, but in case of denial, to avenge the slaughter. The messenger was received with a shower of arrows, and twenty-four ships of Calicut and other places prepared to receive ours. Don Lorenzo, after pouring in his shot liberally, burnt them all, only a few of the Moors were saved by swimming. Don Lorenzo then went to load in another port." (*Portuguese Asia*, vol. i. p. 102.) I presume that it was about this time that Varthema met the Viceroy's son at Cannanore.

he sent me with a galley to the Viceroy his father in Cuccin,[1] of which a knight named Joan Sarrano[2] was captain. The Viceroy was exceedingly pleased when I arrived, and showed me great distinction, because I had informed him of all that was doing in Calicut; and I also said, that if his lordship would pardon Ioan-Maria and Piero Antonio, who made artillery in Calicut, and assure me of their safety, that I would induce them to return, and that they would not do that injury to Christians which they had done, although against their will, and that they were afraid to return without a safe conduct. The Viceroy was extremely pleased and much satisfied, and gave me the safe conduct; and the captains of our ships and our vicar promised for the Viceroy; and at the end of three days he sent me back with the said galley to Canonor, and gave me a letter which he addressed to his son, that he should give me as much money as I required for payment of the spices to be sent to Calicut. When we had arrived at Canonor, I found a Pagan, who gave me his wife and children as a pledge, and I sent him with my letters to Calicut, to Ioan-Maria and Piero Antonio, by which I advised them how the Viceroy had pardoned them, and that they might come in safety. You must know that I sent the spy five times backwards and forwards, and that I always wrote to them that they should be on their guard, and should not trust their wives or their slave; for each of them had a wife, and Ioan-Maria had a son and a slave. They always wrote to me that they would come willingly. In the last letter they said to me thus: "Lodovico, we have given all our goods to this spy; come on such a night with a galley or brigantine where the fishermen are, because there is no watch in that part, and, if it please God,

---

[1] Cochin.

[2] This João Serrão subsequently accompanied the expedition under D. Antão de Noronha to El-Catif and the island of Hormuz in the Persian Gulf. See De Couto, *Decadas*, vol. iii. pp. 247, 439.

we will both come with all our party." You must know
that I wrote to them that they should come alone, and that
they should leave their wives, their son, their goods, and
the slave, and that they should only bring their jewels and
money. And you must know that they had a diamond
which weighed thirty-two carats, which they said was worth
thirty-five thousand ducats; and they had a pearl which
weighed twenty-four carats; and they had two thousand
rubies, which weighed a carat and a carat and a half each;
and they had sixty-four rings with set jewels; and they had
one thousand four hundred *pardai;* and they also wished to
save seven *spingarde* and three apes, and two civet-cats,
and the wheel for repairing jewels; so that their avarice
caused their death. Their slave, who was of Calicut, saw
that they wanted to escape, and immediately went to the
king and told him everything. The king did not believe
him. Nevertheless, he sent five Naeri to their house to
remain in their company. The slave, seeing that the king
would not put them to death, went to the Cadi of the faith
of the Moors, and repeated to him those same words which
he had said to the king, and, moreover, he told him that
they informed the Christians of all that was done in Calicut.
The Moorish Cadi held a council with all the Moorish merchants, amongst whom were collected one hundred ducats,
which they carried to the king of the Gioghi,[1] who was at
that time in Calicut with three thousand Gioghi, to whom
the said Moors said: "Sir, thou knowest that in other years
when thou hast come here we have shown thee much kindness, and more honour than we show thee now; the reason
is this: there are here two Christians who are enemies of
our faith and yours, who inform the Portuguese of all that
is done in this country; wherefore, we beseech thee to kill
them, and to take these hundred ducats." The king of the
Gioghi immediately sent two hundred men to kill the said

[1] See note 1 on p. 111, and note 3 on p. 112 *ante.*

two Christians, and when they went to their house, they began by tens to sound their horns and demand alms. And when the Christians saw so many people increasing they said: "These want something else besides alms;" and began to fight, so that these two killed six of them, and wounded more than forty. At last, these Gioghi cast at them certain pieces of iron which are made round like a wheel, and they threw them with a sling, and struck Ioan-Maria on the head and Pietro Antonio on the head, so that they fell to the ground; and then they ran upon them and cut open the veins of their throats, and with their hands they drank their blood. The wife of Ioan-Maria escaped with her son to Canonor, and I purchased the son for eight ducats of gold, and had him baptized on St. Lawrence's day, and gave him the name of Lorenzo, because I baptized him on that same day, and at the end of a year on that same day he died of the French disease. You must know that I have seen this disease three thousand miles beyond Calicut, and it is called *pua*,[1] and they say that it is about seventeen years since it began, and it is much worse than ours.

THE CHAPTER CONCERNING THE FLEET OF CALICUT.

On the twelfth of March 1506,[2] this news of the Christians being killed arrived. On this same day the immense fleet

[1] Probably from the Sanscrit *pûya*, matter from an ulcer. Varthema's remark on the recent appearance of the disease would imply that it was introduced into India by the Portuguese.

[2] The year 1506 here given is somewhat perplexing. In Greene's *Collection* the fleet under Don Francisco de Almeyda is made to leave Lisbon on the 25th of March 1507, whereas the *Modern Universal History*, after Maffei, starts them from that port on the 25th of March 1505, which I take to be the correct date. On the 11th of April following, De Almeyda reached the Cape Verd Islands, from whence he proceeded to the east coast of Africa, and after taking Quiloa (Kilwah) and

departed from Pannani,[1] and from Calicut, and from Capogat, and from Pandarani, and from Tormapatan.[2] All this fleet was two hundred and nine sail, of which eighty-four were large ships, and the remainder were rowing vessels, that is, *paraos*. In which fleet there was an infinite number of armed Moors; and they wore certain red garments of cloth stuffed with cotton, and they wore certain large caps stuffed, and also on the arms bracelets and gloves stuffed; and a great number of bows and lances, swords and shields, and large and small artillery after our custom. When we saw this fleet, which was on the 16th of the month abovementioned, truly, seeing so many ships together, it appeared as though one saw a very large wood. We Christians always hoped that God would aid us to confound the Pagan faith. And the most valiant knight, the captain of the fleet, son of Don Francisco dal Meda, Viceroy of India, was here with eleven ships, amongst which there were two galleys and one brigantine. When he saw such a multitude of

Mombása, steered towards India, visited the island of Anjediva, touched next at Honahwar, and finally arrived at Cannanore, where he received permission to build a fort. I have hitherto supposed it unlikely that these different transactions were accomplished by the end of 1505; nevertheless, it is still more improbable that Varthema should be mistaken in this and the succeeding dates; hence, by postponing the erection of the fort at Cannanore till the end of 1506, (see note 1 on p. 266 *ante*) I have miscalculated by one entire year.

I perceive that Greene also delays the battle recorded in this chapter, and the subsequent attack on Ponani, till 1508, which is unquestionably wrong; for Varthema mentions Guidobaldo, Duke of Urbino, as being alive when he dedicated his book to the Lady Agnesina, the Duke's sister. This was after his return to Europe, and Guidobaldo died on the 11th of April 1508.

Presuming Varthema's dates to be correct, his eastern voyages and travels from the day he left Damascus, 8th April 1503, until his return to India, occupied two years and nine months. If we add thereto the eighteen months during which he acted as factor at Cochin, and the time expended on the return voyage, his total absence from Europe will amount to about five years.

[1] See note 1 on p. 132.   [2] See note 1 on p. 131 *ante*.

ships, he acted like a most valiant captain: he called to him all his knights and men of the said ships, and then began to exhort and beseech them that, for the love of God and of the Christian faith, they would expose themselves willingly to suffer death, saying in this wise: "O sirs, O brothers, now is the day that we must remember the Passion of Christ, and how much pain He endured to redeem us sinners. Now is that day when all our sins will be blotted out. For this I beseech you that we determine to go vigorously against these dogs; for I hope that God will give us the victory, and will not choose that His faith should fail." And then the spiritual father stood upon the ship of the said captain, with the crucifix in his hand, and delivered a beautiful discourse to all, exhorting us to do that which we were bound to do. And then he gave us absolution from punishment and sin, and said: "Now, my sons, let us all go willingly, for God will be with us." And he knew so well how to speak, that the greater part of us wept, and prayed God that He would cause us to die in that battle. In the meantime the immense fleet of the Moors came towards us to pass by. On that same day, our captain departed with two ships and went towards the Moors, and passed between two ships, which were the largest in the Moorish fleet. And when he passed between the said ships, he saluted both of them with very great discharges of artillery; and this our captain did in order to know these two ships, and how they behaved; for they carried very great ensigns, and were captains of all the fleet. Nothing more was done that day. Early on the following morning, the Moors began all to make sail and come towards the city of Canonor, and sent to our captain to say that he should let them pass and go on their voyage, for they did not wish to fight with Christians. Our captain sent to them to say, that the Moors of Calicut would not allow Christians to return who were staying in Calicut in their faith, but killed forty-eight of them, and robbed them of three thousand ducats between goods and money. And then he said to them: "Pass, if pass you can, but first know what sort of people Christians are." Said the Moors: "Our Mahomet will defend us from you Christians;" and so began all to sail with the greatest fury, wishing to pass, and they always navigate near the land, eight or ten miles. Our captain allowed them to come until they arrived opposite the city of Canonor. Our captain did this because the king of Canonor was looking on, and to show him how great was the courage of the Christians. And when it was the time for eating, the wind began to freshen a little, and our captain said: "Now, up brothers, for now is the time; for we are all good knights;" and began to go towards these two largest ships. It would be impossible to describe to you the kinds of instruments which they sounded, according to their custom. Our captain grappled valiantly with one of the ships of the Moors, that is, the largest, and three times the Moors threw off our grappling-irons; at the fourth time we remained fast, and immediately our Christians leaped on board the said ship, in which there were six hundred Moors. Here, a most cruel battle was fought with immense effusion of blood, so that not one escaped from this ship: they were all killed. Then our captain went to find the other very large ship of the Moors, which was now grappled fast by another of our ships; and here also a cruel battle was fought, in which five hundred Moors died. When these two large ships were taken, all the rest of the fleet of the Moors fought with desperation, and divided our sixteen ships, so that there were some of our ships which had around them fifteen or twenty of those of the Moors to fight. It was a beautiful sight to see the gallant deeds of a very valiant captain, Ioan Sarano, who, with a galley made such a slaughter of the Moors as it is impossible to describe. And there was a time when he had around his galley fifty vessels, some with oars and some with sails, and all with artillery. And by the grace of God, neither in the galley nor in the ships was any one of the Christians killed, but many were wounded, for the fighting lasted all that day. Once our brigantine separated a little from the ships, and was immediately placed in the middle of four of the Moorish ships; and they fought her sharply, and at one time fifteen Moors were on the brigantine, so that the Christians had all withdrawn to the poop. When the valiant captain named Simon Martin[1] saw that there were so many Moors upon the brigantine, he leaped amongst these dogs, and said: "O Jesus Christ, give us the victory! help thy faith!" and with the sword in his hand he cut off the heads of six or seven. All the other Moors threw themselves into the sea and fled, some here, some there. When the other Moors saw that this brigantine had gained the victory, four other ships went to succour their people. The captain of the brigantine, seeing the said Moors coming, immediately took a barrel which had contained powder, and then he took a piece of a sail and thrust it in the bung-hole of the said barrel, which appeared like the stone of a mortar, and he put a handful of powder over the barrel, and standing with fire in his hand, made as though he were going to fire a mortar. The Moors, seeing this, thought that the said barrel was a mortar, and immediately turned back. And the said captain withdrew where the Christians were with his brigantine, victorious. Our captain then placed himself amongst these dogs, of whom seven ships were captured, laden in part with spices and in part with other merchandise; and nine or ten were sunk by our artillery, amongst which there was one laden with elephants. When the Moors saw so many of their ships sunk, and that the two ships, the captains of the fleet and others were taken, they immediately took to

---

[1] Though I do not find this officer specially mentioned elsewhere, there appear to have been several Portuguese naval commanders named *Martins* engaged in India at this period. See DE COUTO, *Index*, p. 197.

flight, some one way, some another, some by land, some by sea, some in the port, some in the opposite direction. At the conclusion, our captain, seeing all our ships safe, said: "Praised be Jesus Christ, let us follow up our victory against these dogs ;" and so we all together set ourselves to follow them. Truly, to any one who had seen these dogs fly, it would have appeared that they had a fleet of a hundred ships behind them. And this battle commenced with the hour for eating, and lasted until the evening. And then they were pursued all night, so that all this fleet was put to flight without the death of a single Christian ; and our ships which remained here followed another large ship, which was tacking out at sea. Finally our ships prevailed over theirs, which was surrounded by us, so that all the Moors cast themselves [into the sea] to swim, and we constantly followed them to the shore in the skiff, with crossbows and lances killing and wounding them. But some saved themselves by dint of swimming, and these were as many as two hundred persons, who swam more than twenty miles, sometimes under and sometimes on the water, and sometimes we thought they were dead, when they rose again to the surface a crossbow-shot distant from us. And when we came near them to kill them, thinking that they were exhausted, they dived again under the water ; so that their being able to continue swimming so long appeared like a very great miracle. At last, however, the greater part were killed, and their ship sank from the blows of our artillery. On the following morning, our captain sent the galleys, the brigantine, with some other vessels, along the shore, to see what bodies they could count. They found that those who were killed on the shore and at sea, and those of the ships taken, were counted at three thousand six hundred dead bodies. You must know that many others were killed when they took to flight, who threw themselves into the sea. The king of Canonor, seeing all this battle, said : " These

Christians are very brave and valiant men." And truly I
have found myself in some battles in my time, but I never
saw any men more brave than these Portuguese. The next
day after, we returned to our Viceroy, who was at Cuccin.
I leave you to imagine how great was the joy of the Viceroy and of the king of Cuccin, who is a true friend of the
king of Portugal, on seeing us return victorious.[1]

THE CHAPTER SHOWING HOW I WAS SENT BACK TO CANONOR BY THE VICEROY.

Let us leave the fleet of the king of Calicut, which was
defeated, and return to my own affairs. At the end of three
months, the Viceroy gave me, of his favour, a certain office,
which was that of the factorship of these parts, and I remained in this office about a year and a half. Some months
afterwards, my lord the Viceroy sent me by a ship to Canonor, because many merchants of Calicut went to Canonor,
and took the safe conduct from the Christians by giving

---

[1] De Souza's account of this action is as follows:—"Whilst these
things happened at Zofala, [Sofála, on the east coast of Africa,] the
Zamorin of Calicut had stirred up the Soldan of Cayro, [Cairo,] and
hoped, with his assistance to drive us out of these seas; this was not so
private but that the king of Cochin had intelligence of it, and advertised
the Viceroy Don Francisco, who sent his son Lawrence with eleven sail
to prevent or put a stop to the design. As he visited some ports, news
was brought to him that in the road of Cananor was a fleet of two hundred and sixty *paraos*, whereof sixty exceeded our ships in bulk. He
directs his course towards them, and after a very sharp engagement
they were put to flight, pursued, and some taken, but many sunk and
obliged to run aground, with great loss to the enemy, and of his own
only five or six men." (*Portuguese Asia*, vol. i. p. 108.) Brief as this
description is, it coincides in several particulars with Varthema's more
detailed narrative: as, for example, in ascribing the command of the
Portuguese fleet to the Viceroy's son; in the approximate number of
vessels on both sides; in the trifling loss to the Europeans and the
great slaughter of the native combatants; and in the eventual escape of
many of the enemy's ships.

them to understand that they were of Canonor, and that they wished to pass with merchandise in the ships of Canonor, and which was not true. Wherefore, the Viceroy sent me to these merchants, and to understand these frauds. It happened at this time that the king of Canonor died, and the next king that was made was a great enemy of ours; wherefore the king of Calicut made him [king] by force of money, and lent him twenty-three pieces of artillery (*bocche di fuoco*). In 1507, there commenced a very great war on the 27th of April, and it continued until the 17th of August. Now, you shall understand what the Christian faith is, and what sort of men the Portuguese are. One day, the Christians going to get water, the Moors assaulted them, through the great hatred they bore us. Our people retired into the fortress, which was now in a good state, and no harm was done on that day. Our captain, who was called Lorenzo de Britto, sent to inform the Viceroy, who was at Cuccin, of this new occurrence; and Don Lorenzo immediately came with a *caravella*, furnished with everything that was necessary, and at the expiration of four days the said Don Lorenzo returned to Cuccin, and we remained to fight with these dogs, and we were not more than two hundred men. Our food consisted solely of rice, sugar, and nuts, and we had no water to drink within the castle; but twice a week we were obliged to take water from a certain well, which was a bow-shot distant from the castle. And every time we went for water, we always were obliged to take it by force of arms; and every time we skirmished with them, the least people that came were twenty-four thousand, and sometimes there were thirty thousand, forty thousand, and fifty thousand persons, who had bows, lances, swords, and shields, with more than one hundred and forty pieces of artillery between large and small, and they wore a kind of armour, as I have explained to you in the fleet of Calicut. Their fighting was in this wise: Two or three thousand came on at a time, and bringing with them the sounds of divers instruments, and with fireworks, and they ran with such fury, that truly they would have inspired with fear ten thousand people; but the most valiant Christians went to meet them beyond the well, and they never approached the fortress within two stones'-cast. We were obliged to be on our guard, both before and behind, because sometimes there came of these Moors by sea with sixty *praos* to take us in the midst of them. Nevertheless, every day we fought we killed ten, fifteen, and twenty of them, and not more, because as soon as they saw some of their people killed they took to flight. But on one occasion, amongst others, a mortar called the Serpent, at one discharge killed eighteen of them, and they never killed one of us. They said that we kept the devil, who defended us. This war from the twenty-seventh of April never ceased until the twenty-seventh of August. Then the fleet of the Portuguese came, of which the most valiant knight Tristan da Cugna was captain; to which, when it arrived at Canonor, we signalled that we were at war; and the prudent captain immediately had all the boats of the fleet armed, and sent us three hundred knights all armed in white armour, so that, had it not been for our captain, as soon as they landed we would have gone to burn the whole of the city of Canonor. Think, O kind reader, what was our joy when we saw such succour; for, in truth, we were almost exhausted, and the greater part were wounded. When the Moors saw our fleet arrive, they sent an ambassador, who was named Mamal Maricar, who was the richest man in the country, and he came to demand peace; wherefore we sent at once to the Viceroy, who was in Cuccin, to know what was to be done. The Viceroy sent to say, that we should make peace without delay, and so it was done.[1] And this he

---

[1] De Faria y Souza's account of the origin of this rupture with the Rajah of Cannanore, of the attack made upon the Portuguese fort, and the opportune arrival of Tristan de Cunha, who was on his way to

did only that he might be able to load the ships and send them to Portugal. Four days being past, there came two

Europe after having, in concert with Albuquerque, taken possession of the island of Socotra and left a garrison there, is as follows:—" The king of Cananor, desiring to break with the Portuguese, was encouraged by the Zamorin, and grounded this rupture on finding on the shore the body of the nephew of Mamale, a rich merchant of Malabar, which was one of those Gonçalo Vaz had thrown into the sea sewed up in a sail. This action was not known then, and the blame was laid on Laurence de Brito, captain of the fort, whose pass that ship carried. [This refers to a vessel which Vaz had unjustly seized, putting all the crew and passengers to death, whose bodies he subsequently caused to be sewed up in a sail in order to prevent their floating to land.] The message was delivered to him at church whilst he assisted at the service of Maundy Thursday, and he immediately left the church, and went about taking up from every one what provisions they had, and shipped the men with such haste, [*i.e.* sent them to the fort in boats,] that those who had lent their arms to those who watched at the sepulchre [the imitation of the Sepulchre of Christ which is set up in Roman Catholic churches during Holy Week] went to the church to disarm them. Don Lorenzo was captain, and had orders when he came to Cananor to obey Lorenzo de Brito; but Brito insisted that the other, as the son of the Viceroy, and so famous an officer, should command. Don Lorenzo was positive he would obey Brito as being commander of the fort, and in pursuance of his father's orders; but finding Brito resolved to persist in that courtesie, and that it might prove dangerous, he left the relief, and returned alone to Cochin...The besieged fortified and entrenched themselves, the same was done by the besiegers, who were twenty thousand strong. Much blood was spilt about the water of a well, but our men, by help of a mine, made themselves masters of it. The Moors after this loss retired to a wood of palm-trees, and prepared engines to batter the fort. Our commander had intelligence of it by means of a nephew of the king of Cananor, who endeavoured to gain our friendship. He prepared to receive them, and when they gave the assault, succeeded so well, first with cannon, and then with the sword, that he filled the ditch with their bodies, which they intended to have done with faggots. They returned to the wood, and Brito sending out by night eighty men, commanded by one Guadalajara, a Spaniard, who was his lieutenant, the sally was so vigorously executed by the firing of some small pieces first, in a cold rainy night, that the enemy in consternation knew not where to save themselves: three hundred were killed. But this joy was abated by the magazine of provisions taking fire, so that hunger began to rage, and all vermin was eaten. The garrison, part sick and part famished,

merchants of Canonor, who were friends of mine before war
had been made, and they spoke with me in this manner, as
you shall understand. "Fattore, on maniciar in ghene ballia
nochignan candile ornal patu maniciar patance maniciar
hiriva tu maniciar cia tu poi nal nur malabari nochi ornal
totu ille cura po;" that is, "O factor, show me a man who is
a *brazzo* larger than any of you, who every day has killed
ten, fifteen, and twenty of us, and the Nacri were sometimes
four hundred and five hundred firing at him and never once
could they touch him." I answered him in this manner:
"Idu manicar nicando inghene ille Cocin poi;" that is,
"This man is not here, but is gone to Cocin." Then I
thought that this was other than a Christian, and I said to
him: "Giangal ingabani manaton undo." One of them
answered: "Undo." I said to him: "Idu maniciar nicando Portogal ille." He replied: "Sui e indi." I said:
"Tamarani Portugal idu." He answered: "Tamerani ni
Patanga cioli ocha malamar Patangnu idu Portogal ille
Tamaran Portugal piga nammi;" that is, I said to him:
"My friend, come here, that knight whom thou hast seen is
not a Portuguese, but he is the God of the Portuguese and
of all the world." He replied: "By God, thou sayest the
truth; for all the Nacri said that that was not a Portuguese,
but that he was their God, and that the God of the Christians was better than theirs, and they did not know him, so
that it appeared to all that it was a miracle of God." See
what kind of people they are, who stood sometimes ten and

was reduced to extremity; but the sea being then rough left abundance
of lobsters when it went off the point of land where our chapel was,
which was the only relief the men had. The Zamorin sent a powerful
supply to the king of Cananor, who gave the last assault to the fort by
sea and land with above fifty thousand men, who were vigorously received and repulsed with great loss, not one of our men being killed in
the action. But now arrived Tristan de Cunna, and the king of Cananor,
terrified with his coming, and the defence made by Brito, sues for peace,
which was concluded with great honour to the Portuguese valour."
Portuguese Asia, vol. i. pp. 121-124.

twelve hours to see our bell ring, and looked upon it as
something miraculous, and when the bell did not ring any
longer, they said in this wise: " Idu maniciar totu, idu
parangnu tot ille parangnu ille Tamarani Portogal perga nan
nu ;" that is, " These people touch that bell and it speaks ;
when they do not touch it any longer it does not speak any
more ; this God of Portugal is very good." And, again,
some of these Moors were present at our mass, and when
the body of Christ was shown, I said to them : " That is the
God of Portugal, and of the Pagans, and of all the world."
And they replied : " You say the truth, but we do not know
Him ;" wherefore it may be understood that they sin without
knowledge.[1] There are, however, some of these who are

---

[1] Varthema seems to have rehabilitated himself as a devout Romanist,
as easily as he had doffed his five years' profession of Islàm. His apology
for the ignorance of the natives does him more credit than his pious
fraud to impress them in favour of Christianity. It may fairly be questioned, however, whether these people were as credulous as he represents them ; I think it more likely that, if Muhammedans, they would
have listened to his theology with supreme disgust. The narrative reminds me of the case of a learned and wealthy Tunisian, who visited
Malta about twenty-five years ago on his way to Europe, bent on seeing
something of the civilization of the West. One day he called upon me
in a state of great excitement, and on inquiring the cause, he told me
that he had gone to inspect the Arabic class at the Normal School attached to the Government University, and that while there, an *abbate*,
who was among the pupils, insisted on drawing him into a religious
discussion, in the course of which he ridiculed some of the doctrines of
the Koràn. The young Tunisian, who was remarkably courteous in his
demeanour, quietly asked him to explain the doctrine of the Trinity,
promising in case of conviction that he would at once embrace Christianity. Whereupon the *abbate*, taking up his three-cornered hat, requested him to han lle each corner successively. This done, the zealot
said : " How many angles are there ?" To which the other replied :
" Three." " And how many hats are there ?" The implied deduction
so horrified the pious Mussulman, that he left the school forthwith, and
came to inquire of me whether such blasphemous comparisons formed a
part of Christian theology.

The natives of India were well acquainted with the use of bells long
before the arrival of the Portuguese ; so that our author must have been

great enchanters. We have seen them grasp serpents which, if they touch [bite?] any one, he immediately falls to the earth dead. Also I tell you that they are the greatest and the most expert workmen, I believe, in all the world.

THE CHAPTER CONCERNING THE ASSAULT OF THE PORTUGUESE UPON PANNANI.[1]

Now, the time approached for the return homewards, for the captain of the fleet began to load the ships to return to Portugal, and I, having been seven years from my own house, and from my love and good feeling towards my country, and also in order that I might carry to it an account of a great part of the world, was constrained to ask leave of my lord the Viceroy, which of his grace he granted to me, and said that he wished me first to go with him where you shall know. Wherefore, he and all his company put ourselves in order in white armour, so that few people remained in Cucin, and on the twenty-fourth of November of the year abovementioned we made the assault within the port of Pannani. On that day we came before the city of Pannani. On the next morning, two hours before day, the Viceroy summoned all the boats of the ships with all the people of the fleet, and told them how that was the country which made war upon us more than any other country in India, and

sadly at a loss for an exemplification of Mussulman or Hindû ignorance, when he adduced in proof of it their wonderment on hearing the tolling of the church bell.

[1] This is the *Pananie* of Barbosa, the *Ponani* of Keith Johnstone's *Atlas*, and the *Ponany* of Thornton's *Gazetteer*. It is situated thirty-four miles south-east of Calicut, on the south side of a river of the same name, close to its entrance into the Arabian Sea. This town must not be confounded with Varthema's *Pandarani*, which lies to the north of Calicut, which Baldæus calls *Panane*, and which in Greene's *Collection* is written *Padarane*. (See note 1 on p. 132.)

therefore he begged us all that we would go with a good will to attack that place, which truly is stronger than any other on that coast. When the Viceroy had spoken, the spiritual father made such a discourse that every one wept, and many said that for the love of God they were willing to die in that place. A little before day, we began a most deadly war against those dogs, who were eight thousand, and we were about six hundred. But it is true that the two galleys did not do much, because they could not approach so near to the land as the boats. The first knight who leapt on shore was the valiant knight, Don Lorenzo, son of the Viceroy. The second boat was that of the Viceroy, in which I was, and at the first assault a cruel battle took place, because here the river was very narrow; and on the border of the city there were a great many mortars, of which we captured more than forty pieces. Here, in this assault, there were sixty-four Moors, who had sworn that they would die in that place or be victorious, for each of them was the master of a ship. And so in the first assault they discharged many mortars at us; but God assisted us, so that none of our people were killed here, but of them there were killed about one hundred and forty, of whom the said Don Lorenzo killed six in my presence, and he received two wounds, and many others were wounded. For a short time the battle was very severe. But after our galleys got to the land, those dogs began to retire, and, as the water began to fall, we would not follow them farther. And these dogs began to increase, and therefore we set fire to their ships, of which thirteen were burnt, the greater part new and large.[1] And then the

---

[1] The attack on Ponani is thus described by De Souza:—" Tristan de Cunha was on his return [to Europe] with the merchant ships, and the Viceroy bore him company to fall upon Pauane, a town subject to Calicut, where our enemies landed under the shelter of four ships of the Zamorin commanded by Cutiale, a courageous Moor. The Viceroy and Tristan anchored at the bar, held a council, and then sent both their sons in two barques with several boats, and they in a galley followed

Viceroy withdrew all his people to the headland, and here made some knights, amongst whom, out of his grace, he also made me one, and the most valiant captain Tristan da Cugna was my sponsor. Having done this, the Viceroy began to embark his people, but continued burning many houses of the said place; so that, by the grace of God, without the death of any one of us, we took our way towards Canonor, and as soon as we had arrived, our captain had the ships furnished with provisions.

them. They all went up the river through showers of balls sent from the shore, which is high. The Moors ran into the water to meet the boats, and killed three men; but the dispute was now come to their trenches, which some of ours mounted, and Peter Cam set upon them Don Lorenzo's colours. The colours were flying, when the Viceroy, seeing his son Don Lorenzo climbing with some difficulty, cried out: 'Lorenzo, Lorenzo, what laziness is that?' and he very readily answered: 'Sir, I give way to him that has gained the honour.' A large Moor encountered and wounded Don Lorenzo, and he gave him such a stroke as clove his head to his breast. The town being entered, all were put to the sword. Then all the ships in the harbour and docks were fired. We lost eighteen Portuguese: none of note; of the enemy above five hundred perished." *Portuguese Asia*, vol. i. p. 124,5.

THE BOOK CONCERNING ETHIOPIA.

To those who wish to make any profession of history or cosmography, by which they may contribute both to the common advantage, as already has been many times touched upon, and to the immortality of a laborious life, there is nothing more necessary than to be the tenacious possessors of their memory, in order that, if anything has been promised by them in any previous place, they may be able to perform it free from the defect of forgetfulness; so that there may be no one who may presume to reproach them wantonly with negligence or lack of memory. Wherefore I, having promised you in my proemium to display to you part of Ethiopia on my return from so many involuntary troubles, having now on my return an opportunity of fulfilling my promise, will enter upon it with brevity, in order that you may be able to arrive quickly at the end of the work, and I to take repose in my country.

THE CHAPTER CONCERNING THE VARIOUS ISLANDS IN ETHIOPIA.

On the sixth of December we took our way towards Ethiopia and passed the gulf, a course of about three thousand miles, and arrived at the island of Mozambich, which belongs to the king of Portugal. And before we arrived at the said island, we saw many countries which are subject to my lord the king of Portugal, in which cities the king maintains good fortresses, and especially in Melindi, which is a realm, and Mombaza, which the Viceroy put to fire and flame. In Chilva he has a fortress, and one was building in Mozambich. In Zaphala, also, there is a very good fortress. I do not describe to you what the valiant captain Tristan da Cugna did, who, on his coming into India, took the cities of Gogia and Pati, and Brava, a very strong island, and Sacutara, extremely good, in which the aforesaid king keeps good fortresses. I do not describe to you the war which was waged, because I was not present at it. I am also silent about many beautiful islands which we found on our route, amongst which is the island of Cumere, with six other islands about it, where much ginger and much sugar grow, and many singular fruits, and animal food of all kinds in abundance. I likewise do not speak to you of another beautiful island called Penda, which is friendly towards the king of Portugal, and most fertile in everything.[1]

[1] Mozambique, Malindi, Mombasa, Kilwah, Sofála, Angoxa, Paté, Brava, Pemba, and the Comoro Isles. These places, with a few others not named, had been seized by the Portuguese, on different expeditions to and from India, between the years 1498-1507. Some historical notices respecting the Arab settlers, who appear to have occupied them for centuries before the arrival of the Portuguese, will be found in the Introduction. The island of Socotra, which lies about one hundred and twenty miles off the north-eastern extremity of the African mainland, was captured by the fleet under Tristan de Cunha and Alfonso de Albuquerque towards the end of 1507. De Souza gives the following account of the occurrence:—"De Cunha found here an indifferent fort, not ill manned, nor unprovided. Being provoked by the Sheikh's answer to his message, he resolved, though it were dangerous, to land with Albuquerque. The first who leaped ashore was his nephew Don Alfonso de Noronna, with a few but brave men. The Sheikh received him with no great number, though much gallantry, maintaining his ground, and threatening De Cunha, who, through a shower of bullets and stones, made his approach to the fort, and was briskly repulsed by the Sheikh, whom then Don Alfonso struck down with his lance. Hence ensued a sharp skirmish: the Moors endeavouring to carry off their

THE CHAPTER CONCERNING THE ISLAND OF MOZAMBICH AND ITS INHABITANTS.

Let us return to Mozambich, whence the king of Portugal (as also in the island Zaphala) derives a very great quantity of gold and of oil, which comes from the main-

Prince, and the Portuguese to hinder it: till he and eight more being slain, the enemy fled to the castle, which was scaled, and those who entered opening the gate for the rest, a bloody fight began within, the Moors disputing it to the last man...The Portuguese lost six men. The natives [Christians] who had kept off, hearing of their success, came to thank De Cunna for delivering them from the heavy yoke of the Muhammedans, and were received under the protection of the king of Portugal, who having chosen Don Alfouso de Noronna to command the fort, if taken, De Cunna gave it him, with a hundred men for garrison." It would appear from De Souza that the island at this period was inhabited principally by Christians:—" They are all Jacobite Christians, like the Abissins. The men use the names of the Apostles, the women chiefly that of Mary. They worship the cross, which they wear on their cloathes, and set up in their churches, where they pray thrice a day in the Chaldean language, alternatively, as in a choir. They receive but one wife, use circumcision, fasting, and tithes. The men, comely; the women, so manly, that they follow the war, and live like Amazons. Some of them, for propagation, making use of such men as arrive there, and even bringing some by witchcraft. Their cloathing, some cloth, and some skins; their habitations, in the caves; their weapons, stones and slings. They are subject to the Arabian king of Caxem" [Keshîn]. (*Port. Asia*, vol. i. pp. 116-119.) Dr. Vincent quotes Cosmas Indocopleustes as stating that " the inhabitants of Socotra were Greeks from Egypt. He was not at the island, but conversed with some of the natives in Ethiopia: they were Christians, and their priests were from Persia, that is, they were Nestorians." (*Com. and Navig. of the Ancients*, vol. ii. p. 342 *n.*) El-Edrisi describes the population in his time as being composed chiefly of Christians, and his account of their original settlement there is curious though obviously fabulous:—" Most of the inhabitants of Socotra are Christians, and the cause of this was that Alexander [the Great] after he had overcome the king of Persia, and his fleet had captured the Indian islands, and he had killed Môr, king of India, his preceptor, Aristotle, having enjoined him to discover the Island of Aloes, this subject was on his mind, owing to his preceptor's injunction; so that after he had accomplished the taking of the Indian islands, and had overcome them and their kings, he turned from the Indian Sea

land. We remained in this island about fifteen days, and found it to be small: the inhabitants of it are black and poor, and have very little food here; but it comes to them from the mainland, which is not far distant. Nevertheless, there is a very good port here. Sometimes we went on the mainland to amuse ourselves and to see the country. We found some races of people quite black and quite naked, excepting that the men wore their natural parts in a bark of wood, and the women wore a leaf before and one behind. These people have their hair bristling up and short, the lips of the

to the Sea of Yemen, [which he never did,] and he conquered those islands as far as Socotra, with which he was much pleased on account of its fertility and the temperature of its climate, and wrote to his preceptor accordingly. When this news reached Aristotle, he wrote directing him to remove its inhabitants, and to replace them by Greeks who were to be instructed to take care of the aloes trees, and to cultivate them, on account of the several benefits to be derived therefrom." (Part vi. of *First Climate*.) Marco Polo, a century later, describes Socotra as the seat of an archbishop, who was subject to a *Zatolia* [Catholicos] who resides at Baldak, [Baghdad,] by whom he was elected.

I infer from these several accounts, that the Christians at Socotra were originally Nestorians, but that, following the example of some of their co-religionists in India, they subsequently embraced the Monophysite doctrines of Jacob Baraddæus, whose followers were styled, after him, Jacobites. In that case, De Souza is correct in classing them with the Abyssinians, who hold the same theological views, and some of whose social habits these Socotra Christians appear also to have adopted. On the abandonment of the island by the Portuguese, it reverted to its original native proprietor, the Arab Sheikh of Keshîn, a small town on the north-east coast of Arabia. An attempt was made on the part of the Indian Government in 1834 to obtain the island by purchase, in order to establish a coaling-station there; but 'Amr ibn Tawâri, the then ruling chief of Keshîn, resolutely refused to entertain the proposal, declaring that "as sure as there is but one God, and He is in heaven, I will not sell so much (making a span with his fingers.) It was the gift of the Almighty to the Mahrahs, and has descended from our forefathers to their children, over whom I am Sultan." (*Trans. of the Bombay Geog. Soc.*, vol. vii. p. 148.) The Christian population of the island has entirely disappeared, and there have been no native Christians resident there within the memory of any of the Arabs of the adjoining coast.

mouth as thick as two fingers, the face large, the teeth large and as white as snow. They are very timid, especially when they see armed men. We, seeing these beasts to be few and vile, (we were about five or six companions well armed with *spingarde*,) took a guide in the said island who conducted us through the country, and we went a good day's journey into the mainland; and on this journey we found many elephants in troops, and, on account of these elephants, he who guided us made us carry certain pieces of dry wood ignited, which we constantly made to flame up. When the elephants saw the fire they fled, excepting once, that we met three female elephants who had their young behind them, who gave chase after us as far as a mountain, and there we saved ourselves, and travelled through the said mountain at least ten miles; then we descended on the other side and found some caverns, to which the said negroes resorted, who speak in a manner which I shall have great trouble in making you understand. However, I will endeavour to explain it to you in the best way I can. For example: when the muleteers follow their mules in Sicily and wish to drive them on, with the tongue under the palate they make a certain warble and a certain noise, with which they make the mules go on. So is the manner of speaking of this people, and with signs until they are understood. Our guide asked us if we wished to purchase some cows and oxen, as he would procure them for us cheap. We answered that we had no money, thinking he might have an understanding with these beasts, and might cause us to be robbed. He said: "There is no need of money in this affair, for they have more gold and silver than you have, for it is near here that they go to find where it grows." We asked the guide: "What would they then?" He said: "They are fond of small scissors, and they like a little cloth to bind round themselves." They are also extremely fond of some little bells for their children; they also covet razors." We answered:

"We will give them some of these things, if, however, they would take the cows to the mountain." The guide said: "I will see that they shall take them to the top of the mountain and no farther, for they never pass beyond. Tell me, however, what you will give them?" One of our companions, a bombardier, said: "I will give them a good razor and a small bell." And I, in order to get animal food, took off my shirt, and said that I would give them that. Then the guide, seeing what we would give, said: "Who will drive so much cattle to the sea?" We answered: "We will drive as many as they will give." And he took the things abovementioned and gave them to five or six of these men, and demanded for them thirty cows. The brutes made signs that they would give fifteen cows. We told him to take them, for they were enough, provided they did not cheat us. The negroes immediately conducted fifteen cows to the top of the mountain. But when we had gone a little way from them, those who remained in the caverns began to make a noise; and we, thinking that it might be to follow us, left the cows and all betook ourselves to our arms. The two negroes who led the cows showed us by certain of their signs that we need not be afraid. And our guide said they must be quarrelling, because each would have wanted that bell. We took the said cows again, and went to the top of the mountain, and the two negroes then returned on their way. On our descent to come to the sea-shore we passed through a grove of cubebs about five miles, and discovered part of those elephants which we had met in going, which put us into such fear that we were obliged to leave some of the cows, which fled towards the negroes, and we returned to our island.[1] And when our fleet was fur-

---

[1] The following is Barbosa's description of Mozambique, from which it would appear, that in his time the Arab settlers, though subject to the Portuguese, continued to exercise a separate civil jurisdiction:—
"Passing Angos [Angoxa] on the way towards India, there are three

nished with all that it required, we took our way towards the Cape of Good Hope, and passed within the island of islands very near the land, one of which, called Mozambique, is inhabited by Moors. It has a good harbour, frequented by all the Moors who navigate in the direction of Cefala, [Sofála,] Zuama, and Angos, among which Moors is a *Serife* [Sherif,] who governs them, and administers justice to them; and these use the language and customs of the Moors of Angos. In these islands the king of Portugal has now a fortress, and has these Moors under his sway and government. In this island [Mozambique] the Portuguese ships take in water, wood, fish, and other provisions, and here those vessels that need it are repaired. In like manner, from this island the Portuguese factory at Cefala is provided, both with articles from Portugal and from India, it being situated in the highway. On the mainland opposite to this island there are many very large elephants, and other wild beasts. The country is inhabited by Pagans, who are very ugly men: they go naked, and besmeared with coloured earth, e le lor parti vergognose involte in una braca di drappo di bombagio azurro, without any other covering. Their lips are bored,...each lip with three holes, and in the holes they insert bones, jewels, and other trinkets." (RAMUSIO, vol. i. p. 289.) The oppression of the Portuguese soon converted these comparatively harmless Makuas, as the aborigines are called, into troublesome neighbours; for Purchas records an attack made by them on the colony as early as 1585, (vol. ii. p. 1553.) Their enmity was subsequently embittered by the inhumanity of the slave-dealers, and Salt gives an account of one of their incursions in 1806, when "they destroyed the plantations, burnt the slave-huts, and killed or carried off every person who fell into their hands. They penetrated even into the fort of Messuril, and threw down the image of St. John, which was in the chapel, plundering the one adjoining the Government House, and converted the priest's dress, in which he celebrated mass, into a habit of ceremony for their chief." (*Voyage to Abyssinia*, etc., p. 38.) The atrocities of the slave traffic were revived a few years ago under the operation of the so-called *French Free Labour Emigration Trade*, the Governor-General of Mozambique taking an active part in the undertaking by despatching soldiers into the interior to coöperate with the Arabs in their kidnapping expeditions. "At first they were successful; but, at last, the negroes, exasperated by the bloodshed which had again commenced among them, and attributing it to its correct cause, viz., to the presence of the Portuguese soldiers among them, rose and destroyed some of them, and the survivors escaped only with their lives, to bring to the city of Mozambique the intelligence that all the natives had risen with the intention of driving the Portuguese into the sea." (M'LEOD's *Travels in Eastern Africa*, vol. i. pp. 319-23.)

San Lorenzo,[1] which is distant from the mainland eighty leagues; and I think that the king of Portugal will soon be lord of it, because they have already seized two places and put them to fire and flame. From what I have seen of India and Ethiopia, it appears to me that the king of Portugal, if it please God, and he is as victorious as he has been hitherto, I think that he will be the richest king in the world. And truly he deserves every good, for in India, and especially in Cucin, every fête day ten and even twelve Pagans and Moors are baptized in the Christian faith, which is daily extending by means of the said king; and for this reason it may be believed that God has given him victory, and will ever prosper him in future.

THE CHAPTER CONCERNING THE CAPE OF GOOD HOPE.

Let us now return to our journey. When we had passed the Cape of Good Hope, about two hundred miles distant from the cape, the wind became contrary, and this because on the left hand there is the island of San Lorenzo and many other islands, amongst which there arose a very great storm of wind, which lasted for six days. However, by the grace of God we escaped any accident. When we had passed two hundred leagues we had again a very great storm for six more days, when the whole fleet was dispersed, which went some here and some there. When the storm had ceased, we went on our way, and never saw each other again until we arrived in Portugal. I went in the ship of Bartholomeo Marchioni, of Florence, dwelling in the city of Lisbon,

[1] Madagascar, called San Lorenzo by the Portuguese, who are said to have first landed there on the anniversary of that festival. Some authors assert that the island was discovered by Lorenzo de Almeyda in 1506; others, that it was first visited by the fleet under Tristan de Cunha in 1507, on which occasion they had a skirmish with the Moorish inhabitants of one or more towns on the eastern side of the island.

which ship was called Santo Vicentio, and carried seven thousand *cantara* of spices of all sorts; and we passed near another island called Santa Helena, where we saw two fishes, each of which was as large as a large house, which, every time that they are upon the water, raise a sort of visor, I think three paces (*passi*) wide, which they let down when they wish to go under water. We were so alarmed at the force of these fishes in swimming, that we fired off all the artillery. And then we found another island called Lascension,[1] on which we found certain birds as large as ducks, which perched upon the ship, and they were so stupid and simple that they allowed themselves to be taken by the hand, and when they were taken they appeared very sharp and fierce.[2] And before they were taken they looked at us like something miraculous. And this arose from their never having before seen Christians; for in this island there is nothing but fishes, and water, and these birds. Having passed this island, when we had sailed for some days we began to see the north star, and yet many say that when the north star is not seen it is not possible to navigate save by the Antarctic Pole. Let me tell you that the Portuguese always sail by the north star, although some days the said star is not seen, nevertheless the magnet performs its office and is adjusted to the Arctic Pole. Some days afterwards, we arrived in a beautiful country, that is, at the islands of the Astori,[3] which belong to the king of Portugal. And first we saw the island of Picco, that of Corvo, the island of Flores, that of San Giorgio, La Gratiosa, the island of Faial, and then we arrived at the island of Terticra, at which we remained two days. These islands are very fruitful. We then departed thence and went towards Portugal, and in seven days arrived at the noble city of Lisbon, which is one of the noble and good cities I have seen. I leave you

---

[1] Ascension.   [2] The birds vulgarly known as *Boobies*.
[3] The Azores.

to imagine, O my kind reader, the pleasure and joy I felt when I had arrived on terra firma. And as the king was not in Lisbon, I immediately set out and went to find him at a city called Almada,[1] which is opposite to Lisbon. When I had arrived, I went to kiss his majesty's hand, who caressed me much, and kept me some days at his court, in order to know about the things of India. After some days, I showed to his majesty the patent of knighthood, which the Viceroy had granted me in India, praying him (if so it pleased him) that he would confirm it, and sign it with his own hand, and affix his seal to it. When he had seen the said patent, he said that it pleased him, and so he had a diploma drawn up for me on parchment, signed with his hand, with his seal, and registered; and so I took my leave of his majesty, and came to the city of Rome.

¶ Printed at Rome by Master Stephano Guillireti de Loreno, and Master Hercule de Nani, of Bologna, at the request of Master Lodovico de Henricis da Corneto, of Vicenza. In the year M.D.X. the vith day of December.

---

[1] In the edition of *Ramusio* of 1613 it is "Almeirim," where there was a palace belonging to the kings of Portugal.

INDEX TO THE TRAVELS OF LUDOVICO DI VARTHEMA, AND TO THE NOTES.

ABBASSIDES, xxv; 6
'Abdali tribe of Arabs, 74
Abdallah ibn Muhammed, 91
—— —— Kutb Shâh of Golcondah,195
'Abd er-Razzâk ("India in the xvth century") quoted, l, lxvi; 94, 100, 125, 130, 131, 136, 146, 148, 177
Abercrombie, General, takes Cannanore, 123
Abissins, 291
Aboo 'Abdallah bin Ahmed Muhrim, 58
Abraham (his sacrifice), 36, 41, 43, 44, 45; (and Ephron), 221
Abubekr, (his tomb at El-Medînah), 27, 28, 46, 75, 103
Abulfeda quoted, 80, 82
Abu 'Obeidah, 28
Abyssinia, 47, 86; (bargaining in), 169
Abyssinian army destroyed at Meccah, 32; — mercenaries in India, 118
Abyssinians, 63, 81, 84, 291, 292
Achem, 230; see Achin
Achin, lxxxviii; 229, 231, 232
—— Head, 153
Adam, first builder of the Käaba, 41
Adam's Bridge, 184
——'s Peak, 190, 191
Adders, deaf, 173
Aden, 58; (described), 59, 60; history of the valley of, 58; Varthema's return to, 73; again, 84
Adhân (or call to prayer), 267
'Adil, Shâh of the Deccan, lix, lx, lxiv; 115, 117, 118
Ælian quoted, 241
Ælius Gallus, 21
Africano, Giovan Leoni, xxv
Agag, 22
Agamos in Abyssinia, 47
Agates, 107
Aghâni, El-, author of, quoted, 22, 23, 32

Agila, 235
Agnesina, Duchess, 275
Ahmed ibn el-Imâm en-Nâsir, 80
Ahmed, Shâh of Guzerat, lviii; of Ahmednugger, liv
Aia Chatoteri, 197
Aiam Campetit, 197
Aiaz (city of Yemen), 74
Ainslie's Materia Medica, 163
'Akabet esh-Shâmi, 20
Akbar, the Emperor, lxiv; 111, 211
Akhdar, El-, 33
'Alâ ed-Dîn Husein, Shâh of Bengal, lxiv; 212
Alandrina (Fandaraina) lxxxiv
Albi, Countess or Duchess of, xix; 1
Alexander, fables about, 58, 291
Alexandria, 5
Aleppo, 7
Alla Apostolica (dress so designated), 78, 112, 193, 201, 253
Alberti quoted, 204
Albuquerque, cix; 94, 99; (takes Goa), 115, 184; Commentaries of, (quoted) 224, 254, 283, 290
'Alí, (alleged tomb of), 26, 74, 103
—— Bey quoted, 53
—— Chelebi, 237
—— Muhammed Khân's History of Guzerat. See Bird
Almacarana (El-Makrânah), a city of Yeman 75, 76
Almada, 298
Almadea, (El-Mäadîah), a kind of boat, 154
Almeida. See De Almeyda
Aloes-wood, 235 ; —— Island, of, 291
Am, Amb, Anba, Amba, Amra, (mango) 159, 160
Amalekites, 22
Aman (Hamath), 5
Amanni (Yemen), 57, 83
'Amír ibn 'Abd el-Wahhâb, Sultân, 57, 61

300 INDEX.

Amír Akbai, 76
—— 'Ali el-Bâadâni, 79
—— Bar Sabai, 79
—— el-Muamanin, 57
'Ammân Seyyeds of Máskat and Zanzibar, cxi
'Amr el-Jabraty, 76
Amuck, running, 226
Ananias, 12
Anchors of marble, 153
Andaman Islands, 229
Anecdote of British law as viewed in the East, lxxv
Angediva, Island of, 119, 120, 261, 275
Angos (Angoxa), 290, 294, 295
Animals, at Honahwar, 122; at Calicut, 172; at Tenasserim, 199
Antartic regions heard of by Varthema, xcv; 251
Antelope, 46, 47
Antimony, 102
Antipathy of Hindûs to the sea, 152
Apes, 85, 172
Aqueduct at Aden, 83, 84
Arabia, Deserta, 16; Christianity in, 32; Felix, 31, 37, 53, 54, 57, 151
Arabians, 224
Arabic, Varthema's specimens of, xxvi; 29, 30, 31, 41, 49, 50, 62, 63, 66, 67, 68, 70, 71, 72, 96, 97, 263, 267
—— couplet, quoted, 236
Arabs, of Damascus, 14, 15; of the desert, 17, 19, 20, 21; dress and arms of, 55, 64, 65, 78; fights with, 19, 20, 21, 35; the navigators of India, 152; in India, 178; Christian, 32
Aracan, marriage customs in, 204, 216, 225; king of, 219
Arafât, 36, 41; hurry from, 44, 192
Aream, 22
Archipelago, Indian, navigation to, 153, 170; Varthema's visit to, 223; et seq.
Areca palm and nut, 144, 233
Aristotle, 291, 292
Armenia, 15; writing of, 213
Armenians in Burmah, 217
Arms and dress of Arabs. See *Arabs*.
Arms of soldiers of Calicut, 150; and dress of Ceylonese, 193; of Tenasserim, 198; of fleet of Calicut, 275
Army of King of Calicut, 149; of King of Tenasserim, 198; of Bengal Sultân, 211
Arnaud's travels in Yemen, xlvii

Arrack, 164
Arrian, 152
Arrowsmith's Atlas, lxvi; 132
'Arshiyyîn, 62
Artichokes, 190
Artillery in Ceylon, 193, 255; none in Pulicat, 195; among Javanese, 254; made by Christians for the Zamorin, 261, 276, 278, 279, 281. See *Fire-arms*
Artocarpus integrifolius, 159
Arungzîb, 126, 195
Asas, ('Az'az). See *Aiaz*
Ascension, Island of, 297
Asedegam, (Satgong), cxv
Ashrafi, xlvi; 10, 13. See *Seraphim*
Asiatic Society, Royal, 153
Assemanni Biblioth. Oriental, quoted, 213
Astori Islands, (Azores), 297
'Atar of Roses, 11
Atlas, K. Johnstone's, 286. See *J.*
Aumar, 103. See *'Omar*
Australia, supposed to be referred to, 251
Ava, xxvi; King of, lxxxvi; 216, 217, 218, 219
Azamini, ('Ajami), 7
Azemia, 8
Azores, 297
Azraki, El-, 35

BABACHER. See *Abubekr*
Bab el-Mandeb Straits, legend of, 58, 86
Bab es-Salam at El-Medinah, 27
Babylon, priests from, 180; Patriarch of, 181
Bacam, 216
Bachan, 245
Backwaters of Cochin, lxviii, lxix; 155, 179, 180
Badafattan, 132
Badakhshân, 102
Baduin. See *Bedawîn*
Badulla, 189
Bahâl, 79
Bahar, (a weight), 170
Baharein Island, 94
Bahmâni Dynasty of Kalberga, lix
Bakhtegân, liii
Bakya at El-Medinah, 28
Balachsam, (Badakhshân), 102
Balances, delicate, 168
Balass rubies, liii; 101
Balbi, Gasparo, 213, 220
Baldaeus, Philip, quoted, lxvi; 105, 132, 173, 180, 184, 185, 196, 286
Baldak (Baghdad), 292

INDEX. 301

Balsam, jars of, 40
Balthazar, Sequirius, 197
Bamboos, enormous, 219
Barnó, 190
Banda Islands, (Bandan of V.), lxxvii. xci; 232, 233, 243, 245
Bandar Hokkât (Holket Bay), Aden, 59
Banghella, Bangchella, (i.e. BENGALA), (q.v.). City of, lxxx, lxxxii, cxiv, cxv; 38, 151, 196, 210
Bánias, 20
Bankers in Calicut, 168
Barada River, 9
Barakât, (Barachet of V.), Sherif of Mecca, xxxii; 58
Barbara. See *Berbera*
Barbosa, Odoardo, quoted, lxix, lxxvii, cxiv; 110, 131, 133, 154, 157, 180, 183, 184, 185, 188, 194, 197, 210, 222, 226, 230, 233, 234, 235, 240, 243, 245, 252, 254, 258, 286, 294
Baretti's Dictionary, 107
Bargaining, by fingers, 168; Oriental, 221
Barrygarry, 132
Bartema (Varthema), xviii
Barter with Negroes, 293
Baruti. See *Beyroot*
Baso, 169
Batech (Batta), 256
Batacola or Batcull, 119
Bathacala, (Batheal), Batcoal, or Beitkul), lix, lx; 119, 151
Battle at Cannanore with the fleet of Calicut, 276, et seq.
Bayazid II., xxv
Bebmendo, (I. of Perim), 58
Bedâwin, 15, 20, 23, 24, 34, 42, 43. See *Arabs*
Beef, cow-, 121, 122, 143
Beke's Commerce and Politics of Abyssinia, 169
Bell-ringing impresses the Muhammedans, 285
Bellary, 126
Bendemir, R., lii; 101
Bengal, Bengala, History of, lxiii, lxxx, lxxxii; 38, 151, 184, 196, 197, 198, 210; riches of, lxxxii; 212; Sultâns of, 212; mutilation in, 258; postscript on, cxiv; site of. See *Banghella*
Bengallis, 224
Beni Dhâhir, 76
——— Thamond, 34
Benjamin of Tudela, 1
Bennett, Notes by Mr. J. J., 158, 160, 161, 233

Benzoin, 197, 234
Berbera, 88
Bercy's Map of Asia, cxix
Bergare, 132
Bernier, quoted, 100, 113
Betel leaf, 144
Beyroot, 6
Bhajnugger, or Hyderabad, 195
Bhuta (spirits), 139
Bhutân, 100
Bidar, King of, 117
Bigarrah, see *Mahmúd Sháh*
Bijapúr, lxiv; 115, 117, 186, 194
Bijayanagâr, lx; 116, 125, 177, 194, 212
Biographie Universelle, xvii
Birds; of Calicut, 172; of Java, 253; beaks used for sword-hilts, 200
Bird's Transl. of Ali Muh. Khán's Hist. of Guzerat, lxiv; 109, 110, 111
Bishops, Nestorian, consecration of Indian, 182
Bisinegar (Bijayanagâr), 125
Black damsels of Arabia, 65
——— Arabs, 77
——— and uncivilized people of Mozambique, 292
Blaeu's Cosmography, lxxx; Maps of Asia, &c., cxix
Blair's Map of Hindostan, cxix
Blemishes in British Indian History, c
Blow-pipes, xcvi; 234
Bochor (as a name of aloes-wood), 235
Boghâz Malacca (Straits of Malacca), lxxxvii; 223
Bokhára, 100
Bombay, 113
——— Govt. Selections quoted, 104, 106, 108
——— Quarterly Mag., 117, 166, 168
——— Geog. Society's Transactions, 29, 88, 89
Boobies, 297
Bood-Khana, 111
Books of Muhammed at El-Medinah, 26
Boolâk, 6
Borah merchants of Guzerat, xlix
Bore at Cambay, lviii; 106
Borjëeh Mamlûks, 6
Bornei (Borneo), lxxvii; 247
Bows and arrows, 65, 85, 254
Braccia—what ? 48
Brahminical thread, 139
Brahmins, 129, 134, 138, 140, 141, 142, 143, 173, 176; their feeding, 139; in war, 150; daily ceremonies, 140

Brande's Dictionary of Mat. Medica, quoted, 102
Brava, city of, 290
Brazil-wood, 197, 199, 222; origin of the name, lxxviii; 205
Bread not eaten, 124
Breastwork of camels, 20
Brema (Burmah), 197, 216
Bride assigned to Varthema, lvii; 104
British fleet aids Sháh Abbás, li
—— rule in India, whether it has improved the average position of the people, lxxiii
—— capture of Aden, 59
Brokers, 168
Browne's Travels, quoted, 13
Bubachar. See *Abubekr*
Buceros galeatus, lxxix; 200
Buchanan's Journey through Mysore, Canara, and Malabar, Dr. Francis, quoted, lxvi; 107, 121, 124, 132, 134, 141, 143, 146, 151, 155, 158, 167, 171, 179
Buckingham, J. S., quoted, 12
Buddha, lxxxv; 217
Buddhists, lxxxv; 192
Buddhistic Triad, 217
Buffaloes in Tenasserim, 201
Bunder Abbás, 94, 95
—— Jedid, 88
Burckhardt, quoted, xxvii; 16, 17, 20, 22, 24, 25, 26, 27, 33, 34, 35, 37, 39, 40, 41, 43, 46, 52
Burgara, Bergara, lxvi; 132
Burmah, 216. (See *Tenasserim, Pegu*, and *Ava*.)
Burmas, King of the, 219
Burmese Peninsula, political state of in time of Varthema, lxxvi
—— dress, 201; prayer, 217; countries, their intercourse with the west, 215
Burning the dead, 151, 204, 206; of widows, 206, 222
Burnt Island, 88
Burying the dead, 151
Burton, Capt. R., quoted, xci; 24, 25, 26, 27, 28, 29, 33, 34, 35, 36, 37, 39, 40, 41, 42, 43, 44, 45, 46, 53, 80
—— —— his opinion of Varthema, xxxvi
Bushmen, 47
Buts, 142

CABRAL, Pedro Alvarez, lxv; 123, 156, 178, 260
Cábul, 100
Cadelapalon (sp. of plantain), 162

Cádhi; preaching at Meccah, 43; of Moors at Calicut, 273
Cadjans, 163
Cael, 183, 185. See *Chayl*
Cæsalpina Sappan, 205
Cæsar, Fredericke, quoted, cxvi; 92, 126, 199, 215, 219
Caicolon, Cacolon, Caincoulan, Calecoulang, Coilcoloan (Kayan Kulam), lxviii, lxix; 134, 151, 179, 180, 184
Cain and Abel, legends as to, 12, 59
Cairo, 5, 31, 37, 53, 103
—— Soldan of, 280
—— Fashion of, 226
Calam, 216
Calampat (Calambuco), aloes-wood, 236, 238
Calcutta Govt. Gazette, 48
Calicut, lxii; 133, 134, 143, 260; described, 135; Varthema's stay at, lxvi; ruined by war, 178; fleet of, 274, 275
—— King of (Zamorin), 174, 260, 261, 273
—— Manner of (i.e., Hinduism), 120, 124, 129, 131, 132, 134, 147, 180, 184, 195, 205, 209
Calimere, Point, 187
Caliphs, Abbaside, 6
Calligicum of Ptolemy, lxix; 185
Calmet's Dict. of the Bible, 47
Cam, Peter, 288
Cambay (Combeia of V.), lvii, lviii, lxiv; 91, 92, 105, 184
Camboja, 235
Camels, 17; food, 18; intrenchment of, 20, 31, 33, 37; dung-fuel, 42; of Sultán of Aden, 64
Cammoos, El-, 23
Campar, 230
Camphor, xciv; 248
Camrán, Island of, 65
Canara, North, 119, 120
—— South, 122
—— Rajah of, 121
Canes of Pegu, 218, 219
Canonica, 12
Cannanore, lxi, lxv; 122; described, 123, 131, 133, 261, 265, 266, 268, 272, 274, 275, 276, 288; Varthema goes to, 280; leaves for Europe, c; 289; King of, 281, 283, 284; Portuguese fort at, xcix; 270, 281
Cannibalism in Ind. Archip. 256; alleged, in Java, xcvi; 255, 257
Cape of Good Hope, 295, 296
Capel (Kapal), a kind of ship, 154
Capellan, alleged site of ruby mines, 219

INDEX. 303

Capogatto, lxvi; 132, 133, 275
Capucar, 133
Caravan of Damascus to Meccah, 16, 18, 20, 22; leaves Meccah, 51; of Cairo, 37; of India, 51.
Caravans from Cashmere to China, 100
Cardamums, 124
Carnatic, Kingdom of, lx; 116, 125. See *Bijayanagìr*
—— coinage of, 131
Cas (a coin), 130
Cashmere, 100
Cassia, 124
Castenheda, 179
Castes of Calicut, lxvii; 141
Castle of Damascus, 9; of Portuguese at Cannanore, 270. See *Cannanore*.
Cathai, Cathay, Catai, 101, 204, 236; limits of, 213; Christians subject to, 212
Catigan, lxxxi. See *Chittagong, Chatigam*.
Catholic of Babylon, 181
Catholic missions in India, their success greater than those of Reformed churches, civ
Caussin de Perceval's Hist. des Arabes avant l'Islamisme, 22, 23
Cautley, Sir P. T., 241
Cauvery river, 186
Cave on Adam's Peak, alleged, 191, 192
Caxem (Keshin), 291
Cazazionor. See *Cogiazonor*.
Cefala. See *Sofala*.
Centacola (Uncola), 120
Ceremonies; at the Kâaba, 40, 41; on death of King of Calicut, 144; of Hindû worship, 149, 176
Cevul. See *Chaul*.
Ceylon, lxx; 183, 185, 187, 188; circuit of, 188; described, *ib.*; jewels of, 218
Chaberis, R., cxvi
Chalcedonies, mountain of, 107
Chaldean tongue in Socotra, 291
Chameram (Camrân), an island in the Red Sea, 54, 57
Chapel of the devil at Calicut, 137
Character of Persians, 102
Charts and compasses, alleged, in the Hajj caravan, 31; in the Java Sea, xciv; 249
Chatigam, Catigam (Chittagong), lxxx, cxvii, cxviii, cxix, cxx, cxxi
Chattra (umbrella), 150
Chattrapati, 150
Chaturi (Arab. Shakhtûr ?) a kind of boat, 154

Chaul (Choul Chowul Cevul), a port of Concan, lxiv; 113, 115
Chayl (Cael, Coil), lxiii, lxix; 184
Cheapness of Bengal, lxxxii
Cheo (Jooah on Indus), lv; 104, 105
Chiampana. See *Ciampana*.
Chijs (Chinese), 225
Children, mutilated, 258
Chiloah (Quiloa, Kilwah), cvi, cvii; 290
Chievuli, 151. See *Chaul*.
Chinese umbrella, 150
Chingleput, 194
Chittagong, cxvii
Chivil, 113
Chofole (name app. to Areca), 110
Christians: Arab, 32; restrictions on at Juddah, 52
—— of St. Thomas, lxix; 180, 181, 187
—— merchants from *Sarnau* who accompany Varthema to the farther East, lxxxii, lxxxiv, xc, xcv, xcvii; 212, 214, 219, 220, 235, 238, 241, 242, 244, 246, 248, 249, 257, 258
——, alleged, in Pegu, lxxxv; 217
—— of Socotra, 291
Christianity in Arabia, 32
—— spread of by Portuguese, alleged, 296. See *Missions*.
Chunam, 144
Church, idol temple taken for a, 175, 176
Churchill's Collection of Voyages, 133, 174, 184
Ciampana (Sampan, a kind of boat), 188, 242, 243, 259
Cianchapalon (sp. of plantain), 162
Ciccara (jack-fruit), 159
Cini (King of—here apparently Siam), 224; and Macini, 236
Cinnamon, 188; described, 191
Cioromandel (Coromandel put by author for Negapatam), lxx, xcvii; 151, 259. See *Coromandel*.
Circassian Mamlûks, 6
Circumambulation of the Kâaba, 40
Circumcision, 291
Civet-cats, 199, 218
Cloete, Mr. Henry, 47
Cloves and clove trees, xcii; 245
Cobra, 173
Cochin (Cucin, Cuccin), 134, 260, 272, 286, 296; King of, 280, 281; river or backwater of, 155, 179, 180
—— China, 235
Cock-fighting, 200
Cocoa-palm, described, 162; cutting down, a crime, 166
Coifolo (Areca), 144

Cogiazenor, Cozazionor, etc. (Varthema's comrade from Persia eastward), liii, lxxxiv, xc, xciv, xcvii, xcviii, xcix; 103, 178, 188, 194, 210, 220, 242, 244, 248, 249, 257, 262. 263, 268
Coil. See *Chayl.*
Coilpatam, lxx
Coilcoloan. See *Caicolon.*
Coiloan. See *Quilon.*
Coins of Bijayanagâr, lxv; 130; of Calicut, 151; of Sumatra, lxxxviii; 232
Coir, 164, 165
Cole, Mr., Vice-consul at Juddah, 53
Colombo, lxx; 188, 189, 190
Columbum, 181
Colou, Coulam, Coulang, Coiloan (*Quilon*, q. v.), 134, 151, 182, 183, 184, 187, 259
Colonna; Agnesina, xix; 1; Fabrizio and Vittoria, xix, xxii; Guidobaldo, xx, xxi, xxii; Ascanio, xx
Colosseum, 38
Colossochelys Atlas, 241
Comari, a kind of tree, 245
Combeia (*Cambay*, q. v.), lvii; 105, 106, 107, 151
Commerce, freedom and extent of medieval Indian, lxxi
Comolanga, a fruit of Malabar, 161
Comorin, Cape, lxiii; 153, 183, 187
Comoro islands, 290
Companion of Varthema. See *Cogiazenor.*
Compass. See *Charts and Compass.*
—— Oriental names of, 32; whether derived from Europe by the Arabs, etc., xciv
Compounds, 136
Concan, lix, lxiv
Conti, Nicolò de', quoted, lxxxv; 105, 107, 125, 131, 135, 146, 188, 197, 205, 215, 217, 228, 233, 236, 240, 256
Conversions to Christianity, ci; 296
Copper in Java, alleged, 253
Coptic Monks, practices attributed to, 258
Copyright of Varthema's Itinerary, xxiv. See *Privilege at end of Introduction.*
Corals, 194, 195, 206, 214, 219, 220
Corazani (Khorassân), 99, 102
Corcopal, a fruit of Malabar, 161
Cornelians, 107
Coromandel (polit. state of), lxiii; 125, 184, 186, 187. See *Cioromandel.*
Corroboration of Varthema's descriptions, xxviii, xxix, xxxi, xxxvi, xli, xliv. See *Veracity.*
Corsalis, Andrea, 249, 252
Cortor (a broker), 168
Corvo Island, 297
Cosmos, Indicopleustes, 291
Cotta, Cottica, lxvi; 132, 189
Cotton and cotton stuffs, 8, 38, 107, 111, 114, 153, 198, 212, 222
Cowries, 131
Cows, unicorn, 87, stag-horned, 87
Cow (dung), plaster and fuel, 155
—— killing, a capital crime, 174
—— beef. See *Beef.*
Crawfurd's Descriptive Dictionary of the Indian Islands, quoted lxxvii, lxxxviii, lxxxix; 170, 205, 210, 223, 254, 226, 227, 228, 229, 230, 233, 224, 235, 238, 239, 240, 243, 247, 252, 253, 254, 256
——'s History of the Indian Archipelago, 161
——'s condemnation of Varthema, xcvi, 255
——, J., F.R.S., cxiii
Crecate, 133
Creed, Muhammedam, 63, 66
Crocodiles, 173
Cross, Southern, xcv; 249; apparently referred to by Dante, 250
—— in Socotra, 291
Crowds at Meccah, 38
Crows at Calicut, 140
Cruttenden, Captain, quoted, 88, 89
Cubebs, in Mozambique, 294
Cucin, Cuccin. See *Cochin*
Cucumbers, 42; and melons, 124
Cumere (Comoro) Island, 290
Curia (Ar. *Koraja*, Ang. Ind. *Corje*, a score), 170
Custard-apple, 190
Customs of the Hindûs, domestic, 149

DABUL, Dabuli, lix, 114, 151
Dadin, lxxxiv
Dâl (lentils), 107
Dalîl (guide to holy places), 26
Dallâl (broker), 168
Damar (Dhamâr, city of Yemen), 82
Damascus, 8; described, 8-16
—— lord of, 17
Damota, 47
Dant, see *Dante*
Dankert's Map of Asia, cxix
Dante (Daunt, or Denn), a city of Yemen), xlvii, 75
—— (the Poet)'s mention of the Southern Cross, 250
D'Anville, quoted, 185

INDEX. 305

Darb esh-Sharki, 33
D'Arvieux, quoted, 7
Dates given or implied by Varthema, see xxv, xxvii; 16, 18, 36, 89, 90, 177, 266, 274, 289
Date-trees, 74
Davis, John, 197
Days, short antarctic, heard of by Varthema, 251
De Almeyda, Francisco, Viceroy of India, xcix, c; 266, 271, 274, 280, 281, 282, 286
—— Lorenzo, son of the preceding, xcix; 271, 275, 276, 280, 281, 283, 287, 288, 296
De Barros, J., quoted, lxxvii, lxxxix, cxvii, cxx; 170, 224, 230, 234, 243, 252, 272, 278
De Cabreira, F. de X., cix
De Cunna (Da Cugna), Tristan, c; 282, 284, 287, 288, 290, 296
—— Nunno, 211
De Britto or de Brito, Captain Lorenzo, 124, 281, 283
De Faria y Souza, his Portuguese Asia, quoted, cxvii, cxx; 179, 195, 256, 261, 271, 280, 282, 287, 290
De Gama, Vasco (and Stephen), xxxix, xl, lxv, lxvi, cvi; 24, 132; takes a temple for a church, 175; his first reception at Calicut, etc., 178
De Guzman, Don Alonzo, liv
De la Roque, Voyage de l'Arabie Heureuse, quoted, 80
De Noronna, Alfonso, 290
De Nueva, Juan, 178
De Sala, Juan, his prudent reservation, 176
De Silvoa, P., cx
De Witt's Map of Asia, cxix
Dead, disposal of, 131, 204, 206
Dead Sea, 20
Deaths from thirst, 33
Debtors, treatment of, in Calicut, 147
Decan, Deccan, city and kingdom of (Bijapúr), lix, lxiv; 116, 117, 186
—— king of, 51, 115; his wars, soldiers, etc, 118
Decully, 184
Dedication of Varthema's book, xx; 1
Degradation of low castes in Malabar, 142
Denn, a city of Yemen. See Dante
Dennistoun's Mem. of the Dukes of Urbino, xix
Deumo (Deota), 137, 139, 207

Deuteronomy, quoted, 20, 166
Devil (appearing to Isaac, legend of), 44; —— (worship, supposed), 129, 137, 167; sacrifice to, 220
Devotion, acts of, among Joghees, 112
Devs, 137
Dhâfir, Khân of Guzerat, lviii; 108
Dhamâr, 62
Dhamarmar, 79, 83
Dharma, 217
Dharma Prakrama Bahu, king of Ceylon, 189
D'Herbelot, quoted, xxxi, lv, lvi; 75, 237
Dhura (a grain), 74
Diamond-mines, 107, 118
—— Point (Sumatra), 233
Dictionary, Shakespeare's Hindustani, 172. See also Crawfurd
Difficulties in Varthema's account of Borneo, 247; of Java, 254
Di Solona, Fra Guglielmo, lxxxiii
Diminution of number of frequented ports in India since Varthema's time, lxxi, lxxii
Dimne, see Dante
Diodorus Sic., xc; 148, 241
Diospyrus, 161
Disease, Hindú notions of, 167
Dishes (or discuses), cutting, slung by Joghees, 112
Disposal of dead in Calicut, 131; in Tenasserim, 204, 206
Diu in Guzerat (called by Varthema Dinobandierrumi), xlix; 91
Divers Voyages touching Discovery of America, quoted, 206
Divorces, Muham., 14
Djitel (a coin), 130
Doondies, (kind of boat), 104
Dora. See Dhura
Dormapatam, lxvi; 131
Dove of Muhammed, 45
Doves at Meccah, ib.
Dragon, St. George and, 7
Dress of ladies of Damascus, 14; of King of Joghees, 112; of people of Chaul, 114; of Nairs, 124; of Narsinga, 129; of King and Queen of Calicut, 143, 156; of Ceylonese, 193; of Tenasserim, 201; of Christian merchants of Sarnau, 213; of King of Pegu, 219. See Arabs, etc.
Dromedary journey, 82
Dromedaries, 126
Drum of Damascus, 11
Dutch, rise in the East, cii; in India, 123, 180, 195, 260

X

EAGLE-WOOD, lxxxix; 235
Easter of Indian Churches, 180
Eating, Hindú manner of, 139, 147; in Tenasserim, 201
Ecclesiastical dissensions in Malabar, 181
Eden's old translation of Varthema, 91
Edh-Dháfir, El-Melek, 61
Edom, 20
Edrísi, El-, quoted, 78, 81, 83, 86, 148, 182, 183, 237, 291
Eedur, Rajah of, 111
Egypt, 5, 258
Egyptian expedition to Yemen, 65, 75, 82, 83
Elephant, Elephants; teeth, 86; enormous, 241; of Sultán Mahmúd, 109, 124; how he fights, 126; his intelligence, 127; his dread of fire, *ib.*; employed to beach ships, *ib.*; have joints, *ib.*; described, 128; how they generate, 129; eaten in some countries, *ib.*; varieties of price, *ib.*; great understanding, *ib.*, 149, 151, 172; in Ceylon, 189; in Tenasserim, 198; in Pegu, 218; at Malacca, 225; in Sumatra very large, 232; ship laden with, 278; in Mozambique, 293, 294
El-Fath el-Mubín quoted, 160
Emanuel, King of Portugal, 260
Emeralds, 252; in Java, 258
Enchanters, Indian, 286
English aid to depress Portugal in the East, ciii
—— factory at Dabul, 115; at Karwar Head, 119
Enna, (oil so called), 176
Ephron and Abraham, 221
Eri, (Herat), lii; 99, 100, 102, 104
Esau, 20
Ethersey's account of the Bore, 106
Ethiopia, cvi; 31, 37, 38, 60, 85, 151, 289; King of, 49
Eufra, a large river (?), mistaken for Euphrates, lii; 101
Eunuchs, 258
Eusebius quoted, 32
Expeditions of the Arabs to plunder, 17
Experiment with aloes and benzoin, 238
Ezekiel quoted, 8

FAIAL ISLAND, 297
Fair at Berbera, 89
Fakhr ed-Dín, (of Lebanon) Amír, 7
—— Iskandar of Bengal, lxiii

Falconer, Dr. H., 241
Fanduraina, lxxxiv; 133, 183
Fanom (*Fanam*, a coin), 130
Fantuzzi, Notizie degli Scrittori Bolognesi, xviii
Farasola, (*fàrsala*, a weight), 170
Fath-'Allah Imád, Khán of Berar, lii
Fathers sold and eaten in Java, Story of, 255
Fátihah, El-, Varth.'s version of, 268
Fatomah, (Fátimah), tomb of at El-Medínah, 27
Feet of Adam, impressions of, 191
Female line, succession in, 143
Ferishta Ján (alleged origin of Prester John), 63
Ferishta's History by Scott quoted, 115, 117, 118, 126, 211
Ferrah, (a measure), 170
Ferrier's *Caravan Journies* quoted, 101
Ficus religiosa, 166
Fighting of the people of Calicut, 149, 150
Filagree of Sumatra, 339
Finances, remarks on Varthema's, liii
Finati, Giovanni, 40
Fire-arms in Yemen, 65, 255; introduced in Ceylon, 193; in the Archipelago, xcvii; 239, 254, 255
Fireworks frighten elephants, 127
—— in Sumatra, 239
Fishes, gigantic, 201, 297
Fitch, Ralph quoted, cxvii; 108, 113, 116, 117, 143, 157, 158, 186, 194, 197, 211, 217, 218, 220
Flaming well at Aden, 60
Fleet of Calicut, 274, 275
Flight of Varthema from Calicut, 269
Flora of Ceylon, 193
Florence, Arms of, 9
Flores Island, 297
Floris, Captain John, 197
Food, for Meccah, whence, 37; — of people in India, 124; — of people in Java, 254; — bearing trees not to be cut down, 166
Forbes's *Rás Málá* quoted, 92, 106, 111, 137, 138, 139, 149, 168
Förskal, death of, 77
Fountains of Damascus, 11
Fragments of Portuguese Empire in the East, ciii
Frang (Morb. Gall.), 156
Frasella, see *Farasola*
Fredericke, see *Cæsar*
French disease, 156, 274
—— Free Emigration, 295

INDEX. 307

Fruitfullest tree in the world (cocoanut), 163
Fruits of Damascus, 11; — of Yemen, 54, 55, 75, 78; — of Calicut, 138, et seq.; — of Ceylon, 190; — of Tenasserim, 199

GABRIEL, Don Juan, on the unicorn, 47
Gabriele Sionita, quoted, 81, 83
Gallanga (a root), 106
Gallas, 88
Galleys, 287
Gampola, 189
Ganges, 211
Gangia Regia, ib.
Garnets, 190
Gastaldi's Map of Asia, cxix, cxx
Gautama Buddha, 192
Gaza (Straits of Malacca), lxxxvii, 223
Gems of Ceylon, 190
Generosity, Eastern, liv
Genesis, quoted, 221
Genoa, 50
George, Saint, 7; — martyr, 12
Gezan (Jâzân), city of, 55, 56
Ghâlifkah (a port of Yemen), 81
Ghassân, Ghassanides, 55; Ghassâni, 76
Ghatafân, 23
Ghori dynasty of Hindostan, lviii, lxiii
Giava, 236, 243, etc. See Java
Gilolo, xcii; 245
Ginger, 124; described, 158
Gioghi, see Joghees
Girnar, fort of, 108
Giulfar, see Julfâr
Goa, island of, lix; 115
Goa (Goghâ or Gogo, in Guzerat), xlix; 92
Goats at Damascus, 14, 15; — and sheep in Tenasserim, 199, 200
Gog and Magog, 237
Goga (Goa), 115
Gogo, xlix; 92
Gogia (Angoxa), 290
Golchonda, Methold's Relation of, 215
Golconda, 107, 118, 194
Gold, 86, 291; touchstone for, 168; — work of Sumatra, 238; — and copper in Java, alleged, 253
Gombrûn, Br. Factory at, li; 94
Gorj, see Curia
Goss-hawks, 199
Gour or Luknouti, city of, lxiv, lxxx, cxiv, cxvi, cxviii; 210
Grapes, of Menin and Helbon, 8; Damascus, 11; 67; seedless, 70

Greek Christians, 8, 9
Greeks at Juddah, 52
Gregory the Great, 236
Greene's Collection of Voyages, xxxix; 124, 133, 139, 156, 170, 176, 183, 185, 194, 197, 206, 211, 274, 275, 286
Guadalajara, 283
Guavas, 161
Gnei, a savage people of Siam, 256
Guidobaldo, Duke of Urbino, xx; 275
Gunners in India, Frank and Turk, 261; Gunpowder in the Indian Archipelago, 240. See Fire-arms
Guzerat (Political state of in Varthema's time), lviii; 91, 108, 109, 197
Guzerati tribe, 108, 109, 114, 151
Gujratis, 224
Gypsies, sea-, 227

HADHRAMAUT, xlix; 88
Hadjer (Hagar), 41
Hâfûn, Râs, 88
Hajj route, xxvii; 33
Hakluyt quoted, 92
Halewacko or Kalewacko, 114
Haly, see 'Ali
Hamath, Hamáh, 8
Hamilton, Captain Alexander, quoted, 93, 113, 115, 119, 121, 122, 132, 136, 137, 141, 142, 148, 155, 170, 172, 180, 184, 231, 252
Haram at Meccah, 39. See Mosque
Harîm, morals of the, xlv
Harbour at Sedashevaghur or Bathcal, 119
Hares and partridges in Tenasserim, 200
Hasius, his map of Asia, cxix
Haswah, El-, 26
Hattia Island, cxxi
Haweea tribe, 88
Hawta, El-, 74
Heber's Journal quoted, civ, cv
Hedjer (El-Hijr), 34
Hedye, 22, 33
Helena, mother of Constantine, 8
Heemrâj of Bijayanagâr, lxi; 125
Herât, lii; 99, 100
Heresies and sects, Muhamm., 28
Hieunera lxxxiv
Hidalcan, 117
Hieronomo di San Stefano, 218
Hijâz, European visitors to the, xxvii
—— Jews in the, 22, 23, 24
Hijr, see Hedjer
Hili, 132
Hill, Rev. P. G., cxxii; 236
Hinaur, see Honahwar

INDEX.

Hindú, religion and temple, 137; daily worship and customs, 149; great sacrifice, 176. See Book on Calicut
Hindús not navigators, 151, 152
Hippon, Captain Anthony, 194, 195
Hirava and Poliar, low castes of Malabar, 142, 143, 170, 244
Histoire de Voyages, 91, 95, 99
History, Modern Universal, 197, 198, 274
Hodeidah, 81, 86
Hogs, wild, 122, 172, 175
Homayoon, 211
Honahwar, lxv; 275
Hondius, Map of East Indies, cxix
Hooghly, cxvii
Horaib, King, 121
Hormuz (its trade and history), l, li, lvii. See *Ormus*
Hornbill, Helmet-, lxxix; 200
Horns, coiffure in, 64, 68, 78
Horsburgh's India Directory, 106, 179, 180
Horses, imported to India from Persia, 123; mules and asses not used at Bathacala or Cannanore, 120, 121; not used at Calicut, 149; cost of, 126
Hosh, El-, 26
Hottentots, 47, 48
Houses of Calicut, their small value, 136
Hujrah at El-Medinah, 27
Humaioun-Námeh, 237
Hun (pagoda, a coin), 116, 130
Hunch-backed slaves, 246
Hunting-grounds, 126
Hurrur, xci; 86
Hyder Ali, 122
Hydrabad, 117, 195
Hyenas, 85

IAMGOMA (Zimmé or Changmai), 197
Iana (for Java), lxxxiv
Ibn Batúta, Lee's Trans. of Travels of, quoted or referred to; as to interior of Yemen, xlvii; as to Satgong in Bengal, lxxx; cheapness of Bengal, lxxxii; Muhammed king at Sumatra, lxxxix; Mombása, cvii; as to title of Rasúl, 63; city of Sanáa, 79; Zaila, 86; Goa, 115; Honahwar, 121; Mangalore, 122; Cowries, 131; Dormapatam, 132; Pandarani, 133; Calicut, 135; female line of succession in Malabar, 144; Jack-fruit, 159; Cochin Backwaters, 179; Quilon, 182; journey to Adam's Peak, 192; Sumatra, 228, 229; name of China, 237; Java, 252
Ibn Khaldoon, 22
Ibrahim Pasha, 9
Idols and idol worship of Hindús, 137, 138
Imám, title of, xliii
—— of Máskat, cxi
—— in the Mosque, Varthema acts as, 267
Imáms of Sanáa and Yemen, 55, 74, 75, 78, 80, 81, 82
—— the twelve, 75
Impalement, 147, 209
India, Political State of Western, in time of Varthema, lviii
—— Major and Minor, 38, 51, 60. See *Table of Contents*.
—— in the xvth Century (Hakluyt Soc., edited by Mr. R. H. Major), 94, 105, 107, 125, 127, 131, 158, 177, 205, 240. See also *Major*, 256
Indigo, 107
Indigofera pauciflora, 64
Indus, river, lvii; 104, 105
Inheritance in Calicut, law of, 143
Injection, 264
Inland navigation in Malabar, 179
Inscription on gate of Mombása, cix
Insignia, royal, 150
Irawaddy, river, lxxxvi
Irons put on Varthema, 60, 61
Irrigation works in Ceylon, 193
Isaac, 43, 44
Islám, Varthema's profession of, xxvi, xxvii, lxv, xcvi; 49, 262, 266, 267, 286, etc.
—— in Sumatra, lxxvi; 230, 231; in Java, lxxvi; in Malacca, 223
Isma'il Mulk, a saint of Yemen, 81
—— 'Adil Sháh, 118
Ismayl (for Ishmael, son of Abraham), 41
Island, largest, in the world, 247
Islands, number of, in Indian Archipelago, 259
—— of Ethiopia, 289
Israelites, 20, 22, 166
Istakár, lii; 101
Iunus (the Mussulman name of Varthema), xxvi; 69, 70, 102, 104, 263, 264, 266

JACA, cix
Jack-fruit, 159, 160
Jacinths, 190
Jacob Baraddæus, 292
Jacobite Christians, 291, 292
Jaffnapatam, 189
Jaggery (palm-sugar), 164, 165

Jains of Guzerat, lxiv; 108
Jamâl ed-dín Muhammed, of Honahwar, 121
Janagurh, 108
Janbeah or Arab dirk, 65
Jangomai, 219
Jarafattan, 132
Java, political state of, lxxvii, xciii, xcvi; 228, 247; Varthema's visit to, 248; religion of, 251
—— Minor, 229
Javanese (in Malacca), 226, 227; words, 188, 224; features and character, 253
Jáwah, 228
Jázán. See Gezan
Jebail, 7
Jebel esh-Sheikh, 20
—— Warkan, 34
—— el-Hazna, 35
—— Nikam, 78
—— Sábir, 81
Jerusalem, Lord of, 17; destruction of, 23, 242; — of the Hindûs, 111
Jevkotee or asylum for vermin, 108
Jewel; merchants, 212; —— trade, 195, 218
Jewels at Shiráz, 101; collected by Joghees, 113; of the king of Calicut, 156
Jew beaten by Varthema, 66
—— maker of cannon in India, 262
Jews in Arabia, xxviii; 22, 23, 24, 32, 34
Jezîrah, meaning of, xlviii
Joah or Jooa, a port of Scind. See Cheo
Joan Maria and Pietro Antonio, Milanese at Calicut, 260, 272; lose their lives through avarice, 273, 274
Joghis (ascetics), lxiv; 111, 167
—— the king of, 111; bribed to kill the two Christians just named, 273
John Baptist's church at Damascus, now a mosque, 12
Jones, Sir William, 152
—— Mr. J. Winter, cxiii; 205
Jordanus, Friar, lxx; 181
Joshua, 22
Journal of Royal As. Soc. 200, 201, 206, 208
—— of Indian Archipelago, 205
Juddah, 24, 37, 51, 52, 53, 57, 192
Judea, 22, 23
Julamerk, 182
Julianus, bishop of Alexandria, 32
Julfâr (a port in the Persian Gulf). 1; 93

Junks, 239, 258; origin of the word, 210
Justice in India, lxxiv
—— highly praised by ancient writers, 148
—— in Calicut, 147; in Tenasserim, 209

KAABA at Meccah, 39
Káabiyyín, 62
Kâdhi. See Cadi
Káhira, El-, (in Yemen), 81
Kahra, 62
Kála Nuddi, 119
Kalambak. See Calampat
Kalane gunga river, 190
Kalberga, lix, lx
Kalila wa-Dimnah, 237
Kalkiyán, 183
Kalyam, 86
Kandy, 189
Kapokats, 133
Karwar Head, 119
Kásim Berid, of Bidar, lix
—— el Daulat el Ghori, 25
Kattywar, 92, 108
Kaukammali (Kaulam Mele), 182
Kawlam (Quilon), 179, 182
Kayan-Kulam, 180. See Caicolon
Khaibar, 22, 23, 24, 33
Khalifa. See Caliph
Khán, Great, lxxxiii
Kháns, 13
Khawája, Khôja, 103
Khondemir quoted, 99
Khorassán, 100, 103
Khumbáyat. See Cambay
Khutbat el-Wakfah
Keith Johnstone's Atlas, 155, 179, 180
Keshin, 291, 292
Killakarai (183). See Quilicare.
Killing, Sultán Mahmúd's mode of, 110
Kings; of Corazani, 100; of Sambragante, 103; of the Joghe, 111, 273; of Cevul, 114; of Dabuli, 115; of Deccan, 115, 117, 118; of Narsinga, 116, 119, 122, 125, 129, 134, 187, 194; of Bathacala, 119, 121; of Onor, 121; of Canonor, 123, 281; of Calicut, 133, 139, 143, 155, 261, 269, 273; of Cucin, 134, 280; of Caicolon, 134, 179; of Colon, 134, 182; of Zailon, 188, 190, 194; of Tarnassari, 195, 197, 202, 204, 207; of Pego, 216 et seq.; of Cini, 224; of Malacha, 226; of Sumatra, 230; of Giava, 251; of Portugal, 298

310 INDEX.

Kirillos, Bishop, 181
Kistna, R., 196
Kiswa, or curtain of the Káaba, 40
Knighthood conferred on Varthema, 288; confirmed, 298
Knighton's Hist. of Ceylon, 189
Kock, Jacob, 47
Koerius, map of India, cxix
Kohl, 102
Kolapoor, 173
Koliaki, Kouiaki, Koliki, 186
Kolis, 186
Kolkhi, lxix; 185, 186
Koolee Rájahs, 111
Koord mercenaries in India, 118
Koppera, 164
Koraish, 46
Koran, quoted, 34; committed to memory, 122
Koru of Ptolemy, 185
Kotacull, lxvi; 132
Koulan (*Quilon*), *q. v.*
Kow. See *Cheo*
Krapf's travels and missionary labours quoted, cvii
Kuba, gardens of, 25
Kunduz, 102
Kurrat el-'Ayún (corroborates Varthema), xxxi; 50, 61, 65, 79, 82, 84,91
Kurrum (order of Nairs), 139
Kutb ed-Din of Delhi, lxiii.
—— Sháhi dynasty of Golconda, 195

LA GRATIOSA Island, 297
Lacca, Laera, (Lac dye), 107, 222
—— wood, 238
Ladies of Damascus, manners of, 14
Ladrone Islands, cannibalism, 256
Lagi (Láhej), 73
Láhej, *v. s.*
Lamentation for sin, of pilgrims at Meccah, 43
Lamiyyún, 62
Lâmu, cvi
Langhúti (Hind. garment), 112
Lane's Arab. Lexicon, 170
Lapis lazuli quarries, 102
Lassa, 100
Latter, Major, 48
Lazieva, cix
Lee, Professor S., translator of Ibn Batúta, 63, 182, and see *Ibn Bat.*
Leet (in Red Sea), 54
Legend of Muhammed's coffin and its origin, 25, 31; —— of the Thamudites, 34; —— of sacrifice of Abraham, 44; of Muhammed's dove, 45; of Meccah doves, 46; of spider, *ib.*; of Báb el-Mandeb, 58; of Cain, 59

Legendary sites at Damascus, 12
Lella (Ar. *Dellál*, a broker), 168
Lent of Indian Christians, 180
Lequios (Japanese), 225
Liberality of King of Pegu, 222
Library of the Fathers quoted, 236
Light over tomb of Muhammed, pretended, 30
Lights of the King of Calicut, 174
Lignum-aloes, 235
Ligor, lxxvi; 197
Lions (qu. tigers?), 122, 131, 172, 199; —— animals like (hyenas), 85
Lisbon, author's arrival at, 297
Litta, Famiglie celebri Italiane, xx
Loadstone and Muhammed's coffin, story denied, 31
Loban (Lubán), as a name of aloeswood, 235
Lobo, Father, *Voyage Hist. d'Abyssinie*, 47
Longevity, in Yemen, 78; at Hunahwar, 122
Longor (Ligor), 197
Loheia, 81
Lopez Juarez de Albergaria, 60
—— Journal of Thomé, xxxix
Lords of Meccah, 35
Lorenzo, a Christian boy, 274
Louis XI, 80
Lovers' custom in Tenasserim, 208
Low's History of Tenasserim (in Jour. R. As. Soc.) quoted, 200, 201, 206, 208
Low castes of Malabar, 171
Lubaniabi (*Lubán Jáwí*), 197
Lucknouti, 211
Lucoes (Luzonians), 225
Ludolph's *Hist. Æthiop.*, 47

MAABAR, 183. See *Malabar*
Määzibah, 62
Mace, 244
Machamuth. See *Mahmúd Bigarrah*
Machian, 245
Macin, Machin, Macini, 216, 236
Macleod's *Travels in Eastern Africa*, 295
Mad Prince of Sanáa, 80
Madder, 85
Madness, Varthema feigns, 66
Maffei, 274
Magino Patavino, *Geography of*, See *Patavino*
Magnet. See *Compass*
Mahabar, 184
Mahalfah, 33
Mahagam, 189

INDEX. 311

Mahmúd Bigarrah, Sult. of Guzerat, lix; 107, 108, 109, 111
—— Sháh of Kalberga, lix
Maharras, Mt., 75
Mahratta State, 150
Maina (bird), 172
Majapait, 252
Major, R. H., Editor of *India in the XVth Century*, *q. v.*; also xxiv, xc, xcv, cxiii; 240, 241, 249, 251
Makránah, El-, (city of Yemen). See Almacarana
Malabar, History of, lxii; 122, 123, 125, 135; low castes of, 171; inland navigation of, 179; Christians of, 181. See *Christian*
—— of Polo, its limits, 183 See also *Calicut*, etc.
Malabars, Malabaris (people of M.), 180, 224
Malabathrum, 234
Malacca (Malacha of V.), lxxvi, lxxxii; 184, 197, 210; Varthema goes there, 223; once subject to Siam, 224; climate of, 228, 243; its capture by Albuquerque, 254, 258
—— Straits of, lxxxvii, 223
Malapolanda (*Valei-pullum*) a plantain, 162, 163
Malatesta, Elisabetta, xx
Malayalim, Varthema's specimens of, 145, 146, 147, 150, 161, 168, 170, 185, 202, 203, 204, 284, 285
Malays, lxxxvii; 226, 227
Malcolm's Hist. of Persia, Sir John, quoted, li; 101, 150
Maldive Islands, 131
Maliapoor, 186
Malikiah, 76
Malindi, cix
Maluco, Maluka (Molucca), 245
Mamal Miricar, envoy to the Portuguese fleet, 282
Mamale, a Malabar merchant, 283
Mamlúks, Mamelukes, xxv, xxvi; 6, 9, 10; at Damascus, their ways, 13; Browne's account of, *ib.*; Varthema's enrolment among, 16; in the Pilgrim caravan, 16, 18, 21; skill in warlike exercises, 19, 37, 51; 76; in India, 116, 117
Manaar, 185, 186
Mandelslo's Travels quoted, cxvi; 115, 195, 198, 211
Mandra, cix
Mangalore, 122
Mango, Manga, Mangga, descript. of; origin of the name; introduced into Arabia, 160, 161
Manjerún (Mangalore), 122

Manners of Calicut. See *Calicut*
Mansúri Heights, 59
Manu, laws of, 152, 166
Manzi, Mangi, lxxxiv
Maps, early, showing Australia, 251; of India from 1561 to 1740, cxix
Mar Athanasius, 181; Shimón, 182; Yúsuf, *ib*.
Marchioni, Barth., ci, 296
Mardin, 181
Mares, none in Narsinga, 126
Mariam (for fire-arms), 239, 240
Mariette's map of India, cxix
Markham, Mr. C. R., xciv, cxiii; note by, 249; his trans. of life and acts of Don A. de Guzman, lix
Marriage customs of Calicut, 141, 145, 146; —— of Tenasserim, lxxix; 202, 203; of Aracan, 204
Marsden's Numismata Orientalia, 116, 232
—— history of Sumatra, 236
Martaban, 215, 216; —— Lac of, 222
Máskat (*Meschet* of Var.), 1; 93, 94; —— Sultán of, 95, 182
—— Imám of, cxi
Mass, The, of Indian Christians, 180
Masulipatam, 194, 195, 196
Matchlock, 65
Mathys's map of Asia, cxix
Maulla, cannibals of, 256
Mayer's map of India, cxix
Mebor, lxxxiv
Meccah, (its politics in Varthema's time), xxxii; 16, 18, 24; arrival of Varthema with the caravan at, 35; description of, *ib*.; its barrenness, 37; food whence, *ib*.; crowds at, 38; merchandize at, *ib.*; the pardoning, *ib.*; the Temple, *ib.*: the Káaba, 39; sacrifices at, 42; Sultán of, 49; Varthema escapes from, 52; 102; 151; 192
Mechuas (fishermen), 142
Medáyen Sáleh, 34
Medical thaumaturgy, 167, 168
Medical practice, Varthema's, 264
Medinathalnabi (*Medinat en-Nabi*), 25. See *Medinah*
Medinah, El-, 22, 23; described, 25
Medlar, fruit like, 161
Medressahs (colleges), 83
Melacha, 223. See *Malacca*
Melinde, 290
Melintay, 216
Melons, 124
Menacheaz, captain of Diu, 92
Menancabo, 230
Menin, 8

INDEX.

Merghâb, lii ; 101
Mergui, English factory at, 198
Meschet. See *Máskat*
Methold, Master William, 197, 215
Mezeribe (El-Mezarib) 16, 17, 18
Milan referred to, 129
Milanese at Calicut, xcviii ; 260, 272
Military matters at Calicut, 149
Minau, 95
Miräat Sikandari, 110
Mirabilia Descripta. See *Jordanus*
Mirabolans } 107, 124, 158
Myrobalans }
Miracle at tomb of St. Thomas, 187, 188
——, Varthema invents a, 284
Mirandu, 216
Mirzel, for *brazil*, lxxviii
Misr el-'Ateeka, 6
Missions in India, Roman Catholic, civ, cv ; 181, 206
Mistake in distance, lxxxiv
Miswâk (*Mesuech* of Varthema), a toothstick, 64
Modern Univ. History quoted, 197, 198, 274
Mogoung, 219
Mogul, Great, 119
Mokha, 81
Molaga, 233
Molan (*ammonan*, a Ceylon measure), 190
Moluccas, xcii ; 245. See *Monoch*
Mombása, Portuguese inscription at, cix ; cvi, cvii, cviii ; 275, 290
Money, of Narsinga, etc. See *Coins*
Money-changers, 168, 239
Mongolia, 100
Monoch (the Moluccas), xcii ; 244, 245
Monophysites, 202
Monsoons, 89, 153
Montefeltro, Battista, xix
Moondus (*hod.* Zaila), 82
Moors—*passim* for civilized Arabs and Muhammedans generally; so Moorish merchants, 114, 115, 119, 121, 124, 127, 132, 143, 151, 185, 187, 191, 194, 195, 197, 200, 209, 263, 273
—— language (for Arabic), 9
Moplahs, 123, 132
Môr, king of India, 291
Moresby's Sailing directions for Red Sea, 55
Mortars, 262, 278, 282, 287
Mosaic work, 12
Moses, 22
Mosques ; of Damascus, 12 ; of El-Medînah, 25, 26 ; of Arafât, 36 ; —

great at Meccah, 38; of Muzdalifah, 44 ; of Juddah, 52
Mosul, patriarch of, 181
Mosullon of the Periplus, 89
Motel, 245
Mozambique, cvi ; 289, 290, 291, 295
Muadh-dhin (caller to prayer), 267
Muckwas. See *Mechua*
Muhammed, the prophet, 23, 34, 45, 103 ; his tomb, 25, 26, 27, 28
—— Kutb Shâh of Hyderabad, 194
—— Shâh of Bijapûr, 194
—— Toghlâk of Delhi, lix
—— Bakhtiâr Khilji of Bengal, lxiii
Muhammedan history in East Africa, cvii
—— arrogance, 15
—— sects, 74, 75. See *Sects*
—— travellers of the ninth century, 182 ; —— legend of Adam in Ceylon, 192. See *Legends*
—— call to prayers, 267
—— saint, Varthema sets up for a, 263, 265, 269, 270
Muhammedanism. See *Islám*
Mukdîshu, cvi, cvii
Mul-Jâwah, 228, 229
Mummies, 33
Muna, valley of, 42
Munâsika, 62
Murâd II. of Anatolia, lix ; 117
Musáhhirs, 11
Music of Sultân Mahmûd, 109
Musk, 102
Mustachioes of Sultân Mahmûd of Cambay, lxiv ; 109
Mutabhir, 76
Mutilation of children, xcvii
Muzáffir Shâh, lviii
Muzáwwir, 26
Muzdalifah, mosque of, 44
Muzungulos, cix
Myhee river, lviii ; 105
—— Kanta, 111

NABI JERGEES (St. George), 7
Naeri. See *Nairs*
Nairs of Malabar, lxvii ; 124, 134, 137, 139, 141 ; marriage customs of, 146, 150, 151, 176, 269, 273, 284
Namburi, lxvii ; 141, 142
Names of Indian Christians, 180
Naples referred to, 126, 129
Narsinga, or kingdom of Bijayanagâr, lxxi ; 124, 125, 151
—— King of, lxi ; 116, 119, 122, 125, 129, 187, 188, 192, 194, 198, 212

Naitravutty, 122
Nâsir ed-Dîn Muhammed Shâh, lvii
———————— Baghra of Bengal, lxiii
Navigation of Indian seas, times of, 153
———————— in Calicut, manner of, 152
Nebuchadnezzar, 22
Negapatam, lxx, xcvii, 173, 184, 186. See *Cioromandel*
Negroes described, 292; their manner of speaking, 293
Nekrokis, 1
Nerbudda river, 107
Nestorian Christians, lxix, lxxxv; 181, 212, 213, 291, 292
Neuera-kalawa, 189, 192
Neyrin, liii
Nezwa, 94
Niadis (a caste), 142
Nicobar Islands, 229
Nicoverra (*id.*) lxxxiv
Niebuhr (the elder) quoted, xlvi; 24, 25, 42, 47, 52, 53, 55, 65, 74, 75, 77, 78, 79, 81, 82, 83, 85, 170
Nigraes (Negrais), 215
Nikitin, quoted (from India in the xvth cent.), 107, 111, 113, 115, 127, 236
Noises, supernatural, 35
North-east monsoon, xlix
North star; steering in absence of, 249
Nose, bleeding, a test of musk, 102
Nueva, Juan de, 123
Nutmegs, and mace, xcii; 244
Nutmeg Islands, 243
Nuts, Indian (cocoa), 132

OAKUM not used in Calicut ships, 152
Odia (Yuthia), 197
Odorico, Fra, quoted, lxxxii, xc, xci; interest of his travels, lxxxiii
Odours in Mosque at Mecca, 39
Oil (zerzalino), 86, 166; (cocoa-nut), 164; —— called enna, 176; from Mozambique, 291
Oman ('Ammân) province of, 93, 160
'Omar, 23; (his tomb) 27, 28, 75
Onor. See *Honahwar*
Onyxes, 107
'Ood (aloes-wood), 236
Ophir (question about), cvi
Opium, 100
Oppressions, Mamlûk, 10, 13, 15
Orang-laut, or Sea-Malays, lxxxviii; 227
Oranges, 190
O'Riley's Vegetable productions of Tenasserim, 205
Ormus, 94, 104, 151; pearl-fishery,

95; story of Sultân and his family, 96-99
Oryx, 46
'Othmân (his alleged tomb), 27, 28, 75, 103
—— ez-Zenjily, 59
Ottens, map of Asia, cxix
Outram, Sir James, 159
Ovis Ammon, 200
Oxen not eaten in Tenasserim, 201
Owen, Professor Richd., lxxix, cxiii; notes by, 48, 200

PACANET JOGHIS, 167
Pacem (Pazem), 197, 230
Padarane. See *Pandarani*
Padripatam, 133
Pagan kings of Dabuli, 115; of Bathacala, 119; lord of Centacola, 121; of Honahwar, 121, 122; of Cannanore, 123; of Bijayanagâr, 126; of Calicut, 136; of Caicolon, 180; of Pegu, 216; —— wives of king of Moluccas, 246
Pagans of Calicut, their classes, 141; of Bandan, 244; of Bornei, 248; in Java, 252
Pagoda (a coin), 130, but see *Pardai*
Pahang, 224
Palace at Bijapûr, 117; at Capogatto, 134; of the Zamorin, 136, 155
Paleachet, 194. See *Pulicat*
Palk Strait, 187
Palm-trees at El-Medînah, 25
Palma, what it is, 48
Pambam Passage, lxix
Panane, Pannany, Ponany, *etc.*, 132, 179, 275; assault upon, 286, 287
Pandarane, Pandarane, lxvi, lxxxiv; 132, 133, 175, 275, 286. See *Fanduraina*
Panteunus, 32
Papau, 161
Parah (a measure), 170
Parao (Prahu, a kind of vessel), 154, 269, 270, 275, 280
Pardai (*Pardao*, or pagoda, a gold coin), 115, 120, 130, 175, 218, 243, 258, 259, 273
Pardoning at Meccah, 8
Parrakad, 155. See *Porkah*
Parrots, 122, 172, 199, 218, 225
Patavino, Geog. of Magino, xxx, cxix; 196, 215, 219, 230
Paté, Pati, city of, cix; 290
Patriarchs, Nestorian and Jacobite, 181; Chaldæan, 181, 182
Paul, St., legendary sites at Damascus, 12

Y

Pay of Mamlûks, 13 ; of soldiers at Calicut, 151
Peacocks, 122, 172, 198
Pearls, 94, 273 ; fishery of, 1 ; 93, 95, 185, 186
Pedir (*Pider* of Varthema), xxvi ; 197, 228, 230
Pegu (*Pego* of Varthema), lxxvi, lxxxiv ; 151, 184, 194, 197 ; deterioration of, 199, 214 ; described, 215, 217 ; history of, *ib.*
—— king of, lxxxvi ; 219 ; his pomp, wealth, and liberality, 220-222
Peguans, 224
Pemba, Penda, island of, cvi, cix ; 290
Pennaconda, 126
Pepper, lxxxix ; 124 ; described, 157 ; in perfection, 180, 233
—— long, 233
Peradenia, 189
Percatti, 155, 180
Perchoara, 197
Periplus of the Erythræan Sea, 185, 196, 219. See *Vincent*
Persepolis, 47, 150
Persia, remarks on Varthema's travels in, lii ; 38, 60 ; book concerning, 91, 94, 99 ; ambassador from
—— to India, 115, 151, 197
—— Malcolm's History of. See *Malcolm*
Persian, Varthema passes for a, 220, 242
Persians trading at Aleppo; 7, 101, 102, 214, 224
Perim or Mayún, island of, 58
Perumbh, island of (Guzerat), 93
Perwuttum, 111
Petra, 20
Phœnix, beak of, 200
Phaseolus Aconitifolius, 107
Physician, Varthema acts as, 263
Physicians in Calicut, 167
Picco Island, 297
Pider. See *Pedir*
Piero Antonio, a Milanese. See *Milanese*
Pigafetta quoted, lxxvii ; 102, 233, 243, 245, 256
Pilgrimages of the king of Joghees, 111
Pilots of the desert, 31, 33
Pinjreepols or Brute-hospitals, 108
Pinkerton's Collection of Voyages, quoted, cxvii ; 94, 100, 102, 105, 107, 108, 113, 115, 118, 119, 121, 124, 127, 132, 134, 136, 137, 139, 141, 143, 144, 146, 148, 152, 155, 157, 167, 170, 172, 180, 182, 184,

186, 188, 193, 195, 198, 200, 201, 204, 209, 216, 218, 220, 231, 252
Pinto, F. Mendez, 206, 208, 209, 213
Piracies of Porcat, 155
Pitch in ship-building, 152
Pitts, Joseph, Faithful account of the religion and manners of the Mahometans, 38, 43
Piyadàsi, edicts of, 108
Plantain, 162, 163
Pliny quoted, 47, 152, 241
Pococke quoted, 7
Poison eaten daily by Sultàn Mahmúd, 109
Poisoned darts, 254
Poliars, Poulias, Poulichees (a low caste of Malabar), lxvii, lxxiii ; 142, 143, 171, 244
Polo, Marco, quoted, 1, xci ; 94, 139, 148, 152, 153, 183, 185, 188, 193, 213, 229, 292
Polyandry in Malabar, lxvii ; 146
Polygamy, Muhammedan, 14
Pomp of the king of Decan, 118
Pompey, 23
Ponany, Ponany. See *Panane*
Population of Juddah, 53 ; of Aden, 59 ; of Herât, 100 ; of Bijapúr, 117 ; of Quilon, 182 ; of Tenasserim, 198
Porkah, Porca, Porcai (Parrakad), 154, 180
Portugal, king of, lord of the ocean, 50, 122, 123 ; Emanuel, 260 ; receives Varthema, 298
Portuguese in India, their piracies, xxxix ; expelled from Hormuz, li ; at Cannanore, lxv ; at Negapatam, xcvii ; —— Catholicism in India, ciii ; their fanatical violence, c ; rapid rise and decay of their commercial empire, ci, cii ; first appearance in Indian Seas, 61 ; on Arabian coast, 65, 93, 94, 95 ; at Diu, 92 ; capture Dabul and Goa, 115, 118, 119, 121, 122, 123, 124, 131, 132 ; at war with king of Calicut, 156, 175, 178, 182, 184, 187 ; arrived in Ceylon, 193 ; at Pulicat, 195 ; in Bengal, 211 ; in the Archipelago, 233, 260 ; their ships and castle at Cannanore, 266, 274 ; bravery, 280, 281, 282
—— in East Africa, cviii ; decay of their power there, cx
—— Asia, by De Faria y Souza, translated by S evens. See *De F.*
Prayer, Varthema set to lead, in mosque, 267
Prester John, 63, 86, 96

Pridham's Ceylon and its Dependencies, 190, 191
Prinsep, J., quoted, 116, 130, 170
Prison, Varthema in, 65
Prisoners of Sultan of Aden, 84
Privileges of Mamlûks, 13
—— Joghees, 112
Profligate customs of Tenasserim, 202-204
Pròm, 216
Property, change in distribution of, in India under British, lxxiii
Prosperity of India in Varthema's time, lxxiii
Ptolemy, 185, 211, 230
Pua (*Morbus Gallic.*), 274
Pulicat, lxxi; 194
Pulwan, lii; 101
Punishments in Sumatra, 231
Purbi dynasty in Bengal, lxii
Purchas quoted, cxvi; 197, 198, 295
Pygmies, alleged Jewish, 23, 24

QUARTERLY REVIEW on unicorns, 48
Queda, lxxvi; 197
Queen of Aden, and her dealings with Varthema, 65, 66, 68, 70, 71, 72, 73
Quelijos (Chulias or Telugus), 224
Quilicare (Killacarai), lxix; 183, 185
Quiloa (Kilwah), 274 See *Kilwah*
Quilon (Colam, Colon, etc.), lxii, lxiii, lxix, xcvii; 179, 180, 181, 182, 183, 186, 271
Quintus Curtius, 166

RABBI KIMCHI, 205
Radää el-'Arsh, 61, 62, 67
Raglan castle referred to, 117
Rainy season, 153
Rájah. See *King*
Rajavali quoted, 189, 193
Rajemal, 211
Rajim ("the Lapidated"), 45
Rajpeepla Hills, 107
Rakik, a slave, 81
Ram, 185
Rama Point, 185
Rama's Bridge, 185
Ramadhán, 11, 13
Ramanad-buram, 185
Rami-Ceram (Rameswaram), 185
Ramlah, El-, 26
Ramonan Coil, Raman-Koil, Rammanana Kojel, 185, 186
Ramraj of Bijayanagar, lx
Ramtha, 17
Ramusio, his Preface to Varthema, xxi
—— quoted, cxv, cxvii; 107, 110, 132, 133, 159, 180, 183, 184, 185, 197, 205, 211, 222, 223, 226 230, 246, 249, 252, 254, 256, 258, 295, 298
Rao Mandalik, 108
Raoleonda diamond mines, 118
Ras Haffun, 88
Ratnapoora, 190
Reame (*Verôn*—in Yemen), 77
Red Soil of Sodom, 19
—— Sea, difficult navigation of, 54, 57
Renegade Christians, 13, 16
Rennell's Mem. of a Map of Hindostan quoted, lxxxi, cxx; 211
Reservoirs near Meccah, 36
—— ancient, 95
Rhada. See *Radää*
Rhavan, 185
Rhinoceros, 87
Rhubarb, 100, 101
Richard quoted, 204
Rice, cultivation of, 166; abundant, 120, 121, 187, 195; imported into Ceylon, 192
Robertson, Dr., xxiv
Robinson, Dr. Ed., quoted, 47
Roman Catholic. See *Missions*
Rome, Varthema reaches, 298
Roses of Damascus, 11, 122
Rose-water, 81
—— Apple, 161
Route of Varthema in Yemen, xlvii
Roxburgh's Flora Indica, 160, 163
Roya (*Coir*), 164
Ruah er-Ruah, quoted in corroboration of Varthema, xxxv, xliii; 65, 76, 79, 91, 92
Rubies; Balass, 101; of Pegu, 218, 219; of the King of Pegu, 220, 221, 243
Ruby-mines, 102, 190
Rupat, island of, 223
Rutnagherry, 114

SACHIA LAMA, 48
Sacrifices on the Meccah Pilgrimage, 37, 42; Hindû, 138, 139, 176
Sacrifice Rock, 132
Sacutara—Socotra, q. v.
Sâdkâwân (Satgong), lxxx
Safetica (*Assafœtida*), 106
Saffragam, 190
Saffron, 194, 195
Sahlah, 80
Sahn, El-, 26
Said, grandson of 'Ali, cvii
Sails of Indian ships, 153
Saint Peter and St. Paul, xcvi; 248
—— Paul quoted, 130

Saint Thomas, tomb of, 186, 187;
  miracle of, 187; Christians of, see
  Christian
Saints, Mussulman, 73; Varthema
  sets up for one, 263 *et seq.*
Saláh ed-Dín (Saladin), 59
Salamander, 173
Sáleh the prophet, 34
Sale's Korán, 75, 192
Salt made, 57
Salt's visit to Abyssinia, 295
Samara, 229
Samarcand, liv; 100, 103
Sambragante, *Samarcand*, *q. v.*
Sambuchi (*Sanbúk*), a kind of ship, 154
Samiyyín, 62
Samis, a damsel offered in marriage
  to Varthema, lvii, xc; 104
Samory, Sammoryn. See *Zamorin*
Sampan (kind of boat). See *Chiampani.*
Samuel, 22
Sanáa, city of, 57, 61; besieged, 62, 63; described, 78
—— Imám of, 74, 75, 76
San Giorgio, Island, 297
—— Giovanni in Fonte referred to, 175
—— Lorenzo (Madagascar), 296
—— Vicenzo, ship, ci; 297
Santa Helena Island, 297
—— Maria Rotondo referred to, 81
Santo Stephano, Hieron. di, 158
Sanay or Sandoy, lxxxiii
Sand, sea of, 33
Sandal-wood, lxxxix; 121, 222, 225
—— powder, 112
Sanga, 217
Saniyah Kuda, at Meccah, 35
Sanson's Map of Asia, cxix
Sapeto, Padre, xci
Sappan, 205
Sapphires, 190, 218
Saraphi, Sarafi (gold coin). See
  Ashrafi and *Serafim*)
Sarana Perimal of Malabar, lxii
Saris, 107, 170, 206, 212
Sarnau and its Christians, lxxxii;
  212, 213, 235, 236, 237, 259. See
  Christians
Sarrano, Joao, 272, 277
Saru (a starling or maina?), 172
Satan, 59
Satgong, Satigan, lxxii, lxxx, lxxxi,
  cxv, cxvi, cxvii, cxviii, cxix, cxxi
Sathanas (Hindu idol), 138, 176
Satí in Tenasserim, 206, 208, 222
Satrap, etymol. of, 150
Sattara district, 117

Saul, 22
Savain, Capt., of Goa, 116
Scaliger, J. C., 161
Schirazo (*Shiráz*), *q. v.*
Sciamuthera, 228
Scorpions, 173
Scott's Ferishta, 115, 116
Scutella or Scodella, 204
Sea, men of the, lxxxviii; 227; Red.
  See *Red.* —— fighting of Javanese, 254
Seaports of India in Varthema's
  time, lxxi
Seasons in Tenasserim, 202
Sechamir (Sheikh 'Amir), 83, 84. See
  Sultán of Aden
Sects, Muhammedan, lv; 75, 103, 119
Sedashevaghur, lx; 119, 121
Sedashwa, Rao of Soonda, 119
Seemann's Pop. Hist. of Palms, 163-4
Seerah, Island of (Aden), 59
Selim I., xxv
Semi-white people, 201
Seraphim of gold, 29, 73, 115. See
  Ashrafi
Serindib, 183
Sermon at Meccah, 43; —— before
  battle, 287
Serpent, mortar called, 282
—— charmers, 286
Serpents in Calicut, protected, 173,
  174; very large in Sumatra, 241
Seutter's map of India, cxix
Seyyeds of Máskat, xliii, cxi
Sforza, Battista, xix
Sháh Abbás, 94
—— Ismaí'l es-Súfi, 103
Shakespeare's Hind. Dict., 172
Shamsán range at Aden, 59
Shaytan el-Kabir, 45
Sheep killed by Varthema, 66; fat-
  tailed, 77; Berbera, 87; twist-
  tailed, *ib.*; 122; and goats in Te-
  nasserim, 199; with deer's horns, 200
Sheikh Mahmúd, 35
Shells of turtle, great, 240
Sheravatty river, 121
Sherif of Meccah, xxx; name defined, 36; of Mozambique, 295
—— a coin. See *Ashrafi*
Sherjebi tribe, 81
Shi'áhs. See *Sects*
Shibriyah, 33
Shields, Arab, 64
Ships, of Honahwar, 122; building
  of, in Malabar, 152; of Tenasserim,
  210; of Pegu, 219
Shiráz, liii; 100, 101, 102, 103
Shravakas, a caste of Jains, 108

Shugduf, 33
Siam, lxxvi; 196, 198, 200, 201, 213, 215, 224; funeral of king of, 213; cannibals in, 256
Siamese, their use of elephants, 127; 224
Sick, how treated at Calicut, 167
Sickness feigned by Varthema, 52, 72, 83
Sikander Shâh, of Malacca, 224
Sikkim, Râjah of, 48
Silam, lxxxiv
Silk, 38, 75, 100, 107, 111; in Burmah, 199, 222; in Sumatra, lxxxix; 234; in Java, 252
Silken stuffs, 212, 225
Silon (Siam), 213
Simon Martin, valour of, 278
Sin and Machin, what they stand for, 236
Sinabaff, 212, 269
Sinai, Mount, 34
Sinbad, 240
Singani (*Zingani*—gypsies), 112
Sio, cix
Sirian, 218
Siva and Parbati on a coin, 116, 192
Slaves, Abyssinian, 63
—— trade, 86
Slings, 56, 64, 65, 85
Soarez, Lope, 179
Socotra, Is., of, 58, 283; and its Christians, 290-292
Sodom and Gomorrah, 19, 20
Sofâla, cvi; 290, 291, 295
Soffi, liv; 103
Soldan of Cairo, 280. See *Sultân*
Somâlis, 88, 89
Somario de' Regni, in Ramusio, lxxxiv, cxv; 197
Song birds of Calicut, 172
Sornau, empire of, 213
Sosikooré, 186
Southern Continent, xcv; 251
—— cross, *ib.*
Speed's Map of Asia, cxix
Spelling of Varthema's name, xviii
Spice Islands, Varthema's voyage to, xc, xci; 241
Spices, in Yemen, 80, 82; in India, 124; —, navigation for, 153; in Malabar, 157, 187; trade in, at Malacca, 224
Spider and Muhammed, legend of, 46
Spikenard, 106
Spinelles, 218
Spingarde, 262, 293
Spodium, 102
Sree Pada, 191

Stags, 122
Standard of King of Calicut, 150
Stature of Adam and Eve, 192
Steering by Southern Stars, 249
Stern, Rev. Mr., quoted, 79
Stevens's Translation of Portuguese Asia. See *De Faria*
Stewart's History of Bengal, 211
Stone pile near Meccah, 44
—— houses in Pegu, 217
Strabo quoted, 21, 241
Stuffs of Bengal, 212
Stupidity of Banda people, 244
Submarine ruins at Calicut, 136
Sudras, 124, 134
Sûfî, Sheikh, lx
—— 'Isma'il Es-, Shâh of Persia, lv
—— sect and dynasty, 103
Sugar, 82, 120; cocoa-palm, 164, 165
Sulacho, 256
Suleimân Pâsha, 65, 92
—— the Voyager, 237
Sultân, of Meccah, 36, 49; of Aden and South. Yemen, 'Amiribn' Abd-el-Wahhâb, 57, 61, 63, 71; his riches, 77; he besieges Sanâa, 79, 80, 81, 82; his history and monuments, 83; his prisoners, 84; of Egypt, Kansooh el-Ghoree, xxv; 6, 7, 9, 10, 17, 36, 52, 53, 59, 65; Bin Seif, of Omân, 94; Husein Mîrza of Herât, 99; Mahmûd of Cambay, see *Mahmûd*, *etc.*; of Ormus and his family, 98, 99
Sultan's palace on Bosphorus, 150
Sumatra, lxxvi, lxxxiv, lxxxviii; 151, 153, 184, 197, 223; name of, 228, 229; copper in, 253; cannibalism in, 256
Sumba, 225
Sumoltra (Sumatra), lxxxiv
Sumpitan or blow-pipe, 254
Sun, gender of, lvii; casts shadow to south, 257
Sundas, country of, 252
Sundeep, Island of, cxxi
Sunnis and Shi'âhs. See *Sects*
Superstitions about serpents, 174
Swimming of the Moors, wonderful, 279
Sydenham's account of Bijapûr, 117
Symes's Ava, Col. Michael, lxxxiv; 201, 216
Syria, Varthema goes to, 6, 38, 151
Syriac ritual, 181
Syrian Jacobites, 181

Ta'ez (*Taesa* of Varthema), 76, 80
Taghtakîn, 59

Tagliacozzo, Duchess of, xix; 1
Takruri, 43
Takhtrawân, 33
Tala-côri of Ptol., 185
Talikote, battle of, 125
Tamboli, Pân leaf, 110
Tamerani (Tambarân), 137
Tamuri Râjah, (Zamorin), 134
Tanda (in Bengal), 211
Tangu, 216
Taujong Parlak, 233
Tank, temple in a, 175
Tannah, 113
Taprobane (identified by Varthema with Sumatra), 185, 197, 229
Tar, Tare, a coin, 130
Tardiness of British justice, lxxiv
Tarikh Thagr 'Aden, 58
Tarnassari (Tenasserim), 188, 195, 196, 198, 216, but see *Tenasserim*
Tartary, 101, 102
Tavernier quoted, 100, 118, 218
Tavoy, 215
Tawâf at the Kâaba, 40
Teeth, black, 151
Telingana, 194, 195
Tellicherry river, 131
Telugu, 229
Temple, at Meccah, 38; at Calicut described, 137; in a tank, 175; taken for a church, ib.
Tenacerim, 197
Tenasserim, lxxvi, vide lxxviii; 196, 215. See *Tarnassari*
Tenga (Tânghâ—the cocoa-nut), 163
Tennent, Sir J. E., Ceylon by, lxx; 189, 190, 193
Teraphim (gold coins). See *Ashrafi, Serafim*
Termapatani, 132, 133. See *Dormapatam*
Terminalia, species bearing edible fruits, 158
Ternassari, 151, 216. See *Tarnassari* and *Tenasserim*.
Ternate, xcii; 245
Terra Australis, early voyages to, 249
Tertiera Island, 297
Test of an able recruit, 116
Teyva. See *Tiva*
Thamudites, legend of, 34
Thana, Tana, lxxxiv
Theism, Hindû, 136
Theology, Varthema's, 285
—— injudicious illustrations of, ib.
Thibet, 48, 100, 102
Thirst, death from, 20, 33
Thor, cave at, 28; mount, 46
Tides at Cambay, 106

Tidor, xcii; 245
Tihâma, 62, 80, 81
Tikodi, 132
Timber for ship-building (Malabar), 132, 153; Pegu, 218
Timor, 225
Tin, 225
Tippoo Sultân, 123
Tircari, 133
Titus, 23
Tiva (class of artisans), 142
Toddy, 163, 164, 165, 172
Toongabudra river, 125
Toorán Shâh bin Ayyûb, 59
Topazes, 190
Tormapatam, 131, 275. See *Dormapatam*
Tortoise, enormous, 240
Touchstone for gold, 168
Toungoo, lxxvi; 218, 219
Traditions, local, at Damascus, 12
Travancore, 182
Travel, advantages of, cxxii
Treasure of king of Calicut, 156
Triad, the Buddhistic, 217
Trick on the caravan at El-Medinah, 29
Trinity, supposed belief in, lxxxv, lxxxvi; 217
Tripoli (Syrian), 7
Triumpara, Râjah of Cochin, 260
Truffles, 15
Tsopo, 48
Tucia (*Tótyâ*—antimony), 102
Turbide (*Turbith*), a drug, 106
Turkestân, 100
Turkey, 7, 8, 10, 15, 151
Turkish merchants, xlix; matchlocks, 65; forces in Yemen, 65; mercenaries in India, 118
Turks, their toleration, 52
Turpin quoted, 127, 198, 200, 201, 204, 209
Turquoises, 101
Turtle, roofs made of shells of, xc; 240
Turtle-doves in desert, 24
Tuticorin, lxix; 183, 184, 186

Ulala, 132
Ulema, danger of meddling with, 84
Ultra-marine, 102
Umbrella, royal, 150
Uncalvet (impalement), 147
Unkilwara, kings of, 92
Unicorns at Meccah, discussed, 46
Unicorn cow, 87
Upham's Rajavali, 189
Urbino, dukes of, xix, xxii; 2, 275
Usbeck mercenaries in India, 118

INDEX. 319

VADACURRY, lxvi; 132
Valour of the Portuguese, 280, 281, 282
Varaha (a coin), 130
Varana, Costanza, xx
Variety of nations at Calicut, 151
Varthema, his style, i; editions and translations of his travels: Italian, iii; Latin, ix; German, xi; Spanish, xiii; Dutch, xv; English, xvi; defective information regarding his previous history, xvii, xxii; his dates, see *Dates*; his accuracy, see *Veracity*, and see *Table of Contents*
Vartomannus (form of Varthema's name), xvii, xix
Vaz, Gonzalo, 283
Veddahs, 189
Veiled ladies in India, 118
Velvet, 195
Venice referred to, 129
Venomous reptiles, 173, 174
Veracity of Varthema, i, ii; corroboration of, lvii, lxiv, lxvii, lxx, lxxviii
Verdure, perpetual, of Malabar, 172
Verzino (or brazil-wood), lxxviii; 205
Vessels of India, 152, 188
Viceroy of India. See *De Almeyda*
—— Sultán of Aden, 60
Victory over fleet of Calicut, 274-280
Vincent's Commerce and Navigation of the Ancients quoted, xxiv; 86, 106, 183, 185, 186, 196, 219, 291
—— allocation of Ternassari, lxxviii
Visapour. See *Bijapúr*
Visscher's map of Asia and India, cxix
Volcanic crater at Aden
Volto Santo, xcv; 248

WADA (cowrie), 131
Waddakarree, 132
Wádi 'Araba, 20
Wamáh, 62
Wanny, 189, 192
Wars, of the king of Decan, 118; of Narsinga with Tenasserim, lxxi; 195; between Pegu and Ava, 219, 220, 222
Washings of the Hindús, 149
Washishtee river, 114
Watch of Damascus, 10
Water, in the desert, 18, 20, 21, 24; dearth of, at Meccah, 37; and Juddah, 53
—— melon, 161
Wealth of king of Pegu, 222
Weaving in Bengal, 214

Weevils, charity for, 108
Well of St. Mark near Meccah, 32
Whales, 201
White men, partiality of Arab women for, 65, 69; enlisted in India, 116; in Tenasserim, custom as to, 202
Wight and Arnott, Prodromus Floræ Penins. Ind. Orient., 158
Wilks's Hist. Sketches of the South of India, 121, 158
Wine (for toddy), 172
Wives exchanged in Malabar, 145
Wolves, 122, 172, 199
Women burnt in Tenasserim, 207; and Pegu, 222
Worship of Pagans of Calicut, 149; of Java, 251

XAQUEM DARSA, 224

YAHIA, Ibn Khold ibn Barmak, 35
Yandaboo, treaty of, 198
Yathrib, 22
Yembo, 24
Yemen, politics of, in Varthema's time, xli; scarcity of authorities on, xlvi; Jews of, 22; history of, 50, 54, 57; saints of, 73; Sultán of, see *Sultán*; sea of, 292
Yezd, 101
Yule, Colonel Henry, lxx, lxxviii, lxxx, lxxxv, xcviii, cxix; —— mission to Ava, 199, 215, 217, 219; —— Friar Jordanus, 181
Yúnas, Varthema's Mussulm. name. See *Iunus*
Yunan, 199
Yúsuf 'Adil, Khán of Bijapúr, 117. See *Adil Shah*
Yuthya, lxxvi

ZAALIYYÎN, 62
Zachariah, St., 12
Záhir Jamál ed-Dín, king of Sumatra, 228
Zaid, son of 'Ali, 75
Zaidis, a sect, 75, 79, 83
Zambei (Ez-Zaïbi), 17
Zamorin of Calicut, history of, lxii; 132, 134, 156, 178, 260, 280, 283, 284, 287
Zani, Valerio, xviii
Zanzibar, coiffure of, cvi, cx; 64
Zapa, xc
Zaphala (Sofála), 290, 291, 295
Zealand Acad. of Sciences, Trans. of, 47
Zebair Islands, 60
Zedekiah, 22

Zedler's Universal Lexicon, xvii
Zeilan, Zalan, Zeilon (Ceylon), 151, 183, 184, 187, 188, 230, 245. See Ceylon
Zeila (Zaila), a port of Africa, 58, 85, 86
Zemzem (the well), 37, 40

Zerzalino (sesamum), 86, 87, 166
Zebid (Zibit of Varthema), 80, 81, 83
Zida. See Juddah
Zofala. See Zaphala and Sofāla
Zuama, 295
Zunde, 230
Zurla, Dissert. di M. Polo, etc., xvii

CORRIGENDA.

Page	line	for	read
xlvi	25 of text	N.E.	N.W.
lxiv	27 ,,	*dele,* the	
lxxvii	8 of notes	twelve hundred	two hundred
lxxxviii	13 of text	Blean	Blaeu
lxxxi	24 ,,	*Bangella*	*Bengalla*
xc	5 of notes	is	are
13	3 ,,	1722	1792
23	2 of text	spans	*palmi*
38	1 of notes	1608	1680
55	1 ,,	Jeezân or Gheezân	Jázán or Gázán
56	6 ,,	Jeezân	Jázán
58	8 ,,	Mendeb	Mandeb
62	24 ,,	*iji*	*aji*
79	6 ,,	3	1
112	4 ,,	inapt	unapt
115	8 ,,	Mandeslo	Mandelslo
139	6 ,,	*poonoob*	*jane'a*
158	18 ,,	Wright	Wight
161	8 ,,	on the coast	or on the west coast
163	16 ,,	Seemans	Seemann
199	7 ,,	*dele,* "	
,,	19 ,,	purveyors	surveyors
216	18 ,,	*Losmin* [sic in orig.]	Col. Yule remarks that this should be *Kosmin,* a port of Pegu, near Bassein, not now traceable.
247	23 ,,	*Moluch*	*Monoch*
271	1 ,,	Cananore	Cannanore
299	32 ,,	Yeman	Yemen

N.B. The Translator having entrusted the revision of the proof-sheets to the Editor, the latter is solely responsible for all typographical errors in the text.

In romanizing foreign names and words occurring in the annotations, the Editor has endeavoured to steer a middle course between a pedantic adherence to the original on the one hand, and a servile copying of the ordinary lax orthography on the other. The attempt, he fears, will be found chargeable with many inconsistencies.

The work quoted in the earlier portion of the annotations under the title of *A Collection of Voyages* is that generally known as CHURCHILL'S.

In like manner, VINCENT'S *Periplus* is quoted, whereas the book meant is VINCENT'S *Commerce and Navigation of the Ancients,* in two volumes, which comprises the *Periplus.*

The *Collection* quoted as GREENE'S is that more generally known as ASTLEY'S.

z

www.ingramcontent.com/pod-product-compliance
Lightning Source LLC
Chambersburg PA
CBHW051856300426
44117CB00006B/416